complete book of

Indian

cooking

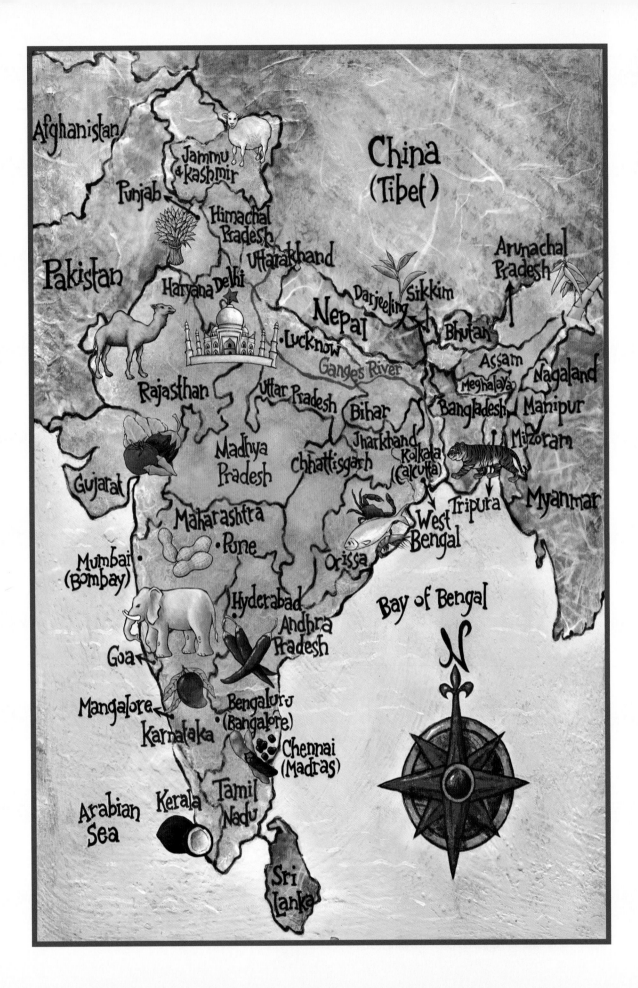

complete book of

Indian
cooking

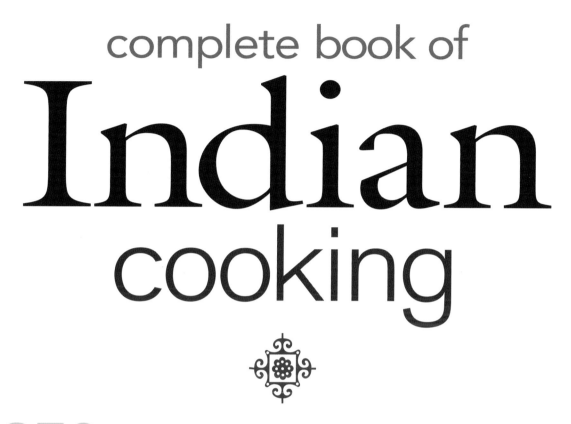

350 recipes from the regions of India

Suneeta Vaswani

Robert
ROSE

Photographs of India: 8 © iStockphoto.com/Eduardo Bombareli Marin; 14 © iStockphoto.com/Kristen Johansen; 20 © iStockphoto.com/John Peacock; 26 © iStockphoto.com/Vera Bogaerts; 38 © iStockphoto.com/Alija; 54 © iStockphoto.com/Emma Saunders; 100 © iStockphoto.com/HighlanderImages; 112 © iStockphoto.com/Robert Churchill; 124 © iStockphoto.com/Ooyoo; 142 © iStockphoto.com/Vera Bogaerts; 148 © iStockphoto.com/Jeremy Edwards; 156 © iStockphoto.com/Vera Bogaerts; 174 © iStockphoto.com/Sunil Menon; 210 © iStockphoto.com/Ron Sumners; 238 © iStockphoto.com/Loic Bernard; 244 © iStockphoto.com/Pabis Studio; 250 © iStockphoto.com/Ashwin Kharidehal Abhirama; 278 © iStockphoto.com/Leeman; 284 © iStockphoto.com/Vassili Koretski; 296 © iStockphoto.com/Robert Churchill; 318 © iStockphoto.com/Loic Bernard; 338 © iStockphoto.com/Terraxplorer; 354 © iStockphoto.com/Alija; 366 © iStockphoto.com/Vivek Khare; 378 © iStockphoto.com/Marco Manzini; 404 © iStockphoto.com/Markandeya ; 412 © iStockphoto.com/Ravi Tahilraman; 420 © iStockphoto.com/Ewen Cameron; 426 © iStockphoto.com/Melissa Schalke; 458 © iStockphoto.com/Suhasini Dharmalingam.

For complete cataloguing information, see page 473.

Disclaimer
The recipes in this book have been carefully tested by our kitchen and our tasters. To the best of our knowledge, they are safe and nutritious for ordinary use and users. For those people with food or other allergies, or who have special food requirements or health issues, please read the suggested contents of each recipe carefully and determine whether or not they may create a problem for you. All recipes are used at the risk of the consumer.

We cannot be responsible for any hazards, loss or damage that may occur as a result of any recipe use.

For those with special needs, allergies, requirements or health problems, in the event of any doubt, please contact your medical advisor prior to the use of any recipe.

Editor: Carol Sherman
Recipe Editor: Jennifer MacKenzie
Copy Editor: Christina Anson Mine
Indexer: Gillian Watts
Design & Production: Daniella Zanchetta/PageWave Graphics Inc.
Food Photography: Colin Erricson
Food Styling: Kate Bush and Kathryn Robertson
Prop Styling: Charlene Erricson
Map Illustration: Lisa Ström (Three in a Box)

Cover image: Kerala Chicken Stew (see recipe, page 230)

We acknowledge the financial support of the Government of Canada through the Book Publishing Industry Development Program (BPIDP) for our publishing activities.

Published by Robert Rose Inc.
120 Eglinton Avenue East, Suite 800
Toronto, Ontario, Canada M4P 1E2
Tel: (416) 322-6552 Fax: (416) 322-6936

Printed in Canada
1 2 3 4 5 6 7 8 9 TCP 15 14 13 12 11 10 09 08 07

Contents

Acknowledgments

WHEN I WROTE *Easy Indian Cooking* in 2003, my only goal was to publish a cookbook that was simple and accessible to all. At the time, Indian cooking was not the "hot" cuisine it is today. However, as India began to gain recognition in the business world, and travel to the country increased tremendously, so did interest in the cuisine of the subcontinent. With many international companies based in Bengaluru (until recently known as Bangalore), the food of the south became familiar. The difference between the cooking of the north and south is tremendous, and the idea for this book was born out of a need to explain these differences. Thus began a fascinating culinary journey, and I soon realized that the more I learned, the less I knew. The journey took two years and would not have been possible without the encouragement and help of wonderful friends and family, all of whom were immensely supportive but also patient in answering my myriad questions.

To my most patient and wonderful husband, Nanik, and to my sister-in-law, Suzie, go my deepest thanks for allowing me the space to grow and the freedom to do what I most love, teaching and writing about the pleasures of the kitchens of India. Along the way, they have had to endure weeks of eating nothing but fish or vegetables or an assortment of flatbreads as I went through the rigors of testing each recipe. Another sincere thank-you to my friends and their friends, in many parts of the world, who were always there with answers when I called with questions about a technique, or the use of particular spices, or even the relevance of a particular recipe in the culture of their ethnic community. Amongst them is Sunanda Nath, Vasu Reddy, Damayanthi Reddy and Gayatri Haragopal in Hyderabad; Saveeta Mohanty in Orissa; Rakhi Mukerji for her insights into the foods of Assam; Jimmy Kapoor, who taught me about the East Indian community of Mumbai; Nalini Prakash, a passionate home cook in the magical little town Coonoor, tucked away in the Nilgiri Hills in the south; Usha Peddamatham; Sudha Mani; Sushila Mathew; Nilima Sethi; Sheela Rao; and so many others who so generously shared their insights.

To Lisa Ekus, literary agent par excellence, whose power of suggestion is impossible to ignore, I owe a deep debt. Were it not for her gentle but constant prodding, I would not have embarked on this project. I am also grateful to Bob Dees, who saw the potential for this book and almost immediately accepted the proposal. Thanks go to Jennifer MacKenzie, a knowledgeable and meticulous recipe tester, and to the amazing team at PageWave Graphics, especially the book's designer Daniella Zanchetta. Thanks also to photographer Colin Erricson, food stylists Kate Bush and Kathryn Robertson and prop stylist Charlene Erricson. My thanks also go to Tina Anson Mine for her thoughtful copy editing, and Gillian Watts for her indexing skills. Words cannot express my deepest thanks to my editor, Carol Sherman, who has endured all the pressures of this project with fortitude, patience and good humor. Her editing skills were apparent in my first book, *Easy Indian Cooking,* but were truly challenged this time, when, in spite of the gaggle of Indian languages in the names of traditional dishes, she retained her calm.

Introduction

R EGIONAL FOODS AROUND THE world tend to be distinctive and influenced by local ingredients. In India, the size and geography of the country, coupled with the impact of history and religion, have accentuated this distinctiveness. The vast and ancient land of India is almost a continent in itself. With more than one billion inhabitants of multiple ethnic backgrounds, it is no surprise that the diversity of its cuisine is equally staggering.

The purpose of the *Complete Book of Indian Cooking* is to illustrate the differences and similarities between Indian regional foods. Although spices are the common denominator, the way they are used is vastly different in each area. That, combined with local ingredients and religious beliefs, means a distinctive cuisine exists in every part of the country. And there are other differences. In general, the north has a grain-based diet of wheat, millet and sorghum, but rice is not the main event as it is in the south, which is almost 100 percent rice-based. In North India, pan-frying is a common cooking method, while in the south, steaming is a much-used method. Generally, gravies (curry sauces) in North India are thicker, with a base of onions, tomatoes, puréed nuts, puréed lentils and, occasionally, cream. Southern cooks use coconut milk and tamarind in their dishes. The gravies are light and broth-like, which is one of the reasons why the cuisine of the south has not become as popular in North America. The soupy dals are too thin and watery for the non-Indian palate and would qualify as soups rather than main courses. The other issue is rice served in multiple courses, which, again, is too repetitive for non-Indians. The exception is *dosa* (crêpes), made of a light rice-and-lentil batter, which are extremely flavorful when eaten with just a smattering of lightly spiced potatoes and coconut chutney. The food of the eastern regions, too, is rice-based. The diet is also rich in fish and seafood, except in the far northeastern states, where pork is the main protein and seasonings tend to be very simple, devoid of oil and spices. The western states share many commonalities with the north, but each has a distinctive cuisine. Rice, a variety of grains, goat, poultry and seafood along the coast — usually cooked with a plethora of spices and using a variety of different cooking techniques — are common to all these states.

My interest in food, which began when I was a young homemaker trying to be a good housewife and mother many decades ago, has developed into a passion, as has my interest in the background and evolution of Indian cuisine. As I delved into the foods of India, partly out of curiosity but mostly to research the antecedents of particular recipes, I became aware of the many differences in the way spices and other ingredients are used in different regions. This, coupled with the fact that there are regional vegetables, fruits, herbs and oils (to mention just a few points of difference), led me to believe the time was right to introduce more people to the richness and diversity of the regional foods of India.

My hope is that this book will help to explain some of the mysteries surrounding the cuisine of this ancient land and encourage you to embark on a culinary adventure that is as astonishing as it is satisfying.

— Suneeta Vaswani

The Changing Face of Indian Food

THE APPRECIATION OF INDIAN food has come a long way in the last few years. At one time, Indian restaurants around the world were small mom-and-pop operations, serving tandoori foods, naan and rich creamy kormas and curries with plenty of fat floating in the gravy. The menus in large part were almost identical, and this food came to be recognized as "Indian food." While somewhat true, it represented only a very small geographical area in North India, which was influenced by Moghlai cuisine. The Moghuls ruled India for three centuries (until the British replaced them in the 1800s) and they brought with them a sophisticated cuisine with Persian influences. Saffron, rich gravies made of puréed nuts and the use of cream were all the results of Moghul influence. This food is particularly appealing to the Western palate. Naan bread, made in a tandoor — a clay oven buried in the ground up to its neck — is the everyday bread of Afghanistan, where it is baked every morning by women in their village's communal oven. Naan is not the daily bread of Indians and is not homemade. Yet, for decades, this was the perception of Indian food outside the country. Mercifully, this misconception is changing, thanks in large part to travel, both business and leisure, and to the fact that Indian food has finally arrived on the haute cuisine scene in the form of excellent restaurants that serve authentic dishes from different parts of India. South Indian food, a world apart from its counterpart in the north, is now available in small local eateries in several cities in North America. Its distinctive rice crêpes and delicate steamed rice cakes have gained a loyal following, particularly among those who have traveled to South India. As more westerners travel outside the "golden triangle" of Delhi, Agra and Rajasthan, all in the north, they realize the astonishing variety of foods in other parts of the country and are happy to try something different.

The two most life-changing occurrences in the world of Indian food have been the advent of food shows on Indian television and the enormous increase in leisure travel by Indians in their own country. The former has transformed cooking from the world of housewives toiling over a kerosene-fired single burner to one where celebrities and socialites rub shoulders with chefs and high-profile restaurateurs at mega-events. It has spawned celebrity TV chefs and cookbook authors, and the profession has gained a respectability hitherto unknown. Cooking is finally recognized as an art form. And travel has broadened the culinary horizons of ordinary folk, who now know the difference between the foods of Gujarat and Bengal, Goa and Tamil Nadu. This two-pronged exposure to the regional foods of India has resulted in an explosion of small family-owned restaurants specializing in the cuisine of not only their state but often that of their ethnic community within the state. The food scene in India is not only alive and well but pulsating with excitement.

Lifestyle changes, too, play a big role in the India of today. The almost total disappearance of full-time help and the simultaneous appearance of quality prepackaged spice mixes are together changing the way Indians cook. Gone are the days when every Indian kitchen had a grinding stone on the kitchen floor. (It was a large slab of soapstone, which had dents chiseled into the surface regularly by the "stone-chiseling man," who came by every month to renew the dents.) Spices and pastes were ground every day with a heavy torpedo-shaped stone by squatting on the floor and working the stone back and forth on the dented surface. The dents facilitated the grinding. Except in rural areas, these stones have been replaced with powerful appliances, indigenously manufactured, which make short work of this laborious process. And the last few years have seen an even greater change in the world of spices, as food companies have built state-of-the-art facilities that package excellent-quality spices and spice powders in vacuum-sealed pouches.

The greatest change that I see on my annual visits to India is not altered flavors but new and different methods for achieving those results. The food remains true to its roots, but there has been a streamlining of the process.

One popular category of Indian food, recognized until recently only by Indians, is street food, or *chaat*. I have never met a person, Indian or otherwise, who did not love chaat from the first bite. The only negative about chaat is that it is impossible to do it justice in words. Casual-eating places serving chaat abound in most cities with a decent-size Indian population. The names of the various chaat dishes have no English counterpart, so it is best to go with an Indian friend on your first chaat expedition. I have included a chapter on chaat, including a chaat primer to help you navigate the maze of dishes with a little more ease.

Soy in all its myriad forms is not an ingredient usually associated with Indian food. It made its appearance in India in the middle of the last century and has gained in popularity as its nutritional value has been recognized. It provides vital protein to the vegetarians so prevalent in India. I felt it was time to include recipes using the many forms of soy products, because vegetarianism is becoming more accepted worldwide.

As I've explored the different regions, I have come to realize that no Indian can claim complete knowledge of all the cuisines of this vast subcontinent. We can only try.

The Regional Cooking of India

✹ NORTH

THE CUISINES OF KASHMIR, PUNJAB, HARYANA, Rajasthan and Sindh (which is now part of Pakistan) are distinctive among the northern states. Uttar Pradesh and Madhya Pradesh share similarities with neighboring states and lean toward a vegetarian diet, with the exception of their Muslim population, who favor meat.

Saffron is the standout spice in the north. It is a legacy of the Moghuls, and some of the finest in the world is grown in Kashmir. It is used on special occasions in pilafs, lamb and chicken dishes and also in desserts. Coriander and cumin seeds are used whole, toasted and powdered, or untoasted and powdered. Black cardamom, grown in the cooler climes of Kashmir, is also unique to North Indian dishes. A variety of dried red chile known as Kashmiri red chile is not as hot as some southern varieties but provides some heat and a brilliant red color to dishes. *Garam masala* (*garam,* meaning "warm," and *masala,* meaning "mixture") is a mix of aromatic powdered spices and is used as a finishing spice in northern dishes.

Some unusual northern vegetables include lotus root and lotus seeds. Sliced crosswise, the root reveals a pretty pattern that is visually exotic. It is used in meat and vegetable dishes and also made into fritters. Lotus seed puffs, airy as popcorn, are cooked with vegetables and used in milk-based desserts.

In Kashmir, lamb plays a major role. It is not uncommon to have between seven and 12 lamb dishes at a wedding feast, and even everyday meals include at least a couple. Dried fruits and vegetables are another important component to ensure a varied winter diet. Kashmiri cooking is clearly divided into two distinct cuisines: Muslim food, which uses onions and garlic freely, and the food of the Hindus (known as Kashmiri pandits), who eat meat but for religious reasons shun garlic and onions, substituting instead asafetida (the gum resin of a plant), which is prevalent in their cuisine.

Throughout India, greens of all varieties are eaten with gusto. In Punjab, the arrival of mustard greens is eagerly awaited in the winter months — the Punjabi staple of mustard greens and corn bread, washed down with a tall glass of buttermilk, is legendary. Spinach, too, is a favorite, sautéed with seasonings, cooked with *dals* or meat, or even in a spinach *pulao*.

Punjab is the granary of the country, and wheat is the major crop. Corn, millet and sorghum, too, are grown in the north and are the basis of some of the tastiest and healthiest flatbreads. Basmati rice, grown exclusively in the foothills of the Himalayan mountain range, is world famous for its distinctive aroma and nutty taste. Expensive even in India, it is reserved for special pulaos and festive occasions.

Beans and lentils play a major role in the Indian diet, and, although several varieties are eaten, each area has its preferences. In the north, east and west, beans are soaked overnight and ground into a paste the next day. Spices are added and the paste is sun-dried in the form of nuggets or balls, known as *wadi, bori* or *baadi,* depending on the region. These dried bean nuggets add texture and flavor to a variety of dishes from curries to rice pilafs. In Punjab, red kidney beans (*rajma*) and chickpeas (*kabuli channa* or *chole*) are by far the most popular. Sindhis favor yellow mung beans and split yellow peas (*channa dal*) and love chickpea flour–based dishes. In Rajasthan, where most dals are eaten, chickpea flour (*besan*) reigns, and Rajasthanis' creative recipes for this ingredient are truly impressive.

The people of Sindh fled as refugees when India was divided in 1947 and settled throughout India. Six decades later, they continue to maintain their culinary heritage. The cuisine is simple, and one defining factor is that it does not use complicated ground spice mixes and pastes. The use of basic ground coriander, cumin, turmeric and cayenne is what defines the cuisine. Cardamom is another favorite spice and is used in meat dishes as well as desserts.

Rajasthan is a desert state and has little by way of fresh vegetables. *Ker*, a berry from a local shrub, is popular, as it can be dried and stored for later use. A green bean known as *sangri* is another delicacy. It, too, is dried and saved for year-round use in a special dish known as *ker sangri*.

One of the most frequently asked questions related to Indian cuisine is about the use of ghee, or clarified butter. Though it varies from state to state, it is safe to say that ghee plays a bigger role in vegetarian diets and in certain communities. Although much maligned as a saturated fat and, therefore, an unhealthy option, ghee plays a major role in Ayurvedic diets. A small amount consumed daily is considered beneficial. Among the Marwaris of Rajasthan and the Jains of Gujarat, both of whom follow vegetarian diets, its use is more prevalent. And, of course, in traditional Indian sweets, ghee is a must. Many vegetarian households serve warm melted ghee at each meal to drizzle over steamed rice. I find that tempering spices in ghee at the end of the cooking process adds tremendous flavor to dals. A little ghee goes a long way and elevates the dish to another level.

A variety of cooking oils is used throughout the country, depending on what is grown locally. In Kashmir, where vast fields of mustard provide a visual treat, mustard oil is used in many dishes, particularly with vegetables. In other areas, peanut and various vegetable oils are the most commonly used.

◈ EAST

THE EASTERN STATES ENCOMPASS SIKKIM, Bihar, Chhattisgarh, Jharkhand, West Bengal, Orissa and, in the remote northeast, the seven sister states of Assam, Arunachal Pradesh, Manipur, Mizoram, Meghalaya, Nagaland and Tripura. Bengali cuisine is refined and subtle, with fish and rice as the center of the diet. The estuary of the mighty Ganges and Brahmaputra rivers provides a wealth of river fish as they flow into the Bay of Bengal, and these are prized by the discerning Bengali palate. A unique feature of Bengali cuisine is that it is served in courses, unlike in the rest of the country, which serves family-style. There is a very proper protocol for a Bengali meal: The first course is mixed vegetables with a bitter flavor, believed to enhance the appetite. This is followed by dal and rice accompanied by a fried vegetable, such as eggplant. Fish and rice come next, then a meat dish with rice. Next is a sweet-and-sour condiment, made either of green mango, tomato or pineapple, known as *tauk*. This is served by itself as a digestive. Then comes the famous *mishti doi,* a sweet, rich, slightly smoky yogurt. The meal ends with a rich milk-based sweet for which Bengali cuisine is justly famous. The main seasonings in Bengali food are mustard seeds, and poppy seeds, which are made into a paste known as *posto*. *Panch phoran,* a mixture of five seeds — mustard, cumin, fennel, fenugreek and nigella — typically flash-fried and not powdered, is the signature seasoning of Bengali cuisine. Another distinctive aspect of Bengali food is the addition of a little sugar to many dishes.

Mustard oil is used extensively in the food of the eastern states. It is made of cold-pressed mustard seeds and is not an infusion of crushed mustard seeds in oil. It has an assertive flavor and is the preferred oil used in Indian pickles — the fiery, salty, oily condiments that line an entire row in most Indian grocery stores.

The northeastern states remain remote and mysterious for most Indians, who know little about their tribal cultures and food habits. Assam, better known because of its tea estates, shares a love of beef and pork with the others. Local river fish is also enjoyed. Their food, for the most part, is devoid of spices and oil, except for rendered pork fat in some areas. Turmeric is used sparingly and is usually scraped fresh turmeric root grown in kitchen gardens. Several varieties of local chiles are grown and used frequently. Local greens and herbs abound, but perhaps the one defining ingredient is bamboo shoot. It is used fresh and fermented and is frequently cooked with other ingredients. A variety of sticky rice is the basis of the diet and relished with most dishes.

The food of Orissa is similar in flavor to Bengali food but perhaps not as refined. The *panch phutana* of Orissa is similar to the *panch phoran* seed mix of Bengal, but the distinctive nigella seeds are replaced with red chile flakes. Rice is the staple, and cooked rice is often submerged in water and left overnight to ferment slightly. A large variety of vegetables and greens are found in Orissa. Squash blossoms are a popular treat, dipped in a paste made with rice and deep-fried or made into patties. There are many other local vegetables that have no equivalents in the rest of India. Fish and seafood are the base of the Oriya (as the people of Orissa are known) diet. Chicken is almost never eaten, and meat plays a minor role.

The cuisines of Bihar and Jharkhand have no particular defining features, as their dishes are influenced by neighboring states. Hearty breads, beans and vegetables are the staple diet.

SOUTH

THE FOUR SOUTHERN STATES — KARNATAKA, Kerala, Tamil Nadu and Andhra Pradesh — share many similarities. They have primarily rice-based diets, and the staple breakfast foods — rice crêpes (*dosa*) and steamed rice cakes (*idli*), accompanied by the signature lentil-and-vegetable stew (*sambhar*) — are common to all four states. Rice is eaten at all meals, and lunch is often three courses, each served with rice. Seafood is relished by all the coastal people, though there are vegetarian communities in the area as well.

Karnataka, with a homogenous population, shares many food traditions with its southern neighbors, and there is no one defining factor to identify this state's cuisine, as there is in Kerala.

Kerala, the lush tropical paradise on the southwest tip of the subcontinent, is the spice coast of India. There was a bustling Arab trade in spices, particularly black pepper, long before it drew the attention of the Europeans. The world-renowned Tellicherry and Malabar peppercorns are grown there, along with cloves and green cardamom. The population of Kerala has three distinct communities. The Muslim descendants of Arab traders who married local Kerala women are known as Mophlas. They are a wealthy trading community, so their cuisine is rich and features many heavily spiced meat dishes. They are well known for the famous Kerala *biriyani*, a dish of basmati rice layered with braised meat cooked with a host of spices. The Syrian Christians also have a distinct cuisine. Perhaps not as spice laden and with slight Western overtones, theirs is a cuisine that uses beef, pork, goat and chicken. And then there are the Hindus, who are divided into two groups: vegetarians and meat eaters. Each has their specialties. The one common link between all the cuisines of Kerala is coconut, the culinary symbol of the state.

The Brahmins of Tamil Nadu are vegetarian, while the non-Brahmins favor goat (mutton, cabrito). Chicken is a special-occasion dish. Coconut and tamarind are used in both vegetarian and meat-based dishes. White rice is the staple, and it is usually just steamed. There is a tradition of serving it with small quantities of hot, dry spice powders called *podi* (pronounced *pori*) and a little warm ghee. Yogurt is also a must in the Tamilian's diet. As in the three other southern states, rice crêpes (*dosa*) and steamed rice cakes (*idli*) and their many variations are the basic breakfast food, always served with coconut chutney and lentil-and-vegetable stew (*sambhar*). Although the ubiquitous sambhar is eaten daily all over the south, there are definite regional differences. Equally important is the broth-like tangy, spicy rasam made with yellow lentils and, in most cases, tamarind or tomatoes for tang, seasoned with flash-fried mustard seeds, chiles and curry leaves and traditionally served as a second course with rice. It is considered to be a digestive and although traditionally served with steamed rice, I like to sip it from the bowl.

Andhra Pradesh, the very large state that shares a border with Maharashtra and an extensive border with Karnataka, has three distinct cuisines. Its capital, Hyderabad, has a strong Muslim influence because its ruler was descended from noblemen who had settled there in the last days of the Moghuls. The cuisine of Hyderabad has Moghul overtones and South Indian undertones, making it unique. The result is a rich, highly spiced, complex cuisine that, though mouth-watering, is laborious to reproduce. Though there are still a few families with old-time help who can produce the lavish meals of yesteryear, it is only a matter of time until the cuisine evolves into something simpler.

Next there is the food of northern Andhra Pradesh, known as Rayalaseema. This area is dry, and the food is simply spiced and not rich. Finally, there's coastal Andhra cuisine, which focuses on the wealth of seafood available from the Bay of Bengal. Tamarind and chiles are used freely. In fact, with the exception of Hyderabadi food, Andhra Pradesh has the hottest food in the country. For very good reason, too. Fiery Guntur chiles are grown in the area and used with abandon. Asafetida is another ingredient used extensively. Whereas in North India pickles are served with meals, in Andhra Pradesh, *podis* (dry spice powders) reign supreme. Plain steamed rice is mixed with a spoonful or two of a *podi,* then a little ghee is drizzled on top and mixed in with the warm rice. This is often a first course. *Dosa* and *idli* are also often eaten with *podis.*

WEST

THE WESTERN STATES OF GUJARAT, Maharashtra and Goa could not be more different from one another — each provides a unique food experience.

Gujarat is home to Muslims, Parsis, Hindus and Jains, each, of course, with their own particular cuisine. The Parsis are Zoroastrians originally from Iran (known then as Persia), who fled religious persecution and arrived by boat on the shores of Gujarat centuries ago. They were accepted by the Hindu ruler and allowed to pursue their religion on the condition that they adopt the local customs and language. Parsis are well assimilated, but their food habits have changed little. Their diet is rich in meat, chicken and seafood, unlike the local Jains, who, for religious reasons, are strictly vegetarian, many shunning any food that grows underground, such as onions, garlic, potatoes and carrots. Interestingly, Parsis eat an astonishing number of eggs. Their vegetable dishes are almost always topped with them. Their wedding banquets are legendary and feature a set menu of fish, chicken and meat dishes, accompanied by pilaf, condiments, flatbreads and desserts.

Gujaratis are predominantly vegetarian and, in my opinion, create the best vegetarian food in the world, often without the use of onions and garlic. I speak from many years' experience

feasting at Gujarati tables and am always amazed at their creativity. A cuisine that shuns excessive use of spices, it relies instead on the freshness of its ingredients. Their variety of breads, snacks and condiments is unparalleled.

One of the most important ingredients in Gujarati food is asafetida. This is the gum resin of a plant, with an offensive odor that is neutralized by cooking. It serves a dual purpose: to replace the flavor of onions and garlic and to help to break down indigestible elements in beans and cruciferous vegetables. Also of note is the fact that, like Bengalis, Gujaratis use a little sugar in most dishes, giving their food a distinctly sweetish taste.

Maharashtra is an immense state, both geographically and in its diversity. Its capital, Mumbai (Bombay), is a melting pot of all that is India. Home to some of the wealthiest Indians, it also has some of the poorest of the poor. Five-star restaurants in five-star hotels boast chefs from culinary meccas around the world. They have access to the finest ingredients worldwide, and their well-traveled, well-heeled clientele are a discerning lot. Yet some of the best food in the city is served in people's homes and in some of the small restaurants that have sprung up in the last decade, which specialize in particular ethnic cuisines from remote areas. Not known for sophisticated décor or service but rather for their authentic flavors and ingredients, these are often tucked away in unpretentious surroundings and are little known by anyone except the most serious food lover.

In Maharashtra, there is a coastal cuisine that abounds in seafood dishes, usually spiked with red chiles and generous amounts of coconut. The variety of seafood fished in the waters of the Indian Ocean defies description. Everything from rock lobster to clams to crab are found, and there is a thriving export trade in frozen seafood. Around the coast of Mumbai, the local favorite is, of course, pomfret, a delicate, flounder-like flatfish that is highly prized. Mackerel, sardines and a local fish known as Bombay duck are other favorites. Between Mumbai and Mangalore, there is the Konkan coast, which boasts several distinct cuisines. Seafood is, of course, the focus, and coconut plays an important role. This food

is different from the seafood dishes of Mumbai and Goa and of late there has been tremendous interest in the specialties of this area.

In Mumbai, there is the indigenous community known as East Indians. They were the original inhabitants of the seven islands that comprise the current city, and they now live in small pockets of Mumbai and its environs. They were converts to Catholicism and remain a distinct group, different from Goans, with whom they are often confused. I have included some recipes from this community as well.

In the interior of Maharashtra, dals, vegetables, and meat and chicken dishes are the focus. There are specific spice blends used in different areas; for instance, the famous black (*kala*) masala of Nagpur families. Fiery blends of a host of spices, these mixtures are well-guarded family secrets and not usually found commercially.

Goa, the tiny state on the west coast wedged between Maharashtra and Karnataka, is a paradise for beach lovers. With a long history of Portuguese rule (461 years to be precise), it is little wonder that the people of Goa are a blend of both cultures. The Portuguese had an ongoing plan to convert the local population to Catholicism, and today Catholics and Hindus live in harmony, their churches and temples side by side. Nowhere is Portuguese influence more apparent than in the food, and it is most prevalent in their baked goods and desserts. Long before the British arrived, Goa had thriving bakeries making Western-style breads, cakes and pastries.

The people of Goa are known for their love of music, drink (wine was introduced by the Portuguese) and food. Seafood is the hands-down favorite of both Hindus and Christians, and coconut is the common denominator. Parboiled rice is the staple food, with hot curries to accompany it. Goan food uses an abundance of garlic, dried red chiles and cumin. They are often made into a paste with vinegar, an ingredient introduced by the Portuguese, to create the signature seasoning blend of Goa. Unlike in the rest of India, pork is a favorite meat, again a result of Portuguese influence. Chicken dishes are equally popular, but mutton (goat), the meat of choice in the rest of India, is not.

General Guidelines

Cookware and Tools

INDIAN COOKING DOES NOT REQUIRE A LOT OF special equipment, but a few essentials make it easier. Wide-bottomed pans with tight-fitting lids are a must so that foods brown evenly from contact with the pan and the moisture in the foods will condense inside the lid and drip back into the pan to cook the food without adding more liquid. This intensifies the flavors. Stockpots do not work very well for Indian cooking.

I prefer good-quality nonstick cookware, which necessitates minimal fat, usually about a quarter of what's called for in a traditional recipe.

Even though this small amount is not always adequate to "fry" foods like onions, it is acceptable to augment the oil with spoonfuls of water or stock to help the onions brown to the desired degree. This process requires a little more "pot watching," but the end results are worth the extra effort to retain the authenticity of the flavors with considerably less fat.

In recent years, several good brands of heatproof silicone spatulas have appeared on the market. I find these invaluable, as they allow you to stir into the curve of the pot.

Common Ingredients

AN ORGANIZED KITCHEN IS THE KEY TO A positive kitchen experience. Stock it with basic ingredients to make your cooking adventures hassle-free.

Beans and Legumes

Beans and lentils occupy an exalted position and are arguably the most versatile food in the Indian culinary repertoire. Here's a sampling of some of them: kidney beans (*rajma*), chickpeas (*chole*, *kabuli channa*), small green chickpeas (*hara channa*) or brown chickpeas (*kala channa*, also known as *kadala* or *kulthi*), black-eyed peas (*lobhia*), brown lentils (*sabat masoor*), Indian black beans (*sabat urad*), green mung beans (*sabat mung*), red lentils (*masoor dal*), split yellow peas (*channa dal*), yellow lentils (*toor dal*), yellow mung beans (*mung dal*), split white lentils (*urad dal*) and dried black-eyed peas (*lobhia*, *chawli*). Beans and dals should be stored in airtight containers.

Bean nuggets, used throughout the north, east and west and known by different names,

such as *wadi*, *mangodi* or *bori*, are dehydrated nuggets made from beans soaked for several hours and ground with a little water to a paste. The paste is seasoned with spices from mild to very spicy. It is then dropped in little clumps on mats and sun-dried. These nuggets can be stored for several months. They are added to curries, rice and vegetable dishes for added flavor and texture, and soften as they cook. The nuggets are also available in Indian markets and should be stored in a container in the refrigerator for one year or longer.

Coconut

Coconut is synonymous with coastal India, particularly the west coast. The food of Goa uses coconut in all seafood preparations, all ground masala mixes used as a curry base, and several desserts. Besides adding flavor, grated coconut is a thickening agent and, when ground with spices and herbs, it is the defining taste of each dish. In Kerala, its use is ubiquitous — it is ground into pastes and chutneys, sprinkled over vegetable salads, and coconut chips are toasted and used as a garnish. And, of course, in both areas, coconut milk is the liquid of choice for many curries. Both Goa and Kerala use coconut oil in several dishes, although its use is being discouraged by the health conscious. In coastal Maharashtra, too, coconut is an important ingredient. Surprisingly, on the east coast coconut is not as prevalent. Coastal Andhra food does not use coconut, and Orissa and Bengal use it sparingly. Packages of frozen fresh grated coconut are available in many supermarkets and all Indian markets. Canned coconut milk is also readily available. Always shake the can vigorously before opening, as the high fat content in coconut milk causes separation when stored.

Buying and using a fresh coconut

1. Hold the coconut to your ear and shake to make sure there is plenty of liquid inside. If there is no liquid, it is a sign that the coconut is not fresh and will be rancid. Look for a heavy coconut because it is usually freshest.

2. Break the coconut with a hammer and discard liquid. Pry the meat from the shell with the tip of a knife. Using a vegetable peeler, remove all the brown inner skin, leaving only the white meat. Cut in pieces and process as fine as possible in a food processor.

Extracts

Rose extract (essence) is a commonly used ingredient in special rice dishes and in sweets. It is concentrated and is not to be confused with rose water, which, being water-based, dissipates over time.

Kewra extract is from the pandanus plant, with long sword-like leaves growing from the base of the plant. This floral extract is used in meat and rice dishes in the north but is unknown in the south. All extracts should be tightly sealed and can be stored indefinitely in the pantry.

Flours

All-purpose flour is used sparingly in Indian recipes. The exceptions are Bengal's basic balloon bread (*puri*), called *luchi* in Bengal, and in Goan desserts, a result of Portuguese influence.

Chapati flour (*atta*) is very finely milled whole wheat flour, usually sold in 5 lb (2 kg) or larger bags. It is used for most North Indian flatbreads. Store in the refrigerator for up to eight months.

Chickpea flour (*besan*) is a high-protein gluten-free flour, a staple in pantries throughout the country. It is a versatile flour used in breads, to make batters, as a binder in place of eggs and to make sweets. Store in the refrigerator for an indefinite period.

Millet (*bajri*) and sorghum (*jowar*) are winter crops and are ground into flour to make wholesome peasant breads flavored with onion, chiles and spices. These are popular all over North India and are eaten in the cooler months. Store for up to four months in the refrigerator.

Semolina/Cream of Wheat (*sooji*, *rava*) are used for breads, savory pancakes and desserts. Cream of Wheat is a little more coarse than semolina and therefore unsuitable for certain recipes.

Ghee and Oils

Ghee, the ancient cooking medium of India, is clarified butter. It is essential in Indian sweets and certain dishes, particularly in the north. Although a saturated fat, ghee is considered healthy when used in moderation.

Available in Indian grocery stores and many health food stores, it is quite simple to make at home. Melt 1 lb (500 g) unsalted butter in a wok or saucepan over low heat. As the melted butter bubbles, reduce heat to very low and let it simmer, without stirring, until foam covers the top. Skim foam with a wire mesh strainer, without disturbing the melted butter. Continue to simmer until liquid begins to look clear and the milk solids that have collected at the bottom turn light brown, 50 to 60 minutes. Pour the melted butter through a very fine mesh strainer or fine cheesecloth into a clean jar. Let cool and cover tightly. Store in the refrigerator for up to one year.

Many different oils are used in Indian cooking, depending on the region. In Kashmir and Bengal, where mustard seeds play a major role, mustard oil is predominant. It is cold-pressed, not an infusion, and has a strong distinctive flavor. It is used extensively in the preparation of Indian pickles — the very hot, salty and oily condiments. It has medicinal uses as well, and is warmed and used topically to relieve joint pain.

Safflower, sunflower and peanut oils are popular in West India, as peanuts are widely cultivated in Maharashtra. The south uses these oils and also untoasted cold-pressed sesame oil, known as *gingelly oil.*

Coconut oil, used as the main cooking medium in Goa and parts of Kerala, is now acknowledged as a health risk and is being discouraged. However, recent studies indicate coconut oil is very high in antioxidants and lauric acid, which some researchers believe make it an excellent immune-system booster.

Ginger and Garlic

Ginger and garlic are staples in Indian cuisine. A shiny, smooth, thin-skinned "hand" of ginger indicates freshness. Fresh ginger is juicy, but as it ages, the skin becomes wrinkled and the flesh fibrous. When I find really fresh ginger and particularly fresh garlic, I process large amounts of each and store them in an airtight container in the refrigerator for up to four weeks. I do not add any oil or salt. Or you can spread the finely chopped ginger or garlic on a dish, form a 1/2-inch (1 cm) thick brick and score into four pieces. Freeze and transfer the frozen pieces to a resealable freezer bag to freeze for up to 12 months. As needed, scrape off the necessary amount with a sharp knife.

Alternatively, keep a prepared mixture. In a food processor, combine cloves of four large heads of garlic (about 6 oz/175 g) and 2 oz (60 g) peeled gingerroot. Pulse until finely chopped but not puréed. Refrigerate, tightly closed, in a glass jar, for up to one month.

Jaggery *(Gur)*

This is unrefined cane sugar, which is used extensively in lentil dishes, breads and, of course, sweets. It is rich in minerals, with a molasses-like flavor. You can substitute brown sugar in recipes where jaggery is called for in small amounts. The color and texture vary from tan to brown and from solid to semisoft, depending on the time of year when it was processed. The taste, however, does not vary with color or texture. It

can be stored indefinitely in an airtight container in the pantry.

Nuts

Nuts are used freely in Indian cooking. They should be bought in small quantities and stored in the refrigerator or freezer for no longer than one year. Buy them from a store with a high turnover because they are more likely to be fresh. I prefer to buy them from an Indian store because the price is usually better. Also, certain nuts, such as cashews and pistachios, called for in Indian dishes are not toasted or salted. Raw cashews are almost white and very sweet — very different in taste from the roasted variety. Raw, unsalted pistachios are also sweetish and completely different in taste from roasted ones. Cashews are grown in Kerala and used in several preparations, including rice and the semolina mash (*upma*), the famous breakfast preparation. In the north, almonds and pistachios are the most popular and are used in curries, pulaos and desserts. Maharashtra has an abundance of peanuts, and these are used in snacks, vegetables and lentil dishes, and sweets. Whole nuts are used as a garnish for many preparations. Puréed nuts are a popular addition to North Indian curries, both for flavor and also as a thickener.

Papadum *(Papad)*

A *papadum* is a lentil-based cracker-like accompaniment. Papadums are made of different lentils and come in many flavors, from plain to highly spiced. While papadum is often mistaken for a bread, its role in the Indian meal is purely as a crunchy accompaniment. In North America, papadums are served in Indian restaurants accompanied by two dipping sauces: a green cilantro-based savory one, the other a sweetish brown one with a tamarind and jaggery base. This new role is a result of the ubiquitous chip-and-dip culture we have come to expect. Papadums can be deep-fried in very hot oil for less than 10 seconds and drained on paper towels before serving. Or toast them on an open flame by holding them with tongs and rapidly flipping back and forth until cooked, about one minute. They can also be cooked in the microwave:

place two papadums between paper towels and cook on High power for 30 to 35 seconds. Once cooked, they will remain fresh for 24 hours if stored in an airtight container.

Puffed Lotus Seeds (Phool Makhana)
Light, airy puffed lotus seeds, somewhat like popcorn but larger, are used in North Indian vegetable dishes and milky desserts purely for texture. They have little flavor. They can be stored for up to six months in the pantry.

Rice
Basmati rice is a must, but all basmati rice is not created equal. Even though "basmati" is often used in a generic manner to denote extra-long-grain white rice, true basmati rice can only be cultivated in the foothills of the Himalayas, where the growing conditions and the type of soil contribute to its unique nutty flavor and unmistakable aroma. And there is certainly nothing that remotely resembles "brown basmati" rice, which is a creation of rice farmers in California and is quite unsuitable for use in Indian cooking.

It is more economical to buy large bags of basmati rice at the Indian store, as you will pay the same for an 11-lb (5 kg) bag as you would for 3 lbs (1.5 kg) in a supermarket, where basmati rice is sold in a 12-oz (340 g) box. It does not spoil; in fact, aged basmati is more desirable and prized for its superior flavor. In India, basmati aged two to three years is more expensive than newly harvested rice. Look for bags or boxes that state that they are a product of India or Pakistan; the growing conditions are similar.

South India grows a very large variety of rice, localized and in limited quantities. Basmati rice is almost unknown in the south. In Hyderabad, where the cuisine is based on Moghul traditions, the exceptional *pulaos* and *biriyanis* are made with a good-quality long-grain rice known simply as pulao rice. In Kerala, the dishes of the Mophlas (the Muslim population who are the descendants of Arab traders who came several centuries ago and subsequently married local women) also call for fine long-grain rice for their special pulaos.

South Indian rice is suited to the batters used for *idli* (rice cake) and *dosa* (crêpes) and for the slightly stickier rice preferred in the cuisine of the region. Flatbreads and puris, similar to North Indian chapati and puris, are made in the south with rice flour. In Kerala, *puttu* is a popular breakfast food. It is made of moistened ground rice, layered with grated coconut and packed in a cylindrical container designed to steam the contents. When cooked, it is pushed out of the cylinder and broken up with the fingers. It is served with sweet mashed bananas, sweetened coconut milk or with a spicy curry for breakfast.

Sev
Sev is a vermicelli-type snack made from chickpea flour (*besan*). It comes ready to eat in different thicknesses, from almost as thin as a strand of hair to the thickness of kitchen twine. It should not be confused with the vermicelli used for making a type of dessert. It is available in Indian stores.

Soy
Soy is used in many forms in Indian vegetarian dishes. Soy flour is often mixed with whole wheat (chapati flour) for flatbreads. Soy granules, also know as textured vegetable protein or TVP, resemble fresh bread crumbs and are used to make patties and rolls and also cooked to resemble ground meat. Soy nuggets and chips come in varying sizes and are small chunks or chips from 1/2 inch (1 cm) to 1 inch (2.5 cm) in size. They are cooked in curries, with vegetables and also in elaborate rice pulaos. They are available in health food stores and in Indian markets. Follow directions on package for use. Store in a cool dry place for up to one year.

Spices (see also page 21)
Stock the basic spices. As a rule, spices in their seed form have an almost indefinite shelf life if correctly stored. Powdered spices, on the other hand, are fragile and deteriorate with exposure to air, much like coffee and pepper. We know now that when we grind small quantities of these just before using, they are far more fragrant and flavorful. I realize that grinding spices for each dish is not practical, but I suggest a compromise. Buy only small quantities of

ground aromatic spices, such as coriander, cumin and *garam masala*, from a reliable source where they are stored in airtight jars. Avoid buying them from bulk containers, which are exposed to air. On the other hand, coriander seeds, cumin seeds, mustard seeds, fenugreek seeds, sesame seeds and poppy seeds can be stored for a year or two. Delicate spices, such as saffron, cardamom, cloves and bay leaves, which are used primarily for their fragrance, should also be bought in small quantities. Turmeric and cayenne do not deteriorate.

Yogurt

Plain yogurt is a must. It is used extensively in marinades and for flavor and texture. I find nonfat, low-fat and full-fat yogurt all suitable for cooking purposes, with no difference in the end result. It is necessary to stabilize yogurt with 1 tsp (5 mL) cornstarch per 1 cup (250 mL) yogurt to prevent it from curdling when heated. To prevent total separation, it is important that the yogurt be at room temperature before adding it to a dish while cooking. In most cases, if there is partial curdling in the beginning, by the time the dish is ready, the appearance is remedied.

Spices, Spice Blends and Herbs

UNDERSTANDING SPICES AND HERBS and their correct use is the essence of understanding Indian cuisine. Spices are derived from roots, bark, leaves, buds and seeds of plants. Most are aromatic. Some need to be roasted to release the essential oils that impart their aroma and flavor, while others need to be flash-fried in hot oil to achieve the same result. Spices play a dual role in Indian food. They not only add flavor and impart aroma and color to the dishes, but most have additional attributes as well; namely, their effect on the body. Some have a cooling effect, while others are heat producing. Understandably, appropriate ones are used during particular seasons. Some act as blood purifiers, some as digestives, and still others as antiseptics. That spices make Indian food hot is not necessarily true. Only the peppers — both black peppercorns and the various dried red peppers, such as cayenne — add fire, but most spices will cause the body to perspire and thereby lower body temperature. This explains why the farther south one travels in India, the hotter the food.

Indian cuisine allows the cook to be creative, and seldom is a recipe written down with precise measurements. One of the tasks I had in my self-appointed role of translating traditional recipes into acceptable North American format was to gather recipes on my frequent trips to India from older relatives and family friends, who would name ingredients and provide a concise method of preparation. There was no mention of quantities, much less precise measurements! The most I could get would be a "guestimate" or, as we say in India, "*andaz.*" When I was fortunate enough to get a hands-on lesson, I would watch carefully to see how big a pinch and how large a fistful. Over time, I became a seasoned "eyeballer"; on returning to my kitchen in Houston, I would be able to duplicate fairly accurately the dishes I had eaten. I would then write them up with precise measurements and instructions.

Using spices and herbs correctly is essential to the success of a dish. However, there is a rationale, which, once understood, will make Indian cuisine less mysterious and daunting to the novice Indian cook. In the list that follows, I have mentioned the attributes of each spice, the most frequently used combinations, the regions each is used in and everything else you need to know.

Spices

Allspice *(Kabab Chini)*
Allspice berries, when dried, resemble black peppercorns. They are indigenous to Jamaica and grow in Central American countries, too. They have an aroma that is reminiscent of cloves.

In all likelihood, allspice was introduced to India by the trade route in the 17th century and is used in certain spice blends today. The berries have a shelf life of two to three years, after which the volatile oils dissipate and the berries shrivel and lack aroma. Store away from heat and light.

Asafetida *(Hing)*
This is the gum resin of a plant, and its use dates back to the days of the Greeks and Romans. It comes in lump form, dark brown and rocklike; in this form, it has no particular aroma. Lumps are used as a preservative, to keep weevils and bugs out of dry foods and spices that are stored for a long period. To use in a recipe, break off a pea-size piece and crush to a powder. The powdered form, pale yellow in color and packaged in small plastic containers, is more common. In this form, it is mixed with rice flour to keep it free-flowing. The powdered form has a strong, distinctive aroma, a cross between onion and garlic, which lingers and can become pervasive. However, once it is used in a dish, it blends with the other flavorings and is not offensive. The most important attribute of this spice, apart from its being used by people who eschew onions and garlic for religious reasons, is that it breaks down the indigestible element in beans, lentils and vegetables of the cruciferous family that causes flatulence, thereby making them easy to digest.

Asafetida has an indefinite shelf life if stored tightly closed in an airtight container. If using asafetida powder, be sure to seal it well and store the container in a resealable plastic bag.

Bay Leaf *(Tej Patta)*
Bay leaves are usually used in rice dishes as an aromatic, most often in a combination that includes cinnamon, cloves and cardamom. The Indian bay leaf is derived from the cassia tree and is a little softer. However, I prefer to use the more readily available bay laurel leaves that are grown in California, as I find them more aromatic than the dried leaves imported from India. Store in an airtight container away from heat and replace when the aroma has dissipated.

Black Cumin *(Shah Jeera)* (see Cumin)

Black Salt *(Kala Namak)* (see Salt)

Cardamom *(Elaichi)*
After saffron, green cardamom pods are the most expensive spice and one of the most important in the Indian kitchen. This three-sided pod enclosing fragrant black seeds is grown in South India. It was introduced to Saudi Arabia by Arab traders, where it is widely used as an addition to coffee. In the Indian context, cardamom is used in rice pilaf, or pulao, as it is called in India, in meat and chicken dishes, and very often in desserts and sweets. Often cardamom pods are chewed after a meal, usually with cloves, as a mouth freshener.

There are two varieties of cardamom: green, which are small, about $\frac{1}{4}$ inch (0.5 cm) long; and the large thick-skinned black variety, which is about $\frac{1}{2}$ inch (1 cm) in diameter and $\frac{3}{4}$ inch (2 cm) long. The green ones are called for in most recipes and are readily available, both as whole pods and powdered. Some Indian stores now carry cardamom seeds, which saves time and labor when a larger quantity of seeds alone is called for. Be wary of the beautiful white puffed cardamom pods. Though they are esthetically appealing, they lack flavor because they have been bleached, a process that destroys the essential oils.

Large black cardamom pods, woody and with an earthy aroma, are only available in Indian stores and have limited use. They are usually used in certain rice and meat dishes, never in desserts. In most recipes, green pods are an acceptable substitute.

Cardamom is an essential ingredient in the famous north Indian spice blend garam masala. Look for the largest and brightest green pods available and store in an airtight container away from light and heat. If stored properly, they will last for about two years.

Carom *(Ajwain, Ajowan)*
Carom seeds, also referred to as lovage, resemble celery seeds in appearance but have a sharper, more pronounced bite. Their flavor is somewhat like thyme. They are used in North Indian breads and savories and in some vegetable dishes. Carom seeds are used in small quantities for flavor and as a digestive aid. Refrigerate in a resealable freezer bag for up to three years.

Cinnamon (Dalchini)

North Americans are familiar with the beautiful, reddish brown rolled cinnamon quills that often come neatly tied in little bundles. Used extensively in baking and as an aromatic during the holidays, cinnamon is a familiar and popular spice. It is a member of the laurel family. The cinnamon used in Indian cooking comes from the cassia tree, also a member of the laurel family. It is a dull grayish color and comes in rough, uneven pieces, some as long as 6 or 7 inches (15 to 17.5 cm). It is sweeter and softer, and easier to grind into a powder. It is an essential ingredient of garam masala (see page 28). The sticks are used in rice and meat curries, often in combination with the other aromatics, cloves and cardamom. Interestingly, Indians do not use cinnamon in desserts and sweets. That role belongs to cardamom and, occasionally, nutmeg. Store cinnamon in an airtight container away from heat and light and, if possible, grind to a powder in a spice grinder just before using to achieve maximum flavor and aroma.

Clove (Lavang, Laung)

Cloves are used whole to flavor rice and meat dishes. The powdered or ground variety is mixed with other spices in elaborate blends created for specific recipes. It, too, is an important ingredient in garam masala, and is used as an ingredient in spiced tea (masala chai) and chewed as a mouth freshener. Freshly harvested cloves are plump and very aromatic and are best used within two years of harvesting. Beyond that, they shrink and shrivel as the essential oils dry out. Clove oil is used in dental emergencies, as it dulls the pain of toothaches. Store away from heat and light.

Coriander (Dhania)

Of all the Indian spices, coriander is one of two most widely used. A seed about the size of a peppercorn, golden brown in color, it is a versatile spice with a sweet, perfume-like aroma and a distinctive, sweetish taste. It is used in three forms in Indian cooking: the seeds, whole or crushed; the seed, roasted and powdered, which makes it pleasantly nutty; and the leaves, referred to as fresh coriander, Chinese parsley or cilantro (see page 28). The leaves and seeds are not interchangeable, as they have very different properties. Coriander is used in meat, seafood, vegetable and lentil dishes. Coriander seeds can be stored indefinitely in the pantry. Since ground spices deteriorate rapidly with exposure to air, roast and grind just enough to last six to eight weeks.

Cumin (Jeera)

Cumin, along with coriander, shares the distinction of being widely used throughout the country. It is a grayish, slightly thick seed about ⅛ inch (0.25 cm) long, often referred to as "white" cumin. This is to distinguish it from the "black" cumin, called *shah* (royal) *jeera*.

Black cumin is distinctly different in flavor from common cumin. It is dark colored — hence the name — and finer, with a sharper flavor. It is also more expensive. It is used in northern meat and rice dishes. It is grown in Andhra Pradesh and is an essential component of the local garam masala, making it distinctly different from the garam masala of the north (see recipe, page 28.)

Cumin seeds are used whole, usually flash-fried in hot oil, or toasted and powdered. Toasting releases the essential oils in the seeds, making them highly aromatic and mellow. Cumin is considered a digestive aid. The seeds have an indefinite shelf life.

Fennel (Saunf)

Fennel seeds resemble white cumin seeds but are slightly larger and greenish yellow, with a flavor that is more like anise. They are usually used crushed or powdered in cooked dishes but are toasted when they are offered at the end of a meal as a mouth freshener and digestive aid.

In Indian restaurants, fennel seeds are often placed in a dish mixed with small pieces of rock sugar for diners to take as they leave. An infusion of fennel seeds in boiling water is a well-known remedy for an upset stomach. Fennel seeds can be stored indefinitely.

Fenugreek (Methi)

Fenugreek seeds and leaves are very important in Indian cooking. The seeds are small, flat sided and bean-like, yellowish brown and very bitter. The leaves are also bitter but have a very different flavor; the two are not interchangeable. The seeds are used whole, at the beginning of a dish, when they are flash-fried, or powdered and used in pickles and spice blends. Fenugreek seeds are an important ingredient in *sambhar* powder, the seasoning mix of South India. They are used in small quantities; about ½ tsp (2 mL) is usually sufficient to flavor a recipe for eight.

Kokum
Kokum is the fruit of a tropical tree that grows in the western states of Maharashtra, Goa and Karnataka and parts of Kerala in the south. It is a very sour, small, plum-like dark purple fruit with a soft, leathery skin. Kokum is available in two forms — the dryish star anise-like seed pod and the moist, thick, leathery skin pieces. The latter have better flavor and a tangier taste. Kokum is simmered in lentil (dal) dishes and fish and seafood curries to add a note of tang. It is made into a signature bright pink coconut drink in Mangalore, called *solkadi*, which has a cooling effect on the body. Store in an airtight jar for up to two years to retain maximum freshness. After that it is still usable but will tend to be dry and less flavorful. Kokum is an important ingredient in the cooking of Goa.

Mace (*Javitri*)
This is the orange-colored lacy outer covering of nutmeg, with a fragrance and taste similar to nutmeg, only milder.

Mango Powder (*Amchur*)
Unripe green mango is peeled, sliced and sun-dried before being powdered. The powder is grayish, mildly scented and sour. It is used in place of lemon juice in dry vegetable dishes and is always folded in at the end of cooking. It comes prepackaged and, unlike most other powdered spices, has an indefinite shelf life when stored in an airtight container in the refrigerator. It is an important ingredient in North Indian *chaat* (street food) dishes.

Mustard (*Rai*)
Dark mustard seeds are used throughout the country and are the primary seasoning in the food of the south and the eastern state of Bengal. Mustard greens (*sarson*) are a popular winter dish in the Punjab, where they are teamed with a griddle-baked corn bread.

The seeds are reddish brown but are commonly called black. Used whole, they are flash-fried in very hot oil until they pop. Popping is essential to release flavor and taste. Just adding the seeds to a boiling pot will do nothing for the dish. The seeds are also crushed and added to pickles, and, when added to a brine-based pickle, act as a souring agent. Mustard seeds should be stored in a cool, dark place; they will remain fresh for up to two years.

Mustard oil is cold-pressed from dark mustard seeds and has a strong flavor. It is not an infusion. It is used as the primary oil in Indian pickles and is also the preferred cooking oil in Bengal. It has medicinal uses as well; it is even warmed and used topically to relieve joint pain.

Nigella (*Kalaunji*)
Nigella, often mistakenly called onion seed, is a small, intensely black seed that is not actually onion seed at all! It only resembles it — hence the misleading name. It is flash-fried in hot oil to release its aroma and has a pleasant, distinctive taste. Nigella is used mainly in North Indian vegetable recipes and is also sprinkled on top of breads. It is always used whole. It is an important pickling spice and is part of the Bengali five-spice blend known as *panch phoran* (see page 28). Nigella seeds do not deteriorate with extended storage.

Nutmeg (*Jaiphul*)
Nutmeg is a gray-brown nut about ¾ to 1 inch (2 to 2.5 cm) in size that is enclosed in a hard, lacy covering called mace (*javitri*). It has a distinctive sweetish aroma and taste when powdered and is used mainly in North Indian dishes. It is best to buy whole nuts and freshly grate them as needed; nutmeg loses its aroma rather quickly when exposed to air. Store nutmeg in an airtight container for two to three years.

Pomegranate (*Anardana*)
The seeds of the bright red pomegranate are dark and about ¼ inch (0.5 cm) long when semi-dried. These are used whole, crushed, or roasted and powdered in dishes from the north, imparting a blackish color and sour taste. They are sold in small packages, often in the refrigerated section of Indian stores. Reddish seeds that are plump are an indication of freshness. Store package in a resealable freezer bag in the refrigerator for up to one year.

Poppy Seeds (Khus-Khus)

Indian poppy seeds are tiny, creamy white and without any aroma. They are added to spice blends or ground up in curry pastes to act as thickeners. Their use is more prevalent in North India and in Bengal, where they are an important ingredient and, in certain dishes, the primary seasoning, providing a distinctive taste and texture. Toasting poppy seeds before grinding into a paste enhances their nutty flavor. Store in an airtight container in the refrigerator for up to one year.

Red Chile (Lal Mirch)

Red chilies are a broad category in the world of Indian spices and one of the most important. Red chiles are usually used in their dry form, and the potency varies with the variety. Some are used for their heat and can be searing. Others are used for their flavor and color, without the searing quality. Some have both. For the recipes in this book, I have used cayenne where I would use hot red chile powder, and paprika where I was looking for color without the heat. Peppers, both red and green, are what give Indian food its piquancy; simply reduce or eliminate to make the cuisine acceptable for people who cannot tolerate hot food. Most Indians develop not only a tolerance but also a craving for heat, and some even travel with their own supply of the hot stuff.

Saffron (Kesar)

Saffron, called the king of spices, is also the world's most expensive one. It is cultivated in Spain, Iran and Kashmir, India. It is the stigma of the crocus flower and is still harvested by hand. It takes more than 60,000 blooms to yield 1 lb (500 g) of saffron; hence the prohibitive cost. Saffron is sold as threads and as powder. I recommend using only the threads, as that is the purest form of saffron. The darker the threads, the better the quality.

To use saffron, it is best to soak it in a little hot water or hot milk before adding to the dish. Saffron has a delicate aroma and imparts a beautiful color to rice pulaos, desserts and sweets. It is also used in meat preparations in North India. It has a two-year shelf life and is best purchased at a reputable store that does a good business in spices, as that will ensure high turnover and, therefore, freshness.

Salt (Namak)

I prefer to use kosher salt, but any table salt is just as good. I believe salt is a matter of personal taste, so I hesitate to specify exact amounts.

Black salt (kala namak) is sulfuric and an important flavor enhancer in North Indian street/snack foods (chaat). It is pinkish brown and has a strong, almost offensive odor. However, it has a pleasant taste and certainly adds oomph to the chaat dishes of the north, and to certain chutneys and relishes.

Sesame (Til, Gingelly)

White sesame seeds are used throughout the country, both toasted and untoasted, as whole seeds and also ground into a paste. The taste and flavor of sesame is nutty and distinctive, and the seeds provide a pleasant crunch. Sesame seed sweets are popular at festival times and are also used in Hindu temple rituals. Refrigerate sesame seeds in an airtight container for up to two years.

Sesame oil is used as a cooking medium and is also used to make Indian pickles.

Star Anise (Badian)

Star anise is the unique star-shaped fruit of a tree native to China. It made its way to India via the ancient trade routes and is now grown in parts of India. It has a distinctive strong anise-like aroma and taste and a little goes a long way. It is used mainly in meat dishes. As with all aromatic spices, the essential oils will dry over a period of time, and should be stored for about two years in an airtight container away from light and heat.

Tamarind (Imli)

The tamarind tree is indigenous to India and is a large shade tree that lines the ancient travel routes in the south. The pod is knobby and flattish, about 4 to 5 inches (10 to 12.5 cm) long and tan colored. When the pod is ripe, the papery outer skin splits, revealing a soft, dark brown pulp on the inside that covers four or five large shiny brown seeds. The pods are processed commercially; the outer skin and seeds are removed and the flesh compressed into a brick about 8 inches (20 cm) long and 4 inches (10 cm) wide. It is very sour and is an important flavoring agent in lentil (dal) and seafood dishes, chutneys and relishes. To use

tamarind brick, break off the specified amount from the brick and break into small pieces. Soak in hot water for 20 minutes to soften. Soften pods further with fingers and pour into a large-holed sieve set over a bowl. Strain, pressing down to push through as much of the thick pulp as possible. Discard the residual fibrous material in the strainer.

There are several brands of tamarind pulp and concentrate on the market. I like the Thai tamarind pulp best, as it is ready to use and similar to the tamarind pulp made from the brick. If you are unable to find this, Indian tamarind concentrate will do, but the dark color tends to alter the color of the dish. Store the brick tightly covered in the pantry; the prepared pulp and concentrate should be refrigerated after opening.

Turmeric *(Haldi)*

Turmeric, which gives Indian food its characteristic yellow color, is the rhizome of a plant of the ginger family, which is indigenous to India. Turmeric is bought and used in powder form, as the root is too woody to be powdered in the home kitchen. The rule with turmeric is that a little goes a long way. When doubling a recipe, I suggest that you do not double the turmeric, just increase by half again. Too much turmeric in a dish will result in a bitter aftertaste.

Turmeric is used throughout the country in meat, seafood, vegetable and lentil preparations. It is used in Hindu religious and social rituals and also as a vegetable dye. It has antiseptic properties and is considered to be a blood purifier. It is used in making beauty products and also for tinting butter and prepared mustard. Be careful when using, as turmeric stains are very difficult to remove. This spice can be stored indefinitely in the pantry in an airtight container.

Spice Blends

Andhra Podis

Podis (pronounced pori) are a distinctive part of the cuisine of Andhra Pradesh and, to a lesser degree, Tamil Nadu. Podis are powdered mixtures of dried spices with a base ingredient such as toasted lentils and beans (dals), peanuts, sesame seeds or desiccated coconut. These are known as "dry chutneys" and are mixed into hot steamed rice with a little melted ghee as a first course of a multi-rice course meal. They are also an essential element of South Indian "tiffin" dishes, such as *dosa* (the signature paper-thin rice crêpes of South India) and *idli* (feather-light steamed rice cakes). Podis are often mixed with a little oil when eaten as a condiment with these dishes.

Andhra Garam Masala
Makes about 3$\frac{1}{2}$ tbsp (52 mL)

> 3 tbsp (45 mL) black cumin (shah jeera),
>   preferably Andhra variety
> 1 tbsp (15 mL) cinnamon pieces
> 5 whole cloves
> 5 green cardamom pods
> 5 allspice berries (kabab chini)

Combine cumin, cinnamon, cloves, cardamom and allspice and grind in a coffee mill. Store in an airtight container.

Andhra Spicy Lentil Powder *(Karapodi)*

This mixture is a staple in Andhra kitchens. If storing for longer than one week, refrigeration is recommended.

Makes $\frac{3}{4}$ cup (175 mL)

> $\frac{1}{4}$ cup (50 mL) split yellow peas (channa dal)
> 1 tbsp (15 mL) split white lentils (urad dal)
> $\frac{1}{4}$ cup (50 mL) dried coconut powder
> 5 dried Indian red chiles, broken in pieces
> 1$\frac{1}{4}$ tsp (6 mL) mustard seeds
> $\frac{1}{4}$ tsp (1 mL) asafetida (hing)
> $\frac{1}{2}$ tsp (2 mL) salt or to taste

In a dry skillet over medium heat, toast each dal separately. Let cool and grind in a blender to a powder. Toast coconut until just beginning to color and become fragrant. Add to blender. Toast chiles, mustard seeds and asafetida separately until slightly darker in color and aromatic, and add to blender. Add salt. Blend mixture until finely powdered. (If you prefer a hotter mix, increase red chiles.) Transfer to an airtight container.

Andhra Spicy Peanut Powder
Makes ¾ cup (175 mL)

½ cup (125 mL) skinned peanuts
½ tsp (2 mL) coriander seeds
½ tsp (2 mL) cumin seeds
1 tsp (5 mL) oil
2 tbsp (25 mL) chopped garlic
5 dried Indian red chiles, broken in pieces

In a dry skillet over medium heat, toast peanuts until brown spots appear. Transfer to a blender. In the same skillet, toast coriander and cumin seeds until slightly darker, 30 to 40 seconds. Add to blender and blend to a powder. In same skillet, heat oil over medium heat. Add garlic and chiles and sauté for 2 minutes. Add to blender. Grind as fine as possible. Transfer to an airtight container and refrigerate for up to two months.

Chaat Masala
This quintessential North Indian mixture is salty and sour and is sprinkled on snacks and street foods. It's particularly popular in Delhi and Mumbai (Bombay). The main ingredient is black salt, the sulfuric salt previously mentioned. This is mixed with mango powder (*amchur*) or ground pomegranate seeds (*anardana*), powdered cumin and a little cayenne. As always, there are variations, but the main flavor profile remains the same. It is usually store-bought, and there are several good brands available. Store the package in a resealable plastic freezer bag in the refrigerator. This is a delicious blend to sprinkle on salads, fish, french fries and baked potatoes.

Garam Masala
The most-recognized Indian spice blend is no doubt garam masala, literally meaning "warm mixture." A blend of aromatic spices, the basic recipe varies slightly, as it is customized by individual families. It is a North Indian mixture and not used in South Indian dishes. There are several good brands on the market, but avoid buying spices from bulk bins as exposure to air causes them to deteriorate.

Makes about ¼ cup (50 mL)

2 tbsp (25 mL) coriander seeds, toasted
   in a dry skillet (see Tip, page 194)
1 tbsp (15 mL) cumin seeds, toasted in a
   dry skillet (see Tips, page 198)

1 tsp (5 mL) peppercorns
3 sticks cinnamon (each 3 inches/7.5 cm long)
35 green cardamom pods
35 cloves

Combine coriander, cumin, peppercorns, cinnamon, cardamom and cloves and grind in a coffee mill. Store in an airtight container.

Panch Phoran
This spice mix from Bengal is unique, as it combines five very distinctive seeds. Literally translated, panch phoran means "five seeds." It is one of my favorite seasonings for a variety of vegetables. The mix can be stored in an airtight container for a year or two. Mix together equal quantities of dark mustard seeds, cumin seeds, fenugreek seeds, fennel seeds and nigella seeds. This mix is always flash-fried in a little oil before adding the next ingredients.

Sambhar Powder
Sambhar powder is a South Indian blend used extensively in southern food. Its laundry list of ingredients includes fenugreek, peppercorns, red chiles, coriander, cumin, mustard seeds, turmeric, curry leaves and asafetida, among others. There are several good brands on the market that will remain fresh for one year if stored tightly closed and refrigerated.

Herbs

Cilantro (*Hara Dhania*)
In India, cilantro, also known as fresh coriander or Chinese parsley, holds pride of place. Indian food without cilantro is unthinkable. The delicate, lacy leaves are used during cooking and as a garnish, and correct handling is important. I like to keep my cilantro in a bowl of water while cooking, to keep the leaves from wilting, and just before using I shake off the excess water and chop coarsely before adding to the dish. Fine chopping results in discoloration, as the cilantro oxidizes, turns blackish and develops an offensive odor. Cilantro is the main ingredient in the famous fresh "green chutney," the ubiquitous dipping sauce served in Indian restaurants. To keep cilantro fresh, spread on a paper towel and remove any rotting matter. Cover with a second paper towel

and set aside for one hour. Roll up both towels together, jelly-roll fashion, and store in a plastic bag in the refrigerator. Stored this way, cilantro will remain fresh for more than a week. Cilantro grows from coriander seeds; the two are not interchangeable.

Curry Leaves (*Kari Patta*)

Curry leaves, also known as kari leaves, are much prized in Indian dishes, particularly in south India, for their unmistakable fragrance and flavor. Multiple-leaved citrus-smelling sprigs grow on a tree that can reach 15 feet, but they also thrive as potted plants in a sunny location. It is not to be confused with the feathery gray-green herbaceous plant that is known as curry plant and has a faint aroma of "curry." Fresh leaves are readily available in Indian markets. They should be refrigerated but will dry when kept for several weeks; however, they still retain their aroma. I prefer not to use the dried leaves available in packages from India; they lack aroma. If fresh leaves are unavailable, omit from recipe. There is no substitute.

Fresh Dill (*Sua*)

Used as a herb and also as a green, when mixed greens are called for, dill is used freely with vegetables and lentils.

Fresh Fenugreek (*Methi*)

After cilantro, fresh fenugreek leaves are the most utilized herb. The gray-green three-part leaves have a distinctive bitter flavor and are used in breads, with vegetables and also with meat and fish. The plant is used in Ayurvedic medicine, the ancient science of Indian herbal medicine, and is surprisingly good when dried. Dried fenugreek leaves, known as *kasuri methi,* are available in packages and should be stored in resealable plastic bags in the refrigerator for up to one year. Fenugreek seeds and leaves have very different tastes and are not interchangeable.

Hints and Tips

LEFTOVERS ARE A FACT OF LIFE. HOW YOU handle them can turn you into a kitchen wizard or relegate you to the category of practical but boring. Food, for me, is a source of joy and an opportunity to be creative, rather than a chore that cannot be avoided. I would like to share my ideas so you, too, can have as much fun in the kitchen and, at the same time, become a hero to your family and friends.

Indians are by nature and necessity frugal. Nothing, in particular something as sacred as food, is wasted. Every morsel of food, cooked or otherwise, is made use of. Even peels, such as those from bananas and squashes, are turned into chutney! Leftovers, no matter how much or how little, are used in myriad ways. Leftover vegetables are coarsely mashed and mixed with a binding agent, such as boiled and mashed potato or dampened slices of bread, and pan-fried as patties. Pieces of boneless cooked meat or chicken are shredded and stir-fried with onions, tomatoes and sliced bell pepper, seasoned with a good dose of ginger, garlic and as many green chiles as the tongue can bear. A popular dish in Bombay kitchens, it is known as chili fry.

One of my favorite tricks is cooking twice as much rice as I need for a meal. The cooking time will not change, and you have a versatile staple to transform into a new dish a day or two later. Cooked rice reheats with great success in a microwave. It can also be turned into a stir-fried dish or a layered one-dish meal. If you have a leftover curry that is on the dry side, it can be layered with the cooked rice. Accompanied with raita, it becomes a quick and delicious meal. When the two components — rice and curry — are layered in this manner, the sum of the components goes far beyond boring rice with leftovers. When the "new" dish is heated, the flavors combine, resulting in a far more complex-tasting dish and a new taste experience.

Leftover dals can be handled in various ways. They can be served as soup by adding a little water, fresh seasonings and herbs. Alternatively, leftover dal can be reduced over low heat to a thick paste and used as a filling for stuffed breads and vegetables.

Enjoy learning about Indian spices and flavors and then let your creativity soar as you incorporate these into your everyday cooking.

Basic Techniques

THE FEW SIMPLE TECHNIQUES USED IN Indian cooking are easy to grasp. Understanding them will ensure success. Here's one basic tip to start: while stirring, cooking and browning food, scrape down the sides of the pan often to keep food from sticking. This prevents burnt food bits from falling into the pan. I find heatproof silicone spatulas work best.

Braising (*Pakana*)

This technique is one of the most important to understand and master. In Indian cooking, meat and poultry are sometimes marinated in a mixture of spices and seasonings, often moistened with yogurt or sometimes vinegar or lemon juice. The marinade then forms part of the finished dish and is incorporated into the sauce or gravy. The other ingredients of the gravy, such as onions, tomatoes and so on, are sautéed and the meat or poultry added to the pan to brown. Then the marinade is added and the dish is simmered or braised, as specified in the recipe, to allow the meat to cook, the gravy to thicken and the flavors to combine. The correct pan size and cooking temperature are also important factors, as they will affect the texture of the meat and the gravy in the finished dish.

Browning (*Bhoona*)

This is an important technique and crucial for achieving the desired flavor and appearance. Adequate browning of onions is particularly important in certain North Indian meat and poultry dishes; in many cases, the recipe calls for dark brown, almost blackened, onions. When combined with spices and other ingredients, the resulting gravy is rich and appealing. Browning of meats for certain curries is also important.

I have developed a technique to brown onions in minimal oil, usually about 2 tbsp (25 mL) for eight servings instead of the usual 1/2 cup (125 mL) in traditional cooking. Although this method requires a little more effort, the result is healthier because less oil is used without comprising flavor. When browning onions, it is best to coat them in hot oil and spread them in a single layer in the pan. To start out, maintain a medium-high heat to allow the inherent moisture in the onions to evaporate. Turn the onions every two minutes, spreading them in bottom of pan to cook evenly. As they begin to color, reduce heat and continue browning, maintaining an audible sizzle at all times to indicate the onions are cooking. At this stage, the browning is a result of the natural sugars caramelizing. A slow process, it is the key to a successful mouthwatering gravy.

Deep-Frying (*Talna*)

Indians love deep-fried foods. They are easy to whip up in a hurry, and vegetarian snacks, such as fritters (bhajias and pakoras), patties and assorted balls, are made with simple ingredients that are staples in every Indian kitchen. Puffy steam-filled whole wheat breads (puris) are a favorite around the country; they are used to scoop up morsels and are a must on picnics and train journeys. And, of course, there are the famous papadums served in Indian restaurants in North America, often with brown and green dipping sauces. There are a few simple rules for successful deep-frying. Use a wok or electric skillet and add 2 to 3 inches (5 to 7.5 cm) of vegetable oil so that the food does not touch the bottom of the pan. It is important to maintain a steady temperature, which is why an electric skillet or wok is ideal. For best results, cook food in batches, without crowding, and do not stir. Allow two to three minutes of cooking (in most cases), then turn each piece to finish cooking according to directions. Avoid removing and adding individual pieces one at a time. Use a wire-mesh strainer or large-holed scoop to remove as many pieces as possible at one time and shake gently over pan to allow oil to drip before draining on paper towels. Do not use a slotted spoon, as it does not drain adequately, resulting in greasy food.

Steam Cooking (*Dum*)

Dum (steam) cooking is a versatile technique that has more than one meaning. The term is often used to describe the last few minutes of rice cooking, when the rice has absorbed all liquid but needs to firm up before serving. Once the rice is cooked, reduce the heat to as low as possible and let stand, undisturbed, for several minutes. This allows the starch in the rice to firm up and form a protective coating on each grain so the grains remain separate and do not become gummy.

The technique is particularly important in vegetable dishes, allowing one to cook wholesome, nutritious dishes without the addition of liquid. After sautéing vegetables in the seasoned oil, add a spoonful or two of water to help start the condensation process. Cover with a tight-fitting lid to retain the condensed moisture in the pan and prevent evaporation. Stir periodically to ensure even cooking and to prevent burning. The finished dish is not only full of flavor and complexity but also highly nutritious. This method of cooking foods in their inherent moisture is called cooking on "dum" or by using the trapped steam.

Tempering (*Tadka, Baghar*)

The instant flash-frying of whole spices and seeds in a small amount of very hot oil is an essential step in the cooking of every region of the country. When seeds and spices are tossed into very hot oil, within seconds they release their volatile oils and essences. This does not occur when they are just stirred into a dish while cooking. In the case of meat, vegetable and rice dishes, the flash-frying is usually done at the beginning of the dish. Lentils, on the other hand, are often boiled until soft, then the flash-fried seasonings are added.

Toasting and Grinding Spices

Toasting spices releases their essential oils and intensifies their flavors. Toasting changes the flavor and aroma of spices such as coriander and cumin; when either of these seeds is toasted then ground, the resulting taste is completely different than when ground without toasting. Whereas whole spices have an almost indefinite shelf life, powdered spices are fragile, and with exposure to air they will lose their freshness and fragrance over a period of time. I suggest you toast and grind small quantities so that you use them within eight to ten weeks.

Heat a dry heavy skillet on medium heat for two to three minutes. Place whole spices, such as coriander or cumin seeds, in a single layer in the pan. Shake pan periodically to brown seeds evenly. Within three to four minutes, the spices will begin to darken and release their aroma. Stir for a few more seconds and transfer to a bowl to cool. Grind in a coffee mill reserved for spices. Store in an airtight jar away from heat and light.

A Note about Hot

I'VE DESIGNATED THE RECIPES THAT are truly hot to the palate with the word HOT so you'll know which ones they are. It is not always easy to tell if a dish is hot simply by reading the list of ingredients. Some recipes may list a lot of chiles — dry red ones, hot green ones, such as serranos, and maybe even cayenne pepper. Yet the dish may not be designated hot, because it may have a large quantity of onions, sautéed until they are caramelized to concentrate the natural onion sugars, yogurt, or coconut milk, which adds a rich and sweet taste. Ingredients such as these make the dish much milder and balance the heat of the chiles. If you need to make a dish milder, reduce the green chiles and cayenne to suit your palate. This will not alter the integrity of the dish.

Appetizers

INDIANS LOVE FRIED FOODS, so traditionally, appetizers and fried foods were synonymous. When I was growing up in India, no meal was complete without a fried appetizer, such as potato or meat patties, vegetable fritters or, my all-time favorite, homemade fries. It was served with the main meal and there was always a chutney or two and, of course, the ubiquitous ketchup, which in India is known as tomato sauce. When family and friends dropped by to visit, courtesy demanded that they be offered a snack. It was always some homemade nibbles, sweet or savory, either ones that had been prepared earlier or any one of a huge assortment of fritters that could be whipped up at short notice.

Times and lifestyles have changed. As people become aware of healthy eating, fried foods are being eased out of the daily diet. Nevertheless, put a dish of fried goodies on the table or a bowl of one of the myriad store-bought crispy snacks like *sev* or *papri* — both made of chickpea flour — and they magically disappear.

KABABS, A NORTH INDIAN FAVORITE, have always enjoyed pride of place in the world of appetizers. However, there is a North American misconception about the kabab: it is believed to be the shish kabob, chunks of meat interspersed with vegetables on a metal skewer and served on a bed of rice. In fact, kababs are simply bite-size morsels and can be chunks of boneless meat, seafood or vegetarian. And they are not always skewered. The word *shish* is derived from *sheekh* meaning "skewer," and that is just one of many different kinds of kabab. A kabab can be grilled, pan-fried, broiled, cooked in a tandoor or deep-fried. It can be a chunk of meat or ground meat shaped into a patty or a cigar. Arguably one of the most beloved is the *sheekh kabab*, made of well-seasoned ground meat — either lamb or goat — wrapped around a skewer. Grilled foods are a northern specialty and do not exist in the south or east. They were introduced by the invaders who entered India through the mountain passes of the northwest, from Central Asia and places farther west. These were meat-loving people, and grilling was the preferred method of cooking. The art of marinating and grilling foods to perfection was mastered and raised to another level by royal chefs who served the Moghul court. Today puréed nuts, rich cream and cheese enhance these morsels, and the result is melt-in-your-mouth bliss.

THE EASTERN STATES DO NOT HAVE A large variety of appetizers. In Bengal, the favorite snack is a bowl of puffed rice dressed up with a little chopped tomato, onion, some green mango if available and a drizzle of mustard oil. *Singara*, a triangular savory stuffed pastry known as *samosa* in the rest of the country, is also popular.

Appetizers

———— ❧ ————

SOUTH INDIA HAS SOME UNIQUE appetizers. Batter-coated potato balls called *bondas*, now a popular street food in the large cities, are a signature snack. Throughout the south there are a variety of fritters, such as the well-known and popular onion *bhajia*.

Equally popular are an assortment of *vadai*. These patties are made of coarsely ground dals, sometimes with the addition of grated vegetables such as cabbage (see Cabbage Vadai, page 63).

THE WEST HAS MANY OPTIONS. GUJARATI cuisine abounds in vegetarian snacks. For religious reasons many Gujaratis prefer to avoid food prepared in kitchens not completely devoted to vegetarian cuisine. As a result, many travel with boxes of homemade snacks that fill in for meals, if necessary. These include crisp shelf-stable wafer-like breads, oodles of chickpea flour crispies and an assortment of other goodies. This food is known as *farsan,* and no other ethnic group has anything that compares. At home they have a vast array of stuffed patties, vegetable rolls and morsels made from whole wheat and various types of dals.

An assortment of meat preparations, such as meat patties, is relished in other parts of western India. In Goa, pork sausages are popular. Shrimp is a particular favorite, as are many other seafood appetizers. Potatoes are also popular, and there is no dearth of variations on the humble tuber, all of them beautifully seasoned and spiced. Potato patties, both stuffed and plain, are a popular choice. In Mumbai, there is no typical appetizer per se. Everything from *samosas* to elaborate meat dishes grace the tables of accomplished home cooks, and, more recently, many a caterer has come up with wonderful morsels that are derived from both Indian and non-Indian lineage. One of my favorite appetizers is Chickpea Flour and Cilantro Squares (*Kothambir Vada*; see recipe, page 79) — cilantro-flavored baked squares, a specialty of Maharashtra. Onion Fritters (see recipe, page 77), my father's favorite, are also delicious. Once you try them, you will never go back to onion rings again.

Vegetable Pakoras
Batter-Dipped Vegetable Fritters

- Wok or deep-fryer
- Candy/deep-fry thermometer

2 cups	chickpea flour (besan)	500 mL
1 tsp	salt	5 mL
½ tsp	cayenne pepper	2 mL
½ tsp	baking soda	2 mL
8	eggplant slices, unpeeled, ¼ inch (0.5 cm) thick	8
8	red or green bell pepper slices, ¼ inch (0.5 cm) thick	8
8	zucchini slices, unpeeled, ¼ inch (0.5 cm) thick	8
8	potato slices, peeled, ¼ inch (0.5 cm) thick	8
	Oil for deep-frying	

1. In a bowl, mix together chickpea flour, salt, cayenne and baking soda. Slowly pour in 1 cup (250 mL) water, stirring to a smooth consistency and adding up to ¼ cup (50 mL) more water, a little at a time, until batter is slightly thinner than pancake batter. Set aside for 15 minutes.

2. In a wok or deep-fryer, heat oil to 375°F (190°C). One at a time, dip slices of eggplant, pepper, zucchini and potato into batter. Add to hot oil in batches of 5 or 6 and deep-fry until golden, 3 to 4 minutes. Remove with a large-holed strainer and drain on paper towels. Serve immediately with a chutney of your choice.

Makes 32

Pakoras, *or* bhajias *as they are called, are a favorite snack. There are numerous kinds of pakoras, this being one of the simplest and most popular. You can use a variety of vegetables, including cauliflower, sweet potato and even fresh spinach.*

Tip
These pakoras are best eaten as soon as they are cooked; they lose their crispness as they sit.

Urad Dal ke Pakore

Black Bean Fritters

Serves 8

Black beans (sabat urad) *are used extensively in the northern state of Uttarakhand, and these fritters are a favorite at weddings and celebrations. The black skin adds to the unique taste of the crunchy morsels.*

- Wok or deep-fryer
- Candy/deep-fry thermometer

1 cup	Indian black beans (sabat urad)	250 mL
2 tsp	salt or to taste	10 mL
1 tsp	cayenne pepper	5 mL
½ tsp	cumin powder	2 mL
½ tsp	cumin seeds	2 mL
½ tsp	fennel seeds (saunf)	2 mL
¼ tsp	turmeric	1 mL
¼ tsp	carom seeds (ajwain)	1 mL
	Oil for deep-frying	

1. Clean and pick through beans for any small stones and grit. Rinse a few times in cold water. Soak at room temperature overnight in 3 cups (750 mL) water.

2. Drain beans. Place half of the beans in a blender or food processor. Add ¼ cup (50 mL) water and grind coarsely. Transfer to a bowl. Repeat with remaining beans. Add to bowl. Add salt, cayenne, cumin powder, cumin seeds, fennel, turmeric and carom. Mix well.

3. In a wok or deep-fryer, heat oil to 350°F (180°C). Drop mixture by heaping teaspoonfuls (5 mL) into hot oil and fry, in batches, without crowding, until golden, 2 to 3 minutes. Remove with a large-holed strainer and drain on paper towels. Serve hot with a chutney of your choice.

Panir Soy ke Roll

Cheese and Soy Rolls

- *Wok or deep-fryer*
- *Candy/deep-fry thermometer*

1/3 cup	soy granules	75 mL
8 oz	all-purpose potatoes (about 2)	250 g
1/4	recipe Lower-Fat Panir, grated (see recipe, page 312)	1/4
3 tbsp	cilantro, chopped	45 mL
3 tbsp	raw cashew pieces	45 mL
1 tbsp	raisins	15 mL
1 tbsp	toasted sesame seeds	15 mL
2 tsp	minced peeled gingerroot	10 mL
2 tsp	minced green chiles, preferably serranos	10 mL
2 tsp	mango powder (amchur)	10 mL
1 1/2 tsp	salt or to taste	7 mL
1/2 tsp	garam masala	2 mL
	Oil for deep-frying	

Makes 12

Tasty and nutritious, these rolls are ideal for a buffet table or a cocktail party. Make them bite-size if serving as a finger food with a dipping sauce.

1. In a bowl, soak soy granules in 1 cup (250 mL) water for 30 minutes. Drain thoroughly.

2. Meanwhile, in a saucepan of boiling water, cook whole potatoes until tender, 20 to 25 minutes. Drain and, when cool enough to handle but still warm, peel and break into chunks.

3. In a food processor, process potatoes for 30 seconds to mash. Add soy, panir, cilantro, cashews, raisins, sesame seeds, ginger, chiles, mango powder, salt and garam masala and process for 30 seconds, until mixture holds together. (This is best done before potatoes get cold.)

4. Divide mixture into 12 portions. Roll each into a cigar shape approximately 3 inches (7.5 cm) long.

5. In a wok or deep-fryer, heat oil over medium heat to 350°F (180°C). Drop rolls into hot oil and fry, in batches, without crowding, until golden, 2 to 3 minutes. Remove with a large-holed strainer and drain on paper towels. Serve hot with a chutney of your choice.

Reshmi Murg Kabab

Pan-Fried Chicken Kababs

1 lb	skinless boneless chicken breasts	500 g
½ cup	chopped onion	125 mL
¼ cup	plain nonfat yogurt	50 mL
3 tbsp	cilantro	45 mL
2 tsp	minced peeled gingerroot	10 mL
2 tsp	minced garlic	10 mL
2 tsp	minced green chiles, preferably serranos	10 mL
1 tbsp	tandoori masala (see Tips, right)	15 mL
1½ tsp	salt or to taste	7 mL
2 tbsp	oil (approx.), divided	25 mL

1. Rinse chicken and pat dry thoroughly. Chop into chunks and place in food processor. Add onion, yogurt, cilantro, ginger, garlic, chiles, tandoori masala, salt and 1 tbsp (15 mL) of the oil. Pulse at first and then process until mixture holds together, about 1 minute.

2. Transfer to a shallow bowl and spread mixture. (It will be soft and sticky.) Chill for 30 minutes, uncovered, or cover bowl with plastic wrap and refrigerate for up to 8 hours.

3. Divide mixture into 15 portions. Lightly oil hands and, using a light touch, make into rolls.

4. In a large nonstick skillet, heat ½ tbsp (7 mL) of the remaining oil over medium heat. Fry half of the rolls (kababs) to brown evenly, shaking pan to loosen rolls, about 3 minutes. Drain on paper towels. Repeat with remaining rolls, adding more oil as necessary. Serve hot with a chutney of your choice.

Makes 15

Delicious and easy to make, these delicate, silky kababs are the perfect finger food.

Tips

Tandoori masala is a prepared mix of spices used to marinate poultry and seafood for tandoori cooking (Indian grilling). There are several good brands on the market.

Kababs can be cooked the day ahead, cooled and then wrapped in foil and refrigerated. Reheat in foil in preheated 300°F (150°C) oven until heated through, 10 to 15 minutes. Kababs can also be frozen for up to 3 months and reheated in a 300°F (150°C) oven for about 30 minutes.

Hara Bhara Kabab

Green Kababs

Makes 12

These scrumptious patties are perfect for a buffet table. They are tasty and healthy, too.

Tips

Chaat masala is a blend of several spices, including ground dried pomegranate seeds and ground unripe dried green mango *(amchur),* which add sourness to the mix. It is used in the street foods of North India and the area around Mumbai. Packages of chaat masala are available in Indian stores.

Leftover kababs can be refrigerated in an airtight container for up to 3 days. Reheat in the microwave.

8 oz	russet or gold potatoes (about 2)	250 g
2 cups	loose frozen spinach, cooked and squeezed dry	500 mL
¼ cup	frozen peas, thawed, drained and coarsely mashed	50 mL
1½ tbsp	chopped green chiles, preferably serranos	22 mL
1 tbsp	finely chopped peeled gingerroot	15 mL
3 to 4 tbsp	cilantro, leaves and soft stems, chopped	45 to 60 mL
2 tbsp	cornstarch	25 mL
1 tbsp	chaat masala (see Tips, left)	15 mL
¾ tsp	salt or to taste	4 mL
3 to 4 tbsp	oil, divided	45 to 60 mL

1. In a saucepan of boiling water, cook whole potatoes until tender, 20 to 25 minutes. Drain. When cool enough to handle but still warm, peel and mash.

2. In a bowl, mix together potatoes, spinach, peas, chiles, ginger, cilantro, chaat masala, cornstarch and salt, until well blended. Divide into 12 portions. Form into 2-inch (5 cm) round patties.

3. In a large nonstick skillet or griddle, heat 2 tbsp (25 mL) of the oil over medium heat. Add 6 patties and fry on both sides until golden brown, about 2 minutes per side. Drain on paper towels. Repeat with remaining patties, adding more oil as necessary. Serve hot with a chutney of your choice.

Galavat ke Kabab
Lucknowi Griddle Kababs

1 lb	ground lamb or beef	500 g
1 tsp	salt	5 mL
½ cup	yellow split peas (channa dal), rinsed and drained	125 mL
2 tsp	coriander seeds	10 mL
3	black cardamom pods, seeds only	3
12	whole cloves	12
20	black peppercorns	20
1 tsp	cayenne pepper	5 mL
1 cup	puréed onion (about 2 medium)	250 mL
⅓ cup	oil (approx.)	75 mL

Makes 24

Galavat *literally means "melt" and these are truly melt-in-your-mouth kababs, as the Hindi name suggests. They are unforgettable served in small rolls brushed with your favorite chutney.*

1. In a saucepan, combine lamb and salt. Add water to cover meat and bring to a boil over high heat. Skim scum off top. Reduce heat to medium. Cook, uncovered, until water is completely absorbed. Drain off any fat and let meat cool slightly. Transfer to a food processor and pulse 4 to 5 times until slightly chopped. Set aside.

2. Meanwhile, spread dal in a dry skillet. Place over medium heat and toast, stirring continuously, until slightly aromatic and toasted, 3 to 4 minutes. In a spice grinder, grind dal into a powder. Divide powder into 2 equal portions. Set aside.

3. Working with one spice at a time, add coriander, cardamom, cloves and peppercorns to dry skillet and toast, stirring continuously, until toasted. (Time varies with each ingredient, which is why they are toasted separately. Coriander takes about 2 minutes and the other spices from 20 to 40 seconds.) Mix together and transfer to a spice grinder; grind into a powder. Add one portion of the powdered dal to spices. Stir in cayenne and add powdered spice/dal mix to meat.

4. Transfer meat mixture to food processor. Add onion and process to a paste. Transfer to a shallow container and chill, uncovered, about 2 hours. Just before cooking, add remaining powder to mixture and mix well. Adjust salt.

5. Using 1½ tbsp (22 mL) of the mixture at a time, form into 1½-inch (4 cm) small flat patties. (Patties will be soft.) In a skillet, heat 1 tsp (5 mL) of the oil over medium heat. Add patties, 2 to 3 at a time, and fry until browned, about 2 minutes. Flip to brown other side. Handle patties carefully as they are fragile. Drain on paper towels. Repeat with remaining patties, adding more oil as necessary. Serve with a chutney of your choice.

Mathri

Savory Crisps

Makes about 36

These crisps are a favorite in Punjab. Eaten out of hand like potato chips or packed to take on a trip to eat with a hot pickle, they are delicious.

Tips

Indian markets carry *sooji* or *rava*, which is much finer than instant or quick-cooking Cream of Wheat. It is a must in an Indian pantry, used to make dough products crisp. American Cream of Wheat is too coarse for this purpose.

When cool, puris can be stored in an airtight container for several weeks.

- *Wok or deep-fryer*
- *Candy/deep-fry thermometer*

1 cup	all-purpose flour	250 mL
2 tbsp	fine Cream of Wheat (sooji or rava) (see Tips, left)	25 mL
1 tbsp	ghee	15 mL
1 1/2 tsp	salt	7 mL
1 tsp	carom seeds (ajwain)	5 mL
1/2 tsp	cracked black peppercorns	2 mL
	Oil for deep-frying	

1. In a food processor, combine flour, Cream of Wheat, ghee and salt and pulse 2 to 3 times until blended. Add carom seeds and peppercorns and pulse 2 to 3 times until evenly combined.

2. With the motor running, gradually add 3 tbsp (45 mL) water through the feed tube. Gradually add up to 1 tbsp (15 mL) more water until mixture holds together and makes a stiff dough. Process dough for 2 minutes, stopping machine and scraping down sides once. Transfer to a bowl. Shape into a ball. Cover and set aside to rest at room temperature for at least 30 minutes or for up to 2 hours.

3. In a wok or deep-fryer, heat oil to 325°F (160°C).

4. Meanwhile, knead dough by hand for 2 minutes. Divide dough into 4 portions. Keep 3 portions covered with a dry cloth away from heat. Sprinkle work surface lightly with flour and roll 1 portion of dough into a ball. Pat down into a thick disk and roll into a circle, about 7 inches (17.5 cm) in diameter. Prick entire surface with a fork. Using a cookie cutter, cut out 1 1/2-inch (4 cm) circles (puris). Gather up remnants of dough and roll again until all of the dough is used. Repeat with remaining 3 balls of dough.

5. Slip into hot oil, 6 to 8 puris at a time, and fry until crisp and golden, 3 to 4 minutes per batch. Remove with a large-holed strainer and drain on paper towels.

Methi Palak Pakoras

Fenugreek and Spinach Fritters

- Wok or deep-fryer
- Candy/deep-fry thermometer

²/₃ cup	split yellow peas (channa dal)	150 mL
4 cups	loosely packed spinach, coarsely chopped	1 L
1 cup	fresh fenugreek leaves (methi), chopped or ¹/₃ cup (75 mL) dried fenugreek (kasuri methi)	250 mL
1 cup	finely chopped cauliflower	250 mL
¹/₂ cup	finely chopped onion	125 mL
¹/₂ cup	finely chopped potato	125 mL
2 tsp	minced green chiles, preferably serranos	10 mL
1 tsp	mango powder (amchur)	5 mL
1 tsp	salt or to taste	5 mL
³/₄ tsp	garam masala	4 mL
¹/₂ tsp	coriander powder	2 mL
¹/₂ tsp	cumin powder	2 mL
	Oil for deep-frying	
¹/₂ to ³/₄ cup	chickpea flour (besan)	125 to 175 mL

1. Clean and pick through dal for any small stones and grit. Rinse several times in cold water until water is fairly clear. Soak in 4 cups (1 L) warm water at room temperature for at least 2 hours or for up to 6 hours. Drain and transfer to a food processor. Purée coarsely and return to bowl. Add spinach, fenugreek, cauliflower, onion, potato, chiles, mango powder, salt, garam masala, coriander and cumin. Mix well.

2. In a wok or deep-fryer, heat oil to 350°F (180°C).

3. Sprinkle ¹/₂ cup (125 mL) of the chickpea flour into split pea mixture and using a light touch, mix with finger tips. Squeeze a small handful to see if mixture will hold together. Incorporate as much flour as needed to be able to drop mixture by spoonfuls into oil. Using the tip of a tablespoon, scoop up a walnut-size ball of mixture. With the tip of another tablespoon, gently press mixture together and ease into oil. Fry in batches of 4 to 5 pakoras at a time, without crowding, until golden brown, 2 to 3 minutes. Remove with a large-holed strainer and drain on paper towels. Serve hot with a chutney of your choice.

Serves 6 to 8

Fritters such as these are served with tea or coffee, as hors d'oeuvres, or as part of a meal, accompanied always by a chutney or a dipping sauce. The split yellow peas need to be soaked for 2 hours so take that into account when making these fritters.

Tip
The amount of chickpea flour required will depend on the amount of moisture in the mixture. If sufficient flour is not used, the ingredients will come apart in the oil. If this happens while you're testing one, remove particles with a mesh strainer before continuing.

Pyaz Pudinay ke Pakore

Mint and Green Onion Fritters

Serves 4 to 6

These unusual fritters (pakoras) are a great summer treat when gardens are spilling over with mint. They are light, easy to make and very tasty.

❧

Tip

Pakoras are best served freshly made but can be fried ahead, cooled, covered and left at room temperature for up to 6 hours. Reheat in a 200°F (100°C) oven for 10 minutes.

- *Wok or deep-fryer*
- *Candy/deep-fry thermometer*

2 cups	thinly sliced green onions	500 mL
2 cups	mint leaves, chopped	500 mL
2 tsp	minced peeled gingerroot	10 mL
2 to 3 tsp	minced green chiles, preferably serranos	10 to 15 mL
¾ tsp	salt or to taste	4 mL
½ tsp	carom seeds (ajwain)	2 mL
6 to 8 tbsp	chickpea flour (besan)	90 to 120 mL
	Oil for deep-frying	

1. In a bowl, mix together green onions, mint, ginger, chiles, salt and carom seeds. Rub mixture together gently with fingers and set aside for 10 minutes.

2. Sprinkle ⅓ cup (75 mL) of the chickpea flour over mixture. Toss with fingers. Squeeze a heaping tablespoonful (15 mL) to see if it holds together. If not, work in additional chickpea flour, 1 tbsp (15 mL) at a time, until a heaping tablespoon (15 mL) of the mixture holds together. Do not compact.

3. In a wok or deep-fryer, heat oil to 375°F (190°C). Using the tip of a tablespoon, scoop up a walnut-size ball of mixture. With the tip of another tablespoon, gently press mixture together and ease into oil. Fry in batches of 4 or 5 pakoras at a time, without crowding, until golden brown, 1 to 2 minutes. Remove with a large-holed strainer and drain on paper towels. Serve hot with a chutney of your choice.

Panir Fingers
Fried Cheese

- Wok or deep-fryer
- Candy/deep-fry thermometer

1	recipe Lower-Fat Panir (see recipe, page 312)	1
½ cup	chickpea flour (besan)	125 mL
1 tsp	carom seeds (ajwain), rubbed between fingers	5 mL
1 ½ tsp	cayenne pepper, divided	7 mL
½ tsp	salt or to taste	2 mL
3 to 4 tbsp	freshly squeezed lime or lemon juice	45 to 60 mL
½ tsp	mango powder (amchur)	2 mL
	Oil for deep-frying	

1. Cut panir into 2-by 1-by ¼-inch (5 by 2.5 by 0.5 cm) fingers. Set aside.

2. In a dish, mix together flour, carom seeds, 1 tsp (5 mL) of the cayenne and salt. Place lime juice in a shallow glass dish. In a small bowl, combine mango powder and ½ tsp (2 mL) cayenne. Set aside.

3. In a wok or deep-fryer, heat oil to 400°F (200°C).

4. Soak panir, a few pieces at a time, in lime juice, about 1 minute. Dip in seasoned flour and deep-fry in hot oil until golden, for 1 minute. (Panir should be crisp on the outside and soft on the inside.) Remove with a large-holed strainer and drain on paper towels. Sprinkle with mango powder mixture. Serve hot with a chutney of your choice.

Makes 25 pieces

HOT

Panir comes from the north, but these cheese fingers are popular eats at upscale cocktail parties in Delhi and Mumbai and are an elegant vegetarian option.

Mustard-Flavored Chicken Tikka

Makes 15 to 20
Serves 12

Boneless chicken chunks infused with complex flavors are a hit with young and old. Mustard oil adds that extra special touch.

Tips

Ginger and garlic pastes are available in jars in Indian and Asian markets. Making your own is a simple matter of grating peeled gingerroot or garlic cloves on a Microplane grater.

Pure mustard oil is available at Indian grocery stores. Although the bottle will probably advise against culinary use, it is perfectly safe to use provided it is heated to the smoking point. Do not use unheated, as in a vinaigrette.

If using an indoor contact grill, the cooking time will be shorter.

• *Metal skewers or 20 long bamboo skewers, soaked in water for 30 minutes*

2 lbs	skinless boneless chicken breasts	1 kg
¼ cup	freshly squeezed lime or lemon juice	50 mL
3 tbsp	ginger paste (see Tips, left)	45 mL
3 tbsp	garlic paste (see Tips, left)	45 mL
1 tbsp	hot mustard, preferably English mustard	15 mL
1 tsp	salt or to taste	5 mL
¼ cup	chickpea flour (besan)	50 mL
¼ cup	pure mustard oil (see Tips, left)	50 mL
3 tbsp	thick plain yogurt	45 mL
1 tbsp	minced green chiles, preferably serranos	15 mL
1½ tsp	cayenne pepper	7 mL
	Oil for oiling grill	

1. Rinse chicken and pat dry thoroughly. Cut into 1½-inch (4 cm) pieces.

2. In a bowl, mix together lime juice, ginger, garlic, mustard and salt. Add chicken and toss to coat.

3. In another bowl, mix together chickpea flour, mustard oil, yogurt, chiles and cayenne into a paste. Coat chicken evenly with mixture. Cover and marinate for at least 1 hour in refrigerator, preferably 3 to 4 hours.

4. Preheat charcoal grill, barbecue or indoor grill to medium heat.

5. Thread chicken pieces onto metal skewers, 3 to 4 per skewer. Insert a second skewer parallel to the first, about ½ inch (1 cm) apart. Cook on well-oiled charcoal grill or indoor grill, turning once and basting with additional oil or mustard oil, until pieces are no longer pink inside and are slightly charred outside, about 10 minutes. Serve immediately.

Potato-Coated Lamb Chops

It is important to use the smallest chops available, as it is difficult to coat and pan-fry large ones. In India, we prefer to use cabrito (young goat) chops, which are no more than a bite or two. Cabrito is available in specialty meat markets.

12	small lamb chops (about 1 ¼ lbs/625 g)	12
½ cup	packed thinly sliced onion (lengthwise slices)	125 mL
2 tbsp	minced peeled gingerroot	25 mL
2 tbsp	minced garlic	25 mL
8	black peppercorns	8
6	whole cloves	6
2	black cardamom pods, cracked open	2
1	piece cinnamon, about 1 inch (2.5 cm) long	1
¾ tsp	salt	4 mL

Potato Coating

1 ¼ lbs	all-purpose or baking potatoes (4 to 5)	625 g
2 tbsp	cilantro, chopped	25 mL
2 tsp	grated peeled gingerroot	10 mL
2 tsp	minced green chiles, preferably serranos	10 mL
1 tbsp	coriander powder	15 mL
1 ½ tsp	chickpea flour (besan)	7 mL
1 tsp	salt or to taste	5 mL
¾ tsp	cayenne pepper	4 mL
½ tsp	freshly ground black pepper	2 mL
	Oil for pan-frying	
	Dry bread crumbs to coat	

1. In a saucepan, combine lamb chops, onion, ginger, garlic, peppercorns, cloves, cardamom, cinnamon and salt. Add 3 cups (750 mL) water and bring to a boil over medium-high heat. Reduce heat to medium-low. Cover and cook on a gentle boil until lamb is tender, 50 minutes to 1 hour. (Check water periodically, and add a little additional hot water if necessary to cook until tender. There should be no water left in pan when lamb is cooked.)

2. *Potato Coating:* Meanwhile, in a saucepan of boiling water, cook whole potatoes until tender, 20 to 25 minutes. Drain. When cool enough to handle but still warm, peel and mash.

3. Sprinkle cilantro, ginger, chiles, coriander, chickpea flour, salt, cayenne and pepper over potatoes and knead by hand to mix thoroughly.

4. Divide mixture into 12 portions. Place one portion in cupped palm of hand and, with fingers of other hand, press into a cup. Place a portion of the meat into potato cup and cover by gently pressing cup to enclose meat. Leave the bone uncovered to act as a "handle." Repeat until all chops are covered with potato mixture.

5. In a large skillet, heat $\frac{1}{2}$ inch (1 cm) oil over medium heat.

6. Press bread crumbs into potato-coated chops to coat evenly. Add chops to skillet in batches, without crowding, and fry, until bottoms are golden, about 3 minutes. Gently turn and fry other side until golden, about 2 minutes. Drain on paper towels. Serve hot with a chutney of your choice.

Aloo Tikkis
Potato Patties

These patties appear in various guises throughout the country with variations in seasonings. They are served as snacks throughout the day but are equally at home on a banquet table.

2½ lbs	all-purpose or baking potatoes (about 10)	1.25 kg
2½ tsp	salt or to taste	12 mL
3 tbsp	chickpea flour (besan)	45 mL
4 to 5 tbsp	oil, divided	60 to 75 mL
2 tsp	cumin seeds	10 mL
2 cups	chopped onion	500 mL
1 cup	frozen peas, thawed	250 mL
2 tbsp	minced peeled gingerroot	25 mL
2 tsp	minced green chiles, preferably serranos	10 mL
1 tsp	coriander powder	5 mL
1 tsp	cayenne pepper	5 mL
1 tsp	garam masala	5 mL
1 tsp	chaat masala (see Tips, page 40)	5 mL
2 tbsp	cilantro, chopped	25 mL

1. In a saucepan of boiling water, cook whole potatoes until tender, 20 to 25 minutes. Drain. When cool enough to handle but still warm, peel and mash. Sprinkle with salt. Set aside.

2. In a heavy dry skillet over medium heat, toast chickpea flour, stirring continuously, until fragrant and slightly browned, 3 to 4 minutes. Sprinkle over potatoes.

3. In the same skillet, heat 2 tbsp (25 mL) of the oil over medium heat. Sauté cumin seeds for 1 minute. Add onion and sauté until golden, 6 to 8 minutes. Add peas, ginger, chiles, coriander, cayenne, garam masala and chaat masala. Mix well and sauté until flavors combine, 2 to 3 minutes. Let cool. Stir cilantro into mixture and add to potato and mix well.

4. Divide mixture into 12 portions and roll into balls. Flatten each ball into a 3-inch (7.5 cm) patty.

5. Heat remaining oil in a clean heavy skillet and fry patties, 4 at a time, turning to brown evenly on both sides, 2 to 3 minutes per side. Repeat with remaining patties, adding more oil as necessary. Drain on paper towels. Serve with a chutney of your choice.

Shaami Kababs

- *Wok or deep-fryer*
- *Candy/deep-fry thermometer*

½ cup	split yellow peas (channa dal)	125 mL
1 lb	ground beef chuck (see Tips, right)	500 g
4 oz	ground beef round	125 g
2½ tsp	minced peeled gingerroot, divided	12 mL
1½ tsp	minced garlic	7 mL
3	dried Indian red chiles, broken into pieces	3
2	black cardamom pods, cracked open	2
8	whole cloves	8
2	sticks cinnamon, each 2 inches (5 cm) long	2
½ tsp	black peppercorns	2 mL
1½ tsp	salt or to taste	7 mL
1	egg	1
4 tsp	minced green chiles, preferably serranos	20 mL
2 tbsp	cilantro, chopped	25 mL
2 tbsp	chopped mint	25 mL
	Oil for deep-frying	

1. Clean and pick through dal for any small stones and grit. Rinse several times in cold water until water is fairly clear. Soak in 2 cups (500 mL) water in a bowl for 15 minutes.

2. In a saucepan, mix together ground chuck and round. Drain dal and add to meat. Add 1½ tsp (7 mL) ginger, garlic, red chiles, cardamom, cloves, cinnamon and peppercorns. Add water to cover and bring to a boil over medium heat. Skim any scum that may form. Cover and cook until water is absorbed and dal is soft. Partway through cooking, add salt.

3. Remove cardamoms and cinnamon. Transfer mixture to a food processor and process until mixture is a smooth paste. Add egg and process to incorporate. Transfer mixture to a bowl. Add green chiles, 1 tsp (5 mL) ginger, cilantro and mint and mix well. If mixture is too soft, chill for 15 minutes.

4. Form mixture into walnut-size balls and press into patties about 2 inches (5 cm) in diameter.

5. In a wok or deep-fryer, heat oil to 400°F (200°C). Fry, in batches, without crowding, until golden brown, about 2 minutes. Remove with a large-holed strainer and drain on paper towels. Serve with a chutney of your choice.

Makes 20 pieces

Shaami kababs *are a classic North Indian appetizer. Delicious and easy to make ahead, they are a favorite at cocktail parties and on buffet tables.*

Tips

The fat in ground chuck is necessary to keep the kababs from being too dry. Do not use all lean ground round.

To freeze: Arrange cooked patties in rows in an airtight container. Layer if necessary, placing foil between layers. Freeze for up to 3 months. Thaw in refrigerator and fry.

Sindhi Chops

Serves 8

I've had this family recipe for more than 40 years and have served it many times, as a cocktail appetizer and also as part of a buffet. The chops are moist, melt-in-your mouth, flavorful but not spicy. Buying small chops with a single bone is important.

Tips

Cabrito (young goat) chops, which are no more than a bite or two, are available in specialty meat markets.

Spices must be sprinkled while chops are still being fried, as the heat of the skillet is important. Any masala that ends up in the skillet is then scraped up and sprinkled on top of chops in dish.

4 lbs	cabrito (young goat), about 30 chops (see Tips, left)	2 kg
1 ¼ cups	finely chopped onion	300 mL
¼ cup	minced green chiles, preferably serranos	50 mL
2 tbsp	minced peeled gingerroot	25 mL
2 tbsp	chopped garlic	25 mL
½ cup	cilantro, chopped	125 mL
1 cup	plain low-fat yogurt	250 mL
1 cup	cider vinegar	250 mL
1 tbsp	coriander powder	15 mL
2 tsp	cumin powder	10 mL
2 tsp	salt or to taste	10 mL
4 to 5 tbsp	oil	60 to 75 mL

Spice Mixture

1 tbsp	coriander powder	15 mL
1 ½ tsp	cumin powder	7 mL
1 tbsp	garam masala	15 mL

Garnish

	Juice of 2 limes or lemons	
⅓ cup	cilantro, chopped	75 mL
	Cilantro sprigs	
	Lemon or lime wedges	

1. Trim all excess fat from chops. Rinse and pat dry. Place in a large saucepan.

2. In a bowl, mix together onion, chiles, ginger, garlic, cilantro, yogurt, vinegar, coriander, cumin and salt. Pour over chops and mix well. Cover and marinate for 30 minutes at room temperature or longer in refrigerator.

3. Bring saucepan with chops to a boil over high heat. Reduce heat to medium-low. Cover and simmer, shaking pan every 15 minutes to make sure meat is not sticking to pan. Cook until chops are tender and just a very small amount of thick gravy remains in the pan, about 1½ hours. If there is still too much liquid when chops are tender, uncover pan and increase heat to allow liquid to reduce. (Do not stir chops while cooking, as meat will fall off the bones. Make sure chops remain intact and are tender.)

4. *Spice Mixture:* In a bowl, combine coriander, cumin and garam masala. Sprinkle mixture over chops. Set aside.

5. In a large skillet, heat 2 tbsp (25 mL) of the oil over medium heat. Carefully place chops in a single layer in skillet in batches and brown, turning once, 6 to 8 minutes. After turning, sprinkle browned side with some of spice mixture (see Tips, left). Transfer to a plate and continue with remaining chops, adding more oil as necessary.

6. *Garnish:* Squeeze lime juice over chops. Sprinkle any leftover masala in pan over chops. Sprinkle chopped cilantro over top. Garnish with cilantro sprigs and lemon wedges.

Tip

Chops can be frozen after cooking and before frying in an airtight container for up to 3 months. Thaw in refrigerator and fry (see Step 4). Leftover chops can also be frozen. To reheat fried chops, thaw in refrigerator and place in foil. Sprinkle generously with lemon juice, seal foil tightly and heat in a 300°F (150°C) oven, about 20 minutes.

Sindhi Masala Bread Hash

1 ½ tbsp	oil	22 mL
1 tsp	cumin seeds	5 mL
½ cup	finely sliced green onions, including some green	125 mL
2 cups	puréed onion	500 mL
1 tbsp	minced peeled gingerroot	15 mL
1 tbsp	minced garlic	15 mL
1 tbsp	minced green chiles, preferably serranos	15 mL
1 tsp	coriander powder	5 mL
½ tsp	cumin powder	2 mL
½ tsp	turmeric	2 mL
3 to 4	plum (Roma) tomatoes, puréed (about 1 cup/250 mL)	3 to 4
1 ½ tsp	salt or to taste	7 mL
1 tbsp	sambal oelek (Asian hot chili sauce) or to taste	15 mL
1 cup	cilantro, chopped	250 mL
8 oz	soft French bread, torn into 2- to 3-inch (5 to 7.5 cm) pieces	250 g
	Plain yogurt	

1. In a saucepan, heat oil over medium-high heat. Sauté cumin seeds for 30 seconds. Add green onions and sauté for 30 seconds.

2. Add onion and sauté until just beginning to color, 4 to 5 minutes. Reduce heat to medium. Add ginger, garlic and chiles and sauté for 2 minutes. Add coriander, cumin and turmeric and sauté for 2 minutes.

3. Add tomatoes, salt and 2 cups (500 mL) water. Cover and bring to a boil. Reduce heat to low and simmer until mixture thickens, 6 to 8 minutes. Stir in cilantro and cook for 1 minute.

4. Remove from heat and mix in bread, making sure all pieces are completely soaked. (Mixture resembles hash.) Serve hot or at room temperature with plain yogurt.

Serves 4

Indian frugality was one of the reasons for this dish, but it is now a recognized Sindhi specialty. Western-style bread is used extensively in Sindhi cuisine, so this dish was created to use leftover bread. I love to serve it for a late Sunday breakfast with plain yogurt. Although not traditional, it would definitely jazz up a serving of scrambled eggs and bacon.

Tip
Hash can be made through Step 3 up to 1 day ahead and refrigerated in an airtight container. Reheat on stove top before adding bread.

Stuffed Lamb Patties

This is a variation on the classic North Indian appetizer shaami kabab. *In this version ground meat is cooked with split yellow peas* (channa dal) *and seasonings to make patties.*

Tip

Patties can be made ahead, fried and frozen in an airtight container for up to 3 months. Reheat without thawing on a baking sheet in a 250°F (120°C) oven for 15 to 20 minutes or until heated through.

- *Wok or deep-fryer*
- *Candy/deep-fry thermometer*

¼ cup	split yellow peas (channa dal)	50 mL
1 lb	ground lamb or lean ground beef	500 g
4 to 5	dried Indian red chiles, halved with seeds removed	4 to 5
1 ½ cups	chopped onion	375 mL
2 tsp	minced peeled gingerroot	10 mL
2 tsp	garam masala	10 mL
1	egg, lightly beaten	1
1 ½ tsp	salt or to taste	7 mL

Stuffing

¼ cup	finely chopped onion	50 mL
2 tbsp	slivered almonds	25 mL
2 tbsp	raisins	25 mL
2 tbsp	cilantro, chopped	25 mL
1 tbsp	chopped green chiles, preferably serranos	15 mL
	Oil for deep-frying	

1. Clean and pick through dal for any small stones and grit. Rinse several times in cold water until water is fairly clear. Soak in 2 cups (500 mL) water in a bowl for 15 minutes.

2. In a saucepan, combine lamb and just enough water to cover. Bring to a boil over medium-high heat. Skim any scum off the top. Drain dal and add to saucepan with red chiles, onion and ginger. Reduce heat to medium. Cover partially and cook until all liquid is absorbed, about 20 minutes. Brown for 3 to 4 minutes and remove from heat. Let cool for a few minutes.

3. Transfer lamb mixture to a food processor. Add garam masala, egg and salt and process to make a smooth, paste-like mixture. Transfer to a bowl.

4. *Stuffing:* In a bowl, mix together onion, almonds, raisins, cilantro and green chiles. Divide into 12 portions.

5. Divide lamb mixture into 12 portions. Place one portion in palm of hand and press into a $\frac{1}{2}$-inch (1 cm) thick layer. Cup the palm and place a portion of the stuffing in the middle. Cover by gently pressing cup to enclose stuffing and flatten patty gently between palms. Make sure edges are smooth and there are no cracks. Repeat process to make remaining patties.

6. Meanwhile, in a wok or deep-fryer, heat oil to 350°F (180°C). Fry patties, in 3 batches, without crowding and turning once, until brown, 2 to 3 minutes. Remove with a large-holed strainer and drain on paper towels. Serve hot with a chutney of your choice.

Spicy Sesame Eggs

The incredible sesame topping on these eggs is a treasure trove of flavors. I think it would make a wonderful topping for a baked potato and a knockout dip for boiled shrimp. Thinned a little, it would be dynamite drizzled over grilled shrimp. How about mixing it into mashed potato!

Tip

Eggs can be cooked, peeled and cut ahead and refrigerated in an airtight container. Sauce can be made several hours ahead and held at room temperature. Before serving, pour sauce over chilled eggs.

6	eggs	6

Sesame Topping

3½ tbsp	sesame seeds	52 mL
2 tsp	cumin seeds	10 mL
1 tbsp	thick plain yogurt	15 mL
2 tbsp	freshly squeezed lime or lemon juice	25 mL
½ tsp	salt or to taste	2 mL
2 tbsp	mustard oil	25 mL
½ tsp	fenugreek seeds (methi)	2 mL
3 to 4	green chiles, preferably serranos, slivered	3 to 4
2 tbsp	slivered peeled gingerroot	25 mL
½ tsp	cayenne pepper	2 mL
¼ tsp	turmeric	1 mL

1. Hard-cook eggs and peel. Cut in half lengthwise and set aside.

2. Spread sesame seeds in a layer in a heavy dry skillet. Toast over medium heat, stirring occasionally, until pale golden, 2 to 3 minutes. Do not overbrown. Transfer immediately to a bowl and let cool. Toast cumin seeds in same skillet over medium heat, 2 to 3 minutes. Add to bowl. Transfer seeds to a spice grinder and grind to a fine powder. Return to bowl. Stir in yogurt, lime juice and salt. Add 2 tbsp (25 mL) water to make a paste.

3. In a small skillet, heat mustard oil over high heat until smoking. Remove from heat and let cool for 1 minute (see Tips, page 46). Return to medium heat. Add fenugreek, chiles, ginger, cayenne and turmeric and sauté for 20 seconds. Pour mixture over paste and stir to mix thoroughly to make a thick sauce.

4. Arrange eggs on serving platter. Spoon sauce over top and serve at room temperature.

Muri
Bengali Puffed Rice

E

- Wok

4 cups	puffed rice (muri)	1 L
1 tbsp	mustard oil	15 mL
½ cup	hot mix or sev (see Tips, right)	125 mL
¼ cup	chopped onion	50 mL
¼ cup	chopped seeded tomato, juices drained	50 mL
¼ cup	peanuts	50 mL
2 tbsp	minced green chiles or to taste	25 mL
2 tbsp	hot mango pickle, chopped, or to taste (see Tips, right)	25 mL
2 tbsp	cilantro, chopped	25 mL
2 to 3 tbsp	freshly squeezed lime or lemon juice	25 to 45 mL
¼ cup	diced boiled potato, optional	50 mL
¼ cup	diced peeled cucumber, optional	50 mL
2 tbsp	diced fresh coconut, optional	25 mL

1. In a wok over medium heat, toast puffed rice until it smells toasty, 4 to 5 minutes. Transfer to a bowl.

2. In a small saucepan, heat mustard oil over high heat until smoking. Remove from heat (see Tips, page 46). Let cool for 1 minute. Drizzle over puffed rice.

3. Add hot mix, onion, tomato, peanuts, chiles, mango pickle, cilantro and lime juice. Add potato, cucumber and/or coconut, if using. Toss to mix. Serve in individual bowls.

Serves 4

Puffed rice is enjoyed in many parts of India, but nowhere as much as in Bengal. Known as muri, *it is a popular snack and the poor man's staple. This "dish" (I call it* Bengali bhel, *after the famous street food of Mumbai* bhel puri, *as both share a base of puffed rice) can be customized to suit your palate, and these proportions are guidelines. My friend Sunanada served this one evening and I couldn't stop eating it.*

Tips

Hot mix and sev are available as ready-to-eat packaged snacks in Indian markets.

Several brands of hot mango pickles are sold in Indian markets. All are oil-based, fiery, bright red and equally good.

Nimki
Crispy Bites

Makes 25 to 30

Crispy snacks such as these are popular in India. Seasonings vary, but the concept remains the same. This is the Bengali version, using one of its favorite seasoning ingredients, nigella.

Tips

To achieve best results, fry slowly over medium heat to cook through the layers and to make them crispy.

These delicious *nimkis* can be cooled and stored in an airtight container for several weeks.

- Pizza pan
- Wok or deep-fryer
- Candy/deep-fry thermometer

1 ½ cups	all-purpose flour	375 mL
4 tsp	nigella seeds (kalaunji)	20 mL
1 ½ tsp	salt	7 mL
2 tbsp	ghee	25 mL
¼ cup	all-purpose flour (approx.) for rolling	50 mL
	Oil for deep-frying	

1. Place flour in the center of a pizza pan. Sprinkle in nigella and salt evenly. Rub in ghee and mix with fingers to a cornmeal texture. Drizzle approximately ¼ cup (125 mL) lukewarm water over mixture. Mix well to form a smooth dough. Knead well. Shape into a ball, cover and set aside for 1 hour.

2. Knead dough again for 2 minutes. Pinch portions of dough and form into 1-inch (2.5 cm) size balls. There should be 25 to 30. Keep covered with a clean towel away from heat.

3. On a clean work surface, sprinkle a tiny pinch of flour. Spread with palm. Flatten a ball of dough into a disk and roll on floured surface into a 4- to 5-inch (10 to 12.5 cm) circle. (It is important to roll the dough very thin.) Sprinkle a tiny pinch of flour and lightly fold circle in half, then in quarters, resulting in a 4-layered triangle shape. Make sure layers are not stuck together except at the center point. Set aside on a baking sheet. Continue to make remaining "nimkis" in the same way.

4. In a wok or deep-fryer, heat oil over medium heat to 325°F (160°C). Fry nimkis, in batches, turning frequently, until crisp and pale golden, 4 to 5 minutes. (Do not allow to brown.) Remove with a large-holed strainer and drain on paper towels. Serve hot or at room temperature.

Alur Chop
Fish-Stuffed Potato Patties

1 lb	baking potatoes (about 4 small)	500 g
3 tsp	salt or to taste, divided	15 mL
8 oz	fish fillet (any variety), skinned	250 g
½ tsp	turmeric	2 mL
1 tsp	cider vinegar	5 mL
1 tbsp	oil	15 mL
¾ cup	finely chopped onion	175 mL
1 tbsp	raisins, chopped	15 mL
1 tbsp	minced green chiles, preferably serranos	15 mL
1 tsp	soy or Worcestershire sauce	5 mL
1 tsp	cayenne pepper	5 mL
½ tsp	freshly ground pepper	2 mL
½ tsp	granulated sugar	2 mL
3 tbsp	cilantro, chopped	45 mL
	Oil for pan-frying	
1	egg, lightly beaten	1
¾ cup	dry bread crumbs	175 mL

Makes 6

This is a classic Bengali recipe. The fish stuffing can be substituted with ground meat, which traditionally would be ground goat.

Variation
Feel free to make the stuffing using ground chicken or turkey instead of the fish if you prefer.

1. In a saucepan of boiling water, cook potatoes until tender, 20 to 25 minutes. Drain. When cool enough to handle but still warm, peel and mash. Mix in 1 tsp (5 mL) of the salt. Divide into 6 equal balls.

2. Place fish in a saucepan with 1 cup (250 mL) water. Add turmeric, vinegar and ½ tsp (2 mL) of salt. Bring to a gentle boil over medium heat. Cook until fish flakes easily with fork. Drain and flake fish.

3. In a skillet, heat oil over medium heat. Add onion and sauté until golden, 6 to 8 minutes. Add fish, raisins, chiles, soy sauce, cayenne, remaining salt, pepper and sugar. Mix well and remove from heat. Mix in cilantro. Divide mixture into 6 portions.

4. *To make patties:* Flatten a potato ball between your palms. Supporting flattened disk in the one hand, press gently with fingers of other hand to make a cup. Place one portion of the stuffing into cup. Cover by gently pressing cup to enclose stuffing. Press filled patty between palms to even out shape. Make sure sides are sealed. It should be 3½ to 4 inches (9 to 12 cm) in diameter. Continue to make remaining mixture into patties in the same way.

5. In a skillet, heat ½ inch (1 cm) oil over medium heat. Dip each patty into beaten egg, then press into bread crumbs. Fry, in batches, without crowding, until bottoms are golden brown, 2 minutes. Flip and fry until golden brown, 2 to 3 minutes. Drain on paper towels.

Bengali Shrimp Cutlets

Serves 8

These "cutlets" are prized morsels in Bengal and are served as an appetizer. I particularly enjoy the combination of strong mustard served with the shrimp.

- *Wok or deep-fryer*
- *Candy/deep-fry thermometer*

16	jumbo shrimp	16
1 cup	coarsely chopped onion	250 mL
1	piece (1 ½-by 1-inch/4 by 2.5 cm) gingerroot, peeled and coarsely chopped	1
2 tsp	white vinegar	10 mL
¾ tsp	salt or to taste	4 mL
	Oil for deep-frying	
1	egg, lightly beaten	1
¾ cup	dry bread crumbs	175 mL
⅓ cup	hot mustard, preferably English mustard	75 mL

1. Peel shrimp, leaving tails intact. Rinse and drain. With a sharp knife, slit through back of each shrimp, pulling out the vein. Continue to cut carefully, until shrimp can be laid flat, without separating the 2 halves. Lay shrimp on paper towels and pat dry.

2. In a food processor, purée onion and ginger. Squeeze purée in cheesecloth over a bowl to extract as much juice as possible. You will need about ½ cup (125 mL) juice (discard solids). Stir in vinegar and salt.

3. In a nonreactive dish, arrange shrimp in a single layer. Pour onion juice mixture over shrimp. Cover and refrigerate for 1 to 2 hours.

4. In a wok or deep-fryer, heat oil to 375°F (190°C). Dip each shrimp into beaten egg, dredge in bread crumbs to coat. Deep-fry, 2 to 3 at a time, until golden, 3 to 4 minutes per batch. Drain on paper towels. Serve hot with mustard.

Cabbage Vadai
Savory Cabbage Donuts

- *Wok or deep-fryer*
- *Candy/deep-fry thermometer*

½ cup	split white lentils (urad dal)	125 mL
½ tsp	asafetida (hing)	2 mL
2 tsp	minced green chiles, preferably serranos	10 mL
¾ tsp	salt or to taste	4 mL
½ cup	finely chopped cabbage	125 mL
½ cup	finely chopped onion	125 mL
1 tbsp	frozen peas, thawed	15 mL
¼ cup	chopped cilantro	50 mL
	Oil for deep-frying	

Makes 8

Split white lentils (urad dal) have a high starch content and are used to make many South Indian fried snacks instead of the chickpea flour commonly used in the north.

1. Clean and pick through lentils for any small stones and grit. Rinse several times in cold water until water is fairly clear. Add water to cover by 3 inches (7.5 cm) and soak in a bowl at room temperature overnight.

2. Drain and transfer to a blender. (Do not use a food processor.) Purée to a fine paste. Scrape sides down several times to ensure paste is smooth and to incorporate as much air as possible. This may take 6 to 8 minutes.

3. Fold in asafetida, chiles and salt. Add cabbage, onion and peas and mix well. (Mixture will be a little soft.)

4. In a wok or deep-fryer, heat oil to 375°F (190°C). Cut a 6-inch (15 cm) piece of foil. Place 2 tbsp (25 mL) of the mixture on foil. Wet palm and pat to form a disk about ½ inch (1 cm) thick. Make a hole with finger in the center of vadai. Using a wide spatula, gently ease one vadai at a time into oil. Fry until golden brown, 2 to 3 minutes. Remove with a large-holed strainer and drain on paper towels. Repeat with remaining mixture. Serve hot with a chutney of your choice.

Pesarattu

Savory Mung Bean Pancakes

Makes 8 to 10

South Indian "tiffin" is famous throughout India. It consists of breakfast and snack foods made with an assortment of lentil- and-rice batters. This pancake is special because it is the only one made with an unhusked bean, giving it a unique flavor.

Tips

Any long-grain rice is fine in this recipe except basmati, which has a lower starch content. Here you need more starch to act as a binder.

To serve as finger food, make 2-inch (5 cm) pancakes and serve with a dollop of chutney on top.

1 cup	split green mung beans (chilkewali mung dal)	250 mL
¼ cup	long-grain white rice (see Tips, left)	50 mL
2 tbsp	chopped green chiles, preferably serranos	25 mL
1 cup	finely chopped onion	250 mL
1	small potato, boiled, peeled and mashed	1
½ cup	cilantro leaves and soft stems, chopped	125 mL
2 tsp	minced peeled gingerroot, optional	10 mL
1 tsp	salt or to taste	5 mL
¼ tsp	asafetida (hing)	1 mL
¼ cup	oil (approx.)	50 mL

1. Clean and pick through beans for any small stones and grit. Rinse several times in cold water until water is fairly clear. Soak beans and rice in 2 cups (500 mL) water at room temperature for 45 minutes or for up to 3 hours. Drain well. Add to a food processor and process coarsely. Transfer to a bowl. Add chiles, onion, mashed potato, cilantro, ginger, if using, salt and asafetida and mix well. Add ¾ cup (175 mL) water, adding just enough to make a batter slightly thicker than pancake batter.

2. Heat a nonstick skillet over medium-high heat until a drop of water flicked on it sizzles. Add 1 tsp (5 mL) of the oil and tilt skillet to spread oil. Ladle ½ cup (125 mL) batter into center and spread quickly with back of ladle to form a pancake about ¼ inch (0.5) thick. Make a hole in the center. Spoon 1 tsp (5 mL) of the oil in the center and some around edges. Cook, turning once, until browned on both sides, about 2 minutes per side. Transfer to a plate. Continue with remaining batter and oil.

3. Serve with a chutney or Indian pickle of your choice.

S

Plantain and Potato Patties

Makes 24

*Plantains are very
popular in South India
and are used in several
ways, in addition to
the ubiquitous plantain
chips. These patties are
a delicious example.*

Tip

These can be made
into small balls and
deep-fried. Serve
with toothpicks.

4	unripe plantains	4
8 oz	baking potatoes (about 2)	250 g
1 ½ tsp	salt or to taste	7 mL
2 tbsp	oil	25 mL
1 ½ cups	finely chopped onion	375 mL
2 tbsp	minced green chiles, preferably serranos	25 mL
2 tsp	minced peeled gingerroot	10 mL
1 tbsp	coriander powder	15 mL
2 tsp	mango powder (amchur)	10 mL
1 tsp	cumin powder	5 mL
1 tsp	garam masala	5 mL
½ tsp	each cayenne pepper and turmeric	2 mL
¼ cup	chickpea flour (besan)	50 mL
¼ cup	cilantro, chopped	50 mL
¼ cup	oil for pan-frying	50 mL

1. Place plantains in a large pot with water to cover by 2 inches (5 cm). Bring to a boil over high heat. Reduce heat to medium-low and cook until soft, about 1 hour. Drain. When cool enough to handle, peel and mash.

2. In a saucepan of boiling water, cook whole potatoes until tender, 20 to 25 minutes. Drain. When cool enough to handle but still warm, peel and mash. Mix with mashed plantain. Sprinkle with salt. Set aside.

3. In a skillet, heat 2 tbsp (25 mL) oil over medium-high heat. Add onion and sauté until soft, 3 to 4 minutes. Add chiles and ginger and sauté until no moisture remains, 3 to 4 minutes.

4. Reduce heat to medium. Add coriander, mango powder, cumin, garam masala, cayenne and turmeric. Mix well and cook for 2 minutes. Let cool.

5. Mix chickpea flour into onion mixture and add to plantain mixture. Add cilantro and mix well to combine.

6. In a clean skillet, heat 2 tbsp (25 mL) of the oil. Divide plantain mixture into 24 portions and roll each into a ball. Flatten into a patty about ½ inch (1 cm) thick. Add to hot oil and fry, in batches, without crowding, until golden, 2 to 3 minutes. Flip and fry other side until golden, 2 to 3 minutes more. Drain on paper towels. Repeat with remaining mixture, adding more oil as necessary. Serve with a chutney of your choice.

Aloo Bondas
Batter-Dipped Potato Balls

- Wok or deep-fryer
- Candy/deep-fry thermometer

1 lb	all-purpose potatoes (about 4)	500 g
1 tbsp	oil	15 mL
1 tsp	dark mustard seeds	5 mL
1 tsp	split white lentils, picked over and rinsed	5 mL
1	dried Indian red chile	1
1	sprig fresh curry leaves, stripped, optional	1
3 cups	finely chopped onion	750 mL
2 tbsp	minced green chiles, preferably serranos	25 mL
1 1/2 tsp	salt or to taste	7 mL
1/2 tsp	turmeric	2 mL
1/2 cup	cilantro, chopped	125 mL

Batter

2 1/2 cups	chickpea flour (besan)	625 mL
2 tsp	cayenne pepper	10 mL
1 tsp	salt to taste	5 mL
1/4 tsp	asafetida (hing)	1 mL
	Oil for deep-frying	

1. In a saucepan of boiling water, cook whole potatoes until tender, 20 to 25 minutes. Drain. When cool enough to handle but still warm, peel and mash. Set aside.

2. In a skillet, heat 1 tbsp (15 mL) oil over high heat until a couple of mustard seeds thrown in start to sputter. Add all mustard seeds and cover quickly. When seeds stop popping, uncover, reduce heat to medium and add lentils, red chile and curry leaves. Sauté 30 seconds. Add onion and green chiles and sauté until softened, 3 minutes.

3. Add potatoes, salt, turmeric and cilantro. Mix well and cook, stirring, for 2 minutes. Let cool. Divide into 14 portions. Form into balls.

4. *Batter:* In a bowl, stir together chickpea flour, cayenne, salt and asafetida. Whisk in 3/4 cup (175 mL) water to make a thick lump-free batter resembling pancake batter, gradually adding up to an additional 1/4 cup (50 mL) water as necessary.

5. In a wok or deep-fryer, heat oil to 375°F (190°C). Dip a potato ball (bondas) in batter to coat evenly. Remove from batter with tip of spoon and gently ease into hot oil, taking care batter does not get scraped off as bonda is dropped into oil. Fry, 3 to 5 at a time, until golden, 2 to 3 minutes. Remove with a large-holed strainer to paper towels. Serve hot with a chutney of your choice.

Makes 14

A popular snack, these potato balls are served in tea and coffee shops all over South India. Equally popular in elegant dining rooms as part of a buffet, they make great picnic food as well.

Tip
Potatoes can be shaped into balls (Steps 1 through 3) and refrigerated for up to 2 days in an airtight container. Bring to room temperature before dipping in batter and frying.

Kerala Beef Cutlets

Makes 12

This type of patty (cutlet) is very popular in India and has a counterpart in every region. The type of meat, the seasonings and the name varies, but the concept remains the same. This is a recipe from the Syrian Christian community in Kerala, one of the few who eat beef and pork.

Tip

Cutlets can be made ahead and refrigerated in an airtight container for up to 2 days. Reheat in a 250°F (120°C) oven until heated through.

1	all-purpose potato (about 4 oz/125 g)	1
1	stick cinnamon, about 2 inches (5 cm) long, broken into pieces	1
½ tsp	each cumin seeds and black peppercorns	2 mL
¼ tsp	cardamom seeds	1 mL
6	whole cloves	6
1 tbsp	oil	15 mL
½ cup	finely chopped onion	125 mL
4 tsp	minced green chiles, preferably serranos	20 mL
1 tbsp	minced peeled gingerroot	15 mL
1 lb	ground beef or lamb	500 g
2 tbsp	apple cider vinegar or malt vinegar	25 mL
1 tsp	salt	5 mL
1 cup	loosely packed cilantro, coarsely chopped	250 mL
1	egg, separated	1
½ cup	oil for pan-frying (approx.)	125 mL
¼ cup	dry bread crumbs (approx.)	50 mL

1. In a saucepan of boiling water, cook whole potato until tender, 20 to 25 minutes. Drain. When cool enough to handle but still warm, peel and mash. Set aside.

2. In a spice grinder, mix together cinnamon, cumin, peppercorns, cardamom and cloves. Grind to a powder. Set aside.

3. In a skillet, heat 1 tbsp (15 mL) oil over medium heat. Sauté onion until translucent, 3 to 4 minutes. Add chiles and ginger and sauté for 2 minutes. Add beef, spice mixture, vinegar and salt. Sauté, breaking up beef with a spoon, until meat is browned and no moisture remains, 12 to 14 minutes. Let cool and transfer to a food processor.

4. Add potato, cilantro and egg yolk and process for 30 seconds. If mixture is too soft, spread in a dish and refrigerate for 30 minutes. Divide mixture into 12 equal portions. Form each portion into a ball and flatten into a disk about ½ inch (1 cm) thick.

5. In a skillet, heat 2 tbsp (25 mL) of the oil over medium heat.

6. Spread bread crumbs in a dish. In a bowl, whisk egg white. Dip each cutlet into egg white to coat and press into bread crumbs.

7. Fry cutlets, in batches, without crowding, turning once, about 2 minutes per side. Drain on paper towels. Repeat with remaining cutlets, adding more oil as necessary.

Bread Upma
Bread and Vegetable Stir-Fry

3 tbsp	oil	45 mL
2 tsp	dark mustard seeds	10 mL
½ tsp	cumin seeds	2 mL
2 cups	coarsely chopped onions	500 mL
1 tbsp	minced green chiles, preferably serranos	15 mL
¾ tsp	cayenne pepper	4 mL
¾ tsp	turmeric	4 mL
2 cups	frozen mixed vegetables or leftover cooked vegetables	500 mL
8 cups	cubed (½ inch/1 cm) sourdough bread, fresh or stale	2 L
2 tsp	granulated sugar	10 mL
1 tsp	salt or to taste	5 mL
	Juice of 2 limes or lemons	
¾ cup	cilantro, chopped, divided	175 mL
¼ cup	raw peanuts, toasted and crushed	50 mL
¼ cup	grated fresh coconut, optional	50 mL

1. In a large wok or deep skillet, heat oil over high heat until a couple of mustard seeds thrown in start to sputter. Add all the mustard seeds and cover quickly. When the seeds stop popping, in a few seconds, uncover, reduce heat to medium and add cumin. Sauté for 30 seconds. Add onions and chiles and sauté until onions are lightly golden, 6 to 8 minutes.

2. Add cayenne and turmeric. Mix well and sauté for 2 minutes, adding 2 tbsp (25 mL) water to prevent burning if necessary.

3. Stir in vegetables and mix well. Reduce heat to low. Cover and cook, stirring often, until vegetables are tender, 5 to 7 minutes. If using leftover cooked vegetables, reduce cooking time.

4. Stir in bread cubes, sugar and salt and toss to mix. Pour 1 cup (250 mL) water over top and mix well. Cover and heat through, about 5 minutes. Add lime juice, ½ cup (125 mL) of the cilantro and mix well. Cover and cook until hot, 6 to 8 minutes.

5. Spoon mixture onto a platter and garnish with remaining cilantro, peanuts and coconut, if using.

Serves 6 to 8

This simple dish is typical of the innovative use of leftovers that the frugal Indian housewife is known for. Quick and easy, it can be whipped up at a moment's notice to feed unexpected guests, to stretch a meal or to provide a healthy after-school snack.

Fiery Shrimp-Stuffed Patties

Makes 7

HOT

Patties such as these are very popular in India and are called tikki. *The potato casing can be stuffed with any mixture of your choice, such as mushrooms, mashed seasoned beans or, as many Indians do, with a mixture of leftover cooked vegetables. Leftover meat loaf also makes a tasty filling.*

Tips

The cooked patties can be refrigerated in an airtight container for up to 2 days. Reheat in 200°F (100°C) oven for 15 minutes or until heated through.

Make patties as thin as possible without splitting the sides. This allows them to fry properly.

1 lb	baking potatoes (about 4 small)	500 g
2	slices firm white bread, crusts trimmed	2
1 ½ tsp	salt	7 mL

Stuffing

1 tbsp	oil	15 mL
½ tsp	nigella seeds (kalaunji)	2 mL
½ cup	finely chopped red onion	125 mL
1 tsp	each minced gingerroot and minced garlic	5 mL
½ tsp	each coriander powder and cumin powder	2 mL
2 tbsp	tomato sauce or 1 tbsp (15 mL) tomato paste	25 mL
2 tbsp	Asian hot sauce	25 mL
4 oz	cooked salad shrimp, coarsely chopped	125 g
3 to 4 tbsp	cilantro, chopped	45 to 60 mL
2 tsp	mango powder (amchur)	10 mL
½ cup	dry bread crumbs (approx.)	125 mL
4 to 5 tbsp	oil for pan-frying (approx.)	60 to 75 mL

1. In a saucepan of boiling water, cook potatoes until tender, 20 to 25 minutes. Drain. When cool enough to handle but still warm, peel and mash. Dip bread, one slice at a time, in water and squeeze between palms. Break over potato. Sprinkle in salt. Mix well with hands, until smooth. Divide into 7 portions and roll into balls.

2. *Stuffing:* Meanwhile, in a skillet, heat 1 tbsp (15 mL) oil over medium heat. Add nigella and sauté until fragrant, about 30 seconds. Add onion and sauté until golden, 5 to 6 minutes.

3. Add ginger and garlic and sauté for 1 minute. Add coriander and cumin and sauté for 1 minute. Stir in tomato sauce and hot sauce and cook until mixture looks dry, 1 to 2 minutes. Stir in shrimp and heat through. Remove from heat. Stir in cilantro and mango powder. Divide filling into 7 portions.

4. *To assemble:* Place one potato ball in cupped palm of hand and, with fingers of other hand, press into a cup about ½ inch (1 cm) thick. Spoon one portion of shrimp filling into potato cup. Carefully enclose filling, making sure there are no cracks. Gently press into a patty between palms. Press both sides into bread crumbs.

5. In a large skillet, heat 2 tbsp (25 mL) of oil over medium-high heat. Fry 4 patties at a time, turning once, until evenly browned, 2 to 3 minutes. Drizzle a little more oil around edges of patties if they seem dry. Repeat with remaining patties, adding more oil if necessary. Serve hot with a chutney of your choice.

Dhansak na Kabab
Parsi Meatballs

- *Wok or deep-fryer*
- *Candy/deep-fry thermometer*

8 oz	ground lamb or beef (see Tip, right)	250 g
1 cup	mashed peeled all-purpose potato	250 mL
¼ cup	finely chopped green onions, with some green	50 mL
¼ cup	cilantro, chopped	50 mL
2 tsp	minced green chiles, preferably serranos	10 mL
1 tsp	minced peeled gingerroot	5 mL
1 tsp	minced garlic	5 mL
1 tsp	salt or to taste	5 mL
1 tsp	coriander powder	5 mL
1 tsp	cumin powder	5 mL
1 tsp	sambhar powder (see page 28)	5 mL
½ tsp	cayenne pepper	2 mL
1	egg, slightly beaten	1
½ cup	dry bread crumbs	125 mL
	Oil for deep-frying	

1. In a bowl, mix together lamb, potato, green onions, cilantro, chiles, ginger, garlic, salt, coriander, cumin, sambhar, cayenne and egg. Mix well.

2. Divide into 16 equal portions and roll into balls. Roll each in bread crumbs.

3. In a wok or deep-fryer, heat oil to 350°F (180°C). Fry meatballs, in batches, without crowding until browned and no longer pink inside, 4 to 5 minutes. Drain on paper towels. Serve hot with a chutney of your choice if serving as an appetizer.

Makes 16 pieces

These meatballs are a traditional accompaniment to the famous Parsi stew (Dhansak) and Parsi brown rice. They are also an excellent cocktail snack.

Tip
Traditionally, ground lamb, or more correctly goat, is the meat used. However, I have tested the recipe with extra lean ground beef and it works just as well.

Sabzi Soy ki Tikki

Vegetable and Soy Patties

Makes 12

Patties such as these are served both as snacks and with meals. The addition of soy has gained popularity, particularly with vegetarians, as it is a good source of protein.

¼ cup	soy granules	50 mL
12 oz	all-purpose potatoes (about 3)	375 g
1 cup	diced green beans	250 mL
1 cup	diced peeled carrots	250 mL
½ cup	frozen peas, thawed	125 mL
3 tbsp	cilantro, chopped	45 mL
2 tsp	minced peeled gingerroot	10 mL
2 tsp	minced green chiles, preferably serranos	10 mL
1½ tsp	salt or to taste	7 mL
1 tsp	coriander powder	5 mL
½ tsp	cumin powder	2 mL
½ tsp	cayenne pepper	2 mL
½ tsp	garam masala	2 mL
2 tbsp	lime or lemon juice	25 mL
¼ cup	dry bread crumbs	50 mL
6 tbsp	oil	90 mL

1. In a bowl, soak soy granules in 1 cup (250 mL) water at room temperature for 30 minutes. Drain thoroughly.

2. In a saucepan of boiling water, cook whole potatoes until tender, 20 to 25 minutes. Drain. When cool enough to handle but still warm, peel and mash.

3. In a separate saucepan, combine beans, carrots and 1 cup (250 mL) water. Bring to a boil over high heat. Reduce heat to low, cover and cook until vegetables are tender and water is absorbed, 8 to 10 minutes. Add peas and mash together.

4. In a bowl, mix together soy granules, potato, vegetable mixture, cilantro, ginger, chiles, salt, coriander, cumin, cayenne, garam masala and lime juice. Mix well using hands.

5. Divide mixture into 12 portions. Form each into a disk ½ inch (1 cm) thick. Place on a work surface and shape disk into a pear shape. Coat each in bread crumbs.

6. In a skillet, heat ¼ cup (50 mL) oil, adding more as required, over medium heat. Fry patties, in 2 batches, without crowding, until browned on both sides, 2 to 3 minutes per side. Serve hot with a chutney of your choice.

Sabudana Vada

Tapioca Pearls and Potato Patties

- Wok or deep-fryer
- Candy/deep-fry thermometer

8 oz	baking potatoes (about 2 small)	250 g
1 1/4 tsp	salt or to taste	6 mL
1/4 cup	tapioca pearls (sago, sabudana)	50 mL
1/2 cup	skinned raw peanuts	125 mL
1/2 cup	cilantro, coarsely chopped	125 mL
1/3 cup	chopped green onions, with some green	75 mL
1/4 cup	finely chopped onion	50 mL
1 1/2 tsp	minced green chiles, preferably serranos	7 mL
	Oil for deep-frying	

1. In a saucepan of boiling water, cook whole potatoes until tender, 20 to 25 minutes. Drain. When cool enough to handle but still warm, peel and mash. Sprinkle on salt. Transfer to a large mixing bowl.

2. Place tapioca in a sieve and place in a bowl of water. Swirl fingers to loosen excess starch. Drain and repeat process 3 to 4 times until water is fairly clear. Place in a bowl and add water to cover by 2 inches (5 cm). Soak for 20 minutes. Drain, rinse and drain very well. Add to potatoes.

3. In a dry skillet over medium heat, toast peanuts, shaking pan and stirring frequently, until flecked with light brown spots, 3 to 4 minutes. Chop coarsely and add to bowl. Add cilantro, green onions, onion and chiles. Mix well using hands.

4. Wash hands. Pinch off walnut-size pieces. Roll each into a smooth ball and flatten between palms to make a patty about 2 inches (5 cm) in diameter and 1/2 inch (1 cm) thick.

5. In a wok or deep-fryer, heat oil to 375°F (190°C). Fry patties, a few at a time, without crowding, until golden, 2 to 3 minutes. Drain on paper towels. Serve hot with a chutney of your choice.

Makes 18 to 20

Tapioca pearls are used in many different ways, from savory to sweet. This is a very popular snack from Maharashtra. It is best eaten freshly prepared and hot. The textures of mashed potato, chewy tapioca and crunchy peanuts combine to make an outstanding snack.

Tip

These patties do not reheat well, as the starch in the tapioca gets slightly gummy. They're best served as soon as they are made.

Mirchi Pakoras
Batter-Dipped Stuffed Long Peppers

Fried stuffed peppers are a very popular appetizer and also sold as a street food. Personally, I like to use hot chiles for this dish, but mild ones are just as good.

Tip

Pick peppers such as pale green banana peppers, which are about 2 to 3 inches (5 to 7.5 cm) long and approximately ¾ inch (2 cm) around, so there is room for stuffing.

- *Wok or deep-fryer*
- *Candy/deep-fry thermometer*

8 oz	all-purpose potatoes (about 2)	250 g
1 tbsp	cayenne pepper	15 mL
1 tbsp	garam masala	15 mL
1 tbsp	chaat masala (see Tips, page 40)	15 mL
2 tbsp	cilantro, chopped	25 mL
1½ tsp	salt or to taste	7 mL
1 lb	any mild green peppers, except bell peppers (see Tip, left)	500 g
1 cup	chickpea flour (besan)	250 mL
1 tsp	baking powder	5 mL
1 tsp	cayenne pepper	5 mL
1 tsp	salt	5 mL
	Oil for deep-frying	

1. In a saucepan of boiling water, cook whole potatoes until tender, 20 to 25 minutes. Drain. When cool enough to handle but still warm, peel and mash. Add cayenne, garam masala, chaat masala, cilantro and salt. Mix well.

2. Slit peppers lengthwise and scrape out all seeds. This is best done with the tip of a small spoon. (Take care not to break peppers apart.) Stuff with potato mixture.

3. In a bowl, mix together flour, baking powder, cayenne and salt. Stir in ¼ cup (50 mL) water to make a thick lump-free batter resembling pancake batter, gradually adding more water if necessary.

4. In a wok or deep-fryer, heat oil to 375°F (190°C). Dip peppers in batter. Fry, in batches, without crowding, until golden brown and crisp. Drain on paper towels. Serve warm with a chutney of your choice.

Spicy Egg Fritters

W

Makes 16

HOT

Hard-cooked eggs are versatile. These are tasty tidbits to serve with cocktails, and I have used them to top a salad.

- *Wok or deep-fryer*
- *Candy/deep-fry thermometer*

1 cup	loosely packed cilantro, leaves and soft stems	250 mL
12 to 14	mint leaves	12 to 14
2 tsp	chopped green chiles, preferably serranos	10 mL
½ tsp	minced peeled gingerroot	2 mL
½ cup	chickpea flour (besan)	125 mL
¾ tsp	salt	4 mL
Pinch	baking powder	Pinch
1 tsp	black salt (kala namak)	5 mL
½ tsp	cayenne pepper or to taste	2 mL
4	hard-cooked eggs, quartered	4
	Oil for deep-frying	

1. In a mini food processor finely chop cilantro, mint, chiles and ginger, adding 1 to 2 tbsp (15 to 25 mL) water if necessary to make a smooth paste.

2. In a bowl, stir together chickpea flour, salt and baking powder. Add cilantro mixture and 1 tbsp (15 mL) water to make a thick lump-free batter resembling pancake batter, gradually adding more water if necessary. Set aside.

3. In a small dish, mix together black salt and cayenne. Place 4 to 6 egg quarters in dish and press into mixture to coat.

4. In a wok or deep-fryer, heat oil to 375°F (190°C).

5. Transfer spice-coated egg quarters to batter. Using 2 teaspoons, one at either end, lift one egg quarter and slip into the oil. Fry, turning once, until golden, about 2 minutes. Drain on paper towels. Repeat with remaining eggs, spices and batter.

Kande ka Bhajia
Onion Fritters

- *Wok or deep-fryer*
- *Candy/deep-fry thermometer*

3	large onions	3
2 tsp	salt or to taste	10 mL
	Oil for deep-frying	
½ cup	chickpea flour (besan) (approx.)	125 mL
¼ tsp	cayenne pepper or to taste	1 mL

1. Cut onions in half from tip to stem, then thinly slice with the grain. Place in a bowl. Sprinkle with salt and work into onions with fingers. Set aside for 30 minutes to allow onions to sweat and soften.

2. Meanwhile, heat oil in deep-fryer to 375°F (190°C).

3. Drain off any onion juice that accumulates in bowl. Sprinkle ¼ cup (50 mL) of the chickpea flour and cayenne over onions and rub lightly with fingers (see Tips, right). Continue adding chickpea flour, 1 tablespoon (15 mL) at a time, until onions begin to hold together in clumps.

4. Drop clumps into hot oil and fry, in batches, without crowding, until crisp and golden, 4 to 5 minutes. Remove with a large-holed strainer and drain on paper towels. Serve hot with a chutney of your choice.

Serves 8

These onion clusters are light and crunchy, with just a hint of batter. Serve them hot or at room temperature — they're great with cocktails or to pack for a picnic.

Tips

The secret to these ethereal nibbles is no water in the batter. Lightly rubbing the chickpea flour into the softened onion shreds, using the onion juices produced by salting and draining the excess onion moisture, is what makes these so crisp and crunchy.

Fritters are best eaten when freshly made, but they can be made up to 3 hours ahead, loosely covered and held at room temperature. Reheat at low temperature in the oven until crisp, 10 to 12 minutes.

APPETIZERS   77

Makki ke Pakore

Corn Fritters

Serves 6

These light-as-a-feather fritters are heavenly with a touch of your favorite chutney. They are best made with fresh sweet summer corn, but thawed frozen or canned corn is an acceptable substitute.

Tip

These are best served as soon as they are made, as they lose their crispness and get soft if kept for longer than 15 minutes.

- *Wok or deep-fryer*
- *Candy/deep-fry thermometer*

5 tbsp	all-purpose flour	75 mL
3 tbsp	chickpea flour (besan)	45 mL
1/2 tsp	freshly ground pepper	2 mL
1/2 tsp	salt or to taste	2 mL
1/4 tsp	baking soda	1 mL
2 cups	corn kernels	500 mL
3	finely sliced green onions, with some green	3
1/4 cup	cilantro, chopped	50 mL
2 tsp	minced green chiles, preferably serranos	10 mL
	Oil for deep-frying	

1. In a bowl, whisk together all-purpose and chickpea flours, pepper, salt and baking soda. Stir in corn, green onions, cilantro and chiles. Gently stir in 3 to 4 tbsp (45 to 60 mL) water until batter is thick enough to hold its shape when dropped into hot oil.

2. In a wok or deep-fryer, heat oil to 375°F (190°C). Drop heaping teaspoonfuls (5 mL) of the batter into oil and fry, in batches, without crowding, until golden, 2 to 3 minutes. Drain on paper towels. Serve hot with a chutney of your choice.

Kothambir Vada
Chickpea Flour and Cilantro Squares

- 8-inch (20 cm) square cake pan, sprayed with vegetable spray

1 cup	chickpea flour (besan)	250 mL
1 tbsp	minced peeled gingerroot	15 mL
1 tbsp	minced green chiles, preferably serrano	15 mL
1 tsp	salt or to taste	5 mL
1/4 tsp	turmeric	1 mL
1 cup	cilantro, leaves only, very coarsely chopped	250 mL
3 tbsp	oil, divided	45 mL
1/3 cup	chopped onion	75 mL
1 tbsp	minced garlic	15 mL
Scant 1/2 tsp	asafetida (hing)	Scant 2 mL

Serves 4 to 6

A traditional appetizer from Maharashtra, these are delicious served as cocktail party finger food. Equally good in a picnic hamper or at a pool party, they can be made ahead and warmed slightly in the microwave.

1. In a bowl, whisk together chickpea flour, ginger, chiles, salt and turmeric with 1 1/3 cups (325 mL) water. (Mixture will be thicker than cake batter.) Stir in cilantro and set aside.

2. In a nonstick saucepan or deep skillet, heat 1 1/2 tbsp (22 mL) of the oil over medium heat. Add onion and garlic and sauté until golden, 3 to 4 minutes. Add asafetida and sauté for 1 minute.

3. Remove from heat. Whisk chickpea flour mixture and pour slowly into pan, stirring vigorously.

4. Return saucepan to medium-low heat. Cook, stirring continuously and cleaning sides of pan as you go, until mixture comes together in a lump, 3 to 4 minutes. Transfer to prepared pan and pat into a smooth cake. Let cool completely. Cut into 2-inch (5 cm) squares.

5. In a large nonstick skillet, heat 1 tbsp (15 mL) of oil over medium heat. Arrange half the squares in skillet and pan-fry until brown, for 2 minutes. Flip and brown other side. Transfer to a serving dish. Repeat with squares and oil. Serve with a chutney of your choice.

W

Dhokla
Steamed Semolina Squares

Serves 18

These fluffy, light appetizers have almost become my signature dish. This adapted recipe came to me via a young Indian friend whose family settled in East Africa several decades ago. The original recipe is from Gujarat — known for its excellent vegetarian offerings — but it takes 2 days to prepare. This version takes only 30 minutes and not even the most die-hard purist has been able to tell the difference.

Tips

Refrigerate leftovers in an airtight container. Warm in microwave to restore freshness.

Eno fruit salts are a digestive and are used in this recipe to aerate the batter while steaming, in lieu of the fermentation that helps to lighten the batter in the traditional recipe. They are available in Indian grocery stores.

- *Steamer with very hot water*
- *9-inch (2.5 L) square cake pan*

1 cup	quick-cooking Cream of Wheat	250 mL
1 cup	plain nonfat yogurt	250 mL
1/4 cup	lemon juice	50 mL
2 tbsp	chickpea flour (besan)	25 mL
1 tsp	minced green chiles, preferably serranos	5 mL
1 tsp	grated peeled gingerroot	5 mL
1 tsp	salt	5 mL
1/2 tsp	granulated sugar	2 mL
1/4 tsp	turmeric	1 mL
2 1/2 tbsp	oil, divided	32 mL
1 tsp	Eno fruit salts (see Tips, left)	5 mL
1 tsp	dark mustard seeds	5 mL
2 tbsp	cilantro, chopped	25 mL

1. In a mixing bowl, stir together Cream of Wheat, yogurt, 1/2 cup (125 mL) lukewarm water, lemon juice, chickpea flour, chiles, ginger, salt, sugar and turmeric.

2. In a saucepan, heat 1 1/2 tbsp (22 mL) of the oil until very hot. Pour into batter and stir well.

3. When ready to steam, stir Eno fruit salts into batter and pour into pan. Place pan in steamer and cover. Steam until top springs back when touched, 12 to 15 minutes. Let cool slightly.

4. In a small saucepan, heat remaining oil over medium heat until very hot. Add mustard seeds and cover immediately. When seeds stop popping, in a few seconds, pour over bread. Sprinkle with cilantro. Cut into 1 1/2-inch (4 cm) squares or diamond shapes and serve with a chutney of your choice.

Masala Cheese Toast

Spicy Cheese Toast

- *Preheat oven to 350°F (180ºC)*

6	slices thin sandwich bread	6
1	egg	1
1½ tsp	strong hot mustard	7 mL
2 tbsp	all-purpose flour	25 mL
1 tsp	cayenne pepper	5 mL
¾ tsp	fresh ground pepper	4 mL
¾ tsp	salt or to taste	4 mL
2 cups	grated sharp Cheddar cheese	500 mL
1 cup	cilantro, chopped	250 mL
3 tbsp	diced tomato	45 mL
3 to 4 tsp	minced green chiles, preferably serranos	15 to 20 mL
	Masala ketchup (see Tips, right)	

1. Trim crusts off bread and set aside.

2. In a bowl, whisk together egg, mustard, flour, cayenne, pepper and salt. Stir in cheese, cilantro, tomato and chiles to make a paste.

3. Divide mixture into 6 portions. Spread one portion on each piece of bread. Cut each slice diagonally in half to make 2 triangles. Set on baking sheet and bake in preheated oven until cheese is bubbly, 10 to 12 minutes. Serve hot with masala ketchup.

Makes 12

HOT

I remember so well the taste of this spicy snack that greeted us when we returned home from school in the late afternoon. It was prepared fresh around the time we were to walk in the door, and the hot toast sent us into squeals of joy as we bit into it.

Tips

Traditionally, these toasts were deep-fried. However, I prefer to bake them, as they are not so greasy and have better flavor.

Masala ketchup is a spicy Indian variation of American ketchup and is available in Indian stores.

Chaat

ICALL CHAAT "LOVE AT FIRST BITE" because that is the reaction of every person I have seen taking the first bite. Chaat is the ubiquitous street food dearly loved in India, particularly in the western city of Mumbai (Bombay) and in the north in Delhi. Only recently has it gone upscale and made an appearance on the restaurant scene, and more non-Indians than ever are enjoying it. Traditionally, chaat was always vegetarian, but now the concept has expanded to include seafood and chicken. Freshly cooked, soft with crunchy, dry with sweet, sweet with hot — this is the essence of chaat: a combination of unlikely textures and consistencies. Layers of contrasting textures are topped with liquid chutneys, the dish finally sprinkled with crispy, crunchy noodles and strange spices such as dried pomegranate seed powder and chaat masala. The result is always delightful and surprising. And while it may appear that chaat is composed of disparate ingredients randomly thrown together, there are a few ground rules (see Chaat: A Flavor Profile, right).

THE FAMOUS BHEL PURI FROM MUMBAI is perhaps the easiest to assemble. The main ingredient is feather-light puffed rice. Add to that crushed wheat puris, chopped red onion, diced boiled potato, chopped green mango, green chiles and cilantro. Spoon in the liquid seasonings — sweet tamarind chutney, cilantro chutney and fiery red chile chutney — then toss them all together. Throw in a handful of very thin chickpea flour noodles and a large squeeze of lime juice and you have heaven on a dish fashioned from a large dried leaf. This unusual but practical container is brilliant. The street vendor, carrying his wares in a basket on his head, avoids the issue of washing up and wastes nothing! That was how it was when I was growing up in Mumbai, but now it is a little different. Although there are still vendors who roam the streets with their wares, a great

many have found permanent locations for sanitary reasons. The taste of their offerings, thankfully, has altered little.

Pani puri literally translates to "water puri," the puri being a crisp walnut-size hollow wheat puff. In the hands of an expert, the puri is held in the palm and deftly punctured in the middle with the thumb. This hole is then filled with chickpeas, sprouted mung beans, boiled potato and a smattering of sweet tamarind chutney. The stuffed puri is then dipped momentarily in a huge terra-cotta vessel swaddled in red cotton fabric that contains the mint-and-cumin-seasoned water that gives the dish its name. The entire operation takes about 15 seconds. Then the whole thing is popped into the mouth, which all at once is flooded with a myriad of magical tastes. This is a very popular dish, known in many parts of the country by various names, such as *gol gappa* in Delhi, *pani puri* in Mumbai and *puchka* in Calcutta. The fillings vary slightly, but in all cases the tamarind chutney and mint-and-cumin water are essential.

THE CHAAT OF DELHI, EQUALLY delicious, is very different. One of the most popular is *aloo tikki chaat,* a potato patty that is slightly smashed and topped with spicy chickpeas, chopped onion, chiles, chutneys and a special blend of spices that includes black salt, dried mango powder and powdered dried pomegranate seeds. For the ultimate pleasure, the whole is then smashed together a little bit more. The mélange of textures and tastes in each mouthful is the epitome of culinary bliss.

Other chaat dishes consist of miniature crispy puffs filled with sprouts and crunchies, and soft lentil dumplings or puffs topped with tamarind chutney, sprinkled with spices and drizzled with seasoned yogurt, each puff exploding with astonishing tastes as you bite into it. Although I've mentioned just a small sample, these clearly demonstrate the diversity of chaat.

CHAAT: A FLAVOR PROFILE

Texture
A cooked ingredient, such as potato, pigeon pea or wheat *puri* (cracker), is the base. Fresh ingredients, such as chopped onion, green chiles and cilantro, are added to complement the cooked ingredient.

Crushed wheat crackers (flat puris) and crispy chickpea flour noodles (*sev*) are thrown in for crunch. Fried lentils and occasionally a few fried peanuts are also added.

Consistency
The mix is then topped with liquid chutneys (see Chutney Primer, page 84), which add a contrasting consistency — the dry ingredients are pulled together by the liquid.

Sweet tamarind chutney is almost always a must. This is often enhanced with green cilantro chutney and sometimes with searing red chile–garlic chutney if a hardy soul opts for it. In some cases, yogurt mixed with a little water is drizzled on top.

Spice Powders
The spice mixes that are sprinkled on top are the identifying feature of chaat. Sometimes it's just one spice, other times two or three, and yet other times a complex mix known as chaat masala (see below).

Pomegranate seeds (*anardana*). Dried pomegranate seeds, ground into a coarse dark brown powder, add a tart, slightly smoky taste.

Mango powder (*amchur*). Ground from sun-dried slices of tart unripe mangos.

Black salt (*kala namak*). Not black at all but rather pinkish gray, a sulfurous compound with a high mineral content and distinctive taste that cannot be substituted. It replaces common table salt in many chaat dishes. It is always sprinkled on top and never used to season a dish during cooking.

Chaat masala. A combination of several ingredients such as ground pomegranate seeds, mango powder, black salt, cumin powder, cayenne pepper and black pepper. An essential ingredient in many chaat dishes, it is also used to enhance grilled foods.

Chaat

Puri Primer

Puris come in many varieties and sizes. They are always deep-fried. Those served with meals to scoop up sauces are 3 to 5 inches (7.5 to 12.5 cm) and are most often made of whole wheat flour. They are fried for about 1 minute and puff up magically with steam. They deflate within minutes but are still soft and delicious.

The bite-size crisp, puffy puris that are the basis of *pani puri* are unique. They are made of fine semolina and are usually store-bought in airtight bags. They will remain crisp for several days.

Puris for *bhel puri* and *sev puri* are made of whole wheat flour and are about 2 inches (5 cm), flat and crisp. They are crushed into shards to add to bhel puri. For sev puri, they are arranged in a single layer in a dish and topped with the same ingredients used for bhel puri, minus the puffed rice. The ingredients are layered, rather than tossed, and each sev puri is then carefully lifted and popped in the mouth.

Chutney Primer

The word *chutney* in the Indian lexicon encompasses a world of different meanings. Not all chutneys are cooked, nor are all chutneys sweet. The word is used to denote any condiment that is used to enhance or complement a dish. The three chutneys synonymous with chaat — although all three are not always used together — are sweet tamarind, slightly hot green (made from cilantro and mint) and fiery red chile–garlic chutney. They are diluted with water to make them pourable.

Aloo Tikki Chaat
Potato Chaat

2 lbs	baby new potatoes or all-purpose potatoes (see Tips, right)	1 kg
2 to 3 tbsp	oil, divided	25 to 45 mL
¾ cup	plain yogurt	175 mL
⅓ cup	Cilantro Mint Chutney (see recipe, page 417) or store-bought coriander chutney	75 mL
⅓ cup	Sweet Tamarind Chutney (see recipe, page 424) or store-bought	75 mL
2 tsp	chaat masala (see Tips, right and page 86)	10 mL
1½ tsp	salt or to taste	7 mL
1 tsp	cumin powder	5 mL
½ to ¾ tsp	cayenne pepper	2 to 4 mL
½ cup	finely chopped red onion	125 mL
½ cup	Punjabi mix (see Tips, right)	125 mL
½ cup	fine sev (see Tips, right)	125 mL
3 tbsp	cilantro, chopped	45 mL

1. Place potatoes in a saucepan and cover with water. Bring to a boil over high heat. Reduce heat to low and simmer until potatoes are tender, 8 to 10 minutes. Drain and set aside until cool enough to handle but still warm. Place each unpeeled potato in the palm of your hand. Press gently with the other palm to flatten, forming a patty about ¼ inch (0.5 cm) thick. (Edges will split, but that's fine.)

2. In a skillet, heat 1 tbsp (15 mL) of the oil over medium heat and swirl to coat. Add potatoes and fry, in batches, until brown on both sides, 2 to 3 minutes, adding more oil as necessary between batches. Arrange potatoes in a single layer in a shallow dish or platter.

3. Place yogurt in a bowl and stir in ¼ to ½ cup (50 to 125 mL) water to make it a thick pouring consistency. Set aside.

4. Place cilantro and tamarind chutneys in separate bowls and stir a little water into each as necessary to make a pouring consistency.

5. In a small bowl, mix together chaat masala, salt, cumin and cayenne pepper. Sprinkle mixture over potatoes. Drizzle yogurt evenly over potatoes. Drizzle both chutneys over top.

6. Sprinkle onion on top, followed by Punjabi mix, sev and cilantro. Serve immediately.

Serves 6 to 8

Delhi and Mumbai are famous for their street foods. There is a difference in the chaat of the two cities, and there are a few that are synonymous with each. Delhi is famous for its aloo tikki chaat. Here is my adaptation of this old favorite.

Tips
If using all-purpose potatoes, cook in boiling water just until tender. Drain and peel when cool enough to handle but still warm. Let cool completely and cut into 2-inch (5 cm) pieces.

Chaat masala, Punjabi mix and sev are all available in Indian, Pakistani and Middle Eastern stores. Punjabi mix and sev are made of chickpea flour and are snack foods eaten out of hand like corn chips and potato chips.

Fruit Chaat

Serves 8

Fruit chaat is popular all over India and is particularly refreshing in summer, when the fruit is placed on a block of ice on the vendor's cart. Any tropical fruit is good — the sweeter the better — but bananas are a must.

❧

Tip

Chaat masala is a mixture of salty, hot and tart powders, including black salt (*kala namak*), cayenne, cumin and mango powder.

1	apple, cut into ¼-inch (0.5 cm) thick slices	1
2	ripe bananas, sliced	2
2	oranges, sectioned or 1 can (11 oz/310 g) mandarin oranges, drained	2
1	pear, cut into ½-inch (1 cm) thick slices	1
2 cups	diced ripe papaya, optional	500 mL
1 cup	seedless grapes	250 mL
3 to 4 tbsp	freshly squeezed lime or lemon juice	45 to 60 mL
¼ tsp	salt or to taste	1 mL
¼ tsp	freshly ground black pepper	1 mL
2 tsp	chaat masala (see Tip, left)	10 mL
1 tsp	cumin powder	5 mL
½ tsp	cayenne pepper	2 mL

1. In a bowl, mix together apple, bananas, oranges, pear, papaya, if using, and grapes. (You may add other tropical fruits that are available.) Sprinkle with lime juice, salt and pepper. Toss to mix.

2. In a small bowl, mix together chaat masala, cumin and cayenne. Sprinkle over fruit and toss again.

3. Chill for up to 3 hours before serving.

Dahi Pakodi Chaat

Fried Dumplings with Yogurt and Chutneys

Makes about 25

A favorite chaat in both Mumbai and Delhi, it also keeps company on many a banquet table.

Tips

Dumplings can be frozen in an airtight container after being fried, but before soaking in water, for up to 3 months. To use, thaw and proceed with recipe.

If you can't find self-rising flour, use ½ cup (125 mL) all-purpose flour instead and increase the baking powder to ¼ tsp (1 mL).

- *Wok or deep-fryer*
- *Candy/deep-fry thermometer*

½ cup	split white lentils (urad dal)	125 mL
1 cup	chickpea flour (besan)	250 mL
½ cup	self-rising flour (see Tips, left)	125 mL
2 tbsp	minced green chiles, preferably serranos	25 mL
1 tsp	minced peeled gingerroot	5 mL
1 tbsp	raisins	15 mL
1 tsp	salt or to taste	5 mL
⅛ tsp	baking powder	0.5 mL
	Oil for deep-frying	
3 cups	plain nonfat yogurt	750 mL
2 tsp	granulated sugar	10 mL
1½ tsp	cumin powder	7 mL
1 tsp	black salt (kala namak)	5 mL
¼ cup	tamarind chutney	50 mL
2 tbsp	Cilantro Mint Chutney (see recipe, page 417) or store-bought coriander chutney	25 mL
3 to 4 tbsp	cilantro, chopped	45 to 60 mL

1. Soak dal in water for 1 hour or longer. Drain and grind to a paste in blender with 2 to 3 tbsp (25 to 45 mL) water. Transfer puréed dal to a bowl. Sieve chickpea flour over bowl and add flour. Whisk until smooth and lump-free, adding just enough water to make a thick batter similar to drop cookie batter. Stir in chiles, ginger, raisins, salt and baking powder. Set aside for 15 minutes.

2. In a wok or deep-fryer, heat oil to 350°F (180°C). Drop batter by tablespoonfuls (15 mL) into hot oil and fry, in batches, without crowding, until golden, 3 to 4 minutes. Remove with a large-holed strainer and drain on paper towels. Transfer dumplings to a bowl of very warm water large enough to cover all the dumplings with water. Soak for 10 minutes. Remove, one at a time, and gently squeeze between palms to remove all water. Place on a platter.

3. In a bowl, combine yogurt, sugar, cumin and black salt. Top dumplings with yogurt mixture, reserving ½ cup (125 mL) and chill well for at least 2 hours or for up to 8 hours.

4. Pour remaining yogurt over top. Drizzle with tamarind and cilantro chutneys and sprinkle with cilantro. Wipe any separation of water from yogurt around edges of dish with paper towel.

Dhokla Chaat

1	recipe Steamed Semolina Squares (Dhokla) (see recipe, page 80)	1
1 cup	chopped red onion	250 mL
1 cup	diced peeled green mango (see Tips, right)	250 mL
1 tbsp	minced green chiles, preferably serranos	15 mL
1 cup	cilantro, chopped	250 mL
1 cup	Cilantro and Mint Chutney (see recipe, page 417) or store-bought	250 mL
1 cup	Sweet Tamarind Chutney (see recipe, page 424) or store-bought, divided	250 mL
3 to 4 tbsp	sambal oelek, thinned with 3 to 4 tbsp (45 to 60 mL) water	45 to 60 mL
½ cup	plain nonfat yogurt	125 mL
2 to 3 tbsp	freshly squeezed lime or lemon juice	25 to 45 mL
1 to 2 cups	sev (crunchy savory noodles) (see Tips, right)	250 to 500 mL

1. Make dhoklas up to end of Step 3 in the recipe on page 80. (Or use 2- or 3-day-old dhokla). Cut into 1½-inch (4 cm) squares and place in a large mixing bowl. Add onion, mango, chiles and cilantro. Toss to mix. Set aside.

2. Place green chutney, tamarind chutney and sambal oelek in separate bowls. Thin each with just enough water to make a pourable consistency. In another bowl, stir yogurt with ½ cup (125 mL) water. Set yogurt aside.

3. Drizzle dhokla mixture with ¾ cup (175 mL) of the green chutney, ¾ cup (175 mL) of the tamarind chutney, sambal oelek to taste, and lime juice. Toss again.

4. Divide mixture between individual serving plates and drizzle each with a little of the thinned yogurt. Top each with 3 to 4 tbsp (45 to 60 mL) sev. Serve immediately with remaining chutneys, yogurt and sev on the side.

Serves 8 to 10

Chaat is impossible to define. The common thread is often a semi-substantial base, such as a potato patty, a samosa, crisp fried wheat chips or cooked dried peas. There are an assortment of toppings and chutneys, creating an astonishing array of tastes. I have created this chaat using the popular Gujarati steamed snack dhokla, *following the principles of chaat. The result is quite delicious.*

Tips

Green mango should be rock hard and very sour. It is usually available in Asian markets.

Sev packages are sold in Indian markets and come in many textures. It is often mixed with other crunchy ingredients, such as peanuts, fried lentils and peas. All varieties are suitable.

Pune-Style Peas Chaat

Serves 6 to 8

Pune (pronounced Pu-nay), where this is a popular street food, is a bustling city 120 miles (193 km) from Mumbai.

1½ cups	dry white peas (watana)	375 mL
½ tsp	turmeric	2 mL
2½ tsp	salt	12 mL
¼ cup	unsalted Thai tamarind purée	50 mL
1½ tsp	oil	7 mL
¾ tsp	dark mustard seeds	4 mL
1 tbsp	minced peeled gingerroot	15 mL
1 tbsp	minced garlic	15 mL
1 tbsp	minced green chiles, preferably serranos	15 mL
1 tsp	cayenne pepper	5 mL
½ tsp	garam masala	2 mL
3 to 4 tbsp	cilantro, chopped	45 to 60 mL

Toppings

1 cup	cilantro, coarsely chopped	250 mL
1 cup	plain nonfat yogurt, lightly salted and stirred to a creamy consistency	250 mL
¾ cup	finely chopped red onion	175 mL
3 to 5	green chiles, preferably serranos, chopped	3 to 5
2 cups	store-bought Indian crispy snacks, such as Bombay mix, Punjabi mix, etc.	500 mL

1. Clean and pick through peas for any small stones and grit. Rinse and soak for at least 8 hours in water to cover by 4 inches (10 cm).

2. Drain and transfer to a saucepan. Add 4 cups (1 L) water and turmeric. Bring to a boil over medium-high heat. Reduce heat to low and cook, partially covered, until peas are tender, 20 to 30 minutes. (There should be about 1 cup (250 mL) of liquid remaining in the pan.) Add salt. Cover and simmer for 5 minutes. Remove from heat and stir in tamarind purée.

3. In a small saucepan, heat oil over medium-high heat until very hot. Toss in mustard seeds and cover immediately. When seeds stop popping, in a few seconds, reduce heat to medium and add ginger, garlic and chiles. Sauté for 1 minute. Pour into warm pea mixture. Stir in cayenne, garam masala and cilantro.

4. *Toppings:* Place cilantro, yogurt, onion and chiles in small bowls on the table. Sprinkle the pea mixture with the crispy snacks and allow your diners to add the toppings as desired.

Bhel Puri Chaat

8 oz	all-purpose potatoes (about 2)	250 g
4 cups	puffed rice (mumra)	1 L
12	puris, preferably flat, crushed (see Tips, right)	12
1 cup	chopped red onion	250 mL
½ cup	diced peeled green mango, optional	125 mL
½ cup	cilantro, coarsely chopped	125 mL
1 tbsp	minced green chiles, preferably serranos, or to taste	15 mL
½	lime or lemon	½
⅔ cup	Sweet Tamarind Chutney (see recipe, page 424) or store-bought	150 mL
⅔ cup	green chutney or to taste	150 mL
1 tbsp	Red Chile Garlic Chutney (see recipe, page 419) or store-bought	15 mL
1 cup	sev (crunchy savory noodles) (see Tips, right)	250 mL
8	flat puris, optional (see Tips, right)	8

1. In a saucepan of boiling water, cook whole potatoes until tender, 20 to 25 minutes. Drain. When cool enough to handle but still warm, peel and cut into ½-inch (1 cm) cubes.

2. In a large bowl, toss together puffed rice, crushed puris, potatoes, onion, green mango, if using, cilantro and chiles. Add a healthy squeeze of lime juice.

3. Place tamarind chutney, green chutney and chile-garlic chutney in separate bowls. Add a few spoonfuls of water to each chutney to make them pouring consistency. (They should be the consistency of pancake syrup.) Add chutneys to puffed rice mixture and toss again.

4. Divide mixture into 8 serving bowls and sprinkle generously with sev. Stick 1 flat puri into each, if using, and serve immediately.

Makes 8 cups

The signature chaat of Mumbai, this is served on the beaches to throngs of people out for an evening stroll. It is also served in many "bhel puri houses," as the tiny unpretentious chaat places that dot the city are called.

Tips

Packages of flat puris are available in Indian stores. Or deep-fry 2 whole wheat tortillas and crush as a substitute.

Sev are crunchy savory noodles and come in different thicknesses. I prefer the thinner, more-delicate looking variety, but the thicker ones will also work.

Two-Potato and Corn Chaat

Serves 4

I love the flavors of the sweet and russet potatoes with summer corn in this dish. The zing of chaat spices, black salt and mango powder are enlivened with cayenne pepper and pomegranate seed powder — spicy, salty, sweet and sour — a perfect pick-me-up on a hot summer day.

Tips
Indian markets carry both dried pomegranate seeds and pomegranate seed powder. It is tangy, not sweet, and is used as a souring agent in North Indian recipes. It is an essential seasoning in chaat dishes.

Boondi are crunchy droplets made of chickpea flour. Packages of boondi are available in Indian markets.

12 oz	sweet potatoes (about 2 small)	375 g
12 oz	russet potatoes (about 2)	375 g
1 tbsp	dried pomegranate seeds, powdered (anardana) (see Tips, left)	15 mL
1½ tsp	mango powder (amchur)	7 mL
¾ tsp	black salt (kala namak)	4 mL
½ tsp	cayenne pepper	2 mL
¼ cup	oil	50 mL
2 cups	corn kernels, preferably fresh	500 mL
½ cup	tamarind chutney	125 mL
½ cup	boondi (see Tips, left)	125 mL
¼ cup	finely sliced green onions, with some green	50 mL
¼ cup	cilantro, coarsely chopped	50 mL
2 tbsp	minced green chiles, preferably serranos, optional	25 mL

1. In a saucepan of boiling water, cook sweet potatoes and russet potatoes until tender, about 25 minutes. Drain and peel while still warm. Let cool to room temperature and cut into ¼-inch (0.5 cm) thick slices.

2. In a small bowl, stir together pomegranate powder, mango powder, black salt and cayenne pepper. Set aside.

3. In a large skillet, heat oil over medium-high heat. Fry potatoes, in batches, until slightly browned on both sides and crisp, about 3 minutes per side. Remove with a large-holed strainer and drain on paper towels. Blot tops with more paper towels. Transfer to a shallow bowl. Sprinkle half of the spice mix over warm potatoes. Shake the bowl gently to mix well.

4. In the same skillet, cook corn, stirring, until slightly crisp, about 3 minutes. Drain on paper towels and place in another bowl. Toss with remaining spice mix.

5. Layer potatoes on a serving platter. Top with corn. Drizzle chutney over top. Sprinkle boondi, green onions, cilantro and chiles, if using, over top. Serve immediately.

Chicken Kofta Chaat

Serves 6 to 8

Traditionally, chaat is vegetarian. However, there has been an enthusiastic response to this recipe, and it is quite versatile. I have included it on a buffet table, and it's equally good as a first course or a light lunch.

Tip

Chicken *koftas* can be served with a chutney of your choice for cocktails. Or smother in a tasty gravy and serve with noodles, pasta, rice or as an "Italian style" sandwich in a bun.

- Wok or deep-fryer
- Candy/deep-fry thermometer

1 lb	all-purpose potatoes (about 4)	500 g
1	can (15 to 19 oz/450 to 540 mL) chickpeas (garbanzo beans), drained and rinsed	1
2 tsp	mango powder (amchur)	10 mL
2 tsp	black salt (kala namak)	10 mL
1½ tsp	cumin powder	7 mL
1 tsp	cayenne pepper	5 mL

Kofta

1 cup	bread crumbs, made from day-old white bread	250 mL
½ cup	mint leaves	125 mL
½ cup	cilantro leaves	125 mL
4 tsp	chopped green chiles, preferably serranos	20 mL
1 tsp	ginger paste (see Tips, page 46)	5 mL
1 tsp	garlic paste	5 mL
1 lb	skinless boneless chicken breast, cut into large pieces, or ground chicken	500 g
1	small onion, quartered	1
1 tsp	coriander powder	5 mL
1 tsp	cumin powder	5 mL
1 tsp	salt	5 mL
½ tsp	cayenne pepper	2 mL
	Oil for deep-frying	

Garnish

2 cups	plain nonfat yogurt	500 mL
⅓ cup	tamarind chutney	75 mL
2 to 3 tbsp	cilantro, coarsely chopped	25 to 45 mL
2 to 3 tbsp	mint leaves, coarsely chopped	25 to 45 mL

1. In a saucepan of boiling water, cook whole potatoes until tender, 20 to 25 minutes. Drain. When cool enough to handle but still warm, peel and cut into ½-inch (1 cm) cubes and place in a large bowl.

2. Add chickpeas to potatoes in bowl. In a small bowl, combine mango powder, black salt, cumin and cayenne. Sprinkle half over potato mixture and toss well. Set potato mixture and remaining spice mixture aside.

3. *Kofta:* In a food processor, pulse bread crumbs, mint, cilantro, chiles, ginger and garlic to combine. Add chicken, onion, coriander, cumin, salt and cayenne. Process into a coarse mixture. You should be able to form a small ball that will hold together.

4. Keep a bowl of water at hand. Moisten palms and roll mixture, using a light touch, into 32 to 34 smooth 1-inch (2.5 cm) balls.

5. In a wok or deep-fryer, heat oil to 350°F (180°C). Drop koftas into hot oil, in batches, without crowding. Reduce heat to about 325°F (160°C) and fry until cooked through, 3 to 4 minutes per batch. Remove with a large-holed strainer and drain on paper towels.

6. Add koftas to potato mixture in bowl and toss again. Transfer to a serving dish or platter.

7. *Garnish:* Add remaining spice mixture to yogurt, stirring to a creamy consistency. Pour evenly over kofta mixture. Let stand at room temperature for 30 minutes for flavors and textures to blend.

8. Drizzle tamarind chutney over top. Garnish with cilantro and mint before serving.

Variation

You can omit mango powder, black salt and cumin powders and substitute 2 to 3 tbsp (25 to 45 mL) chaat masala, available in Indian stores.

Beans and Lentils

IN THE VAST WORLD OF INDIAN beans and lentils, confusion reigns supreme when it comes to naming the many varieties. However, the lowly bean occupies an exalted position and is arguably the most versatile food in the Indian culinary repertoire. Nutritional powerhouses with hundreds of seasoning possibilities, beans and lentils are easy to cook and have universal appeal.

Cooked dal is like a blank canvas: you can paint it with a variety of seasonings to create flavors that appeal to your palate. The basic rules for cooking dal are very simple: rinse, soak and cook in water. In most cases, the dal is then mashed or puréed and ready for seasoning. This can be as simple as adding few flash-fried mustard or cumin seeds and chopped garlic, or as elaborate as incorporating a mixture of ginger, green chiles, tomatoes, onions and spices. There are as many ways to season dal as there are recipes for it.

THE ENGLISH PHRASE "DAILY BREAD and butter" can be aptly translated as *roz ki dal roti* — basic dal and flatbread. The most impoverished Indian relies on dal for sustenance. A cup of dal can be stretched to feed a family of eight simply by diluting it with water. Although this reduces the nutritional value, it will fill an empty belly. Dal is the comfort food of all Indians, no matter which economic stratum they come from. Even today when I return from a trip, no matter what exotic locales I've visited, and no matter what exotic foods I've sampled, the one thing I crave when I return is dal.

There are definite regional preferences, with one or two favorites in each area. For the most part, there are traditional recipes for these, with some variations. But what is most confusing, even to Indians, are the many names by which each bean is known. For instance, yellow lentils are known as *toor dal,* sometimes spelled *toovar,* but are also called *arhar dal.* Small black chickpeas, used universally, are known as *kala channa*, *horse gram*, *kadala* or *kulthi* depending on the region (see Common Ingredients, page 16). Each bean or lentil has a unique taste and characteristic, and not all have the same starch content. As a result, in most cases, they are not interchangeable. Most recipes require lentils to be cooked until soft, with almost no seasoning except, perhaps, turmeric. At this point, even though the cooked lentils are soft, it is essential to blend them with their cooking liquid so that the starch and water are homogenized into a creamy soup-like consistency. The seasonings are added after this. American and European bean and lentil recipes do not follow this practice. Rather, they are cooked with liquid that is either absorbed or drained so that the lentils retain their shape. I have found that cooking dal the Indian way seems to be

Beans and Lentils

⁂

confusing for many cooks in North America, yet it is nothing more difficult than understanding the reason for the blending.

Beans, such as kidney beans, chickpeas, black-eyed peas and some others, are not blended. The residual liquid is thickened using various methods, such as mashing a few cooked beans with the back of a spoon against the side of the saucepan and mixing them into the cooking liquid. However, whole beans are also cooked and drained for use in Indian salads.

BEANS AND LENTILS ARE VERY nutritious. They are a complex carbohydrate and a good source of protein, calcium and fiber. They are also extremely versatile. Soaked overnight and ground into a paste or made into a batter, they are seasoned and made into pancakes, crêpes and dumplings. Ground into flour, they are used to make patties, desserts and flatbreads. One of the best-kept secrets of Indian cuisine is an ingredient that is finally gaining recognition worldwide for its versatility. Chickpea flour (*besan*) is found in every part of the country. It is used as a binder in patties, breads, curries and, most magically, an eggless batter for deep-fried foods such as fritters (*pakoras*). It is also transformed into rich fudge-like sweets (each region has its share of sweets made with chickpea flour). A variety of crispy snacks, such as *sev* (fine, crispy noodles), *papri* (flat crispy bites) and *boondi* (droplets), are made from this flour and are as loved by Indians as potato and corn chips are in the West.

Last, but not least, is the all-time favorite *papadum*. In the north, these are made from different varieties of dal, seasoned with cumin, black pepper, garlic, green chiles and other spices. In the south, papadums are made from rice.

IN NORTH INDIA, KIDNEY BEANS, chickpeas and Indian black beans (different from Mexican black beans) are the beans most cooked. The favorite dal dish of Rajasthan, cooked daily, is a mix of split white beans, yellow mung beans and split yellow peas. In the east, it is yellow mung beans and red lentils (*masoor dal*), with split yellow peas (*channa dal*) reserved for special occasions.

Yellow lentils (*toor dal*) are without a doubt the winner in the four southern states. The ubiquitous *sambhar* (made with this dal) accompanies *dosa*, *idli* and rice and is cooked every single day. Dal batter seasoned with herbs and spices is used to make savory pancakes. And the list goes on.

IN THE WEST, THE LINES ARE FUZZY because there is a greater mix of ethnicities. In Gujarat and Maharashtra, mixing three or four dals is common practice, making the texture and flavors more interesting. I love to cook a mix of dals because some turn soupy, some remain whole and yet others take on a silky texture.

Sprouting beans is unique to Gujarat and Maharashtra. Sprouting gives them a nutritional boost, making them a high-quality source of protein. The sprouts are used raw in salads and cooked in curries. Sprouting beans is not difficult — I urge everyone to try and have provided instructions on how to do it (see page 126).

Follow the simple rules for cooking dal the Indian way and you, too, will develop a craving for this most basic of all Indian foods, adding a new world of flavors and versatility to your cooking repertoire.

Punjabi Malai Palak
Punjabi Creamy Yellow Mung Beans

1 cup	yellow mung beans (mung dal)	250 mL
3 cups	chopped fresh spinach	750 mL
2 tbsp	minced green chiles, preferably serranos	25 mL
1 ½ tbsp	minced peeled gingerroot	22 mL
½ tsp	turmeric	2 mL
2 tbsp	oil	25 mL
1 cup	finely chopped onion	250 mL
1 ½ tsp	salt or to taste	7 mL
½ tsp	cayenne pepper	2 mL
¼ cup	plain nonfat yogurt, divided	50 mL

Serves 8

The creamy dal gives this lightly spiced spinach dish a sensually silky texture.

1. Clean and pick through dal for any small stones and grit. Rinse several times in cold water until water is fairly clear. Soak in 3 cups (750 mL) water in a large pot for 10 minutes.

2. Add spinach, green chiles, ginger and turmeric to dal and bring to a boil over medium heat. Reduce heat to medium-low and boil gently, partially covered, until dal is very soft, about 30 minutes. Remove from heat. Using a blender, in batches if necessary, purée dal mixture until smooth. Set aside.

3. In a saucepan, heat oil over medium-high heat. Add onion and sauté until golden, 8 to 10 minutes. Stir in salt and cayenne and sauté for 1 minute. Add dal mixture and mix well.

4. Stir yogurt until creamy. Stir 2 tbsp (25 mL) into dal. If mixture is too thick, add ½ cup (125 mL) hot water. Cover and simmer for 5 minutes. Serve hot. Swirl remaining yogurt over top.

Tip: How to Cook Dal

Beans and lentils, simply called "dal" in India, are unquestionably the basic food of all Indians. The variety of dals used throughout the country is astonishing, and they vary enormously in flavor, texture and starch content. With some exceptions, dal is usually cooked with plenty of water, which is seldom drained. A layer of water will be present on top of the cooked lentils. Instead of draining this off, when the dal is soft, it is mashed or blended with the remaining water, allowing the starch in the dal to break down and act as a thickener. The mashed dal is more often than not the consistency of cream soup. (This technique is uncommon in Western cooking, where lentils and beans are cooked until soft, then drained, retaining their shape.) The cooked dal is then finished with flash-fried spices and seasonings.

Dals with Crispy Onions

1 cup	split yellow peas (channa dal)	250 mL
½ cup	split white lentils (urad dal)	125 mL
2 tbsp	minced peeled gingerroot	25 mL
2 tbsp	minced garlic	25 mL
1 tsp	cayenne pepper	5 mL
½ tsp	garam masala	2 mL
½ tsp	turmeric	2 mL
1 ½ tsp	salt or to taste	7 mL
1 tbsp	oil	15 mL
1 ½ tsp	cumin seeds	7 mL
½ cup	crispy fried onions (see Tip, right)	125 mL
½ tsp	garam masala	2 mL
1	tomato, cut into ¼-inch (0.5 cm) thick slices	1

1. Clean and pick through channa and urad dals for any small stones and grit. Rinse several times in cold water until water is fairly clear. Soak in 5 cups (1.25 L) water in a saucepan for 15 minutes.

2. Bring dal mixture to a boil over medium heat. Skim any froth off top. Reduce heat to medium-low. Stir in ginger, garlic, cayenne, ½ tsp (2 mL) garam masala and turmeric and boil gently, partially covered, stirring periodically, until dal is soft, 40 to 45 minutes. Mash well until combined with any remaining water. (Mixture should be thick, but not semisolid.) If necessary, add ½ cup (125 mL) hot water to loosen. Stir in salt.

3. In a small saucepan, heat oil over medium heat. Fry cumin seeds until aromatic, about 30 seconds. Pour into dal. Stir in fried onions.

4. Pour into serving dish. Sprinkle with ½ tsp (2 mL) garam masala and arrange tomato slices over top. Serve with rice or any Indian bread.

Serves 6

Indians love their dal and get creative with combinations. I particularly like the "silkiness" of the split white lentils (urad dal) in this simple, home-style dal.

Tip

Crispy fried onions are available in Indian and Middle Eastern markets. After the package is opened, they can be refrigerated for up to 1 year.

Chainsoo
Garhwali Black Beans

Serves 4 to 6

Black beans are probably the most favored dal in Uttarakhand state in North India. Toasting the beans before cooking gives them a unique taste and makes them more digestible.

———❦———

Tip
Mustard oil is made from cold-pressed mustard seeds and is not an infusion. It has a distinctive taste. However, it has an element that can be toxic to some. Heating it to smoking point neutralizes this and makes it safe for cooking.

1 cup	Indian black beans (sabat urad dal)	250 mL
2 tbsp	mustard oil	25 mL
2 tbsp	coarsely chopped garlic	25 mL
1 tsp	cumin seeds	5 mL
5	black peppercorns	5
3	dried Indian red chiles	3
1/4 tsp	asafetida (hing)	1 mL
3/4 tsp	coriander powder	4 mL
1/2 tsp	cayenne pepper	2 mL
1/4 tsp	turmeric	1 mL
1 tsp	salt or to taste	5 mL
2 tsp	ghee, melted	10 mL
1/2 tsp	garam masala	2 mL
3 tbsp	cilantro, coarsely chopped	45 mL

1. Rub beans in a damp cloth to wipe clean.

2. In a wok or a saucepan over medium heat, toast dal, stirring continuously, until slightly fragrant, 4 to 5 minutes. Transfer to a bowl and let cool. In a blender, grind dal coarsely in 2 batches.

3. In the same wok, heat oil over high heat until smoking. Remove from heat and let cool for 1 minute (see Tip, left). Return to medium heat. Add garlic and sauté until golden, about 1 minute. Add cumin, peppercorns, red chiles and asafetida and sauté for 1 minute.

4. Add ground beans and sauté for 2 minutes. Add coriander, cayenne and turmeric and sauté for 1 minute. Add 3 cups (750 mL) water and salt. Bring to a boil. Reduce heat to medium-low. Cover and simmer until dal is soft and water is reduced to about 1 cup (250 mL), 20 to 25 minutes.

5. Remove from heat and drizzle ghee over top. Sprinkle with garam masala and cover for 2 minutes to allow aromas to blend. Stir to mix. Garnish with cilantro and serve hot with rice.

Gita's Mixed Beans

⅔ cup	yellow lentils (toor dal)	150 mL
⅔ cup	red lentils (masoor dal)	150 mL
⅔ cup	yellow mung beans (yellow mung dal)	150 mL
¼ cup	split white lentils (urad dal)	50 mL
2 cups	chopped onions	500 mL
2 cups	chopped tomatoes	500 mL
4 tsp	chopped green chiles, preferably serranos	20 mL
1 tbsp	minced peeled gingerroot	15 mL
1 tbsp	chopped garlic	15 mL
½ cup	cilantro, chopped, divided	125 mL
2 tsp	coriander powder	10 mL
1 tsp	cayenne pepper	5 mL
½ tsp	turmeric	2 mL
¼ tsp	asafetida (hing)	1 mL
2 tsp	salt or to taste	10 mL
1 ½ tbsp	oil	22 mL
1 tsp	dark mustard seeds	5 mL
1 tsp	cumin seeds	5 mL

Serves 6 to 8

A visiting cousin from India who excels in "home-style" dishes shared this recipe many years ago. The combination of beans (dals) adds variety to the taste and texture of the dish.

1. Clean and pick through toor, masoor, mung and urad dals for any small stones and grit. Rinse several times in cold water until water is fairly clear. Soak in 6 cups (1.5 L) water in a large saucepan for 10 minutes.

2. Add onions, tomatoes, chiles, ginger, garlic, 2 tbsp (25 mL) of the cilantro, coriander, cayenne, turmeric and asafetida to dal mixture. Bring to a boil over medium heat. Reduce heat to low and boil gently, partially covered, until dals are soft and well blended, about 30 minutes. Add salt.

3. In a small saucepan, heat oil over high heat until a couple of mustard seeds thrown in start to sputter. Add all mustard seeds and cover quickly. When the seeds stop popping, in a few seconds, uncover, reduce heat to medium and add cumin seeds. Sauté for 30 seconds and pour into dal. Cook for 5 minutes longer.

4. Garnish with remaining cilantro and serve hot with rice or bread.

Kale Channe
Blackened Chickpeas with Shredded Ginger

Serves 6 to 8

This is a classic dish in Punjab. The dark color is a result of the tea bags. I got this recipe about 20 years ago from Asha Vohra, who is well known for her great food. It is a popular street food served with giant puffed fried bread called bathura.

1 ½ cups	dried chickpeas	375 mL
½ tsp	baking soda	2 mL
2	black tea bags, Indian or other type	2
12 oz	all-purpose potatoes (about 3)	375 g
6 tbsp	oil, divided	90 mL
2 tbsp	dried pomegranate seeds, powdered	25 mL
1 ½ tbsp	coriander powder	22 mL
1 tbsp	each cumin powder and mango powder	15 mL
2 tsp	cayenne pepper	10 mL
2 tsp	salt or to taste	10 mL
1 tsp	garam masala	5 mL
¼ cup	very finely julienned peeled gingerroot	50 mL
6	green chiles, preferably serranos, cut into 2-inch (5 cm) long julienne, divided	6
⅓ cup	chopped red onion	75 mL
¼ cup	cilantro, chopped	50 mL

1. Rinse chickpeas and transfer to a bowl. Add water to cover by 4 inches (10 cm) and soak at room temperature overnight. Drain chickpeas. In a saucepan, combine with 6 cups (1.5 L) fresh water, baking soda and tea bags. Bring to a boil over medium-high heat. Reduce heat to medium-low and boil gently, partially covered, until chickpeas are tender, about 1 hour.

2. Meanwhile, peel potatoes and cut into thick french fries. In a skillet, heat 1 tbsp (15 mL) of the oil and fry potatoes, in batches until golden on all sides, 3 to 4 minutes. Adding more oil as necessary. Drain on paper towels and set aside.

3. Drain chickpeas, reserving about 1 cup (250 mL) liquid. Return chickpeas to saucepan. Sprinkle with pomegranate, coriander, cumin, mango powder, cayenne, salt and garam masala.

4. In a small saucepan, heat remaining oil. Add ginger and half of the chiles and sauté until crisp, 3 to 4 minutes. Pour over chickpeas. Add potatoes and gently mix all ingredients, taking care not to break potatoes. Drizzle reserved cooking liquid around edges of pan. Return saucepan to low heat. Cover and simmer to allow flavors to blend, gently stirring occasionally, until all liquid is absorbed and potatoes are tender, 6 to 8 minutes.

5. Transfer to a large serving platter and serve hot, garnished with cilantro, onions and remaining chiles.

Channa Dal with Zucchini

Split Yellow Peas with Zucchini

1 cup	split yellow peas (channa dal)	250 mL
2 tbsp	oil	25 mL
1 1/2 tbsp	minced peeled gingerroot	22 mL
2 tsp	minced green chiles, preferably serranos	10 mL
1 cup	finely chopped onion	250 mL
3 cups	chopped zucchini (1/2-inch/1 cm pieces)	750 mL
1 tsp	coriander powder	5 mL
1 tsp	salt or to taste	5 mL
1/2 tsp	turmeric	2 mL
1/2 tsp	cayenne pepper	2 mL
1	can (14 oz/398 mL) tomatoes, including juice, chopped	1

1. Clean and pick through dal for any small stones and grit. Rinse several times in cold water until water is fairly clear. Soak in 2 cups (500 mL) water for 20 to 30 minutes.

2. In a saucepan, heat oil over medium-high heat. Add ginger and chiles and sauté for 1 minute. Add onion and sauté until soft and translucent, 6 to 7 minutes.

3. Add zucchini and mix well. Cover and cook for 5 minutes. Add coriander, salt, turmeric and cayenne. Mix well and cook, stirring, 3 to 4 minutes (see Tips, right).

4. Add tomatoes with juice and dal with soaking liquid, plus enough additional water to cover. Stir to mix well. Cover, reduce heat to low and simmer, stirring every 10 minutes, until dal is soft and a little liquid remains, resulting in a thin gravy (sauce), 20 to 25 minutes.

Serves 8

Sindhis love channa dal and traditionally this dish would be made with turai, a long vegetable with a thick ridged skin but mild like zucchini on the inside. It is often available in Asian markets and is known as Chinese okra, although it bears no resemblance to okra. Unlike zucchini, the skin is peeled before cooking.

Tips

When adding dry spices, it is important to sauté for 3 to 4 minutes to remove the "raw taste" of the spices. The spices will neither soften nor be recognizably fragrant. If anything, they may turn slightly darker.

This dish freezes well. To freeze, transfer to an airtight container and freeze for up to 3 months. Reheat in microwave or on stove top over low heat.

Rajasthani Mixed Dal

Serves 8

This is the dal cooked almost daily in many homes in Rajasthan. It is served with a baked whole wheat ball that is semihard and dry called bati. *When cooked, the balls are soaked in warm ghee to soften. I prefer to serve it with steamed rice.*

Tip

If curry leaves have dried naturally in the refrigerator over several weeks, they are most likely still aromatic. The dried ones sold in Indian markets have no aroma or flavor and I would advise against those.

1 cup	split white lentils (urad dal)	250 mL
½ cup	yellow mung beans (mung dal)	125 mL
¼ cup	split yellow peas (channa dal)	50 mL
½ tsp	turmeric	2 mL
1 ½ tsp	salt	7 mL
2 tbsp	ghee	25 mL
1 tsp	cumin seeds	5 mL
¼ tsp	asafetida (hing)	1 mL
4	bay leaves	4
3	whole cloves	3
3	green cardamom pods, crushed	3
1	sprig fresh curry leaves, stripped (12 to 15 leaves) (see Tip, left), optional	1
1 ½ cups	chopped tomatoes	375 mL
2 tbsp	minced green chiles, preferably serranos	25 mL
1 tbsp	minced peeled gingerroot	15 mL
1 tsp	cayenne pepper	5 mL
1 cup	loosely packed cilantro	250 mL

1. Clean and pick through urad, mung and channa dals for any small stones and grit. Rinse several times in cold water until water is fairly clear. Soak in 7 cups (1.75 L) water in a saucepan for 1 hour.

2. Bring dals to a boil over medium-high heat. Stir in turmeric and boil gently, partially covered, until dals are soft but not mushy and water does not appear to be separated (see Tip, page 99), about 30 minutes. Stir in salt. Set aside.

3. In another saucepan, heat ghee over medium heat. Add cumin, asafetida, bay leaves, cloves, cardamom and curry leaves and sauté for 20 seconds. Add tomatoes, chiles, ginger and cayenne and sauté for 2 minutes.

4. Pour dal into tomato mixture and mix well. If there is excess water, cook, uncovered, over medium-low heat until water looks absorbed but without drying dal too much. (It should be thick but liquidy enough to pour over rice.) Adjust consistency with a little additional warm water if too thick. Sprinkle cilantro over dal before serving.

Three-Bean Medley

Serves 6 to 8

I love the flavors and textures of this mix of beans. The brown lentils break down to make a semi-mushy texture, while the other beans, though soft, tend to remain whole. This dal can be served with rice or an Indian bread.

½ cup	kidney beans (rajma)	125 mL
½ cup	black-eyed peas (lobhia, chawli)	125 mL
½ cup	brown lentils (sabat masoor)	125 mL
2 tbsp	oil	25 mL
½ tsp	asafetida (hing)	2 mL
1	dried Indian red chile	1
1	stick cinnamon, about 2 inches (5 cm) long	1
2	bay leaves	2
1 tsp	cumin seeds	5 mL
2½ cups	thinly sliced onions (lengthwise slices)	625 mL
2 tbsp	slivered peeled gingerroot	25 mL
2 to 3	green chiles, preferably serranos, slivered	2 to 3
1½ tsp	salt	7 mL
1	large plum (Roma) tomato, cut into 8 wedges	1
1 tsp	garam masala	5 mL
3 to 4 tbsp	cilantro, coarsely chopped	45 to 60 mL

1. Combine beans, peas and lentils in a large bowl. Rinse several times in cold water until water is fairly clear. Add water to cover by 4 to 5 inches (10 to 12.5 cm) and soak at room temperature overnight.

2. Drain mixture. Place in a saucepan and add 5 cups (1.25 L) fresh water. Bring to a boil over medium heat. Skim any froth off the top. Reduce heat and boil gently, partially covered, until beans are tender, 30 to 40 minutes. Set aside.

3. Meanwhile, in a skillet, heat oil over high heat. Add asafetida and sauté for 20 seconds. Add red chile, cinnamon, bay leaves and cumin and sauté until spices are aromatic, for 45 seconds.

4. Add onions and mix well. Reduce heat to medium-high and sauté until onions lose their moisture and begin to brown, about 10 minutes. Reduce heat to medium and cook, stirring often, until well browned, 12 to15 minutes. Add ginger and green chiles and cook for 2 minutes.

5. Add to bean mixture. Add salt and simmer, uncovered, for 6 to 8 minutes to combine flavors. Partially mash a few beans against sides of pan to thicken. Stir in tomato and mix gently. Remove from heat. Sprinkle garam masala over top. Cover and let stand for 5 minutes.

6. Stir to blend garam masala into beans. Spoon into serving bowl, arranging some of the softened tomatoes on top as garnish. Sprinkle cilantro over top.

Saag aur Channa Dal
Winter Greens with Split Yellow Peas

1 cup	split yellow peas (channa dal)	250 mL
½ tsp	turmeric	2 mL
2½ tsp	salt or to taste, divided	12 mL
6 to 7 cups	spinach, rinsed and chopped (see Tip, right)	1.5 to 1.75 L
6 to 7 cups	turnip greens, rinsed and chopped	1.5 to 1.75 L
6 to 7 cups	mustard or collard greens, rinsed and chopped	1.5 to 1.75 L
2 tbsp	oil	25 mL
2 tbsp	slivered peeled gingerroot	25 mL
1 tbsp	minced green chiles, preferably serranos	15 mL
2 tbsp	dark mustard seeds, coarsely pounded	25 mL
1 tbsp	cumin seeds	15 mL
1½ tsp	salt or to taste	7 mL
2 tbsp	freshly squeezed lime or lemon juice or to taste	25 mL

Serves 8

Rich in nutrients and equally tasty, this unusual combination is one of my favorite winter dishes when turnip and mustard greens are at their freshest. I like to serve it with a lamb or chicken curry.

Tip

Greens, when cooked, reduce drastically in volume, so a little bit more or a little bit less will not change the dish.

1. Clean and pick through dal for any small stones and grit. Rinse several times in cold water until water is fairly clear. Soak in 2½ cups (625 mL) water in a saucepan for 15 minutes.

2. Bring dal to a boil over medium heat. Reduce heat to low. Stir in turmeric and boil gently, partially covered, until dal is soft but not mushy and water is absorbed, 20 to 25 minutes. Add 1 tsp (5 mL) of the salt in the last 5 minutes of cooking. Set aside.

3. In a large pot, combine spinach, turnip and mustard greens and 2 tbsp (25 mL) water. Cover and cook over low heat, until water is absorbed, about 5 minutes.

4. Meanwhile, in a large skillet, heat oil over medium heat. Add ginger and chiles and sauté for 1 minute. Add mustard and cumin and sauté, stirring continuously, for 2 minutes.

5. Add spinach mixture, dal and remaining salt. Mix well and heat through. Add lime juice to taste. Serve with Indian bread.

Bengali Red Lentils

This everyday dal can be seasoned in different ways to change the flavor profile. Cook the lentils and purée. Refrigerate for up to a week. Before serving, you can take a portion of the dal, bring it back to a boil and finish with a seasoning mix of your choice. The remainder of unseasoned dal can be saved for another meal, when it can be seasoned differently.

Variations

Omit nigella and add 1 cup (250 mL) thinly sliced onions with the chiles in Step 3 and sauté until onions are light golden, 6 to 7 minutes. Add to dal.

Omit nigella and chiles and add 2 cups (500 mL) chopped tomatoes in Step 3 and sauté until soft and mushy, 6 to 7 minutes. Add ½ cup (125 mL) chopped cilantro and 1 tsp (5 mL) granulated sugar and cook for 1 minute. Add to dal.

2 cups	red lentils (masoor dal)	500 mL
1 tsp	turmeric	5 mL
2 tsp	salt or to taste	10 mL

Tempering

1½ tbsp	oil	22 mL
1½ tsp	nigella seeds (kalaunji)	7 mL
2	green chiles, preferably serranos, slit	2

1. Clean and pick through dal for any small stones and grit. Rinse several times in cold water until water is fairly clear. Soak in 6 cups (1.5 L) water in a saucepan for 10 minutes.

2. Bring dal to a boil over medium-high heat. Reduce heat to low. Stir in turmeric and boil gently, partially covered, until dal is soft, about 20 minutes. Using an immersion blender or in a blender, in batches as necessary, purée until smooth. Return to saucepan. Add salt and cook over medium-low heat, stirring often, until consistency of pea soup, about 10 minutes.

3. *Tempering:* In a small saucepan, heat oil over medium heat Add nigella and chiles and sauté, about 1 minute. Add to dal. Serve with rice.

Cholar Dal
Bengali Special Dal

1 cup	split yellow peas (channa dal)	250 mL
½ tsp	turmeric	2 mL
1 tsp	salt	5 mL
1 tbsp	ghee or butter, divided	15 mL
¼ cup	dried coconut chips (see Tips, right)	50 mL
2	dried Indian red chiles	2
½ tsp	cumin seeds	2 mL
1	piece (1 inch/2.5 cm) cinnamon	1
3	green cardamom pods, cracked open	3
3	whole cloves	3
2	bay leaves	2
1	green chile, preferably serrano, cut in half	1
2 tsp	minced peeled gingerroot or ginger paste (see Tips, page 46)	10 mL
1 tbsp	raisins	15 mL

Serves 4 to 6

This dish is a favorite at weddings and special occasions.

Tips

Coconut chips are available at health food stores and in Indian markets.

Leftover dal can be refrigerated for up to 1 week and will almost solidify. It can be reheated in the microwave or on the stove top over low heat. Do not add water to dilute until dal is steaming hot, as starch will liquefy when reheated.

1. Clean and pick through dal for any small stones and grit. Rinse several times in cold water until water is fairly clear. Soak in 3 cups (750 mL) water in a saucepan for 30 minutes.

2. Bring dal to a boil over medium-high heat. Skim any froth off the top. Reduce heat to medium. Stir in turmeric and boil gently, partially covered, until dal is tender and there is about ½ cup (125 mL) water in pan, 35 to 40 minutes. Mash a little dal with the back of a spoon. Add 1½ cups (375 mL) water and salt. Return to a boil. Reduce heat to low, cover and simmer until dal is very soft, 6 to 8 minutes.

3. Meanwhile, heat 1 tsp (5 mL) of the ghee in a skillet over medium heat. Add coconut chips and sauté until golden, 2 to 3 minutes. Transfer to a bowl and set aside.

4. In same skillet, heat remaining ghee over medium heat. Add red chiles, cumin, cinnamon, cardamom, cloves, bay leaves and green chile and sauté, until fragrant, for 1 minute. Pour into dal.

5. Stir in ginger, raisins and coconut chips. Cover and simmer until dal thickens to the consistency of oatmeal, 6 to 8 minutes. If dal gets too thick, add a little hot water to return to desired consistency. Serve with puris or any Indian bread.

Bhaja Mung Dal
Toasted Mung Dal

1 cup	yellow mung beans (mung dal)	250 mL
½ cup	frozen peas	125 mL
½ tsp	turmeric	2 mL
1 tbsp	minced green chiles, preferably serranos	15 mL
1 ¼ tsp	salt or to taste	6 mL
¾ tsp	granulated sugar	4 mL
1 tbsp	ghee or oil	15 mL
3	bay leaves	3
1 tsp	cumin seeds (see Tip, right)	5 mL

1. Clean and pick through dal for any small stones and grit. Rinse several times in cold water until water is fairly clear. Drain thoroughly.

2. In a saucepan over medium heat, toast drained dal, stirring gently, until golden, 12 to15 minutes.

3. Add 1¾ cups (425 mL) water, peas and turmeric. Bring to a boil over medium-high heat. Reduce heat to low and boil gently, partially covered, until water is absorbed, 14 to 15 minutes. Remove from heat and stir in chiles, salt and sugar, taking care not to mash dal.

4. In a small saucepan, heat ghee over medium heat. Add bay leaves and sauté for 20 seconds. Add cumin and sauté until aromatic, about 30 seconds. Pour over dal. Stir to mix and serve hot. Remove bay leaves, but I like to leave them in as they continue to flavor the dish and look decorative.

Serves 4

Toasting gives the dal a delicious nutty flavor and also helps keep the grains of dal intact instead of cooking up soupy, as mung dal usually does. This is a popular everyday dal in Bengal.

Tip
Cumin seeds are used in most dals, as they are an aid to digestion besides being a compatible flavoring agent.

Tomato Pappu

Andhra Yellow Lentils with Tomatoes

Serves 6

A delicious home-style dal without the fire of many Andhra dishes. This recipe comes from the chef at the Taj Banjara hotel in Hyderabad.

1 cup	yellow lentils (toor dal)	250 mL
2	plum (Roma) tomatoes, cut into 1-inch (2.5 cm) pieces	2
1 tbsp	thinly sliced green chiles, preferably serranos	15 mL
½ tsp	turmeric	2 mL
1½ tbsp	oil	22 mL
1 tsp	dark mustard seeds	5 mL
1 tsp	cumin seeds	5 mL
2	dried Indian red chiles	2
1 tbsp	sliced garlic	15 mL
3	sprigs fresh curry leaves, stripped (30 to 40), divided	3
1 cup	chopped onion	250 mL
1 tsp	minced peeled gingerroot	5 mL
1 tsp	minced garlic	5 mL
1 tsp	salt or to taste	5 mL

1. Clean and pick through dal for any small stones and grit. Rinse several times in cold water until water is fairly clear. Soak in 4 cups (1 L) water in a saucepan for 10 minutes.

2. Bring dal to a boil over medium-high heat. Skim any foam off top. Reduce heat to medium-low. Add tomatoes, chiles and turmeric and boil gently, partially covered, until dal is soft and most of the water has been absorbed, 20 to 25 minutes.

3. In another large saucepan, heat oil over high heat until a couple of mustard seeds thrown in start to sputter. Add all the mustard seeds and cover quickly. When the seeds stop popping, in a few seconds, uncover, reduce heat to medium and add cumin seeds, red chiles, sliced garlic and about three-quarters of the curry leaves and sauté for 1 minute. Add onion and sauté until soft and just beginning to color, 3 to 4 minutes.

4. Pour dal over onion masala. Add ginger, minced garlic and salt and stir to mix. Cover and reduce heat to low. Simmer until dal is well mixed and mixture is thickened (see Tip, page 99), about 10 minutes. Sprinkle remaining curry leaves over top before serving over rice.

Kadale Kalu Huli

Brown Chickpea Curry

1 cup	chickpeas (kala channa)	250 mL
1 tsp	salt or to taste	5 mL
1/3 cup	fresh or frozen grated coconut	75 mL
2 tbsp	unsalted Thai tamarind purée	25 mL
1 tbsp	sambhar powder (see page 28)	15 mL
1 tsp	Indian poppy seeds (see Tip, page 219)	5 mL

1. Pick through and rinse chickpeas 2 to 3 times. Add water to cover by 3 inches (7.5 cm) and soak at room temperature in a bowl for 6 hours or overnight.

2. Drain chickpeas. Place in a saucepan with 4 cups (1 L) fresh water. Bring to a boil over high heat. Reduce heat to low and boil gently until chickpeas are tender, 20 to 25 minutes. Add salt just before chickpeas are ready and remove from heat.

3. With a slotted spoon, transfer 1/2 cup (125 mL) of the cooked chickpeas to a blender. Add coconut, tamarind, sambhar powder and poppy seeds. Add 1/2 cup (125 mL) of the chickpea liquid and blend to a purée.

4. Pour purée into remaining chickpeas in saucepan and cook over medium-low heat, stirring occasionally, until gravy thickens to the consistency you prefer, 6 to 8 minutes. If not serving immediately, allow a little extra liquid to remain, as it thickens considerably as it cools. Serve with steamed rice.

Serves 4 to 6

This is a recipe from my friend Usha, who hails from Bengaluru (Bangalore). My family enjoys the flavor and texture of this healthy, easy-to-prepare dish.

Tip
When reheating leftovers, do not add additional liquid until curry is heated through completely, as it will loosen when heated. If still too thick, add a little water to achieve the desired consistency.

Gayatri's Green Mango Dal

Serves 4 to 6

A recipe straight from the heart! On a trip to Hyderabad, I met a woman who was not only a fabulous cook, but also more than happy to share her knowledge and recipes. Her love of food was translated into a hugely successful restaurant set in a beautifully landscaped garden. She prepared this dish in her home and brought it to the restaurant to share with me, and I fell in love with it.

Tip

Green mangoes are not suitable for eating as a fruit and are used for their tartness. Look for one that is dark green and very hard, as it will be sourer. They can sometimes be found in the produce aisle and not in the fruit section of some supermarkets and in Indian or Asian stores.

1 cup	yellow lentils (toor dal)	250 mL
½ tsp	turmeric	2 mL
2 tbsp	oil, divided	25 mL
½ tsp	dark mustard seeds	2 mL
½ tsp	cumin seeds	2 mL
1 tbsp	chopped green chiles, preferably serranos	15 mL
1 tsp	salt	5 mL
½ tsp	coriander powder	2 mL
½ tsp	cayenne pepper	2 mL
1 cup	cilantro, chopped	250 mL
1	green mango, peeled and cut into 3-by 1-inch (7.5 by 2.5 cm) slices	1
5 to 6	cloves garlic, crushed	5 to 6

1. Clean and pick through dal for any small stones and grit. Rinse several times in cold water until water is fairly clear. Soak in 4 cups (1 L) water in a saucepan for 15 minutes.

2. Bring dal to a boil over medium-high heat. Skim any froth off the top. Reduce heat to low. Stir in turmeric and boil gently, partially covered, until dal is soft and mushy, 25 to 30 minutes. Using an immersion blender or in a blender, in batches if necessary, purée dal mixture until smooth. Set aside.

3. Meanwhile, in another saucepan, heat 1 tbsp (15 mL) of the oil over high heat until a couple of mustard seeds thrown in start to sputter. Add all the mustard seeds and cover quickly. When the seeds stop popping, in a few seconds, uncover, reduce heat to medium and add cumin and chiles and sauté for 30 seconds. Add salt, coriander and cayenne and sauté for 1 minute. Add cilantro and sauté for 1 minute.

4. Add mango, including the large seed, and sauté for 4 minutes. Add ½ cup (125 mL) water. Cover and cook until mango softens, 7 to 8 minutes. (Do not let mango get mushy.)

5. Pour dal over top of mango and stir. Cover and simmer to allow flavors to blend, 10 to 12 minutes.

6. In a small skillet, heat remaining oil over medium heat. Add garlic and sauté until golden, about 3 minutes. Add to dal. Do not stir. Remove from heat, cover immediately and let rest for 3 minutes. Stir dal and garlic together before serving. Serve hot with rice or any Indian bread. Remove mango seed before serving.

Sambhar with Drumsticks

Serves 6 to 8

Drumsticks are long green ridged stick-like pods that hang from a tropical tree and are particularly prized in South India. They are usually cut into 2- to 3-inch (5 to 7.5 cm) sections. Eat them as you would artichoke leaves — by holding between two fingers and pulling through the teeth to get to the pulp and leaving behind the fibrous skin. Drumstick leaves are cooked as a vegetable.

Tip
Drumsticks are available frozen in Indian markets.

1 cup	yellow lentils (toor dal)	250 mL
2 tbsp +1 tsp	oil, divided	25 mL + 5 mL
4	dried Indian red chiles, broken into pieces	4
1 tsp	each coriander seeds and cumin seeds	5 mL
1/2 tsp	fenugreek seeds (methi)	2 mL
1/2 cup	fresh or frozen grated coconut, divided	125 mL
1	package (12 oz/375 g) frozen drumsticks, do not thaw (see Tip, left)	1
3 tbsp	unsalted Thai tamarind purée	45 mL
1 tsp	salt	5 mL
1/2 tsp	turmeric	2 mL
1 tsp	dark mustard seeds	5 mL
1/4 tsp	asafetida (hing)	1 mL
2	sprigs fresh curry leaves, stripped	2
1 cup	cilantro, coarsely chopped	250 mL

1. Clean and pick through dal for any small stones and grit. Rinse in cold water until water is fairly clear. Soak in 6 cups (1.5 L) water in a saucepan for 10 minutes. Bring to a boil over high heat. Skim any froth off. Reduce heat to medium-low and boil gently, partially covered, until dal is soft, 25 to 30 minutes. Using an immersion blender or in a blender, in batches if necessary, purée dal until smooth. Return to saucepan if necessary. Cover and leave on lowest heat.

2. Meanwhile, prepare masala. In a skillet, heat 1 tsp (5 mL) of the oil over medium heat. Add chiles, coriander, cumin and fenugreek and sauté until a little darker and fragrant, 1 minute. Transfer to a bowl and cool slightly. Transfer to a spice grinder and grind to a powder.

3. In a blender, combine 1/4 cup (50 mL) of the coconut, powdered spices and 1/4 cup (50 mL) water. Blend to a paste. Add to dal.

4. Add drumsticks, tamarind, salt, turmeric and remaining coconut and mix well.

5. In a small saucepan, heat remaining oil over high heat until a couple of mustard seeds thrown in start to sputter. Add all the mustard seeds, asafetida and curry leaves. Cover quickly. When the seeds stop popping, in a few seconds, uncover and add to dal.

6. Cover and cook over low heat until drumsticks are soft, about 10 minutes. Do not overcook as drumsticks will disintegrate. If dal is too thick, stir in 1/2 cup (125 mL) hot water and mix well. Remove from heat. Add cilantro and serve hot over steamed rice.

Wateli Dal
Crushed Split Yellow Peas

1 cup	split yellow peas (channa dal)	250 mL
2½ tsp	cumin seeds, divided	12 mL
2 tbsp	minced green chiles, preferably serranos, divided	25 mL
3 tbsp	oil, divided	45 mL
¾ tsp	dark mustard seeds	4 mL
½ tsp	asafetida (hing)	2 mL
1¼ tsp	salt or to taste	6 mL
1 tsp	cayenne pepper	5 mL
¾ tsp	turmeric	4 mL
2 tbsp	slivered peeled gingerroot	25 mL
6	green chiles, preferably serranos, slivered	6
½ cup	cilantro leaves, chopped	125 mL

Serves 8

Dals lend themselves to a myriad of textures and consistencies. This is a good example of a dal that is always cooked whole and remains whole after cooking. The coarse grinding translates to a completely different consistency.

1. Clean and pick through dal for any small stones and grit. Rinse several times in cold water until water is fairly clear. Add water to cover by 3 inches (7.5 cm) and soak at room temperature in a bowl for 5 to 6 hours.

2. Drain dal. Transfer half to a food processor. Add 1½ tsp (7 mL) of the cumin seeds and 1 tbsp (15 mL) of the minced green chiles and process until coarsely ground. Transfer to a bowl. Add remaining dal to food processor and process until coarse. Combine both batches and mix together. Set aside.

3. In a large saucepan, heat 1½ tbsp (22 mL) of the oil over high heat until a couple of mustard seeds thrown in start to sputter. Add all the mustard seeds and cover quickly. When the seeds stop popping, in a few seconds, uncover, reduce heat to medium and add asafetida, remaining cumin and remaining 1 tbsp (15 mL) minced chiles and sauté for 1 minute.

4. Add dal mixture, salt, cayenne, turmeric and 1½ cups (375 mL) water and mix well. Cover and simmer until dal is soft and water is absorbed, 10 to 12 minutes.

5. In a small pan, heat remaining oil over medium heat. Add ginger and slivered green chiles and sauté until crisp, about 2 minutes. Pour over dal. Sprinkle with cilantro. Serve hot with Indian bread.

Dhansak
Parsi Chicken Stew with Lentils and Vegetables

Serves 6 to 8

This is the signature dish of the Parsi community and is served with Parsi Brown Rice (Dhansak na Chawal), Parsi Meatballs (Dhansak na Kabab) and Fresh Salad with Dhansak (Kachumbar), a fresh salad of tomatoes, cucumber and cilantro. It is somewhat laborious to make, but well worth the effort.

Tip

Dhansak is best served the next day. It can be frozen in an airtight container for up to 6 months. Reheat over low heat.

1⁄3 cup	red lentils (masoor dal)	75 mL
1⁄3 cup	yellow mung beans (yellow mung dal)	75 mL
1⁄4 cup	yellow lentils (toor dal)	50 mL
2 tbsp	Indian split white beans (val dal), optional	25 mL
12	bone-in skinless chicken thighs, rinsed (3 to 4 lbs/1.5 to 2 kg)	12
1 1⁄2 cups	chopped butternut squash	375 mL
1 1⁄2 cups	chopped eggplant	375 mL
1⁄4 cup	dried fenugreek leaves (kasuri methi)	50 mL
1 cup	chopped onion	250 mL
1	carrot, peeled and chopped	1
2 tsp	salt or to taste	10 mL
6 to 8	dried Indian red chiles	6 to 8
1⁄2 tsp	toasted coriander seeds	2 mL
1⁄2 tsp	toasted cumin seeds	2 mL
1	piece (1 inch/2.5 cm) cinnamon	1
6	whole cloves	6
6	black peppercorns	6
1 tbsp	sambhar powder (see page 28)	15 mL
1⁄2 tsp	turmeric	2 mL
1	cube (1 inch/2.5 cm) peeled gingerroot	1
8	cloves garlic	8
3 tbsp	oil	45 mL
3 cups	thinly sliced onions (lengthwise slices)	750 mL
3 cups	chopped tomatoes	750 mL
1 tbsp	jaggery (gur)	15 mL
3 tbsp	cilantro, chopped	45 mL
	Lemon wedges	

1. Clean and pick through masoor, mung, toor and val dals for any small stones and grit. Rinse several times in cold water until water is fairly clear. Add water to cover by 3 inches (7.5 cm) and soak at room temperature for 1 hour.

2. Drain dal. In a large pot, combine dal, chicken, squash, eggplant, fenugreek, onion, carrot, salt and 3 cups (750 mL) water. Bring to a boil over high heat. Reduce heat to medium-low and boil gently, partially covered, until vegetables are soft and mushy, about 45 minutes. Remove chicken and set aside.

3. Meanwhile, in a spice grinder, grind together red chiles, coriander, cumin, cinnamon, cloves, peppercorns, sambhar powder and turmeric to a powder.

4. In a blender, purée ginger, garlic, spice powder and $\frac{1}{4}$ cup (50 mL) water to a smooth paste. Transfer to a bowl. In the same blender, purée dal mixture in 2 batches. Transfer to a separate bowl.

5. In a large saucepan, heat oil over medium-high heat. Add onions and sauté until dark brown, about 10 minutes. Reduce heat to medium. Add spice paste and sauté, stirring constantly, until mixture darkens and is aromatic, about 5 minutes. (Deglaze pan with 1 tbsp/15 mL water periodically if masala begins to stick.)

6. Add tomatoes, jaggery and cilantro. Cover, reduce heat to medium-low and cook until tomatoes are soft enough to be mashed with back of spoon, 5 to 6 minutes.

7. Add puréed dal mixture and chicken and mix well. Cover and simmer to allow flavors to combine, 15 to 20 minutes. Serve with Dhansak rice and pass lemon wedges to squeeze over top.

Variation

You can use lamb here instead of chicken. Use 4 lbs (2 kg) lamb, preferably with bone, cut into bite-size pieces.

Chevti Dal

Gujarati Mixed Lentils with Vegetables

Serves 8

This recipe is one of the oldest in my repertoire, and I remember vividly the afternoon my Jain friend, Rudra, took me to the home of a relative who was a fabulous cook. We spent many happy hours in her kitchen as she cooked Jain dishes for my benefit. I treasure all those recipes to this day.

Tip

Kokum is the soft, black leather-like skin of a sour tropical fruit. Substitute 2 to 3 tbsp (25 to 45 mL) lime or lemon juice if you can't find it.

¾ cup	split white lentils (urad dal)	175 mL
⅓ cup	yellow lentils (toor dal)	75 mL
¼ cup	split yellow peas (channa dal)	50 mL
2 tbsp	yellow mung beans (mung dal)	25 mL
5	kokum (see Tip, left)	5
1 tbsp	minced peeled gingerroot	15 mL
1 tbsp	minced green chiles, preferably serranos	15 mL
1 ½ tsp	coriander powder	7 mL
1 ½ tsp	salt or to taste	7 mL
¾ tsp	cumin powder	4 mL
2 ½ tbsp	jaggery (gur)	32 mL
2 tbsp	Gujarati Sambhar Masala (see recipe, page 123)	25 mL
3 tbsp	oil	45 mL
1 ½ tsp	cumin seeds	7 mL
¼ tsp	asafetida (hing)	1 mL
2	sprigs fresh curry leaves, leaves stripped (20 to 25)	2
1 cup	diced tomatoes	250 mL
1 cup	diced cucumbers	250 mL
½ cup	diced carrots	125 mL

1. Clean and pick through urad, toor, channa and mung dals for any small stones and grit. Rinse several times in cold water until water is fairly clear. Soak in 6 cups (1.5 L) water in a saucepan for at least 10 minutes or for up to 30 minutes.

2. Bring dal mixture to a boil over medium heat. Reduce heat to low and boil gently, partially covered, stirring frequently, until dals are soft and mushy, 35 to 40 minutes.

3. Add kokum, ginger, chiles, coriander, salt, cumin, jaggery and sambhar masala and cook for 10 minutes.

4. Meanwhile, in another saucepan, heat oil over medium-high heat. Add cumin, asafetida and curry leaves and sauté for 30 seconds. Reduce heat to medium. Add tomatoes, cucumbers and carrots and sauté until slightly softened, 3 to 4 minutes. Add to dal and mix well. Simmer for 5 minutes. Serve with rice.

Lasuni Masoor Dal
Red Lentils with Garlic and Cilantro

2 cups	red lentils (masoor dal)	500 mL
¾ tsp	turmeric	4 mL
2 tsp	salt or to taste	10 mL
1½ cups	chopped tomatoes	375 mL
3 tbsp	minced gingerroot	45 mL
4 tsp	minced green chiles, preferably serranos	20 mL
2 cups	cilantro leaves, chopped	500 mL
2 tbsp	oil	25 mL
12 to 14	cloves garlic, sliced	12 to 14
2	sprigs fresh curry leaves, stripped (20 to 25)	2

Serves 8

A typical everyday dal, this is rather thin and soupy, the way most Indians like their dal. However, you could use 1 cup (250 mL) less water and cook until it is the consistency you prefer.

1. Clean and pick through dal for any small stones and grit. Rinse several times in cold water until water is fairly clear. Soak in 8 cups (2 L) water in a saucepan for 10 minutes. Bring dal to a boil over medium-high heat. Skim any froth off the top. Reduce heat to medium-low. Stir in turmeric and simmer, partially covered, until dal is soft, about 20 minutes. Stir in salt.

2. Using an immersion blender or in a blender, in batches if necessary, purée mixture. Return to saucepan if necessary. Return to a gentle boil over medium heat.

3. Add tomatoes, ginger, chiles and cilantro. Cover, reduce heat to medium-low and simmer for 10 minutes.

4. In a small saucepan, heat oil over medium heat. Add garlic and sauté for 1 minute. Add curry leaves and cook until garlic is golden, 2 to 3 minutes. Pour mixture into dal. Cover and remove from heat. Allow to infuse for 5 minutes before serving with rice.

Gujarati Sambhar Masala

2 tbsp	oil	25 mL
1 tbsp	salt	15 mL
2 tsp	cayenne pepper	10 mL
1 tsp	pounded and semi-crushed dark mustard seeds	5 mL
1 tsp	pounded and semi-crushed fenugreek seeds (methi)	5 mL
½ tsp	asafetida (hing)	2 mL

Makes about 3 tbsp (45 mL)

This mixture is a concentrate used for flavoring otherwise bland dishes such as dals. I have also folded it into cooked, slightly smashed potatoes with great success.

1. In a bowl, combine oil, salt, cayenne, mustard seeds, fenugreek and asafetida. Store in an airtight container at room temperature indefinitely.

Masoor ani Shing
Brown Lentils with Peanuts

2 cups	brown lentils (sabat masoor)	500 mL
⅔ cup	raw peanuts, skinned (see Tip, right)	150 mL
¼ cup	unsalted Thai tamarind purée	50 mL
4 tsp	jaggery (gur)	20 mL
2 tsp	salt or to taste	10 mL
1 tsp	cayenne pepper	5 mL
1 tbsp	oil	15 mL
½ tsp	ground cloves	2 mL
½ tsp	ground cinnamon	2 mL
3 tbsp	cilantro, chopped	45 mL

Serves 8

Peanuts are widely grown and extensively used in the cooking of Maharashtra. This simple home-style dal is typical of the area.

Tip
Roasted peanuts in a jar can be used instead. Omit Step 3 if substituting them.

1. Clean and pick through dal for any small stones and grit. Rinse several times in cold water until water is fairly clear. Soak in 6 cups (1.5 L) water in a saucepan for 10 minutes.

2. Bring dal to a boil over high heat. Skim any froth off the top. Reduce heat to medium-low and boil gently, partially covered, until soft and dal can be mashed with back of spoon, about 30 minutes.

3. Meanwhile, in a heavy skillet over medium heat, toast peanuts, shaking pan often to brown evenly, 3 to 4 minutes.

4. Stir peanuts, tamarind, jaggery, salt and cayenne pepper into dal and simmer for 5 minutes.

5. In a small saucepan, heat oil over medium heat. Add cloves and cinnamon and immediately remove from heat. Pour infused oil over top of dal. Cover and simmer for 2 minutes. Garnish with cilantro. Serve hot with rice or any Indian bread.

W

Mung Usal
Mung Bean Salad

Serves 8

Sprouted beans are very important in the diet of the people of Gujarat, which is primarily a vegetarian state. Sprouts are a high-quality source of protein. Known as kathol, *they are included in at least one meal every day. This is a delightful light salad that is good with plain yogurt or as a bed for grilled seafood.*

Tip
To make a lunch entrée, combine salad with cooked shrimp or cooked shredded chicken. Increase cayenne pepper, salt and lime juice, if desired.

1 cup	green mung beans (sabat mung)	250 mL
1 ½ tsp	salt or to taste	7 mL
½ tsp	turmeric	2 mL
2	green onions, sliced fine with some green	2
½ cup	chopped tomatoes	125 mL
½ cup	chopped cucumber	125 mL
¼ cup	cilantro, chopped	50 mL
½ tsp	cayenne pepper	2 mL
3 to 4 tbsp	freshly squeezed lime or lemon juice	45 to 60 mL

1. Clean and pick through beans (sabat mung) for any small stones and grit. Rinse several times in cold water until water is fairly clear. Add water to cover by 3 inches (7.5 cm) and soak at room temperature in a bowl overnight.

2. Drain beans and tie tightly in double layer of cheesecloth. Hang in a well ventilated place for 2 to 3 days, misting cheesecloth a couple of times a day to moisten well. When ready, sprouts should be about 1 to 1½ inches (2.5 to 4 cm) long.

3. Untie and place beans in a saucepan and cover with water. Add salt and turmeric. Bring to a boil over high heat. Boil until beans are just cooked, 2 to 3 minutes. (Some of the beans will shed their skin, which can be skimmed off.) Drain and let cool.

4. Transfer to a bowl. Add green onions, tomatoes, cucumber, cilantro, cayenne and lime juice to taste. Toss to mix. Chill well before serving.

Mung Beans with Ginger

1 ½ cups	green mung beans (sabat mung)	375 mL
2 tbsp	oil	25 mL
1	dried Indian red chile	1
2 tsp	cumin seeds	10 mL
1 cup	thinly sliced onion (lengthwise slices)	250 mL
2 tbsp	minced peeled gingerroot	25 mL
1 tbsp	minced garlic	15 mL
3	green chiles, preferably serranos, minced	3
1 tbsp	coriander powder	15 mL
1 tsp	cayenne pepper	5 mL
¾ tsp	turmeric	4 mL
2 tbsp	jaggery (gur) or 1 tbsp (15 mL) brown sugar	25 mL
1 ½ tsp	salt or to taste	7 mL
¼ cup	cilantro, chopped	50 mL

Serves 6 to 8

Mung beans are a favorite in Gujarat, and since I grew up eating in the homes of my many Gujarati friends, I am partial to them. I love the texture and enjoy both the whole beans and the sprouted mung beans.

1. Clean and pick through beans (sabat mung) for any small stones and grit. Rinse several times in cold water. Add water to cover by 3 inches (7.5 cm) and soak at room temperature in a bowl overnight.

2. Drain beans and transfer to a saucepan. Add 3 cups (750 mL) fresh water and bring to a boil. Skim any froth off the top. Reduce heat to medium and boil gently, partially covered, until beans are soft, about 10 minutes. Remove from heat.

3. Meanwhile, in another saucepan, heat oil over medium heat. Add red chile and cumin and sauté, until fragrant, for 1 minute. Add onion and sauté until golden, 8 to 10 minutes. Add ginger, garlic and green chiles and sauté for 2 minutes. Add coriander, cayenne and turmeric and sauté for 1 minute. Add jaggery and mix well.

4. Pour mung beans with cooking liquid into onion mixture. Stir in salt and 2 tbsp (25 mL) of the cilantro. Simmer for 3 to 4 minutes. Garnish with remaining cilantro. Serve with bread or rice.

Tarka Dal

Serves 6 to 8

Tarka *refers to the technique of seasoning with flash-fried spices, a technique often used to season bean (dal) dishes. There are innumerable variations of dals used, depending on the region. This recipe is from a friend in Mumbai.*

1 cup	red lentils (masoor dal)	250 mL
½ cup	split yellow peas (channa dal)	125 mL
¼ tsp	turmeric	1 mL
2 tbsp	minced green chiles, preferably serranos	25 mL
2 tsp	minced peeled gingerroot or ginger paste	10 mL
2 tsp	garlic paste (see Tip, page 46)	10 mL
1 ½ tsp	salt or to taste	7 mL
2 tbsp	oil	25 mL
½ tsp	dark mustard seeds	2 mL
2	dried Indian red chiles	2
½ tsp	cumin seeds	2 mL
¼ tsp	asafetida (hing)	1 mL
½ cup	thinly sliced onion (lengthwise slices)	125 mL
1 tbsp	slivered peeled gingerroot	15 mL
1	large clove garlic, slivered	1
1	green chile, preferably serrano, slivered	1

1. Clean and pick through masoor and channa dals for any small stones and grit. Rinse several times in cold water until water is fairly clear. Soak in 4 cups (1 L) water in a large saucepan for 10 minutes.

2. Bring to a boil over medium heat. Skim any froth off the top. Reduce heat to medium-low. Stir in turmeric, minced green chiles, ginger and garlic and boil gently, partially covered, until dal is soft, 25 to 30 minutes. Using an immersion blender, purée or whisk vigorously to a batter-like consistency. Dal should be thick like cream soup. Thin with a little hot water if necessary. Add salt.

3. In a small saucepan, heat oil over high heat until a couple of mustard seeds thrown in start to sputter. Add all the mustard seeds and cover quickly. When the seeds stop popping, in a few seconds, uncover, reduce heat to medium and add red chiles, cumin and asafetida. Sauté for 30 seconds. Add onion, ginger, garlic and slivered green chiles and sauté until onions are golden, 5 to 7 minutes.

4. Pour mixture into dal. Cover and let rest for flavors to infuse, 2 to 3 minutes. Do not stir in until ready to serve. Serve with rice or any Indian bread.

Misal
Three-Bean Mix with Two Chutneys

1/3 cup	brown lentils (sabat masoor)	75 mL
1/3 cup	black-eyed peas (chawli)	75 mL
1/3 cup	green mung beans (sabat mung)	75 mL
1 tbsp	oil	15 mL
3/4 tsp	dark mustard seeds	4 mL
2 1/2 cups	chopped onions	625 mL
1 cup	chopped tomatoes	250 mL
2 tsp	coriander powder	10 mL
2 tsp	garam masala	10 mL
1/2 tsp	cayenne pepper	2 mL
1/2 tsp	turmeric	2 mL
1 tsp	granulated sugar	5 mL
1 tsp	salt or to taste	5 mL

Garnishes

1/2 cup	each chopped onion, tomatoes, cilantro	125 mL
1 cup	sev (see Tips, page 91), optional	250 mL
2 tbsp	minced green chiles, preferably serranos, optional	25 mL
	Tamarind chutney and cilantro-mint chutney	

1. Combine lentils, peas and beans in a large bowl. Rinse several times in cold water until water is fairly clear. Add water to cover by 4 to 5 inches (10 to 12.5 cm) and soak at room temperature overnight.

2. In a large saucepan, heat oil over high heat until a couple of mustard seeds thrown in start to sputter. Add all the mustard seeds and cover quickly. When the seeds stop popping, in a few seconds, uncover, reduce heat to medium and add onions and tomatoes. Sauté until vegetables soften and break down, 6 to 8 minutes.

3. Add coriander, garam masala, cayenne and turmeric. Drain beans and add to saucepan. Add 1/2 cup (125 mL) water, sugar and salt and mix well. Cover and cook until beans are tender, 20 to 25 minutes. If the water has not been absorbed, uncover pan and continue to simmer until beans are dry.

4. *Garnishes:* Place 4 to 5 tbsp (60 to 75 mL) of the bean mixture in center of each serving plate. Garnish with onion, tomatoes and cilantro. Scatter 2 tbsp (25 mL) sev, if using, over top and around mixture. Pass green chiles, if using, and chutneys to be added to taste.

Serves 4 to 6

This dish is a salad but could also be a chaat with the addition of crispy store-bought ingredients such as sev or Punjabi mix. Serve it as a first course to accompany chicken kababs or fried fish.

Variation

Place beans in a mixing bowl. Add 1/4 cup (50 mL) each chopped onion, chopped tomatoes, minced chiles and chopped cilantro and toss to mix. Add 3 tbsp (45 mL) each tamarind and cilantro-mint chutneys and toss to mix. Divide equally between plates. Sprinkle 2 tbsp (25 mL) sev over top of each serving and additional sev decoratively on plates. Serve immediately.

Rice, Cereals and Breads

Rice

RICE REIGNS SUPREME IN INDIA (with the exception of the north and parts of the west). The famous basmati rice is grown only in North India but, because it is in limited supply and therefore expensive, is reserved for special occasions and is not the daily rice of most Indians. Basmati rice is grown in the foothills of the Himalayas, where the soil conditions contribute to its subtle aroma and distinctive nutty taste. There is nothing else in the world that can be called basmati. There are, however, innumerable other varieties of rice grown throughout India, each of which is consumed locally. Parboiled rice is popular in many areas, including Orissa, Goa and parts of South India.

It would be appropriate to mention here the ultimate comfort food of all Indians. Known as *khichri* throughout the country except in the south, where it is known as *pongal,* khichri is basically a mixture of rice and lentils (dal) cooked together. In many instances, it is cooked to a soft, risotto-like consistency.

THE VARIETY OF DAL VARIES WITH THE region, and can even be a mixture of dals. Some of the more elaborate ones are cooked with vegetables, and the simplest ones are just rice and dal very lightly seasoned. In any event, it is a one-dish meal, the essence of simplicity and incredibly comforting.

The eastern states are mainly rice-eating areas. Rice and fish is the main diet of many of these peoples, with vegetables playing an equally important role. All-purpose flour replaces whole wheat to make their signature balloon bread, *luchi*.

RICE IS REVERED IN SOUTH INDIA, AND numerous local varieties of rice are grown there. It is served in multiple courses at all meals and is the main ingredient in breakfast foods as well. South India's main contribution to global food is the *dosa*, the signature rice-and-lentil crêpe. Dosa is fast morphing into a food of immense possibilities. Served in many Indian fast-food places, it has gained popularity as an exotic, tasty preparation, either partially stuffed with delicious potatoes or

eaten plain with coconut chutney and *sambhar* (lentil vegetable stew). Its cousin the *idli* (fluffy steamed rice cake) is also served with the same accompaniments. Traditionally, these are both considered breakfast foods in South India. Outside their home environment, however, they have become all-day, anytime snacks.

The southerner's imaginative use of rice is legendary. Rice flour and rice paste are used in batters. This batter is used to make steamed dumplings and savory pancakes. Then there is the southern version of rice pudding, called *payasam*, which is made with sweetened milk into a light, creamy consistency. This is served at weddings, at celebrations and in temples.

In Andhra Pradesh, meals begin with freshly prepared steamed rice served with a dollop of ghee and a couple of spoons of mixed spice powder (*podi*). These are mixed into the hot rice and give it rich flavor.

Semolina is an important cereal in the south and figures in both sweet and savory dishes. Recently, chapatis, the whole wheat tortilla-like flatbread eaten daily in North and West India,

Rice, Cereals and Breads

have gained acceptance as a healthier alternative to a totally rice-based diet.

THE WEST OFFERS A POTPOURRI OF choices. Rice is the mainstay along the coast and in Goa, where fish and seafood dishes abound. In Maharashtra and Gujarat, both rice and grains share the table with many interesting flatbreads. Flattened dehydrated rice, known as *poha,* is popular and used in desserts as well as savory dishes. A signature snack is the spicy, crisp *chevra,* a mix of flattened rice, cashews, raisins, peanuts, crisp potato shreds and spices. This is usually store-bought and eaten out of hand.

Breads

THE BREADS OF INDIA ARE A WORLD unto themselves. In the cities, white bread plays an important role. The common misconception is that naan is the daily bread of Indians. That is not so. Naan is a restaurant bread requiring the intense heat of a tandoor, the popular North Indian clay oven. The tandoor most likely came to us from Central Asia via Afghanistan, where naan is indeed the daily bread. We owe the popularity of tandoori foods as we know them today to the Punjabi Hindus who came as refugees in 1947 from what is now Pakistan. Punjabis used the tandoor to make their delicious *tandoori roti*, a flatbread made from whole wheat flour and cooked like a naan by slapping it onto the vertical wall of the tandoor, where it cooks in less than a minute.

NORTH INDIA IS THE GRANARY OF THE country. Whole wheat flour, called *gehun ka atta* or *chapati atta,* is used extensively and made into the most astonishing flatbreads. A simple dough prepared with water, a little salt and an optional touch of oil is the basis of many of these breads. *Roti* is the generic Hindi word for all bread, and *chapati* is the daily bread of northern and western India. The same dough is used to make *parathas* (griddle-fried flatbreads), stuffed parathas and deep-fried *puris* (balloon breads).

Parathas are the king of flatbreads in Punjab, Madhya Pradesh and Uttar Pradesh. Plain or stuffed, they make a filling breakfast or a simple lunch, accompanied by yogurt and pickles. Packed in school lunch boxes, carried in "tiffin carriers" on long train journeys or tied in a cloth and carried into fields by farmers for their midday meal, parathas are the mainstay of North Indian breads. Best eaten hot off the griddle, of course, they are good even at room temperature and very filling. The most popular stuffed parathas are made with a potato stuffing (*aloo paratha*), followed by cauliflower (*gobi paratha*) and, in the winter, the flavorful daikon radish (*mooli paratha*) so dear to the hearts of all Punjabis.

In the cooler months, grains such as millet and sorghum are freshly ground into flour, and mouthwatering peasant breads are cooked on the griddle, seasoned with onion, chiles and spices. Robust and tasty enough to be eaten on their own with a little pickle or slabs of onion, these make a hearty lunch for farmers and their field workers because they are sustaining and easy to pack.

THE WESTERN STATES ARE FAMOUS FOR their own plethora of flatbreads. Most are made from whole wheat flour, but there are many combinations, such as whole wheat and chickpea flour, whole wheat and rice flour, whole wheat and semolina, etc. Sweet flatbreads are also popular, made with ghee and jaggery (unrefined brown sugar) or granulated sugar.

Bread is the staff of life, and nowhere is it as true as in India, where people are known to survive on bread, green chiles and chunks of onion. Without rice and grains, Indians could not survive.

Perfect Steamed Rice

- *Large saucepan with tight-fitting lid*

2 cups	Indian basmati rice (see Tip, page 134)	500 mL
1 tbsp	oil	15 mL
2 tsp	salt or to taste	10 mL

1. Place rice in a bowl with plenty of cold water and swish vigorously with fingers. Drain. Repeat process 4 or 5 times until water is fairly clear. Cover with 3 to 4 inches (7.5 to 10 cm) cold water and soak for at least 15 minutes or for up to 2 hours.

2. In a large saucepan, heat oil over medium-high heat. Drain rice and add to saucepan. Stir to coat rice. Add 3½ cups (875 mL) cold water and salt.

3. Cover with a tight-fitting lid and bring to a boil over high heat. Reduce heat as low as possible and cook, covered, without peeking, for 25 minutes.

4. Remove from heat and set lid slightly ajar to allow steam to escape. Let rest for 5 minutes. Gently fluff with fork and carefully spoon onto platter to serve.

There are many ways to cook steamed rice. In some regions, a large pot of salted water is brought to a boil, then drained rinsed rice is stirred in and returned to a boil. After 2 minutes, the water is drained and the rice is covered and left on very low heat to finish steaming. I find the method I use here to be the simplest and healthiest because the minerals and vitamins are retained and absorbed into the water, rather than lost when drained. Plus, it's foolproof.

Tip
Rice is always transferred to a platter, never a bowl, as the weight of the freshly steamed rice would cause the rice on the bottom to get mushy.

Cayenne-Spiked Apricot and Nuts Pulao

Serves 8

The spicy, sweet taste of this rich dish, combined with the texture of nuts and dried fruit, makes it a fabulous party dish. It is good with meat or chicken curry but equally wonderful with roast chicken or turkey.

Tip

True basmati rice comes from the foothills of the Himalayas. There is rice available in the bulk bins of some supermarkets that is marked basmati but it is usually from California and does not work in these recipes. Be sure to use only Indian or Pakistani basmati rice (see also Common Ingredients, page 19).

1 ½ cups	Indian basmati rice (see Tip, left)	375 mL
½ tsp	saffron threads	2 mL
½ cup	granulated sugar	125 mL
1	stick cinnamon, about 3 inches (7.5 cm) long	1
4	whole cloves	4
2 tbsp	cayenne pepper or to taste	25 mL
¼ cup	freshly squeezed lime or lemon juice	50 mL
½ cup	dried apricots	125 mL
½ cup	whole blanched almonds	125 mL
½ cup	walnut or pecan halves	125 mL
2 tbsp	oil	25 mL
1 ½ cups	thinly sliced onions (lengthwise slices)	375 mL
1 ½ tsp	salt	7 mL

1. Place rice in a bowl with plenty of cold water and swish vigorously with fingers. Drain. Repeat process 4 or 5 times until water is fairly clear. Cover with 3 to 4 inches (7.5 to 10 cm) cold water and soak for 15 minutes or for up to 2 hours.

2. In a bowl, soak saffron in ¼ cup (50 mL) very hot water for 15 minutes.

3. In a saucepan, cook sugar, ½ cup (125 mL) water, cinnamon, cloves and cayenne over medium heat until mixture is bubbly and syrupy, 5 to 7 minutes. Stir in lime juice. Mix in apricots, almonds and pecans. Set aside.

4. In a large saucepan, heat oil over medium-high heat. Add onions and sauté until golden, 6 to 8 minutes.

5. Drain rice and stir into onions. Sauté for 2 minutes. Stir in nut mixture and saffron with liquid. Add 1¾ cups (425 mL) cold water and salt. Cover and bring to a boil. Reduce heat to as low as possible and cook, without peeking, for 25 minutes. Remove from heat and set lid slightly ajar to allow steam to escape. Let rest for 5 minutes for rice to firm up. Fluff gently with fork. Gently spoon onto a platter to serve.

Spinach Pulao

Serves 6 to 8

A versatile dish that is an elegant accompaniment to any non-Indian entrée, it is also good as a room-temperature salad. Stir in shrimp or bite-size chicken pieces and you have a main-course salad perfect for summer. I do not like to serve it chilled, as the starch in rice hardens to an unappetizing texture. Stir chicken or shrimp into rice just before serving.

• *Large saucepan with tight-fitting lid*

2 cups	Indian basmati rice (see Tip, page 134)	500 mL
2 tbsp	oil	25 mL
1 tsp	cumin seeds	5 mL
4 tsp	chopped green chiles, preferably serranos	20 mL
1 tbsp	coarsely chopped garlic	15 mL
1 1/2 lbs	fresh spinach, finely chopped (14 cups/3.5 L)	750 g
1 tsp	cumin powder	5 mL
1/2 tsp	turmeric	2 mL
2 tsp	salt or to taste	10 mL
3 to 4 tbsp	freshly squeezed lime or lemon juice	45 to 60 mL

1. Place rice in a large bowl with plenty of cold water and swish vigorously with fingers. Drain. Repeat 4 or 5 times until water is fairly clear. Cover with 3 to 4 inches (7.5 to 10 cm) cold water and set aside to soak for at least 15 minutes or for up to 2 hours.

2. In a large saucepan, heat oil over medium heat. Add cumin seeds, chiles and garlic and sauté for 2 minutes. Add spinach, cumin and turmeric and sauté for 2 minutes. Drain rice and stir into saucepan. Pour in 3 1/2 cups (875 mL) cold water and add salt.

3. Cover and bring to a boil over high heat. Reduce heat as low as possible and cook, covered with a tight-fitting lid, without peeking, for 15 minutes. Lift lid and quickly sprinkle lime juice over rice. Cover and continue to cook for 10 minutes.

4. Remove from heat and set lid slightly ajar to allow steam to escape. Let rest for 5 minutes. Gently fluff with fork and carefully spoon onto platter to serve.

Sindhi Khichri

Rice with Split Green Mung Beans

- *Saucepan with tight-fitting lid*

½ cup	split green mung beans (chilkewali mung dal)	125 mL
2 cups	Indian basmati rice (see Tip, page 134)	500 mL
1 tbsp	oil	15 mL
6	green cardamom pods, cracked open	6
1½ tsp	salt or to taste	7 mL

1. Clean and pick through dal for any small stones and grit. Place dal and rice in a large bowl with plenty of cold water and swish vigorously with fingers. Drain. Repeat 4 or 5 times, until water is fairly clear. Cover with 3 to 4 inches (7.5 to 10 cm) cold water and set aside to soak for at least 15 minutes or for up to 2 hours.

2. In a saucepan, heat oil over medium-high heat. Add cardamom and sauté until fragrant, for 1 minute. Drain rice mixture and add to pan. Sauté for 1 minute. Add 3½ cups (825 mL) cold water and salt. Cover with a tight-fitting lid and bring to a boil. Reduce heat as low as possible and cook, without peeking, for 25 minutes.

3. Remove from heat and set lid slightly ajar to allow steam to escape. Let rest for 5 minutes. Gently fluff with fork and carefully spoon onto platter to serve.

Serves 8

All Sindhis know and love this classic dish, which is traditionally served with the classic Sindhi spinach with vegetables (sai bhaji). It was always accompanied with diced fried vegetables such as potatoes, small cubes of eggplant or okra, but that practice has been abandoned in most homes now. In Sindh, this vegetarian meal was prepared every night in summer and always served with plain yogurt and papadums. Sindhis believe lighter vegetarian meals are better for the digestion in the hot summer months.

Lamb Chop Biriyani

Serves 8 to 10

Traditionally, this dish would be made with baby goat meat, called mutton in India. Biriyani *is best made with meat on the bone, as it enriches the flavors and keeps the meat moist. If you prefer, you can use lamb leg or stewing lamb, preferably on the bone. This special occasion dish, a Muslim specialty, is usually served with a yogurt salad and little else.*

There are many regional variations. Although traditional recipes have at least twice as much rice as meat, I have found that for the Western palate equal portions of rice and meat are more suitable.

━━━━ ❧ ━━━━

- *Preheat oven to 425°F (220°C)*
- *Large deep ovenproof casserole with a tight-fitting lid*

4 cups	Indian basmati rice (see Tip, page 134)	1 L
2 cups	milk	500 mL
1 tsp	saffron threads	5 mL
¼ cup	ghee	50 mL
1 tbsp	minced peeled gingerroot	15 mL
1 tbsp	minced garlic	15 mL
¼ cup	plain nonfat yogurt, at room temperature, stirred to creamy consistency	50 mL
2 tbsp	coriander powder	25 mL
1½ tsp	turmeric	7 mL
12	lamb shoulder chops, trimmed of fat	12
2½ tsp	salt or to taste	12 mL
¼ cup	thinly sliced green chiles, preferably serranos	50 mL
1 cup	mint leaves, coarsely chopped	250 mL
1½ tbsp	garam masala, divided	22 mL
1 cup	crispy fried onions, divided (see Tip, page 101)	250 mL
2 tbsp	white vinegar	25 mL
1 tbsp	oil	15 mL
3 tbsp	salt	45 mL
2 tsp	black cumin seeds (shah jeera)	10 mL
1½ cups	cilantro leaves, coarsely chopped, divided	375 mL
2 cups	chopped tomatoes, divided	500 mL
2 tbsp	julienned peeled gingerroot, divided	25 mL
2 tbsp	sautéed raisins (see Tip, right)	25 mL
2 tbsp	sautéed cashews (see Tip, right)	25 mL

1. Place rice in a large bowl with plenty of cold water and swish vigorously with fingers. Drain. Repeat process 4 or 5 times until water is fairly clear. Cover with 3 to 4 inches (7.5 to 10 cm) cold water and set aside to soak for 15 minutes or for up to 2 hours.

2. In a saucepan or in microwave, heat milk over medium heat until steaming. Add saffron and soak for 10 minutes or for up to 2 hours.

3. In a large saucepan over medium heat, melt ghee. Add ginger and garlic and sauté until fragrant, about 1 minute. Slowly pour in yogurt. Add coriander and turmeric and simmer 2 to 3 minutes.

4. Add lamb chops. Increase heat to medium-high and sauté until partially cooked, 8 to 10 minutes.

5. Add ½ cup (125 mL) water and salt. Return to a boil. Reduce heat to low and cook, stirring periodically, until lamb is tender, 20 to 30 minutes.

6. Stir in chiles, mint and ½ tbsp (7 mL) of the garam masala. Remove from heat and set aside.

7. Meanwhile, in a large pot, bring 12 cups (3 L) water to a rolling boil over high heat. Add 1 tbsp (15 mL) of the crispy fried onions, vinegar, oil, salt and black cumin.

8. Drain rice and stir into water and return to a boil. Cook until grains are half-cooked, tender on the outside and firm in the center, about 2 minutes. Drain in colander and spread in a shallow pan to cool.

9. *To assemble:* In casserole, arrange 4 lamb chops with some of the cooking masala. Sprinkle with a little of the remaining garam masala, one-third each crispy onions, cilantro, tomatoes and ginger. Stir saffron milk and pour ½ cup (125 mL) over top. Layer with one-third of the rice mixture.

10. Make 2 more layers to use remaining lamb and rice. Top with any remaining crispy fried onions and remaining saffron milk. Cover casserole with foil, then tight-fitting lid. Bake in preheated oven for 20 minutes.

11. *To serve:* Remove biriyani from oven and let rest for 5 minutes. Uncover and gently fluff rice around edges with fork. Gently spoon onto a large platter, arranging lamb and rice decoratively. Sprinkle with sautéed raisins and cashews.

Tip

To sauté cashews and raisins, heat 1 tsp (5 mL) oil in a small skillet over medium heat. Add cashews and raisins and sauté until cashews are lightly browned and raisins are puffed up, about 2 minutes

Subzi ka Dalia

Cracked Wheat with Vegetables

⅓ cup	split green mung beans (chilkewali mung dal), with skin, rinsed	75 mL
2 tbsp	oil	25 mL
2	green cardamom pods, cracked open	2
1	piece cinnamon, about 1 inch (2.5 cm) long	1
1	bay leaf	1
5	whole cloves	5
8 to 10	black peppercorns	8 to 10
1½ tsp	cumin seeds	7 mL
1 cup	cracked wheat (dalia)	250 mL
1 cup	sliced carrots	250 mL
1 cup	sliced green beans (½-inch/1 cm pieces) or frozen peas, thawed	250 mL
1 tsp	salt or to taste	5 mL

1. Clean and pick through dal for any small stones and grit. Rinse several times in cold water until water is fairly clear. Drain. Set aside.

2. In a saucepan, heat oil over medium-high heat. Add cardamom, cinnamon, bay leaf, cloves, peppercorns and cumin and sauté until fragrant, about 2 minutes.

3. Add cracked wheat and drained dal and sauté for 2 minutes.

4. Add carrots, green beans, salt and 4 cups (1 L) water. (If using frozen peas, do not add until almost at the end of cooking time). Increase heat to medium-high, cover and bring to a boil. Reduce heat to low and simmer until mixture is soft and the consistency of oatmeal, 10 to 12 minutes. If too thick, add more hot water to dilute to desired consistency.

5. Serve hot, accompanied with plain yogurt, papadums and a pickle or chutney of your choice.

Meetha Dalia
Sweet Cracked Wheat

2 tbsp	oil	25 mL
6	green cardamom pods, cracked open	6
1 cup	cracked wheat (dalia)	250 mL
1 tbsp	wheat berries (haleem wheat), optional	15 mL
½ cup	granulated sugar	125 mL

1. In a saucepan, heat oil over medium heat. Add cardamom, cracked wheat and wheat berries, if using, and sauté until partially cooked, for 8 minutes.

2. Add sugar and sauté until sugar is dissolved, for 2 minutes.

3. Add 3 cups (750 mL) water. Cover and bring to a boil. Reduce heat to low and simmer, uncovered, stirring periodically, until wheat is soft and the consistency of oatmeal, 10 to 12 minutes. Add more hot water if too thick. Serve hot.

Serves 6 to 8

A nourishing breakfast cereal, this is a popular breakfast dish in Punjabi homes.

Atta
Basic Whole Wheat Dough

3 cups	chapati flour (atta) (see Tip, right)	750 mL
½ tsp	salt	2 mL
2 tbsp	oil	25 mL
¾ to 1 cup	lukewarm water (approx.)	175 to 250 mL

Food processor method

1. In a food processor with a metal blade, combine flour and salt. Process for 5 seconds. Drizzle in oil. With machine running, pour in ¾ cup (175 mL) lukewarm water in a steady stream for 30 seconds. Scrape down sides of bowl. Gradually drizzle in more of the water in 3 or 4 additions, stopping every 20 seconds to check consistency of dough.

2. Add just enough water until dough sticks together when pinched between thumb and forefinger. Process until dough forms a ball. Knead for 1 minute longer and turn off motor. The dough should be smooth and soft. Transfer dough to work surface and pat until perfectly smooth. Place in a bowl, cover with a towel and let rest away from heat for at least 30 minutes. (The dough can be made a day ahead and stored in the refrigerator in an airtight container. Let come to room temperature before using.)

Hand method

1. Sift flour and salt onto a large flat pizza pan. Drizzle oil over top and mix with fingertips. Make a well in the center and add lukewarm water, a little at a time, while mixing the flour from the sides into the center. Use a circular motion with your fingers to incorporate all the flour. When you have added enough water to form a crumbly mixture, work it into a smooth dough. Add more water if necessary, a little at a time, kneading until dough is soft and smooth. Place in a bowl, cover with a towel and let rest for 30 minutes. (The dough can be made a day ahead and stored in the refrigerator in an airtight container. Let come to room temperature before using.)

Makes enough dough for 16 chapatis or 10 parathas

This simplest of doughs, made from finely milled whole wheat, is the basis of a variety of everyday Indian breads. Chapati, also called roti *(though that is also the generic word for all breads), is made daily in Indian homes, and parathas — both plain and stuffed — are very popular, too.*

Tip

Chapati flour (*atta*) is whole wheat flour that has been very finely milled. Whole wheat flour from the supermarkets or health food stores is coarsely ground in comparison and lacks the natural sweetness, it is not suitable for chapatis. Chapati flour is available prepackaged in Indian grocery stores.

Whole Wheat Griddle Bread

Makes 16

Chapati flour is very finely milled whole wheat. Chapati is the everyday bread of Indians, made daily in home kitchens.

Tips

The correct temperature of the griddle is very important. If too hot, the chapati will burn before it cooks through. If too cold, it will take too long to brown and will become dry and tough.

Chapatis can be made ahead, wrapped in foil and stored in the refrigerator for several days or frozen for several weeks. To reheat, place a stack of 4 in the microwave, covered, for 40 to 45 seconds. Or wrap in foil and warm in a 250°F (120° C) oven for 6 to 8 minutes.

1	recipe Basic Whole Wheat Dough (Atta) (see recipe, page 143)	1
	Chapati flour (atta) for dusting	
¼ cup	oil or melted ghee	50 mL

1. On a clean surface, knead dough for 2 or 3 minutes. Roll into 1½ inch (4 cm) thick rope. Pinch off 1-inch (2.5 cm) sections and roll into small balls. Place on a plate and cover with a damp towel.

2. Heat a dry nonstick griddle or heavy skillet over medium-high heat for about 5 minutes.

3. Keep chapati flour in a small dish nearby. Sprinkle generous pinch on work surface and spread into a circle with your hand. Flatten ball of dough between your palms to ½-inch (1 cm) thick circle (chapati). Lift a few times while rolling, sprinkling with just a hint of flour so chapati does not stick to surface.

4. Place chapati on hot dry griddle and cook for 1 minute. Flip and make sure some brown spots have appeared on cooked surface. If not, increase heat slightly. Cook other side for 30 to 40 seconds, pressing down on edges with crumpled paper towel. There should be a few brown spots on both sides. Transfer to a piece of foil or dish towel and rub surface quickly with ¼ tsp (1 mL) oil. Repeat with remaining dough, keeping cooked chapatis covered and warm.

Paratha
Whole Wheat Griddle-Fried Bread

1	recipe Basic Whole Wheat Dough (Atta) (see recipe, page 143)	1
1/3 cup	oil, divided	75 mL
	Chapati flour (atta) for dusting	

1. Keep oil in a bowl near griddle, with a pastry brush at hand. Heat a dry nonstick griddle or heavy skillet over medium heat for 5 minutes.

2. Knead dough briefly. Divide into 10 portions and roll into balls. Keep covered and away from heat.

3. Working with one ball at a time, flatten between palms into 1/2-inch (1 cm) thick circle. Dust generously with flour and shake off excess. Place on work surface and use a rolling pin (with a light touch) to roll out into a long oval, about 8 by 4 inches (20 by 10 cm). Brush generously with some of the oil. Place forefinger and thumb on the outer long edge of oval and bring sides together to make a bow-tie shape. Each side of bow tie will roughly be a circle. With pinched section as a hinge, fold one circle over other circle, oiled sides together, to form single circle. Flatten lightly. Brush top with some of the oil and fold to make half-circle. Brush top with some of the oil and fold half-circle in half to make quarter-circle. Roll out to 1/8-inch (0.25 cm) thickness. Paratha will not be circular.

4. Place paratha on griddle and cook, patting down firmly, for 2 minutes and flip. There should be brown spots. Cook other side for 1 minute, making sure there are brown spots. Brush top generously with oil and flip again. Cook, pressing down with a spatula, so oil on underside fries paratha for about 1 minute. Brush top with oil and flip and cook in the same manner. When paratha is cooked through, transfer to a dish and keep warm. Repeat with remaining dough and oil.

Makes 10

Everyone loves a paratha, plain or stuffed. The dough is the same as for chapati, but parathas are flaky. They are ideal to pack for a picnic, a school lunch or, as Indians love to do, for a train journey.

Tip

Adjust heat to cook each paratha in about 4 minutes. If it takes longer, parathas will become stiff. The layers of oil separate the dough and make this bread soft on the inside and crisp and lightly browned on the outside. Parathas can be made several hours ahead, wrapped in foil when cool and refrigerated for up to 2 days or frozen for up to 3 months. Reheat refrigerated parathas in 250°F (120°C) oven until heated through, about 10 minutes.

Garlic, Mint and Crispy Onion Parathas

Makes 8

Although this is not a traditional recipe, the flavors are so exciting I felt compelled to include it. Parathas, the traditional griddle-fried flatbreads of the north, lend themselves to a variety of seasonings.

❧

Tip

The dough can be wrapped in plastic and refrigerated for up to 24 hours. Return to room temperature before proceeding with recipe. The parathas can be wrapped and refrigerated for up to 1 week. Reheat in microwave.

1 tbsp	oil	15 mL
¼ cup	coarsely chopped garlic	50 mL
2 cups	chapati flour (atta)	500 mL
2 cups	loosely packed mint leaves, chopped	500 mL
1 cup	crispy fried onions (see Tip, page 101)	250 mL
2 tbsp	minced green chiles, preferably serranos	25 mL
1 tsp	salt or to taste	5 mL
¼ cup	oil	50 mL
	Chapati flour (atta) for dusting	

1. In a skillet, heat 1 tbsp (15 mL) oil over medium heat. Add garlic and sauté until golden, about 2 minutes.

2. Transfer garlic with any oil in skillet to a food processor. Add flour, mint, crispy onions, chiles and salt and pulse 3 times to combine. With motor running, slowly pour ¼ cup (50 mL) water (more if needed) through feed tube until mixture begins to come together. Process for 30 seconds and add a little more water if mixture does not form a dough. Scrape sides and bottom of bowl and continue to process until smooth dough forms, about 2 minutes. Transfer to a work surface and knead for 1 minute by hand, oiling hands lightly if dough is sticky. Form into a ball. Place in bowl and cover with a towel and let rest away from heat for 1 hour.

3. Heat skillet over medium-high heat for 3 to 4 minutes. In small separate dishes, place ¼ cup (50 mL) oil and flour near the work surface.

4. Knead dough for 2 minutes. Divide into 6 portions. Roll each into a ball. Keep covered, away from heat. Sprinkle work surface lightly with flour. Spread with palm into a large circle. Working with one ball of dough at a time, flatten into a ½-inch (1 cm) thick disk. Place on floured surface and roll into a long oval, about 8 by 4 inches, (20 by 10 cm), lifting dough and dusting as necessary. Spread ½ tsp (2 mL) oil on entire surface. Place thumb and forefinger on the outer long edge of oval and bring sides together to make a bow-tie shape. Fold oiled sides together at pinched center to make a circle. Sprinkle board lightly with more flour. Roll out to a 6-inch (15 cm) circle, lifting circle periodically as you roll and dusting surface with flour as necessary to prevent sticking. Spread ½ tsp (2 mL) oil over top. Fold over into a half-circle. Spread a few drops oil and fold over to a quarter-circle. Roll layered dough until ⅛ inch (0.5) thick. It will not be a circle. Set aside, but do not allow circles (parathas) to touch.

5. Cook on heated skillet until brown spots appear, 1 to 1½ minutes. Flip over and spread ½ tsp (2 mL) oil over top. Flip again and oil top, pressing down with spatula for 30 seconds. Both sides should have crisp brown areas. Keep warm and cook remaining parathas in the same way.

Puri

Whole Wheat Puffed Bread

- *Wok or deep-tryer*
- *Candy/deep-fry thermometer*

	Oil for deep-frying	
1	recipe Basic Whole Wheat Dough (Atta) (see recipe, page 143)	1
	Chapati flour (atta) for dusting	

1. In a wok or deep-fryer, heat oil to 350°F (180°C).
2. Meanwhile, knead dough briefly. Divide dough in half. Keep one half covered. Sprinkle work surface lightly with flour and roll dough as thinly as possible. With a cookie cutter (or lid of a jar about 3 or 4 inches /7.5 to 10 cm in diameter), cut out circles (puris). Slip into hot oil, one at a time. Tap top of puri rapidly with a large-holed strainer; within seconds it will begin to puff up (see Tip, right). Turn over once, and fry for 10 seconds more. Remove with strainer and drain on paper towels. Repeat with remaining dough. Serve hot.

Makes 12 to 14 puris

Puri is a magical bread, puffed and filled with steam. Light as a feather, it almost melts in your mouth when freshly made. Sadly, puris deflate quickly, and though still good, the deflated ones cannot compare with just-made puris. A popular everyday bread, it is wonderful for scooping up food.

Tip

Puris deflate almost immediately. The tapping action is important or else they will not inflate with steam but remain flat.

Gobi Paratha
Cauliflower-Stuffed Griddle-Fried Bread

| 1 | recipe Basic Whole Wheat Dough (Atta) (see recipe, page 143) | 1 |

Stuffing

1½ cups	grated cauliflower	375 mL
3 tbsp	cilantro, chopped	45 mL
2 tsp	grated or minced peeled gingerroot	10 mL
1 tsp	minced green chiles, preferably serranos	5 mL
1 tsp	salt or to taste	5 mL
¾ tsp	garam masala	4 mL
¾ tsp	cayenne pepper or to taste	4 mL
3 tbsp	oil	45 mL
	Chapati flour (atta) for dusting	

Makes 10

Cauliflower is one of the most popular vegetables in the north — mild, crunchy and snow white. Gobi parathas *are popular in school and office lunch boxes and make a delicious light lunch accompanied with plain yogurt and spicy pickle.*

1. Prepare Basic Whole Wheat Dough (Atta). While it rests, prepare stuffing.

2. *Stuffing:* In a bowl, mix together cauliflower, cilantro, ginger, chiles, salt, garam masala and cayenne. Divide stuffing into 10 portions.

3. Knead dough briefly. Place oil in a bowl with a pastry brush and set aside by the griddle.

4. Line a baking sheet with foil. Divide dough into 10 portions. Roll each into a ball. Place in a bowl, cover and set aside, away from heat. Working with one ball at a time, flatten to shape the cup of your palm to a circle about 4 inches (10 cm) in diameter. Place one portion of the stuffing in the center, then pull dough gently to cover filling and make a ball. Seal well and flatten between your palms into a disk, keeping seam on one side. Meanwhile, preheat a dry nonstick griddle or heavy skillet over medium-high heat for 5 minutes.

5. Dust disk with flour. With seam side down, roll out gently into ¼-inch (0.5 cm) thick circle. Make all parathas and lay on prepared sheet, without touching. Cook, one at a time, on griddle until brown spots form, 2 to 3 minutes. Flip and brush cooked side with oil. Cook, pressing down with spatula, until brown spots appear on other side, adjusting heat as necessary to prevent burning, 1½ to 2 minutes. Press edges firmly to cook thoroughly. Flip and pressing with spatula, fry oiled side for 1 minute. Brush other side with oil, flip and fry in same manner. Both sides should be crisp and brown. Transfer to a dish and keep warm. Repeat with remaining parathas.

Tips

Do not hesitate to dust parathas with flour while rolling to prevent sticking and tearing dough. If necessary, press edges gently with fingers to make as thin as possible, to enable edges to cook through.

Parathas can be refrigerated when cool and wrapped in foil for up to 4 days or frozen for up to 3 months. Reheat refrigerated parathas, wrapped in foil, in 250°F (120°C) oven for 10 minutes and frozen parathas for 20 minutes or until heated through.

Aloo ki Roti

Griddle-Cooked Potato Bread

Makes 6

Soft and luscious, these griddle-cooked breads are a favorite at my house. They are wonderful for brunch with scrambled eggs and a spicy chutney. And they are equally wonderful to take on a picnic.

8 oz	all-purpose or russet potatoes (about 2)	250 g
½ cup	all-purpose flour	125 mL
4 tsp	minced green chiles, preferably serranos	20 mL
2 tbsp	cilantro, chopped	25 mL
1½ tsp	mango powder (amchur)	7 mL
1 tsp	hot pepper flakes	5 mL
1 tsp	salt or to taste	5 mL
¾ tsp	cumin seeds	4 mL
¾ tsp	crushed coriander seeds	4 mL
¼ cup	oil or melted ghee, divided	50 mL
	All-purpose flour for dusting	

1. In a saucepan of boiling water, cook whole potatoes until tender, 20 to 25 minutes. Drain. When cool enough to handle but still warm, peel and mash. Sprinkle in flour, chiles, cilantro, mango powder, pepper flakes, salt, cumin and coriander. Mix well with fingertips. Drizzle 1½ tbsp (22 mL) of the oil over top and continue to mix by hand until dough is soft and pliable. Divide into 6 portions. Roll into balls. Place in a bowl, cover with a towel and set aside, away from heat.

2. Lightly dust work surface with flour. Working with one ball at a time, flatten into a 2-inch (5 cm) round patty. Roll out into ¼-inch (0.5 cm) thick circle (roti), lifting and turning dough over to make sure it doesn't stick. Dust lightly with additional flour, if necessary. Repeat process with remaining dough. Set aside, without allowing edges to touch.

3. Heat nonstick griddle or heavy skillet over medium-high heat until a drop of water flicked on it sizzles, 2 to 3 minutes. Carefully transfer a bread (roti) to griddle and drizzle ¼ tsp (1 mL) of the oil around edges, tilting griddle to allow oil to run under roti. Cook until brown spots appear, about 1½ minutes. Turn over and repeat process with ¼ tsp (1 mL) of oil. Cook until brown spots appear, about 1 minute. Transfer to a serving plate and keep warm. Repeat with remaining rotis and oil. Serve with curry or a side dish.

Missi Roti

1 cup	chapati flour (atta)	250 mL
1 cup	chickpea flour (besan)	250 mL
½ tsp	salt	2 mL
2 tsp	oil	10 mL
	Chapati flour (atta) for dusting	

1. In a food processor, pulse together chapati and chickpea flours, salt and oil. With motor running, slowly pour in enough water, about ⅓ cup (75 mL), through feed tube to make a smooth dough. (Dough will be a little stiff.) Process for 1 minute more. Lightly oil hands and knead dough 1 minute by hand. Form into a ball. Cover with a towel and let rest for 30 minutes.

2. Heat a heavy skillet over medium heat for 5 minutes. Meanwhile, knead dough once more, for 2 minutes. Divide into 8 equal portions. Roll each into a ball. Cover and set aside, away from heat.

3. Working with one ball at a time, flatten between your palms into a ½-inch (1 cm) thick disk. Sprinkle ½ tsp (2 mL) flour on work surface and spread with hand. Place disk on top and roll out into a 7- to 8-inch (17.5 to 20 cm) circle, frequently rotating dough one-quarter turn and dusting with more flour as necessary to prevent sticking. Transfer to skillet and cook until puffy spots appear, 1½ minutes. Flip and cook other side, pressing down on the edges with a spatula, for 1 minute. Very lightly oil both sides of roti and keep warm. Repeat with remaining rotis.

Makes 8

This is one of the most popular North Indian breads. The dough can be used as a base for the addition of chopped onion, chiles and spices. Alter the seasonings to suit your palate.

Tip
Wrap rotis tightly in foil, place in resealable plastic bag and refrigerate for up to 4 days or freeze for up to 3 months. Reheat in microwave before serving.

Moongri
Millet, Rice and Lentil Bread

Makes 18

This wonderful earthy griddle-baked bread is from Rajasthan. Delicious and easy to prepare, it can be made ahead and reheated or served at room temperature. It makes a nutritious light lunch with vegetables and yogurt.

❧

½ cup	yellow mung beans (yellow mung dal)	125 mL
½ cup	long-grain white rice	125 mL
1 ½ cups	millet flour (bajri flour)	375 mL
2 tbsp	minced green chiles, preferably serranos	25 mL
1 tsp	coriander powder	5 mL
¾ tsp	cumin powder	4 mL
½ tsp	turmeric	2 mL
1 ½ tsp	salt or to taste	7 mL
3 to 4 tbsp	oil	45 to 60 mL

1. Clean and pick through dal for any small stones and grit. Place rice and dal in a bowl with plenty of cold water and swish vigorously with fingers. Drain. Repeat 4 or 5 times until water is fairly clear. Cover with 3 to 4 inches (7.5 to 10 cm) cold water and set aside to soak for at least 30 minutes.

2. Drain rice mixture. Place in a saucepan and add 1½ cups (375 mL) cold water. Bring to a boil over high heat. Skim any froth off top. Reduce heat and simmer, partially covered, until rice and dal are soft and mushy, 10 to 12 minutes. (The mixture should be moist.) Let cool completely.

3. Transfer mixture to a bowl. Add millet flour, chiles, coriander, cumin, salt and turmeric. Knead until dough is smooth and pliable enough to roll. If mixture is too dry, add a few tablespoons water to make dough. Divide into 18 pieces and roll each into a ball. Cover and set aside away from heat.

4. Heat a nonstick griddle or heavy skillet over medium-low heat for 2 to 3 minutes. Working with one ball at a time, flatten to a thick disk between palms and transfer to a piece of foil. Continue to press or roll into a 4- to 5-inch (10 to 12.5 cm) circle. Invert onto griddle. Drizzle ¼ tsp (1 mL) of the oil around outer edges of bread. Shake pan to allow oil to flow under bread. Cook for 1 minute. Flip, drizzle ¼ tsp (1 mL) of the oil around edges again. Shake pan. Drizzle a few more drops of oil on top. Press down on bread with spatula. Cook for 1 minute. Transfer to a dish and keep warm. Repeat with remaining dough and oil.

Roat
Garhwali Jaggery Bread

¾ cup	jaggery (gur)	175 mL
1⅔ cups	chapati flour (atta)	400 mL
¾ tsp	fennel seeds (saunf), powdered	4 mL
½ tsp	cardamom seeds, ground to a powder	2 mL
¼ cup	cold milk	50 mL
5 tbsp	ghee (approx.), divided	75 mL

1. In a small saucepan, combine jaggery with ½ cup (125 mL) water and melt over low heat. Let cool.

2. In a bowl, combine flour, fennel and cardamom and mix with fingertips. Drizzle in milk and add 1 tbsp (15 mL) of the ghee. Mix until a crumbly dough forms. Make a well in the center and gradually add jaggery mixture and knead for 2 minutes until a smooth, stiff dough forms. Cover and set aside for 10 minutes.

3. Divide dough into 8 equal portions. Roll each into a ball. Place in a bowl, cover and set aside, away from heat.

4. Heat a skillet over medium heat for 5 minutes.

5. Working with one ball at a time, flatten into a disk ½-inch (1 cm) thick. On a lightly floured surface, roll into a circle about 4 to 4½ inches (10 to 12 cm) in diameter. Spread 1 tsp (5 mL) of the ghee in center of heated skillet. Add dough and cook until brown spots appear, about 2 minutes. Flip and spread about 2 tsp (10 mL) ghee around edges, shaking pan to allow it to flow under bread. Fry, pressing down gently with spatula, until brown, 1 to 2 minutes. Repeat with remaining dough and ghee.

Makes 8

These sweet flatbreads from Garhwal in Uttarakhand state are a tradition at wedding feasts and festive occasions. They are easy to make and, although it's not traditional, are wonderful with a cup of tea or coffee.

Tip
When cool, store in an airtight container at room temperature for up to 1 week.

Makki ki Roti

Punjabi Griddle-Baked Corn Bread

2 cups	very fine ground cornmeal (see Tips, left)	500 mL
¾ tsp	salt or to taste	4 mL
2 to 3 tbsp	ghee or oil for brushing	25 to 45 mL

Makes 8

In winter, one of the favorite foods of Punjabis is Sarson ka Saag aur Makki ki Roti — *Mustard Greens and Corn Bread — washed down with tall glasses of thick cumin-laced buttermilk. This recipe is very similar to one from the southeastern United States, except for the glasses of buttermilk.*

Tips

Indian cornmeal has a finer texture and is easier to handle. Punjabis believe that fresh ground corn makes the best rotis and some go so far as to have it custom ground when they plan to make the corn bread.

Leftover rotis can be reheated in the microwave. Do not store for more than 1 day, as bread hardens.

1. Prepare corn mixture just before cooking. (The dough should not be prepared ahead and set aside.)

2. In a shallow bowl, mix together cornmeal and salt. Gradually add about 1 cup (250 mL) hot water and make a smooth dough-like mix. Knead for 1 minute. Divide dough into 8 portions.

3. Heat a dry skillet or nonstick griddle over medium-high heat.

4. Place an 8-inch (20 cm) piece of foil on a work surface. Lift one portion of dough and pat into a ½-inch (1 cm) thick disk. Place disk on foil and pat into a 3½- to 4-inch (9 to 10 cm) circle. Pick up the foil with disk and carefully invert into skillet. Peel off foil.

5. Cover and cook until brown spots appear on bottom, about 2 minutes. Flip and cook second side, pressing down on edges to cook partially, about 1 minute. Spread ½ tsp (2 mL) of ghee on cooked side. Flip again when second side has a few brown spots, about 1 minute. Spread ½ tsp (2 mL) of ghee on second side. Flip again and cook for 30 seconds. Transfer to a dish and spread with a little more ghee and keep warm.

6. Continuing with remaining rotis, taking care not to leave on griddle too long, as rotis will get tough and hard. Serve warm with Punjabi Mustard Greens (see recipe, page 319).

Naan

- *2 nonstick baking sheets*

2½ cups	all-purpose flour	625 mL
2 tsp	granulated sugar	10 mL
1 tsp	baking powder	5 mL
1 tsp	salt	5 mL
6 tbsp	ghee or softened butter, divided	90 mL
1	egg, lightly beaten	1
¾ cup	milk (approx.)	175 mL

1. In a food processor, pulse together flour, sugar, baking powder and salt. Add 2½ tbsp (32 mL) of the ghee and egg and pulse again. With processor running, gradually pour in milk through feed tube and process until dough comes together. Process for 1 minute more. Knead bread for 1 minute. Dough should be very soft and smooth. Form into a ball, cover with a towel and set aside for 1 hour.

2. Preheat oven to 400°F (200°C).

3. Knead dough for 2 minutes. Divide into 5 portions and roll into balls. Cover with a towel. Working with one ball at a time, pat dough into a disk and roll into an oval, about 8 by 4 inches (20 by 10 cm). Gently pull one end to make into a teardrop shape. Transfer to baking sheet. Make remaining naans and place on baking sheet. Bake in preheated oven for 12 minutes. Flip and cook other side until cooked through, for 5 minutes. Remove from oven and brush generously with remaining ghee. Serve immediately.

Makes 5

In the West, naan bread is considered to be the daily bread of Indians. Nothing could be further from the truth. It requires the intense heat of a tandoor, the clay oven you may have seen in Indian restaurants but that is not found in homes. It is one amongst hundreds of mouthwatering breads made in the north but is not a bread made in home kitchens. Although no recipe for homemade naan comes close to the restaurant version, my recipe is simple and a reasonable substitute.

Bhatura

- *Wok or deep-fryer*
- *Candy/deep-fry thermometer*

3 cups	self-rising flour	750 mL
¾ tsp	salt or to taste	4 mL
1 cup	buttermilk (approx.)	250 mL
	Oil for deep-frying	
2 to 3 tbsp	all-purpose flour	25 to 45 mL

1. In a bowl, combine flour and salt. Gradually add buttermilk to make a soft, pliable dough. Add more buttermilk if dough is too dry, 1 tbsp (15 mL) at a time. Knead, like bread dough, until smooth and elastic, 5 to 7 minutes. Roll into a ball and return to bowl. Cover loosely with a towel and let rest in a warm place for 3 to 4 hours.

2. In a wok or deep-fryer, heat oil to 375°F (190°C).

3. Punch dough down and knead again for 2 minutes. Divide into 12 equal portions. Roll each portion into balls. Work with one ball at a time, keeping remaining dough covered. Flatten ball between your palms into a disk ½ inch (1 cm) thick. Place on a lightly floured board. Roll into a circle ⅛ inch (0.25 cm) thick. Slip into hot oil. Splash top of bhatura with oil from the pan and almost instantly it will begin to puff. Cook for 1 minute. Turn over once and cook for 1 minute more. Remove with a large-holed strainer and drain on paper towels. Continue with remaining bhaturas.

4. Serve with Blackened Chickpeas with Shredded Ginger (see recipe, page 104). This is a classic combination, known as *Chole Bhatura*.

Makes 12

This large deep-fried puffy bread is a Punjabi favorite. It is served with chole, *a spicy chickpea preparation. The combination of* chole/bhatura *is a popular roadside snack and is a must at all northern truck stops, known as* dhabbas. *Dhabba food is earthy soul food, life-sustaining stuff that is scrumptious and inexpensive.*

Tip

Bhaturas will not brown. They remain pale. When cool, stack 5 or 6 together and wrap in foil. Store at room temperature for 1 day or refrigerate for up to 3 days. Reheat in a 350°F (180°C) oven for 10 minutes.

Assamese Khichri

Serves 6 to 8

This is a one-dish vegetarian meal and is served at lunch or dinner with a fried appetizer, such as deep-fried eggplant, and tasty pickle as accompaniments. I find it is delicious with a piece of fried or grilled fish, or fried shrimp. Feel free to substitute any vegetables of your choice.

3 tbsp	red lentils (masoor dal)	45 mL
3 tbsp	yellow mung beans (yellow mung dal)	45 mL
1 cup	long-grain white rice	250 mL
3 tbsp	ghee or oil, divided	45 mL
2	bay leaves	2
4	whole cloves, crushed	4
2	green cardamom pods, cracked open	2
1	piece cinnamon, 1 inch (2.5 cm) long, crushed	1
1 cup	chopped onions	250 mL
6	small potatoes (any variety), cut in half, or 2 medium potatoes, quartered	6
½ cup	chopped green beans (1-inch/2.5 cm pieces)	125 mL
½ cup	frozen green peas, thawed	125 mL
1½ tbsp	minced green chiles, preferably serranos	22 mL
1 tbsp	minced peeled gingerroot	15 mL
3	cloves garlic, smashed	3
2 tsp	salt or to taste	10 mL
½ tsp	turmeric	2 mL

1. Clean and pick through masoor and mung dals for any small stones and grit. Rinse several times in cold water. Place rice and dals in a large bowl with plenty of cold water and swish vigorously with fingers. Drain. Repeat 4 or 5 times until water is fairly clear. Cover with 3 to 4 inches (7.5 to 10 cm) cold water and set aside to soak for 15 minutes.

2. In a saucepan, heat 1½ tbsp (22 mL) of the ghee over medium heat. Add bay leaves and sauté for 30 seconds. Add cloves, cardamom and cinnamon and sauté for 30 seconds. Add onions and sauté until softened, 5 to 6 minutes. Drain rice mixture and add to saucepan. Add potatoes, green beans, peas, chiles, ginger, garlic, salt and turmeric. Mix well and sauté for 2 minutes.

3. Add 3½ cups (875 mL) fresh water. Cover and bring to a boil over high heat. Reduce heat as low as possible and cook, covered, without peeking, for 25 minutes.

4. Remove from heat. Drizzle remaining ghee over warm rice. Set lid slightly ajar to allow steam to escape. Let rest for 5 minutes. Gently fluff with fork and carefully spoon onto platter to serve.

Bengali Khichri

1 cup	yellow mung beans (yellow mung dal)	250 mL
¾ cup	long-grain white rice	175 mL
2 tbsp	ghee, divided	25 mL
1 tsp	cumin seeds	5 mL
1 cup	frozen peas, thawed	250 mL
1½ tbsp	minced peeled gingerroot	22 mL
2	bay leaves	2
1½ tsp	salt	7 mL
½ tsp	granulated sugar	2 mL
1 tbsp	minced green chiles, preferably serranos, optional	15 mL

Serves 6 to 8

Khichri is the ultimate comfort food for all Indians. It is a combination of rice and lentils cooked together with enough water to make them soft, resembling risotto. Other ingredients and seasonings vary regionally.

1. Clean and pick through dal for any small stones and grit. Rinse several times in cold water. Drain and spread on dishtowel to dry for 30 minutes or for up to 2 hours.

2. Place rice in a bowl with plenty of cold water and swish vigorously with fingers. Drain. Repeat 4 or 5 times until water is fairly clear. Cover with 3 to 4 inches (7.5 to 10 cm) cold water and set aside to soak for at least 15 minutes or for up to 2 hours.

3. Heat a wok over medium heat and add mung beans. Toast, stirring continuously, until beans turn golden, 8 to 10 minutes. Remove from heat.

4. In a saucepan, heat 1 tbsp (15 mL) of the ghee. Add cumin and sauté for 1 minute. Drain rice and add to pan. Add mung beans and sauté for 1 minute. Add 4 cups (1 L) fresh water. Add peas, ginger, bay leaves, salt and sugar. Cover and bring to a boil over high heat. Reduce heat to low and cook, stirring once, until soft and the consistency of risotto, 20 to 25 minutes.

5. Drizzle remaining 1 tbsp (15 mL) of ghee over top. Sprinkle with chiles, if desired, or pass at table.

Luchi

Makes 16

These puris (balloon breads) are a Bengali favorite and are made of all-purpose flour instead of the whole wheat flour used in the rest of India. They have to be eaten freshly made, as they lose their texture and turn hard, if made ahead.

Tip
The dough can be made a day ahead and stored in the refrigerator in an airtight container. Bring to room temperature before using.

- *Wok*
- *Candy/deep-fry thermometer*

1 ½ cups	all-purpose flour	375 mL
¼ tsp	salt	1 mL
1 tsp	melted ghee or oil	5 mL
	All-purpose flour for dusting	
	Oil for deep-frying	

Food processor method

1. In a food processor, combine flour and salt. Process for 5 seconds. Drizzle in ghee. With processor running, pour in ⅓ cup (75 mL) water in a steady stream through feed tube and process for 30 seconds. Scrape down sides of bowl. Gradually drizzle in more of the water in 3 or 4 additions, stopping every 20 seconds to check consistency of dough. Add just enough water until dough sticks together when pinched between thumb and forefinger. Process until dough forms a ball. Process for 1 minute longer to knead. The dough should be smooth and soft. Transfer dough to a clean work surface and pat gently until perfectly smooth. Place in a bowl, cover with a towel and let rest away from the heat for at least 30 minutes. Proceed with Step 2 below.

Hand method

1. Sift flour and salt onto a large flat pan, such as a pizza pan. Make a well in the center and add lukewarm water, a little at a time, while mixing the flour from the sides into the center. Use a circular motion with your fingers to incorporate all the flour. Add the ghee. When you have added enough water to form a crumbly mixture, work it into a smooth dough. Add more water if the dough won't hold together. Place in a bowl, cover with a towel and let rest away from heat for at least 30 minutes.

2. In a wok, heat oil to 350°F (180°C). Meanwhile, knead dough briefly. Divide into 16 portions. Roll each into a ball and keep covered. Working with one ball at a time, roll as thinly as possible into a circle, lifting dough periodically and dusting very lightly with flour to prevent sticking. Slip into hot oil, one at a time. Tap top of luchi briskly with back of slotted spoon and in a few seconds it will begin to puff up. Turn over once and fry for 20 seconds to cook through. Remove with a large-holed strainer and drain on paper towels. Repeat with remaining dough. Serve hot.

Puliysadam
Tamarind Rice

1 cup	long-grain white rice	250 mL
3 tbsp	oil, divided	45 mL
1 ¼ tsp	salt	6 mL
¾ tsp	coriander seeds	4 mL
¾ tsp	split white lentils (urad dal)	4 mL
3	dried Indian red chiles, divided	3
½ tsp	dark mustard seeds	2 mL
¼ tsp	each asafetida and fenugreek seeds	1 mL
½ tsp	turmeric	2 mL
5 tbsp	unsalted Thai tamarind purée	75 mL
¼ cup	raw cashews	50 mL
1 tsp	split yellow peas (channa dal)	5 mL
1	sprig fresh curry leaves, stripped	1
1 tbsp	ghee, optional	15 mL

Serves 6 to 8

Rice dishes such as this are served throughout South India. Often served just by itself, with crunchy papadums as an accompaniment, I like to serve it with a lightly spiced chicken or meat curry.

1. Place rice in a bowl with plenty of cold water and swish vigorously with fingers. Drain. Repeat until water is fairly clear. Cover with 4 inches (10 cm) cold water and set aside to soak for 10 minutes.

2. In a saucepan, heat 1 tsp (15 mL) of the oil over medium-high heat. Drain rice and add to saucepan. Mix well and sauté for 1 minute. Add 1¾ cups (425 mL) fresh water and salt. Cover and bring to a boil over high heat. Reduce heat as low as possible and cook, covered with a tight-fitting lid, without peeking, for 20 minutes. Remove from heat and set lid slightly ajar to let steam escape and let rest for 5 minutes. Gently fluff with a fork and carefully spoon into a shallow pan. Spread to cool slightly.

3. In a dry skillet over medium heat, toast coriander, urad dal and 1 red chile, broken in pieces, stirring constantly, until aromatic, about 3 minutes. Immediately transfer to a bowl and let cool slightly. In a spice grinder, grind to a powder. Sprinkle over cooked rice in pan.

4. In a saucepan, heat 2 tsp (10 mL) of oil over high heat until a couple of mustard seeds thrown in start to sputter. Add all mustard seeds and cover quickly. When the seeds stop popping, in a few seconds, uncover, reduce heat to medium and add asafetida, fenugreek and remaining red chiles, broken in half. Add turmeric and sauté for 30 seconds. Add tamarind and ¼ cup (50 mL) water. Reduce heat to low and simmer until thickened, about 3 minutes. Pour over rice.

5. In a skillet, heat remaining oil over medium heat. Add cashews and channa dal and sauté until golden, about 2 minutes. Add curry leaves and sauté for 20 seconds. Pour over rice. Mix gently, taking care rice does not get mushy. Melt ghee, if using, and drizzle over rice.

South Indian Vegetable Rice

Serves 8

Rice reigns supreme in South India and is served at every meal. This dish is typical of the pulaos of the region. You can substitute the choice of vegetables with any others that you prefer.

Tips

This a wonderful one-dish meal to take on a picnic or to serve for a light lunch with yogurt and papadums.

Although basmati rice does not grow in the area, it is used in elaborate pulaos and biriyanis of the South.

• *Saucepan with tight-fitting lid*

1 1/2 cups	long-grain white rice, preferably basmati	375 mL
3 tbsp	oil, divided	45 mL
2 tsp	salt or to taste, divided	10 mL
1 tsp	dark mustard seeds	5 mL
2 tsp	split white lentils (urad dal)	10 mL
2 tsp	split yellow peas (channa dal)	10 mL
2	green chiles, preferably serranos, slit lengthwise 1/2 inch (1 cm) from stem end	2
1 tbsp	minced peeled gingerroot	15 mL
3	sprigs fresh curry leaves, stripped (30 to 40 leaves)	3
2 cups	chopped onions	500 mL
1 tbsp	sambhar powder	15 mL
1/2 tsp	turmeric	2 mL
3	bell peppers, green or combination of colors, sliced into thin strips	3
2	medium potatoes (any variety), cut into 3-by 1-inch (7.5 by 2.5 cm) long strips	2
3	tomatoes, cut into wedges	3
1 cup	frozen peas, thawed	250 mL
1/2 cup	cilantro leaves, chopped, divided	125 mL
1/4 cup	freshly squeezed lime or lemon juice	50 mL

1. Place rice in a large bowl with plenty of cold water and swish vigorously with fingers. Drain. Repeat 4 or 5 times until water is fairly clear. Cover with 3 to 4 inches (7.5 to 10 cm) cold water and set aside to soak for at least 15 minutes.

2. In a saucepan, heat 2 tsp (10 mL) of the oil over medium-high heat. Drain rice and add to saucepan. Mix well and sauté for 1 minute. Add 1 1/2 cups (375 mL) fresh water and 1 tsp (5 mL) of the salt. Cover and bring to a boil over high heat. Reduce heat as low as possible, cover with a tight-fitting lid and cook, without peeking, for 25 minutes. Remove from heat and set lid slightly ajar to let steam escape and let rest for 5 minutes. Fluff gently with a fork.

3. Meanwhile, in a large saucepan, heat remaining oil until a couple of mustard seeds thrown in start to sputter. Add all the mustard seeds and cover quickly. When the seeds stop popping, in a few seconds, uncover, reduce heat to medium and add urad and channa dals and sauté until golden, about 1 minute. Add chiles, ginger and curry leaves and sauté for 1 minute.

4. Add onions and sauté until brown, about 10 minutes. Add sambhar powder and turmeric and cook for 2 minutes.

5. Add bell peppers and sauté for 2 minutes. Add potatoes and tomatoes and continue to sauté until slightly soft, about 5 minutes. Add peas, remaining salt and $1/2$ cup (125 mL) water. Cover and simmer until vegetables are cooked and moisture is absorbed, 5 to 8 minutes. Remove from heat and stir in $1/4$ cup (50 mL) of the cilantro and lime juice.

6. Divide rice and vegetables into 2 portions each. Lightly mix one portion of rice with vegetables, taking care not to mush the mixture. Repeat with the remaining rice and vegetables. Combine the 2 mixtures and spread on a platter to serve. Garnish with remaining cilantro.

Kerala Lamb Biriyani

This is the classic biriyani of the Muslims (Mophlas) of Kerala. Their cuisine is a happy blend of southern seasonings with Moghul overtones. Biriyani is arguably the most elaborate of Indian rice dishes and is reserved for special occasions. This would traditionally be made with cabrito (young goat), but lamb is a good substitute. The only accompaniment is a yogurt salad of thinly sliced onion and chopped tomatoes.

Tip

For best results, use hot, freshly prepared rice for this dish. Cool or reheated leftover rice will not absorb flavors to the same extent.

Garam Masala

1	piece (1 inch/2.5 cm) cinnamon, broken into pieces	1
1/4 tsp	cardamom seeds	1 mL
3	whole cloves	3
1/4 tsp	each cumin seeds and fennel seeds (saunf)	1 mL
1/4 tsp	black cumin (shah jeera)	1 mL
1/4 tsp	ground mace	1 mL
1/2 tsp	ground nutmeg	2 mL
1/2 tsp	saffron threads	2 mL

Meat

1 tsp	Indian poppy seeds (see Tip, page 219)	5 mL
2 1/2 tbsp	minced green chiles, preferably serranos	32 mL
2 tbsp	finely chopped peeled gingerroot	25 mL
2 tbsp	finely chopped garlic	25 mL
1/2 tsp	cornstarch	2 mL
1/2 cup	nonfat yogurt, at room temperature	125 mL
1 tsp	salt	5 mL
1 tbsp	each oil and ghee	15 mL
1 cup	thinly sliced onion (lengthwise slices)	250 mL
1 lb	bone-in lamb shoulder meat, cut into 2-inch (5 cm) pieces	500 g
3 tbsp	freshly squeezed lime or lemon juice	45 mL
1 1/2 cups	loosely packed cilantro, chopped	375 mL
1 cup	loosely packed mint leaves, chopped	250 mL

Rice

1 1/4 cups	Indian basmati rice (see Tip, page 134)	300 mL
1 tbsp	oil	15 mL
1 tbsp	ghee	15 mL
1 cup	thinly sliced onion (lengthwise slices)	250 mL
20	cashews, preferably raw	20
3 tbsp	raisins	45 mL
1 tsp	salt	5 mL
2 tbsp	rose water or 3 drops rose extract	25 mL

1. *Garam masala:* In a spice grinder, grind together cinnamon, cardamom, cloves, cumin, fennel, black cumin, mace and nutmeg. Set aside.

2. In a bowl, soak saffron in 1/4 cup (50 mL) very hot water. Set aside.

3. *Meat:* In a smooth mortar, soak poppy seeds in $\frac{1}{2}$ tsp (2 mL) water for 15 minutes. Grind to a paste with pestle. Add chiles, ginger and garlic. Grind all together. Set aside.

4. Stir cornstarch and salt into yogurt and set aside.

5. In a Dutch oven, heat oil and ghee over medium heat. Add onion and sauté until golden, 6 to 7 minutes. Add reserved chile mixture and sauté for 3 minutes. Add lamb and brown lightly, 6 to 8 minutes. Add yogurt mixture and $\frac{1}{2}$ cup (125 mL) water. Mix well and bring to a boil. Cover, reduce heat to low and cook, stirring periodically, for 25 minutes.

6. Add lime juice, cilantro and mint. Cover and simmer until lamb is fork-tender and a thick gravy forms, 20 to 25 minutes. If necessary, add an additional 3 to 4 tbsp (45 to 60 mL) hot water to prevent sticking. Sprinkle $\frac{1}{2}$ tsp (2 mL) garam masala over meat. Cover and set aside.

7. *Rice:* Place rice in a large bowl with plenty of cold water and swish vigorously with fingers. Drain. Repeat 4 or 5 times until water is fairly clear. Cover with 3 to 4 inches (7.5 to 10 cm) cold water and set aside to soak for at least 15 minutes.

8. In a saucepan, heat oil and ghee over medium heat. Add onion and sauté until brown, about 8 minutes. Add cashews and raisins and sauté until raisins puff up, about 1 minute. Remove with a slotted spoon and set aside.

9. Drain rice and add to the same saucepan. Sauté for 1 minute. Add $2\frac{1}{3}$ cups (575 mL) fresh water and salt. Cover, increase heat to medium-high and bring to a boil. Reduce heat as low as possible and cook, covered, without peeking, for 25 minutes. Remove from heat and let rest, uncovered, for 5 minutes. Fluff lightly with fork.

10. Meanwhile, preheat oven to 300°F (150°C).

11. *To assemble:* Spoon one-third of rice over meat. Sprinkle $\frac{1}{2}$ tsp (2 mL) of the garam masala and one-third of the reserved onion mixture over rice. Sprinkle one-third of saffron liquid with threads. Repeat layers, finishing with layer of onion mixture. Use all garam masala and onion mixture. Sprinkle rose water over top. Cover tightly with foil and lid. Bake for 30 minutes. Remove and open a corner of foil to let steam escape. Set aside for 5 minutes and let rest.

12. *To serve:* Spoon gently onto platter, placing a few pieces of meat on top.

Dosa
South Indian Rice and Lentil Crêpes

Makes 12 to 14

This quintessential South Indian food, which has been embraced globally, is a breakfast dish. However, it has morphed into an anytime crêpe and is served with a variety of fillings. The traditional filling is, of course, a soft mix of potatoes and onions.

Tip

Crêpes should be almost translucent — the thinner, the better. Stir batter well before pouring each, as batter tends to settle.

Variation

Potatoes with Two Onions filling: Serve with potato filling (see recipe, page 351). Place about ¾ cup (175 mL) of the stuffing slightly off-center and fold in half. The stuffing does not run the length of the dosa. Serve with chutney.

2 cups	long-grain rice (not basmati)	500 mL
1 cup	split white lentils (urad dal)	250 mL
1 ½ tbsp	fenugreek seeds (methi)	22 mL
1 ½ tsp	salt or to taste	7 mL
3 to 4 tbsp	oil	45 to 60 mL

1. Soak rice overnight in 6 cups (1.5 L) water. Clean and pick through dal for any small stones and grit. Rinse well. In another bowl, combine dal and fenugreek seeds and cover with 4 cups (1 L) cold water. Soak overnight.

2. Drain dal mixture. In a blender, purée mixture, in 2 batches, with ¼ cup (50 mL) warm water for each batch. Blend continuously for 2 to 3 minutes to make a smooth batter. Transfer to a large bowl.

3. Drain rice and add to blender, in 2 batches, adding ¼ cup (50 mL) water to each batch. Blend continuously for about 2 minutes, until batter is very smooth. Pour into lentil batter. Stir in salt and about ¼ cup (50 mL) additional water to make a cake-like batter. Mix well to combine. Cover and set aside in a warm spot to ferment for 10 to 12 hours. Ideally, when ready, batter should be almost doubled and appear light and frothy. (This does not always happen, but, even so, the batter will be fine to use. It will lack the slight tang of a fermented batter.) Batter can be covered and refrigerated for up to 48 hours. Return to room temperature before proceeding with recipe.

4. When ready to make dosas, whip batter vigorously for 2 minutes. Thin batter with additional water as necessary until it resembles heavy cream — thick but pourable.

5. Heat a dry large nonstick griddle or heavy skillet over medium heat. Sprinkle a few drops of water to check if they sizzle and disappear. The correct temperature is very important. Using a ½-cup (125 mL) metal measuring cup, pour batter into middle of griddle and quickly spread with a circular motion using flat bottom of cup, from the inside to outer edge, forming a crêpe about 10 to 12 inches (25 to 30 cm) round. If metal cup is not available, use metal ladle and spread batter with bottom of ladle. This step requires quick action as crêpe (dosa) begins to cook almost instantly. Cover and cook for 2 minutes. Uncover and drizzle ¾ tsp (4 mL) of the oil over top. Cook for 1 minute. Edges will begin to curl. Remove with spatula and fold gently in half. Repeat with remaining batter. Serve immediately with chutney.

Rice Vermicelli with Sesame

Serves 4 to 6

My friend Sudha introduced me to this delightful dish from Karnataka. The essence of simplicity, it shines with the flavors of the south — mustard seeds and fresh curry leaves. I like to serve it as a light lunch with a side of raita (yogurt salad) and papadums.

¼ cup + 1 tsp	split white lentils (urad dal), divided	50 mL + 5 mL
1 tbsp	salt	15 mL
4 oz	rice vermicelli (instant rice sevai)	125 g
3 tbsp	sesame seeds	45 mL
4	dried Indian red chiles, divided	4
2 tbsp	oil	25 mL
1 tsp	dark mustard seeds	5 mL
¼ tsp	asafetida (hing)	1 mL
3	sprigs fresh curry leaves, stripped (30 to 40 leaves)	3
1 tbsp	untoasted sesame oil	15 mL

1. Clean and pick through dal for any small stones and grit. Rinse several times in cold water until water is fairly clear.

2. Fill a large pot three-quarters full with water and bring to a boil over high heat. Stir in salt and reduce heat to medium. Add vermicelli and stir once. Cook until soft but not mushy, 2 to 3 minutes. Drain and transfer to a shallow pan. Separate gently with fingers.

3. In a dry heavy skillet over medium heat, toast sesame seeds, stirring constantly, until seeds turn pale golden, about 2 minutes. Stir in ¼ cup (50 mL) of the dal and 3 of the chiles. Cook, stirring, until lentils turn golden and mixture is faintly aromatic, about 2 minutes. Take care not to burn. Immediately transfer to a bowl. Let cool completely. In a spice grinder, grind to a powder. Set aside.

4. In a small saucepan, heat oil over high heat until a couple of mustard seeds thrown in start to sputter. Add all the mustard seeds and cover quickly. When the seeds stop popping, in a few seconds, uncover, reduce heat to medium and add remaining lentils, asafetida, remaining chile and curry leaves. Sauté for 30 seconds and toss with vermicelli. Sprinkle sesame mixture over top and toss to coat. Drizzle with sesame oil and toss again. Serve at room temperature.

Rava Dosa
Semolina Crêpes

⅓ cup	fine semolina	75 mL
2 tbsp	all-purpose flour	25 mL
2 tbsp	frozen freshly grated coconut, thawed	25 mL
3 tbsp	cilantro, chopped	45 mL
1 tsp	minced green chiles, preferably serranos	5 mL
¼ tsp	salt	1 mL
⅔ cup	water (approx.)	150 mL
1 tbsp	oil	15 mL

1. In a bowl, whisk together semolina, flour, coconut, cilantro, chiles and salt. Slowly mix in enough water to make a thin batter. Batter should resemble cream.

2. Heat a dry large nonstick griddle or heavy skillet over medium heat. Sprinkle a few drops water to check if they sizzle and disappear. The correct temperature is very important. Using a ⅓-cup (75 mL) metal measuring cup, pour batter into middle of griddle and quickly spread with a circular motion using flat bottom of cup, from the inside to outer edge, forming a crêpe about 6 to 7 inches (15 to 17.5 cm) round. If metal cup is not available, use metal ladle and spread batter with bottom of ladle. This step requires quick action, as crêpe (dosa) begins to cook almost instantly. Cover and cook for 2 minutes. Uncover and drizzle ¾ tsp (4 mL) oil around edges of dosa. Cook for 1 minute. Edges will begin to curl. Remove with spatula and fold gently in half. Serve immediately with chutney. Repeat with remaining batter.

Makes 4

Crêpes and pancakes are an important feature of South Indian cuisine. This is the quickest of the savory crêpes, because it does not require a fermented batter. The key is to make these very thin and translucent so the bright flavor of the cilantro comes through. They make a perfect light lunch, and, though unconventional, are delicious with a chicken curry.

Tip
Crêpes should be almost translucent — the thinner, the better. Stir batter well before pouring each, as batter tends to settle.

S

Buttermilk Upma

Savory Buttermilk Semolina Pudding

Serves 6 to 8

Upma *is one of the few dishes in South India made with wheat. Rava or sooji, as it is also called, is used extensively throughout India, and upma is a very nourishing traditional breakfast dish in the south. I love this variation of the original, because I enjoy the slight tang of buttermilk.*

1 cup	Cream of Wheat (sooji or rava)	250 mL
2¼ cups	buttermilk	550 mL
1¼ tsp	salt or to taste	6 mL
¼ tsp	turmeric	1 mL
2 tbsp	oil	25 mL
1½ tsp	dark mustard seeds	7 mL
1 tsp	cumin seeds	5 mL
4	whole cloves	4
2	sticks cinnamon, each 2 inches (5 cm) long	2
6	black peppercorns	6
1 tbsp	minced green chiles, preferably serranos	15 mL
2 tsp	minced peeled gingerroot	10 mL
1¼ cups	sliced mushrooms	300 mL
1	red bell pepper, diced	1
½	green bell pepper, diced	½
2 cups	corn kernels, fresh or frozen	500 mL
1 cup	frozen peas	250 mL
1 cup	cilantro, coarsely chopped, divided	250 mL

1. In a dry skillet over medium-high heat, toast Cream of Wheat, stirring constantly, until slightly darker, 3 to 4 minutes. Transfer to a large bowl and whisk in buttermilk, salt and turmeric to form a smooth batter. Set aside.

2. In a skillet, heat oil over high heat until a couple of mustard seeds thrown in start to sputter. Add all the mustard seeds and cover quickly. When the seeds stop popping, in a few seconds, uncover, reduce heat to medium and add cumin, cloves, cinnamon and peppercorns. Sauté for 30 seconds. Add chiles and ginger and sauté for 1 minute.

3. Add mushrooms and red and green peppers and sauté for 2 minutes. Cover and cook over medium-low heat until vegetables are almost soft, 3 to 4 minutes.

4. Add corn, peas and ¾ cup (175 mL) of the cilantro and mix well. Cover and cook until vegetables are softened, 3 to 4 minutes.

5. Pour in semolina mixture and mix well. Cover and cook, stirring frequently, until moisture is absorbed and grains are cooked, 4 to 5 minutes. Let rest, covered, for 5 minutes. Gently break up any lumps. Garnish with remaining cilantro before serving.

Shrimp Upma
Savory Semolina with Shrimp

Green Masala

4	green chiles (2 inches/5 cm long), preferably serranos	4
5 to 6	cloves garlic	5 to 6
1 tbsp	minced peeled gingerroot	15 mL
¾ tsp	black peppercorns	4 mL
4	green onions, with some green, chopped into pieces	4
3 cups	cilantro leaves	750 mL
3 tbsp	oil	45 mL
3 cups	chopped onions	750 mL
12 oz	shrimp, peeled and deveined	375 g
1 ½ cups	Cream or Wheat (sooji or rava)	375 mL
1 ½ tsp	salt or to taste	7 mL
4 to 5 tbsp	freshly squeezed lime or lemon juice	60 to 75 mL
10	roasted cashews	10

Serves 6 to 8

Upma *is normally a vegetarian dish, using the traditional seasonings of mustard seeds, a teaspoon or two of lentils and a dried red chile. This is a most unusual version using "green masala" and shrimp. It's absolutely delicious, though unconventional.*

1. *Green Masala:* In a food processor, combine chiles, garlic, ginger, peppercorns, green onions and cilantro and process until puréed.

2. In a large wok, heat oil over medium-high heat. Add onions and sauté until golden, 8 to 10 minutes.

3. Add green masala to onions. Reduce heat to medium. Sauté until masala is a shade darker, 3 to 4 minutes, deglazing wok with water, 1 tbsp (15 mL) at a time, to prevent burning.

4. Add shrimp and Cream of Wheat and sauté for 3 to 4 minutes.

5. Add 2½ cups (625 mL) hot water and salt and mix well. Reduce heat to medium-low. Cover and cook until water is absorbed, 4 to 5 minutes. Stir in lime juice while breaking up lumps. Transfer to a serving bowl and sprinkle cashews over top before serving.

Akki Ooti

Coorgi Griddle-Baked Rice Bread

Makes 12

These snow white griddle-baked breads are a specialty of the small southwestern region of Coorg, where rice is the principal grain.

- *Saucepan with tight-fitting lid*
- *Baking sheets, sprayed with vegetable spray*

½ cup	parboiled long-grain rice (not basmati)	125 mL
1 cup	rice flour	250 mL
1 tsp	salt or to taste	5 mL
	Vegetable spray	
	Extra rice flour for dusting	

1. In a saucepan, combine rice and 1½ cups (375 mL) water. Bring to a boil over high heat. Reduce heat to low. Cover with a tight-fitting lid and cook until soft and water is absorbed, about 15 minutes. Transfer to a blender and purée to a paste, adding 1 to 2 tbsp (15 to 25 mL) water, if necessary, to blend.

2. In a bowl, combine rice flour and salt. Add rice purée and mix with a sturdy spoon until dough begins to form. Mixture will be sticky. Spray hands with vegetable spray (rice dough can be very sticky) and transfer mixture to prepared baking sheet. Knead until dough is soft and pliable. If necessary, add more rice flour, a little at a time, until dough is smooth. Divide into 12 portions and roll each portion into a ball. Cover with a towel and let rest for 15 minutes.

3. Heat a nonstick griddle or heavy skillet over medium heat for 4 to 5 minutes. Generously flour rolling surface. Working with one ball at a time, flatten into a disk. Flour rolling pin and roll into a circle about 4 to 5 inches (10 to 12.5 cm) in diameter. Lift dough periodically while rolling and dust with flour as necessary as dough tends to be sticky.

4. Transfer bread to dry griddle and cook first side for 1½ minutes. Flip and press down with spatula to cook second side, pressing around edges, about 1 minute. Bread will puff up slightly. Do not overcook or allow brown spots to appear. Transfer to a plate and cover to keep warm. Repeat with remaining dough.

Kerala Porotas

Kerala Griddle-Fried Bread

1 ½ cups	all-purpose flour	375 mL
½ tsp	granulated sugar	2 mL
¼ tsp	salt	1 mL
¼ cup	plain yogurt	50 mL
2 tbsp	milk	25 mL
2 tsp	ghee	10 mL
1	egg	1
	All-purpose flour for dusting	
¼ cup	melted ghee	50 mL

1. In a food processor, combine flour, sugar and salt. Pulse twice to combine. Add yogurt, milk, ghee and egg and process to make a smooth dough. Continue to process for 2 minutes to knead.

2. Lightly oil hands. Remove dough and form into a ball. Place in a bowl, cover with slightly damp towel and let rest for 4 or 5 hours.

3. Heat dry nonstick griddle or heavy skillet for 5 minutes over medium heat.

4. Knead dough by hand for 2 minutes. Divide into 8 portions. Roll each into a ball. Place in a bowl, cover and set aside, away from heat.

5. Dust work surface lightly with flour. Spread with palm into a large circle. Working with one ball at a time, flatten between palms to make a disk about 2 inches (5 cm) across. Roll on floured surface to a 6- to 7-inch (15 to 17.5 cm) circle. Brush generously with melted ghee. Roll tightly into a cigar shape. Wind "cigar" into a coil, placing end under dough to secure. Roll again into 6- to 7-inch (15 to 17.5 cm) circle, lifting and dusting surface if necessary. Repeat with remaining dough. Set aside, but do not allow circles to touch.

6. Place on heated griddle and cook until brown spots appear, about 2 minutes. Turn and cook other side, pressing down with spatula, for 1 minute. Brush top side with some of the ghee. Turn again and brush second side with ghee. Turn once more and cook, pressing down with spatula, until browned and crisp, 1 to 2 minutes. Transfer to foil to keep warm.

7. Repeat with remaining dough and ghee. While still warm, hold a stack of 4 porotas vertically between your hands and crush sideways so layers appear separated as in a puff pastry. (They won't be evenly separated.)

Makes 8

These rich breads are from the cuisine of the Muslims of Kerala, descendants of Arab traders who came several centuries ago. They married local women, and their food evolved over time to incorporate Arab influences and South Indian ingredients.

Tip

All the rolling in Step 5 is necessary as a way to layer and get fat between the layers to make a tender bread — like puff pastry.

Utthapam

2 cups	long-grain rice (not basmati)	500 mL
1 cup	split white lentils (urad dal)	250 mL
2 tsp	fenugreek seeds (methi)	10 mL
2 tsp	salt or to taste	10 mL
2 cups	finely chopped onions	500 mL
2 cups	finely chopped tomatoes	500 mL
2 to 3 tbsp	minced green chiles, preferably serranos	25 to 45 mL
1 cup	cilantro, chopped	250 mL
4 to 6 tbsp	oil	60 to 90 mL

1. Soak rice overnight in 6 cups (1.5 L) water. Clean and pick through dal for any small stones and grit. Rinse well. In another bowl, combine dal and fenugreek seeds and cover with 4 cups (1 L) water. Soak overnight.

2. Drain dal mixture. Purée in blender, in 2 batches, with ¼ cup (50 mL) warm water for each batch. Blend continuously to make a smooth batter, 2 to 3 minutes. Transfer to a large bowl.

3. Drain rice and add to blender in 2 batches, adding ¼ cup (50 mL) water to each batch. Blend continuously for about 2 minutes. Pour into lentil batter. Stir in salt and about ¼ cup (50 mL) additional water to make a cake-like batter. Mix well to combine. Cover and set aside in a warm place to ferment for 10 to 12 hours. Ideally, when ready, batter should be almost doubled and appear light and frothy. (This does not always happen, but even so, the batter will be fine to use. It will lack the slight tang of a fermented batter.) Batter can be covered and refrigerated for up to 48 hours. Return to room temperature before proceeding with recipe.

4. Add ¾ to 1 cup (175 to 250 mL) water to make a thicker-than-pancake batter. Whip batter vigorously for 2 to 3 minutes to make it lighter. Stir in onions, tomatoes, chiles and cilantro.

5. Heat a large nonstick griddle or heavy skillet over medium heat. Add 1 tsp (5 mL) of the oil and swirl to coat bottom. Using a metal measuring cup, pour a heaping ½ cup (125 mL) batter in center of skillet and, using the bottom of the measuring cup or a ladle, spread rapidly to make a pancake a little less than ½ inch (1 cm) thick. Cover and adjust heat to cook until underside is golden, 2 to 3 minutes. Flip to brown other side lightly, adding a little oil around edges and tilting skillet to allow oil to flow under pancake, about 2 minutes. Do not cover. Repeat with remaining batter and oil as necessary. Serve hot with coconut chutney or any other chutney of your choice.

Makes 12

A much-loved breakfast dish, utthapam *is made of the same batter as* dosa *— the ubiquitous thin rice crêpe that is arguably the most familiar icon of South Indian cuisine.*

Tips

When cool, wrap utthapams in foil, with plastic wrap in between, and refrigerate for up to 4 days. To warm, remove from plastic wrap and foil and microwave, covered, for a few seconds. Cold utthapam is unappetizing as the starch in the lentils and rice stiffens.

Recipe can be halved.

Sabudana Utthapam
Tapioca Pearl Pancakes

Makes 10

Tapioca pearls are popular in several parts of India. A versatile high-starch food, they are made into South and North Indian milk puddings, cooked as a pancake, and in the loose form known as khichri. *Tapioca pearls are a well-known cure to settle a runny stomach.*

❦

Tips

To serve as finger food, make dollar-size pancakes and top with a dollop of chutney. To serve as a first course, make 2½-inch (6 cm) pancakes and serve with spicy shrimp or shredded chicken mounded on top.

Pancakes can be made a day ahead, wrapped tightly in foil and stored at room temperature. Reheat in 250°F (120°C) oven for 10 minutes before serving.

½ cup	tapioca pearls (sago, sabudana)	125 mL
2 cups	buttermilk, divided	500 mL
2 cups	rice flour	500 mL
1 cup	finely chopped onion	250 mL
6 to 8	fresh curry leaves, chopped	6 to 8
3 tbsp	chopped green chiles, preferably serranos	45 mL
2 cups	cilantro, leaves and soft stems, coarsely chopped	500 mL
1 cup	finely chopped tomato, optional	250 mL
1½ tsp	salt or to taste	7 mL
3 to 4 tbsp	oil, divided	45 to 60 mL

1. In a large bowl, soak sago in 1 cup (250 mL) of the buttermilk for 3 hours at room temperature.

2. Stir in rice flour, onion, curry leaves, chiles, cilantro, tomatoes and 1¾ cups (425 mL) water. Stir salt into remaining buttermilk and stir into mixture. Mixture should be as thick as pancake batter. If necessary, add additional water to achieve correct consistency. (For each pancake, stir batter well before ladling into skillet. Batter will thicken while standing and will probably need a little additional water to restore consistency. Pancakes should not be too thick, as they will not cook evenly.)

3. Heat a nonstick skillet or crêpe pan over medium heat. Add ½ tsp (2 mL) of the oil. Swirl to spread evenly. Pour ½ cup (125 mL) of the batter into center and quickly spread with bottom of ladle, using a circular motion to spread evenly to about 6 inches (15 cm) in diameter. Cover and cook for 2 to 3 minutes. Flip and drizzle ½ tsp (2 mL) of the remaining oil around edges. Tilt skillet to spread oil under pancake. Cover and cook for 2 minutes. Remove and keep warm. Repeat with remaining batter and oil as necessary. Serve with a chutney of your choice.

Kala Channa aur Nimbu Pulao

Brown Chickpea and Lemon Rice

W

Fresh dill and lemon bring this sparkling dish to life, the small brown chickpeas adding crunch and boosting nutrition. It is equally good served with a non-Indian entrée.

- *Saucepan with tight-fitting lid*

½ cup	small brown dried chickpeas (kala channa)	125 mL
3 tsp	salt or to taste, divided	15 mL
2 cups	Indian basmati rice (see Tip, page 134)	500 mL
2 tbsp	oil	25 mL
1	stick cinnamon, 2 inches (5 cm) long	1
4	green cardamom pods, cracked open	4
3 tbsp	chopped green garlic (see Tip, right) or 1 tbsp (15 mL) chopped garlic or 4 tbsp (60 mL) chopped garlic chives	45 mL
2 cups	fresh dill, chopped	500 mL
1	lemon, thinly sliced	1

1. Rinse chickpeas and soak overnight in water to cover by 4 to 5 inches (10 to 12.5 cm). Drain and place in a saucepan with 3 cups (750 mL) cold water. Bring to a boil over high heat. Reduce heat and simmer until tender, 20 to 30 minutes. Add 1 tsp (5 mL) of the salt and simmer for 5 minutes more. Drain and set aside.

2. Place rice in a large bowl with plenty of cold water and swish vigorously with fingers. Drain. Repeat 4 or 5 times until water is fairly clear. Cover with 3 to 4 inches (7.5 to 10 cm) cold water and set aside to soak for at least 15 minutes or for up to 2 hours.

3. In a saucepan, heat oil over medium-high heat. Add cinnamon and cardamom and sauté for 30 seconds. Add garlic and sauté for 1 minute. Drain rice and add to saucepan. Stir in dill. Add lemon and reserved chickpeas. Mix well and sauté for 1 minute. Add 3 cups (750 mL) fresh water and remaining salt. Cover and bring to a boil over high heat. Reduce heat as low as possible and cook, covered with a tight-fitting lid, without peeking, for 25 minutes.

4. Remove from heat and set lid slightly ajar to allow steam to escape. Let rest for 5 minutes. Gently fluff with fork and carefully spoon onto platter to serve.

Tip

Green garlic is grown from a single clove of garlic and the clove is pulled up when the shoots are about 9 to 10 inches (23 to 25 cm) long. Green garlic has a milder flavor than mature garlic and is prized in Sindhi and certain Gujarati dishes. Recently, fresh green garlic has appeared in specialty markets and is also available frozen in Indian stores. Garlic chives are a good substitute.

Green Masala Chicken Pulao

Serves 6 to 8

This is an amazingly quick and easy one-dish meal. As pulaos go, this is probably one of the best. Avoid using chicken breasts, as the flavor of the dark meat enriches the dish immensely.

Tip
Serve with papadums, pickles and a salad.

1½ cups	Indian basmati rice (see Tip, page 134)	375 mL
1½ inch	piece peeled ginger, cut into pieces	4 cm
6 to 8	green chiles (2 inches/5 cm long)	6 to 8
2	medium onions, cut into chunks	2
4 cups	mint leaves (about 3 bunches)	1 L
1½ cups	cilantro leaves and soft stems	375 mL
¾ tsp	cornstarch	4 mL
¾ cup	plain nonfat yogurt, at room temperature	175 mL
3 tbsp	oil, divided	45 mL
2	sticks cinnamon, each 2 inches (5 cm) long	2
8	whole cloves	8
6	green cardamom pods, cracked open	6
8 to 10	chicken drumsticks, skinned	8 to 10
1½ tsp	salt or to taste, divided	7 mL

1. Place rice in a large bowl with plenty of cold water and swish vigorously with fingers. Drain. Repeat 4 or 5 times, until water is fairly clear. Cover with 3 to 4 inches (7.5 to 10 cm) cold water and set aside to soak for at least 15 minutes or for up to 2 hours.

2. In a food processor, pulse ginger and chiles until chopped. Add onions and process until coarsely puréed, 30 seconds. Add handfuls of mint and cilantro, processing until mixture is puréed. This is "green masala."

3. Stir cornstarch into yogurt until creamy and set aside. In a large saucepan, heat 2 tbsp (25 mL) of the oil over medium-high heat. Toss in cinnamon, cloves and cardamom and sauté until spices are a shade darker and aromatic, 30 to 40 seconds. Add green masala and reduce heat to medium. Sauté until masala is aromatic, about 10 minutes, adding 1 tbsp (15 mL) water periodically to deglaze pan and prevent burning.

4. Add chicken and 1 tsp (5 mL) of salt. Reduce heat to medium. Mix chicken with masala and spread in a single layer to cook for 5 minutes. Cook, stirring periodically, until chicken absorbs flavors, 10 minutes.

5. Pour in yogurt mixture. Cover, reduce heat to medium-low and simmer until chicken is half-cooked, 6 to 8 minutes.

6. Drain rice and stir into pot. Add 1 cup (250 mL) fresh water and remaining salt. Cover and bring to a boil over high heat. Reduce heat as low as possible and cook, covered with a tight-fitting lid, without peeking, for 20 to 25 minutes.

7. Remove from heat and set lid slightly ajar to allow steam to escape. Let rest for 5 minutes. Gently fluff with fork and carefully spoon onto platter to serve.

Gujarati Khichri
Gujarati Mung Beans and Rice

- *Saucepan with tight-fitting lid*

1 cup	yellow mung beans (yellow mung dal)	250 mL
1 cup	Indian basmati rice (see Tip, page 134)	250 mL
2 tbsp	oil	25 mL
1½ tsp	cumin seeds	7 mL
6	whole cloves	6
8 to 10	black peppercorns	8 to 10
1 to 2	green chiles, preferably serranos, finely sliced	1 to 2
1½ cups	thinly sliced onions (lengthwise slices)	375 mL
1 cup	cubed (1 inch/2.5 cm) potatoes (any variety)	250 mL
1 cup	frozen peas, thawed	250 mL
1¾ tsp	salt or to taste	9 mL

1. Clean and pick through dal for any stones and grit. Place rice and dal in a bowl with plenty of cold water and swish vigorously with fingers. Drain. Repeat 4 or 5 times until water is fairly clear. Cover with 3 to 4 inches (7.5 to 10 cm) cold water and set aside to soak for 10 minutes.

2. In a saucepan, heat oil over medium heat. Add cumin, cloves, peppercorns and chiles and sauté for 2 minutes. Add onions and sauté until golden, 10 to 12 minutes.

3. Add drained rice mixture, potatoes and peas. Mix and add 1¾ cups (425 mL) fresh water. Add salt and increase heat to high. Cover and bring to a boil. Reduce heat as low as possible and cook, covered with a tight-fitting lid, without peeking, for 25 minutes.

4. Remove from heat and set lid slightly ajar to allow steam to escape. Let rest for 5 minutes. Gently fluff with fork and carefully spoon onto platter to serve.

Serves 8

This is one of my favorite rice dishes. I got the recipe from a Gujarati friend when we were both newly married and I barely knew how to boil an egg. She, on the other hand, was an accomplished cook and generously shared many family recipes with me. This meal is always accompanied with a thin broth-like yogurt curry, which is, by American standards, more like a soup.

Jhinga Pulao

Shrimp Pulao

Serves 8

This is a mouthwatering one-dish meal. Feel free to turn it into a mixed seafood pulao if you prefer.

• *Preheat oven to 350ºF (180ºC)*

2 cups	Indian basmati rice (see Tip, page 134)	500 mL
1	onion, cut into chunks	1
1	piece (1 inch/2.5 cm) peeled gingerroot	1
4	cloves garlic	4
1/4 cup	oil, divided	50 mL
1 cup	chopped tomato	250 mL
2 1/2 tsp	salt or to taste, divided	12 mL
1 tsp	Indian poppy seeds (see Tip, page 219)	5 mL
1/2 tsp	each coriander powder and cumin powder	2 mL
1/2 tsp	cayenne pepper	2 mL
1/4 tsp	turmeric	1 mL
1 lb	medium shrimp, peeled and deveined	500 g
1/4 cup	cider vinegar	50 mL
1 tsp	granulated sugar	5 mL
2	sticks cinnamon, each 2 inches (5 cm) long	2
2	bay leaves	2
3 tbsp	freshly squeezed lime or lemon juice	45 mL

1. Place rice in a bowl with plenty of cold water and swish vigorously with fingers. Drain. Repeat until water is fairly clear. Cover with 4 inches (10 cm) cool water and let soak for 15 minutes. In a food processor, purée onion, ginger and garlic.

2. In a saucepan, heat 1 tbsp (15 mL) oil over medium-high heat. Add onion mixture and sauté until golden, 6 minutes. Add tomato and continue to sauté until reduced to a thick purée, 4 to 5 minutes. Add 1 tsp (5 mL) of salt, poppy seeds, coriander, cumin, cayenne and turmeric. Sauté spices for 2 minutes. Add shrimp and mix well. Add vinegar and sugar. Reduce heat to medium-low. Cover and cook until shrimp turns opaque, 4 to 5 minutes. Remove from heat.

3. Fill a large saucepan three-quarters with water. Add cinnamon, bay leaves and remaining salt. Bring to a boil over high heat. Drain rice and add to saucepan. Return to a boil and cook until rice is cooked on the outside but uncooked in the center, 2 to 3 minutes. Do not overcook. Drain immediately and spread in a shallow pan to cool.

4. Heat remaining oil in a Dutch oven over medium heat. Swirl to coat evenly. Add half of rice mixture in a layer. Spread shrimp over rice and cover with remaining rice. Sprinkle with lime juice. Cover casserole tightly with foil and a tight-fitting lid. Bake in preheated oven for 20 minutes. Let rest 10 minutes. Fluff with a fork.

Dhansak na Chawal
Parsi Brown Rice

2 cups	Indian basmati rice (see Tip, page 134)	500 mL
2 tbsp	granulated sugar	25 mL
½ cup	hot water	125 mL
2 tbsp	oil	25 mL
12	cloves	12
10	green cardamom pods, cracked open	10
1	stick cinnamon, 2 inches (5 cm) long	1
12	black peppercorns	12
1½ cups	chopped onions	375 mL
2 tsp	salt or to taste	10 mL

Serves 8

This rice is a must with the famous lentil, vegetable and meat stew known as dhansak, *without doubt the signature dish of the Parsi community. This combination is always served with fried meatballs known as* Dhansak na Kabab.

1. Place rice in a large bowl with plenty of cold water and swish vigorously with fingers. Drain. Repeat 4 to 5 times, until water is fairly clear. Cover with 3 to 4 inches (7.5 to 10 cm) cold water and set aside to soak for at least 10 minutes or for up to 2 hours.

2. In a small saucepan, melt sugar over low heat. Do not stir. When sugar turns brown, in about 30 seconds, carefully add ½ cup (125 mL) hot water and set aside.

3. In another saucepan, heat oil over medium heat. Add cloves, cardamom, cinnamon and peppercorns and sauté for 30 seconds. Add onions and sauté until dark brown, 6 to 8 minutes.

4. Drain rice and add to pan along with sugar water and salt. Sauté for 1 minute. Add 3 cups (750 mL) fresh water. Cover and bring to a boil over high heat. Reduce heat as low as possible and cook, covered, without peeking, for 25 minutes.

5. Remove from heat and set lid slightly ajar to allow steam to escape. Let rest for 5 minutes. Gently fluff with fork and carefully spoon onto platter to serve.

Chicken Baida Roti

Open-Faced Chicken Sandwich

Makes 6

A well-known street food in Mumbai (Bombay), this open-faced chapati sandwich makes a satisfying light lunch and is perfect for brunch.

❦

Tip

Tandoori masala is a prepared mix of spices used to marinate poultry and seafood for tandoori cooking (Indian grilling). There are several good brands on the market.

2 tbsp	oil	25 mL
2 cups	finely chopped onions	500 mL
4 tsp	minced peeled gingerroot	20 mL
1 tbsp	minced garlic	15 mL
2 tsp	cayenne pepper or to taste	10 mL
2	skinless boneless chicken breasts, coarsely chopped (about 1 lb/500 g)	2
¼ cup	plain nonfat yogurt	50 mL
1¾ tsp	salt or to taste	9 mL
2 tsp	tandoori masala (see Tip, left)	10 mL
¼ cup	cilantro, chopped	50 mL
⅓ cup	oil (approx.)	75 mL
6	whole-wheat chapatis or tortillas (about 8 to 9 inches/20 to 23 cm)	6
4 to 5	eggs, lightly beaten	4 to 5

1. In a large nonstick skillet, heat 2 tbsp (25 mL) oil over medium-high heat. Add onions and sauté until golden, 6 to 8 minutes.

2. Add ginger, garlic and cayenne and sauté for 2 minutes. Stir in chicken and cook until lightly browned, 3 to 4 minutes. Add yogurt and salt and stir briskly until yogurt is absorbed, 3 to 4 minutes. Add tandoori masala and continue to cook until there is no liquid left in skillet and chicken is no longer pink inside, for 2 minutes. Remove from heat and stir in cilantro. Divide mixture into 6 portions.

3. Lightly oil a heavy nonstick skillet. Place one chapati in skillet and spread one portion of filling evenly over top.

4. Drizzle 3 to 4 tbsp (45 to 60 mL) beaten egg carefully over top of chicken to "glue" it to chapati. Cook for 1 minute and flip carefully to cook egg so it holds the chicken filling. Cook until egg is set, for 1 minute. Invert onto a dish and keep warm. Repeat with remaining rotis, eggs and oil as necessary. Serve warm with a chutney or raita of your choice.

Fresh Corn Bread

Makes 12

Fresh corn is one of the pleasures of the monsoon season in Mumbai. This quick griddle bread packed with flavor and texture is versatile enough to accompany both Indian and non-Indian meals. It is perfect with spiced scrambled eggs for brunch.

2 cups	corn kernels, fresh or frozen, thawed	500 mL
1¼ cups	all-purpose flour	300 mL
2 tsp	minced peeled gingerroot	10 mL
1 tbsp	minced green chiles, preferably serranos	15 mL
1 tbsp	cilantro, coarsely chopped	15 mL
1 tsp	salt or to taste	5 mL
1 tsp	oil	5 mL
	All-purpose flour for dusting	
¼ cup	melted ghee or oil (approx.)	50 mL

1. In a food processor, pulse corn until coarsely puréed. Add flour, ginger, chiles, cilantro and salt. Process until dough just holds together. Scrape sides and bottom of bowl. Continue to process until dough forms a ball, about 40 seconds. (Dough will be sticky.) Transfer to a shallow bowl. Oil hands and smooth over dough to coat.

2. Divide dough into 12 equal portions. Roll each portion into a ball. Cover and set aside, away from heat.

3. Heat a dry heavy skillet or nonstick griddle over medium heat for 3 to 4 minutes. Working with one ball at a time, flatten into a 2-inch (5 cm) disk. Dust with flour and roll into a 6-inch (15 cm) circle, lifting dough and dusting lightly as necessary to prevent sticking during rolling.

4. Flick a drop of water onto skillet. If it disappears immediately, transfer bread to skillet. Cook until brown spots appear on bottom, for 1½ minutes. Turn over and cook second side for about 1 minute. Brush lightly with ghee and transfer to a dish. Keep warm. Repeat with remaining dough and ghee.

Sabudana Khichri

Tapioca Pearls with Potatoes

2 cups	medium-size tapioca pearls	500 mL
1 ¼ to 1 ½ cups	buttermilk	300 to 375 mL
½ cup	roasted peanuts, coarsely chopped	125 mL
½ to 1 tsp	cayenne pepper	2 to 5 mL
¾ tsp	salt or to taste	4 mL
2 tbsp	oil	25 mL
1 tsp	cumin seeds	5 mL
1 tbsp	chopped green chiles, preferably serranos	15 mL
3 cups	diced potatoes (any variety)	750 mL
½ cup	cilantro, chopped	125 mL
	Lemon wedges	

Serves 4 to 6

This is a popular dish in Maharashtra and is always eaten to end a religious fast period, during which only certain foods are permitted. It is nutritious and filling and can be prepared as spicy as one wants. Peanuts play an important part in the cuisine of Maharashtra.

Variation

Add 1 cup (250 mL) thawed frozen peas with potatoes.

1. Place tapioca in a large bowl with plenty of cold water and swish vigorously with fingers. Repeat 4 to 5 times until water is fairly clear. Drain well. Spread in a shallow nonreactive dish in a thin layer. Pour in enough buttermilk to barely cover tapioca. Cover and soak overnight at room temperature.

2. Fluff with a fork. Mix peanuts, cayenne and salt into tapioca. Set aside.

3. In a wok, heat oil over medium heat. Add cumin and sauté for 30 seconds. Add chiles and potatoes and stir-fry until lightly colored, 3 to 4 minutes. Cover, reduce heat to medium-low and cook until potatoes are soft, 6 to 8 minutes.

4. Add tapioca mixture to wok. Mix well and heat through, stirring often, over low heat. Remove from heat and stir in cilantro. Serve with lemon wedges.

Puran Poli
Sweet Bean–Stuffed Bread

Makes 12

A Maharashtrian favorite, this is a little time-consuming to make but more than worth the effort. There is a similar bread in neighboring Andhra Pradesh that is made without coconut.

Bread

1	recipe Whole Wheat Griddle Bread (see recipe, page 144)	1

Stuffing

1 1/2 cups	yellow lentils (toor dal)	375 mL
1/2 cup	split yellow peas (channa dal)	125 mL
1 1/2 cups	granulated sugar	375 mL
1 1/2 tsp	ground cardamom seeds	7 mL
1 1/2 tsp	ground nutmeg, preferably freshly ground	7 mL
2 tbsp	unsweetened grated coconut	25 mL
1/3 cup	all-purpose flour for dusting	75 mL
1/2 cup	ghee, melted	125 mL

1. *Bread:* Prepare Whole Wheat Griddle Bread recipe. While it rests, prepare Stuffing.

2. *Stuffing:* Clean and pick through dals for any small stones and grit. Rinse several times in cold water until water is fairly clear. Soak in 4 cups (1 L) water in a saucepan for 30 minutes.

3. Bring dal mixture and water to boil, uncovered, over medium-high heat. Skim froth off top. Reduce heat to low, cover partially and simmer until dal mixture is soft, 30 to 40 minutes.

4. Strain. Return dal to saucepan and add sugar. Mix and cook over medium heat, stirring frequently, until mixture is thick enough to mound, 8 to 10 minutes. Let cool.

5. Add cardamom and nutmeg and mix well. Transfer to a dish and spread in a layer. Sprinkle coconut over top.

6. *To assemble:* Heat nonstick griddle or heavy skillet over medium-high heat for 5 minutes.

7. Divide dough into 12 equal portions and roll into balls. Cover and set aside away from heat. Sprinkle a generous pinch of flour on the work surface and spread with palm into a large circle. Working with one ball at a time, flatten between your fingers to a 1/2-inch (1 cm) thick disk. Dust with flour and roll into a 5-inch (12.5 cm) circle, lifting dough and sprinkling with flour as necessary while rolling to prevent sticking.

8. Place about 3 tbsp (45 mL) of dal mixture in center of circle and pull edges towards center to enclose completely. Flatten slightly and reshape gently into a circle. Dust with flour and place, seam side down, on work surface. Roll into a 6- to 7-inch (15 to 17.5 cm) circle, about $\frac{1}{4}$-inch (0.5 cm) thick.

9. Spread 1 tsp (5 mL) of ghee on griddle. Place bread on griddle and cook until brown spots appear on bottom, about 2 minutes. Flip. Drizzle 1 tsp (5 mL) additional ghee around edges. Shake pan to allow ghee to flow under bread. Press down firmly with a spatula and cook for 1 to 2 minutes. Transfer to a dish and keep warm. Continue until all of the dough and dal mixture is used.

Tip

Bread can be made ahead. Let cool and wrap in foil. Refrigerate for up to 2 days. Bring to room temperature and warm in foil in 300°F (150°C) oven, about 10 minutes.

Meetha Thepla

Sweet Griddle Bread

⅔ cup	jaggery (gur)	150 mL
1½ tsp	ghee or butter	7 mL
1⅓ cups	chapati flour (atta)	325 mL
⅛ tsp	salt	0.5 mL
	Chapati flour (atta) for dusting	
2 to 3 tbsp	oil	25 to 45 mL

Makes 10

These wonderful little breads are easy to make and can be made and stored for several days in an airtight container. They are ideal for an after-school snack or to nibble with a cup of coffee.

1. In a small saucepan, melt jaggery over medium-low heat, stirring gently once or twice, 2 to 3 minutes. Stir in ghee.

2. In a bowl, combine flour and salt. Make a well in the center and pour jaggery mixture into well. Mix together. Add water, 1 tbsp (15 mL) at a time, and knead to make a smooth dough. Divide into 10 equal portions. Roll each portion into a ball. Cover and set aside away from heat.

3. Heat a nonstick griddle or heavy skillet over medium heat. Working with one ball at a time, flatten ball into a patty. Dust with flour and roll into a ¼-inch (0.5 cm) thick circle, lifting dough and dusting with flour as necessary to prevent sticking. Set aside, but do not allow circles (theplas) to touch.

4. Spread 1 tsp (5 mL) of the oil on heated griddle. Transfer 2 to 3 breads (theplas) to griddle and cook until brown spots appear on bottom, 1½ to 2 minutes. Flip, drizzle ½ tsp (2 mL) oil around edge and cook until a few brown spots appear, 1 to 1½ minutes. Repeat with remaining theplas and oil. Serve warm or at room temperature with tea or coffee.

Peanut Puris

- *Wok*
- *Candy/deep-fry thermometer*

1 cup	chapati flour (atta)	250 mL
¼ cup	skinned, raw peanuts, toasted and coarsely powdered	50 mL
2 tbsp	sesame seeds	25 mL
¾ tsp	cumin seeds, toasted	4 mL
½ tsp	turmeric	2 mL
½ tsp	cayenne pepper	2 mL
2 tbsp	plain nonfat yogurt	25 mL
¼ cup	cilantro, chopped	50 mL
½ tsp	salt or to taste	2 mL
2 tbsp	hot oil	25 mL
	Chapati flour (atta) for dusting	
	Oil for deep-frying	

1. In a food processor, combine flour, peanuts, sesame and cumin seeds, turmeric, cayenne, yogurt, cilantro and salt.

2. In a small pan, heat oil over medium heat for 2 minutes. Drizzle into processor and pulse to combine. With processor running, slowly drizzle enough water, about ¼ to ⅓ cup (50 to 75 mL) through feed tube, and process to form a smooth dough. Scrape down sides of processor periodically. Process for 2 minutes to knead dough. Form into a ball and place in a bowl. Cover with a towel and let rest away from heat for 30 minutes.

3. Heat oil in a wok to 375°F (190°C). Divide dough into 10 equal portions. Roll each into a ball and flatten into a ½-inch (1 cm) thick disk. Cover and set aside away from heat. Sprinkle a little flour on work surface and spread with palm into a large circle. Working with one disk at a time, roll into a circle about 5 inches (12.5 cm) in diameter, lifting dough and sprinkling with additional flour as needed to prevent sticking. Add one puri at a time to wok and deep-fry for about 40 seconds, tapping top of puri rapidly with a slotted spoon to make it puff up. Flip and fry for 20 seconds. Do not tap second side. Remove with a large-holed strainer and drain on paper towels. Repeat with remaining dough. Serve with a chutney of your choice.

Makes 10

Peanuts feature in many dishes in Maharashtra, and these unusual puris are a good example of the creativity of Maharashtrians.

Tip
Puris are best eaten freshly made because they deflate within minutes. Although not as exotic when they do, they taste just as good as the puffy ones.

Eggs, Chicken and Meat

RELIGION PLAYS A PIVOTAL ROLE in the Indian diet. It is perhaps its most defining factor. In India, religion and daily life are inextricably interwoven. It is the birthplace of four of the world's religions — Hinduism, Buddhism, Jainism and Sikhism — and home to the second largest Muslim population in the world, so it is not surprising that there are a plethora of Indian dietary requirements based on religion. Muslims do not eat pork, and Hindus do not eat beef. Some vegetarians eat eggs, others do not because they have the potential for creating life.

The red meat of choice throughout India is young goat, known as cabrito or mutton. This is an unfortunate appellation, because to the rest of the world mutton conjures up tough leathery meat from an old smelly sheep. Young goat is lean and flavorful and is ideal for braising, the style of cooking most Indians prefer. In the far north, in mountainous Kashmir, people raise sheep, and lamb replaces goat as the meat of choice.

INDIANS PREFER THEIR MEAT AND poultry cut into bite-size pieces rather than large chunks, and on the bone rather than boneless because the result is moist, succulent meat cooked until it falls off the bone. The gravy, too, has better flavor when made with bone-in cuts, and since many people eat with their hands, they find it easier to pick up a piece of meat and chew around the bone, as you do with fried chicken or spareribs. I must confess I am befuddled by the passion for skinless boneless chicken breast in North America. Except in stir-fried dishes, I discourage the use of this in Indian dishes. It is certainly not suitable for braising, as it gets stringy with prolonged simmering and does not absorb flavors well.

Eggs play a unique role in Indian cuisine. Except for the Parsis, who consume an inordinate number, eggs are not a traditional breakfast food. Rather, they are popular hard-cooked and used in curries. I have included several recipes from different regions.

In the north, meat is relished. Kashmiri meals include multiple lamb dishes, and their wedding feasts must include at least eight to 10! Unlike Hindu Brahmins (the priestly class at the top of the caste system), who are primarily vegetarian, Kashmiri pandits, as they are called, are meat eaters. It is to Punjabi Hindus that we owe our passion for *tandoori* (grilled) foods, which today are synonymous with Indian food. This has been both a plus, because it put Indian cuisine on the global culinary map, and also a minus for those less familiar with the wide array of Indian cuisines. Tandoori chicken and *chicken tikka masala* (originally known as butter chicken or *chicken makhanwala*) and naan are mistakenly thought of as Moghlai food,

Eggs, Chicken and Meat

when in fact these dishes come from the Punjabi Hindus, many of whom fled to India as refugees during the partition of India and Pakistan in 1947.

THE VERSATILITY OF GROUND MEAT (*keema*) makes it a favorite with Indians, but it is particularly popular in the north. The Moghuls used it to great advantage, and recipes for melt-in-your-mouth kababs (patties and rolls) abound. Often they include nuts, saffron and exotic extracts, transforming humble hamburger meat into a heavenly mixture fit for a king. These morsels are extremely popular even today, and restaurants specializing in kababs are world renowned.

Cooking meat and chicken with vegetables or dal is a common technique. The resulting dish is substantial and, when eaten with rice or bread (*roti*), makes a satisfying meal.

IN THE EAST, MEAT IS NOT AN IMPORTANT part of the diet. In Bengal, Orissa and the other eastern states, meat plays a secondary role to the main protein, fish. Meat dishes tend to have thinner and lighter gravies and are not as heavily spiced as in the north.

THE MOST SIGNIFICANT DIFFERENCE between the meat and poultry dishes of the north and south is no doubt the extensive use of coconut in the south, an ingredient that is unknown in northern cooking. In the south, coconut replaces ground nuts to enrich gravies. Grated coconut and coconut milk are used freely. There is also an increased use of dried red chiles, which balance the sweetness of the coconut. Yogurt is used in southern curries, but its use is more limited than in the north.

In Coorg, a district in Karnataka in the south, wild boar abounds, and pork is very popular. In Kerala, with a population that includes Muslims, Hindus and Christians, there is a wide variation in the consumption of meats. The three religions have distinct cuisines, and each has its own dietary restrictions. The common thread is, of course, the use of spices and coconut.

Andhra Pradesh has perhaps the hottest food in the country. It is no surprise, because it is home to the chile fields of Guntur, well known for their fiery red chiles. Meats are often enveloped in spicy masalas, and coconut is used sparingly. Instead, tomatoes and onions are the base of gravies, often enhanced with tamarind.

WESTERN INDIA FAVORS GOAT MEAT and a variety of poultry. Gujarat is primarily a vegetarian state, but Maharashtrians are meat eaters. The Marathas in the interior of Maharashtra were warriors who fought and won many a battle against the mighty Moghul armies. Their meat dishes are rich and highly spiced, and dried shaved coconut, known as *copra,* is an important ingredient.

Goan meat dishes have a strong Portuguese influence but have been adapted to include spices, particularly cumin, lots of dry red chiles, garlic and vinegar. Pork is relished, and a local sausage known as Goa sausage is similar to the chorizo of Spain but much spicier.

The Muslims of western India are comprised of three distinct groups. All are meat eaters, though their cuisines are distinct. Among them, the Khojas have a special technique of adding a smoky flavor to certain dishes, a technique known as *dungar.* It is simple but brilliant. A piece of burning charcoal is placed in a cup formed by two or three outer layers of onion and placed in the center of a dish when it has finished cooking. A little warm ghee is poured on top of the coal and set on fire. The lid is replaced immediately and the resulting smoke infuses the dish in a few minutes. Natural and with delicious results.

Blackened Chicken

- *Saucepan or skillet with tight-fitting lid*

½ cup	plain nonfat yogurt	125 mL
3 lbs	skinless boneless chicken thighs	1.5 kg
2 tbsp	minced peeled gingerroot or ginger paste	25 mL
2 tbsp	minced garlic or garlic paste (see Tips, page 207)	25 mL
2 tbsp	minced green chiles, preferably serranos	25 mL
2 tbsp	coriander powder	25 mL
2 tsp	salt	10 mL
¼ cup	oil, divided	50 mL
½ cup	crispy fried onions (see Tip, right)	125 mL
1 tbsp	black cumin (shah jeera)	15 mL
1 ½ tsp	ground cardamom	7 mL
½ tsp	freshly ground black pepper	2 mL

1. Place yogurt in a coffee filter–lined strainer over a bowl to drain excess moisture. Refrigerate for 2 hours. Discard liquid.

2. Rinse chicken and pat dry thoroughly.

3. In a large bowl, mix together yogurt, ginger, garlic, chiles, coriander, salt and 2 tbsp (25 mL) of the oil. Add chicken and mix well. Cover and marinate in refrigerator for 3 to 4 hours.

4. In a nonstick skillet or saucepan, heat remaining oil over medium-high heat. Arrange chicken in a single layer. Shake pan vigorously to make sure pieces are not sticking. Cook, without stirring, until pieces are browned, for 5 minutes. Turn pieces and cook for 5 minutes to brown.

5. Cover with a tight-fitting lid, reduce heat to medium-low (there should be an audible sizzle at all times) and cook until chicken is partially cooked, 6 to 8 minutes. Turn chicken and cook, uncovered, until there is no liquid in the pan and chicken is no longer pink inside, 6 to 8 minutes.

6. Add crispy fried onions and stir to mix. Cook for 2 minutes. Sprinkle with black cumin, cardamom and black pepper. Stir gently to mix and serve.

Serves 6 to 8

Chicken with an attitude. Chicken thighs intensely flavored with aromatic spices make a wonderful party dish served with a vegetable curry or a delicious dal. I also like to serve these stuffed in a pita pocket with yogurt salad (raita).

Tip
Crispy fried onions are available in Indian and Middle Eastern markets. After the package is opened, they can be refrigerated for up to 1 year.

Brandied Chicken with Pomegranate Seeds

I acquired this outstanding recipe when I was visiting my sister-in-law more than 35 years ago. It was lost in my papers for many years until I came across it recently. I am happy to share it, as it's absolutely scrumptious and easy to prepare.

Tip

To toast coriander seeds: In a dry skillet, add 1 tbsp (15 mL) coriander seeds and toast over medium heat, stirring gently, until fragrant and a shade darker, 3 to 4 minutes. Immediately transfer to a bowl. Let cool and grind in a spice grinder.

4 lbs	skinless boneless chicken thighs	2 kg
3 tbsp	oil, divided	45 mL
3 cups	puréed onions (about 3 medium onions)	750 mL
2 tbsp	minced peeled gingerroot	25 mL
1 tbsp	toasted coriander seeds, ground to a powder (see Tip, left)	15 mL
2 tsp	salt or to taste	10 mL
3 tbsp	brandy	45 mL
2½ tbsp	Worcestershire sauce	32 mL
1½ tbsp	dried pomegranate seeds (anardana), powdered in spice grinder	22 mL
1 tbsp	peppercorns, coarsely ground in spice grinder	15 mL
3 tbsp	cilantro, chopped	45 mL

1. Rinse chicken and pat dry thoroughly.

2. In a saucepan, heat 2 tbsp (25 mL) of the oil over medium-high heat. Add chicken, onions, ginger, coriander and salt and mix well. Cover and bring to a boil. Reduce heat to medium and cook for 15 minutes.

3. Uncover and cook, stirring periodically, until almost all liquid is absorbed, 8 to 10 minutes. Add brandy and Worcestershire sauce and mix well.

4. In a small pan, heat remaining oil over medium heat. Add pomegranate and peppercorn powders. Sizzle for 30 seconds and pour over chicken.

5. Toss chicken to coat with masala and reduce heat to low. Cook until no liquid remains and a thick masala coats chicken, 4 to 5 minutes. Garnish with cilantro and serve with an Indian bread.

Badami Murg
Chicken with Almonds

12	skinless bone-in chicken thighs (or thighs and drumsticks)	12
1 cup	plain nonfat yogurt, at room temperature	250 mL
1 tsp	cornstarch	5 mL
10	dried Indian red chiles, broken into pieces, half without seeds	10
20	cloves garlic	20
1	piece (2-by 1-inch/5 by 2.5 cm) peeled gingerroot	1
30	blanched whole almonds, lightly toasted	30
2 tbsp	Indian poppy seeds (see Tip, page 219)	25 mL
2 tsp	garam masala	10 mL
2 tsp	salt or to taste	10 mL
2 tbsp	oil	25 mL
4 cups	thinly sliced onions (lengthwise slices)	1 L
4 tbsp	slivered blanched almonds	60 mL

1. Rinse chicken and pat dry thoroughly.

2. In a bowl, stir together yogurt and cornstarch to a creamy consistency. Set aside.

3. In a bowl, soak chiles in ½ cup (125 mL) water for 15 minutes.

4. In a blender, combine chiles with soaking water, garlic, ginger, whole almonds, poppy seeds and garam masala. Blend to a smooth paste.

5. Transfer spice paste to a nonreactive bowl. Add chicken and salt. Cover and marinate for 30 minutes at room temperature or for up to 2 hours in the refrigerator.

6. In a large saucepan, heat oil over medium-high heat. Add onions and sauté until golden, about 15 minutes.

7. Add chicken with marinade and sauté until lightly browned, about 10 minutes. Do not allow to burn. Add water, 1 to 2 tbsp (15 to 25 mL) at a time, to prevent sticking.

8. Slowly pour yogurt mixture over chicken and mix well. Cover, reduce heat and simmer, stirring gently every 10 minutes, until tender, 35 to 40 minutes. Turn pieces over once during cooking to cook evenly. If necessary, add a little hot water if gravy gets too thick. Garnish with slivered almonds before serving.

Serves 8

This is a classic Moghlai (Moghul) dish, almost always offered on North Indian restaurant menus. I prefer to replace cream (used in the restaurant version) with yogurt and additional almonds for better flavor and consistency.

Tips

Gravies made with puréed nuts tend to burn easily. Adjust heat to prevent burning and stir frequently, scraping bottom.

I have found when cooking large pieces of chicken, as in this recipe, that it is best to simmer the pieces gently until half-cooked, then turn them over so the second side remains submerged in the gravy while simmering. This ensures the chicken is more evenly flavored.

Chicken Korma

Serves 6 to 8

Kormas are mild and creamy, with a sensual mouth feel. Puréed nuts add richness to the gravy, which is enhanced with whole aromatic spices. It is a good dish for entertaining, as it is mild enough for anyone not accustomed to spicy food.

Tip

Small frozen onions (pearl onions) are available and are ideal for this dish.

12	skinless bone-in chicken thighs	12
Marinade		
1 cup	plain nonfat yogurt, at room temperature	250 mL
1 tsp	cornstarch	5 mL
1/3 cup	each blanched almonds, raw cashews and raw pistachios	75 mL
2 tbsp	unsweetened desiccated coconut	25 mL
1 tbsp	Indian poppy seeds (see Tip, page 219)	15 mL
2	cloves garlic	2
2 tsp	cayenne pepper	10 mL
2 tsp	salt or to taste	10 mL
1 1/2 tsp	each cumin seeds and coriander seeds	7 mL
1/2 tsp	saffron threads	2 mL
1/2 cup	very hot milk	125 mL
2 tbsp	oil	25 mL
1	stick cinnamon, about 3 inches (7.5 cm) long	1
4	whole cloves	4
6	black peppercorns	6
2 1/2 cups	thinly sliced onions (lengthwise slices)	625 mL
1 lb	pearl onions or small boiling onions	500 g

1. Rinse chicken and pat dry thoroughly.

2. *Marinade:* In a large nonreactive bowl, stir together yogurt and cornstarch to a creamy consistency.

3. In a food processor, combine almonds, cashews, pistachios, coconut, poppy seeds, garlic, cayenne, salt, cumin and coriander. Process until mixture forms as fine a paste as possible. Stir into yogurt. Add chicken pieces and coat thoroughly. Set aside for at least 30 minutes at room temperature or cover and refrigerate for up to 12 hours.

4. In a small bowl, soak saffron in hot milk and set aside.

5. In a large wide saucepan, heat oil over medium-high heat. Add cinnamon, cloves and peppercorns and sauté for 30 seconds. Add onions and sauté until golden, 6 to 8 minutes. Carefully arrange chicken in pan. Scrape any leftover marinade over chicken. Reduce heat to medium-low. Cover with a tight-fitting lid and cook, stirring gently once, for 15 minutes.

6. Tuck pearl onions in between chicken pieces and pour saffron milk over top. Cover and cook until chicken is no longer pink inside, 25 to 30 minutes, stirring gently and periodically scraping bottom to make sure the nut gravy does not burn.

Nina's Broiled Chicken

- *Broiler pan, lined with foil*

8	skinless bone-in chicken breasts	8
1 ½ tbsp	coriander seeds	22 mL
1 tbsp	black peppercorns	15 mL
1 tbsp	dried pomegranate seeds (anardana) (see Tips, page 92)	15 mL
2 tbsp	minced green chiles, preferably serranos	25 mL
½ cup	cilantro leaves, chopped	125 mL
¼ cup	freshly squeezed lime or lemon juice	50 mL
2 tbsp	oil	25 mL
2 tsp	salt or to taste	10 mL

1. Rinse chicken and pat dry thoroughly.

2. In a small dry skillet over medium heat, separately toast coriander, peppercorns and pomegranate seeds until each is fragrant and a little darker, 2 to 3 minutes.

3. In a spice grinder or mortar and pestle, coarsely crush coriander and pepper. Separately grind pomegranate as fine as possible.

4. In a large bowl, mix together powdered spices, green chiles, cilantro, lime juice, oil and salt. Add chicken and coat well with mixture. Cover and marinate for 30 minutes at room temperature or overnight in refrigerator. Return to room temperature before cooking.

5. Preheat oven broiler to high. Transfer chicken to prepared broiler pan and cook about 4 inches (10 cm) from heat. Mist periodically with water. Cook until crisp on the outside and moist but no longer pink inside, 8 to 10 minutes.

Serves 8

Crushed pomegranate seeds add a new dimension to this recipe that my cousin Nina shared with me many years ago.

Chicken Tikka Masala

This dish was called Chicken Makhanwala (Butter Chicken) until the British adopted it as their favorite Indian dish and its name morphed into this one. Chicken tikka means "bite-size boneless chicken."

Tips

This dish is better prepared ahead. Let cool, cover and refrigerate for up to 4 days or freeze for up to 3 months. Reheat on very low heat or in microwave. (If made ahead, add fresh cilantro and a little additional garam masala and cumin before serving.)

To toast cumin seeds: Spread seeds in a layer in a heavy dry skillet. Cook over medium heat, shaking skillet occasionally to toast evenly, until seeds are a little darker and aromatic, 2 to 3 minutes. Let cool. Grind to a powder in a spice grinder.

12	cooked Tandoori Chicken thighs (see recipe, page 201)	12
3	green chiles, preferably serranos, each 2 inches (5 cm) long	3
1	piece (1 inch/2.5 cm) peeled gingerroot	1
1	can (28 oz/796 mL) whole or diced tomatoes, including juice	1
½ cup	butter, divided	125 mL
2 tbsp	freshly ground toasted cumin seeds, divided (see Tips, left)	25 mL
2 tsp	paprika	10 mL
1 cup	whipping (35%) cream	250 mL
1½ tsp	salt or to taste	7 mL
2 tsp	garam masala	10 mL
¾ cup	cilantro, chopped	175 mL

1. Carefully debone cooked chicken, taking care not to shred it.

2. In a food processor, process chiles and ginger. Add tomatoes with juice and purée until smooth.

3. In a large saucepan, melt ¼ cup (50 mL) of the butter over medium heat. Add one-third of the chicken and sauté until edges begin to brown, 3 to 4 minutes. Transfer with a slotted spoon to a bowl. Brown remaining 2 batches of chicken in the same manner, adding 2 tbsp (25 mL) of the remaining butter as needed to prevent sticking.

4. Turn off heat and scrape up all the browned bits. Return to medium-low heat. Melt remaining 2 tbsp (25 mL) of butter. Stir in 4 tsp (20 mL) of the cumin and paprika. Cook, stirring rapidly, for 1 minute.

5. Pour in tomato mixture and return to a gentle boil. Cook, stirring frequently to allow flavors to blend, about 10 minutes. Add cream, salt, chicken and accumulated juices. Simmer, stirring gently a few times and scraping bottom to prevent burning, until chicken is heated through, 10 to 12 minutes.

6. Stir in garam masala and remaining cumin. Remove from heat and cover. Let stand for 10 minutes before serving. Garnish with cilantro and serve.

Tava Murg

Sheilu's Pan-Fried Yogurt Chicken

Serves 8

My cousin Sheilu, who doesn't cook that often, has some wonderful tasty dishes in her repertoire. She shared this with me several years ago and I recognized its versatility immediately. This is the ultimate finger food. Stuff in pita bread with a dollop of yogurt or make a sandwich with sliced tomatoes and your favorite bread, and you have a winner. It's equally good on the dinner table with spicy smashed potatoes.

12	skinless boneless chicken thighs	12
½ cup	plain nonfat yogurt	125 mL
3 tbsp	minced peeled gingerroot or ginger paste	45 mL
2 tbsp	minced garlic or garlic paste (see Tips, page 207)	25 mL
2 tsp	salt or to taste	10 mL
2 tbsp	oil, divided	25 mL
¼ cup	dried fenugreek leaves (kasuri methi)	50 mL
2 tbsp	coriander powder	25 mL
1 tsp	freshly ground black pepper	5 mL
2 tsp	mango powder (amchur)	10 mL

1. Rinse and pat chicken dry thoroughly.

2. In a nonreactive bowl, mix together yogurt, ginger, garlic and salt. Add chicken. Cover and marinate for 5 to 6 hours in the refrigerator.

3. Heat 1 tbsp (15 mL) oil in a large nonstick skillet over medium heat. Using tongs, transfer chicken to skillet, arranging in a single layer. Reserve any remaining marinade. Increase heat to medium-high. Cook, turning pieces periodically, until juices begin to dry and chicken begins to brown, 8 to 10 minutes. When almost dry, add marinade if any, and continue to cook until marinade is totally absorbed, about 2 minutes.

4. Add remaining oil and fenugreek and mix well. Reduce heat to medium and brown chicken evenly, taking care not to burn, turning periodically, until chicken is well browned and no longer pink inside, 10 to 12 minutes.

5. Sprinkle in coriander and black pepper. Reduce heat to medium-low and cook for 2 minutes. Toss to mix. Remove from heat and sprinkle with mango powder. Mix well and serve.

Tandoori Chicken

- *Shallow baking pan, lined with foil*

16	skinless bone-in chicken thighs (or thighs and drumsticks) (about 5 lbs/2.5 kg)	16
1 cup	plain nonfat yogurt	250 mL
	Juice of 2 limes or lemons	
2 tbsp	minced peeled gingerroot (see Tips, right)	25 mL
2 tbsp	minced garlic	25 mL
2 tsp	coriander powder	10 mL
2 tsp	cumin powder	10 mL
2 tsp	garam masala	10 mL
1½ tsp	salt or to taste	7 mL
1 tsp	paprika	5 mL
1 tsp	cayenne pepper	5 mL
	Few drops red food coloring, optional	
	Juice of 2 limes or additional lemons	
1	onion, cut into rings	1
	Lemon wedges	

Serves 8

A tandoor is a North Indian clay oven that is about three feet (90 cm) high, usually buried in the ground up to the neck. Live coals are placed in the bottom, and skewers with meat and poultry are angled at a suitable distance from the heat to cook them. It's the Indian version of a barbecue.

Tips

Tandoori chicken is best cooked on a charcoal grill. Buy split chickens or leg quarters if using this method. Grease barbecue grill and preheat to medium-high. Place chicken on grill and cook, covered, for 20 minutes. Turn and cook until juices run clear when chicken is pierced, 20 to 25 minutes.

Ginger and garlic can be minced in a blender, grated on a ginger grater or purchased prepared in jars.

1. Rinse chicken and pat dry thoroughly. Cut long diagonal slits, against the grain, almost to the bone.

2. In a large shallow nonreactive bowl, mix together yogurt, lime juice, ginger, garlic, coriander, cumin, garam masala, salt, paprika and cayenne. Add red food coloring, if using. Add chicken, turning to coat and making sure marinade goes into all slits. Cover and marinate in refrigerator for about 2 hours or for up to 12 hours.

3. Preheat oven to 375°F (190°C). Remove chicken from marinade and place in prepared shallow baking pan. Discard any remaining marinade. Bake in preheated oven until juices run clear when chicken is pierced, about 45 minutes.

4. Transfer pieces to heated platter and squeeze lime juice over top while still warm. Discard accumulated juices. Garnish with sliced onion rings and lemon wedges.

Kadhai Murg
Wok-Cooked Chicken

Serves 6 to 8

HOT

A kadhai *(pronounced* ka-ra-hi*) is a must in any Indian kitchen. A multi-purpose pan, it is similar to a wok and is used for stir-frying, deep-frying and toasting spices. Kadhai Chicken is a home-style dish with many variations.*

12	skinless boneless chicken thighs	12
8	dried Indian red chiles, broken into pieces, half without seeds	8
2 tsp	coriander seeds	10 mL
2 tbsp	oil	25 mL
1 cup	chopped onions	250 mL
1½ tbsp	minced garlic	22 mL
1 tsp	carom seeds (ajwain)	5 mL
3 cups	chopped tomatoes	750 mL
2 tbsp	minced green chiles, preferably serranos	25 mL
2 tbsp	minced peeled gingerroot	25 mL
2 tsp	salt or to taste	10 mL
1 tbsp	tomato paste, dissolved in ¼ cup (50 mL) water	15 mL
1 tbsp	dry fenugreek leaves (kasuri methi)	15 mL
3 to 4 tbsp	freshly squeezed lime or lemon juice	45 to 60 mL
1 tsp	garam masala	5 mL
3 to 4 tbsp	cilantro, chopped	45 to 60 mL

1. Rinse chicken and pat dry thoroughly.

2. In a dry skillet over medium heat, toast red chiles and coriander seeds until aromatic, 2 to 3 minutes. Let cool and grind to a powder in a spice grinder.

3. In a large wok, heat oil over medium-high heat. Add onions and sauté until golden, 6 to 8 minutes.

4. Add garlic and carom seeds and sauté for 1 minute.

5. Add tomatoes, green chiles, ginger and salt and mix well. Reduce heat to medium-low. Cover and cook until tomatoes are soft, about 5 minutes. Mash with back of spoon.

6. Add reserved powdered spices, tomato paste and chicken. Mix well. Cover and cook, stirring once, until chicken releases juices, 12 to 15 minutes.

7. Remove cover and continue to cook, stirring periodically, until chicken is tender and juices run clear when chicken is pierced and a very thick gravy coats the pieces, 6 to 8 minutes.

8. Fold in fenugreek and drizzle lime juice over top. Stir to mix well. Remove from heat and sprinkle garam masala over top. Cover and let rest for 2 to 3 minutes for flavors to mingle. Before serving, mix again to incorporate garam masala. Garnish with cilantro.

Kashmiri Chicken

12	skinless bone-in chicken thighs (or thighs and drumsticks)	12
4 cups	plain nonfat yogurt	1 L
4 tsp	cornstarch	20 mL
3 tbsp	minced peeled gingerroot	45 mL
2 tsp	salt or to taste	10 mL
2 tbsp	oil	25 mL
8	cardamom pods, cracked open	8
3	sticks cinnamon, each about 2 inches (5 cm) long	3
1 1/2 tsp	asafetida (hing)	7 mL
2 tsp	cayenne pepper	10 mL
2 tsp	coriander powder	10 mL
1 tsp	cumin powder	5 mL
1 tsp	garam masala	5 mL
1 tbsp	butter or oil	15 mL
1/4 cup	slivered blanched almonds	50 mL

Serves 8

Asafetida replaces garlic in the food of the Hindu Kashmiri pandits. Though they eat meat, they eschew onions and garlic for religious reasons.

1. Rinse chicken and pat dry thoroughly.

2. In a large nonreactive bowl, stir together yogurt, cornstarch, ginger and salt. Add chicken and coat with mixture. Cover and marinate for 30 minutes at room temperature or for up to 12 hours in the refrigerator.

3. In a saucepan, heat oil over medium-high heat. Add cardamom, cinnamon and asafetida. Sauté until asafetida sizzles and turns gray, about 1 minute. Add chicken and marinade. Reduce heat to medium. Cover and cook for 15 minutes.

4. Add cayenne, coriander and cumin and mix well. Cover and cook, stirring gently occasionally every 8 to 10 minutes, until chicken is tender and no longer pink inside and liquid is reduced to a thick gravy, 30 to 35 minutes. Remove from heat and sprinkle garam masala over top.

5. In a small skillet, melt butter over medium heat. Add almonds and sauté until golden, about 2 minutes. Sprinkle over chicken just before serving.

Achar Gosht
Lamb with Peppers

Serves 6 to 8

This elaborate dish is worth the labor, because it is going to be the center of your table. It both looks and tastes extraordinary.

❦

Tip
To powder fenugreek seeds: In a mortar, using a pestle, crush ¼ tsp (1 mL) fenugreek seeds into a powder.

3 tbsp	oil	45 mL
2 tbsp	coarsely chopped garlic	25 mL
1 tsp	nigella seeds (kalaunji)	5 mL
½ tsp	fenugreek seeds (methi)	2 mL
2 lbs	lamb shanks, cut into 1-inch (2.5 cm) thick slices	1 kg
2½ cups	minced onions	625 mL
2 tbsp	minced peeled gingerroot	25 mL
4½ tbsp	coriander powder, divided	67 mL
1 tsp	each turmeric and cayenne pepper	5 mL
1½ tbsp	cumin powder	22 mL
1½ tbsp	mango powder (amchur)	22 mL
¼ tsp	powdered fenugreek seeds (see Tip, left)	1 mL
18 to 20	mild green chiles, such as banana peppers	18 to 20
1 cup	plain nonfat yogurt, at room temperature	250 mL
1 tsp	cornstarch	5 mL
2 tsp	salt or to taste	10 mL

1. In a saucepan, heat oil over medium heat. Add garlic and sauté until lightly golden, 2 to 3 minutes. Add nigella and fenugreek seeds and sauté for 30 seconds. Add lamb. Increase heat to medium-high and brown well, tossing slices periodically, 10 to 12 minutes.

2. Add onions, ginger, 3 tbsp (45 mL) coriander, turmeric and cayenne and sauté until color turns darker, 6 to 8 minutes. Reduce heat to low. Cover and cook, stirring occasionally, until lamb is almost ready to fall off the bone, about 45 minutes.

3. Meanwhile, in a bowl, mix together remaining coriander, cumin, mango powder and fenugreek powder.

4. Slit the chiles horizontally, leaving the ends intact. With the tip of a knife or small spoon, remove seeds and discard. Stuff pepper with spice mixture, reserving a little mixture.

5. Layer stuffed peppers over the meat and sprinkle reserved spice mixture on top.

6. In a bowl, stir together yogurt, cornstarch and salt and pour evenly over peppers. Cover and continue to cook over low heat until peppers and meat are soft, about 15 minutes. Shake pan periodically to make sure meat is not burning and to allow yogurt to seep to the meat layer. Serve with any Indian bread.

Lamb and Potato Hash

Serves 6

*There are many
options for serving this
simple home-style dish.
It can be mixed with
leftover warmed rice
and heated through to
serve as a one-dish meal
with a salad. Or used
as a filling for a wrap,
with a drizzle of hot
sauce. Or made into
a sandwich with
crusty bread.*

Variation
Stewing beef can be
substituted for the lamb.

1 lb	boneless lamb, cut into bite-size pieces	500 g
2 cups	finely chopped onions	500 mL
2 tbsp	minced peeled gingerroot, divided	25 mL
2 tsp	minced garlic, divided	10 mL
1¾ tsp	salt or to taste, divided	9 mL
2 tbsp	oil	25 mL
1	stick cinnamon, about 3 inches (7.5 cm) long	1
4	whole cloves	4
4	green cardamom pods, cracked open	4
2	bay leaves	2
2 cups	thinly sliced onions (lengthwise slices)	500 mL
1 tbsp	minced green chiles, preferably serranos	15 mL
8 oz	all-purpose potatoes, peeled and cut into ½-inch (1 cm) cubes (about 2)	250 g
2 tsp	coriander powder	10 mL
1 tsp	cumin powder	5 mL
2 tbsp	cider vinegar	25 mL
3 cups	mint leaves, chopped	750 mL

1. In a saucepan, combine lamb, chopped onions, 1 tbsp (15 mL)
of the ginger, 1 tsp (15 mL) of the garlic and 1 tsp (5 mL) of the
salt. Add 2½ cups (625 mL) water and bring to a boil over high
heat. Reduce heat to low. Cover and simmer until lamb is tender
and water is absorbed, 45 minutes to 1 hour.

2. In a large skillet or saucepan, heat oil over medium-high heat.
Add cinnamon, cloves, cardamom and bay leaves and sauté until
fragrant, about 1 minute.

3. Add sliced onions and sauté until golden, 10 to 12 minutes.
Add remaining ginger, garlic and chiles and cook for 2 minutes.
Add lamb mixture and brown well, stirring periodically, 8 to
10 minutes.

4. Add potatoes and brown, stirring periodically, for 5 minutes.
Reduce heat to medium. Add coriander, cumin and remaining
salt and cook until potatoes are tender, 3 to 4 minutes. Stir in
vinegar and cook for 1 minute. Mix in mint. Serve hot with any
Indian bread.

Kashmiri Leg of Lamb

5 to 5½ lbs	leg of lamb, bone-in	2.5 to 2.75 kg
1½ cups	plain nonfat yogurt	375 mL
¼ cup	freshly squeezed lime or lemon juice	50 mL
2 tbsp	each ginger paste and garlic paste	25 mL
1 tbsp	salt	15 mL
1 tsp	cumin powder	5 mL
1 tsp	ground cardamom	5 mL
½ tsp	freshly ground black pepper	2 mL
½ tsp	each cayenne pepper and turmeric	2 mL
½ tsp	each ground cinnamon and ground clove	2 mL
2 tbsp	oil	25 mL
¾ tsp	saffron threads	4 mL
2 tbsp	hot milk	25 mL
2 tbsp	blanched almonds, chopped	25 mL
2 tbsp	unsalted pistachios, chopped	25 mL
2½ tbsp	liquid honey	32 mL

Serves 8 to 10

Kashmir raises lamb and it is preferred over goat, which is the meat of choice in the rest of the country. Kashmiri cuisine abounds in rich lamb dishes, and it is well known that no wedding feast would feature less than eight to ten lamb preparations.

Tips

In India, there is a cultural bias against "pink" meat, and all meat is well cooked.

Ginger and garlic pastes are available in jars in Indian and Asian markets. Making your own is a simple matter of grating peeled gingerroot or garlic cloves on a Microplane grater.

1. Trim all fat and silver skin from lamb. Wipe with damp paper towels. With tip of a sharp knife make 3 to 4 deep slits 2 inches (5 cm) apart lengthwise down both sides of leg. Place in a nonreactive container.

2. In a large bowl, stir together yogurt, lime juice, ginger, garlic, salt, cumin, cardamom, black pepper, cayenne, turmeric, cinnamon, clove and oil. Pour half over lamb and work into slits. Turn lamb over and pour remaining marinade over top, working into slits. Cover and refrigerate for 24 to 48 hours. Turn lamb 2 to 3 times as it marinates, spooning marinade over each time.

3. Transfer lamb with marinade to roasting pan and return to room temperature before cooking.

4. In a small bowl, soak saffron in hot milk for 15 minutes.

5. Preheat oven to 450°F (230°C).

6. In a spice grinder, grind almonds and pistachios to a powder. Mix with saffron milk to make a paste. Spread paste over top of lamb. Drizzle honey over top.

7. Cover pan loosely with foil. Roast in preheated oven for 30 minutes. Reduce heat to 350°F (180°C) and continue to roast, allowing 30 minutes per pound (kg), until well done (an internal temperature of 170°F/77°C), about 2½ hours. Remove foil for last 15 minutes of cooking. Let rest for 10 minutes before carving. Spoon any remaining masala over lamb before serving.

Keema Lucknowi
Lucknow-Style Lamb

Serves 6

Lucknow, a predominantly Muslim city in Uttar Pradesh, was the epicenter of gourmet food. Its ruler, the nawab (nabob), *was known to serve the most unusual dishes at his banquets, which were akin to orgies, lasting for several hours.*

3 tbsp	raw unsalted cashews	45 mL
3 tbsp	blanched almonds	45 mL
1 tbsp	sesame seeds	15 mL
¾ tsp	saffron threads	4 mL
¾ cup	plain nonfat yogurt, at room temperature	175 mL
¾ tsp	cornstarch	4 mL
2 tbsp	oil	25 mL
1	stick cinnamon, about 3 inches (7.5 cm) long, broken in half	1
10	whole cloves	10
8	green cardamom pods, cracked open	8
4	black cardamom pods, seeds only, crushed	4
4	flakes mace (see Tips, right) or 1 tsp (5 mL) powdered mace (javitri)	4
4	bay leaves	4
3 cups	chopped onions	750 mL
1 tbsp	minced peeled gingerroot	15 mL
1 tbsp	minced garlic	15 mL
1½ lbs	ground lamb	750 g
1 tbsp	coriander powder	15 mL
2 tsp	salt or to taste	10 mL
1½ tsp	cumin powder	7 mL
1 tsp	cayenne pepper	5 mL

1. In a blender, combine cashews, almonds and sesame seeds and grind to a powder. Add ¾ cup (175 mL) water and blend to a thick batter, adding more water as necessary, in small quantities, and scraping down sides of blender as you go. (The result should resemble cake batter.) Transfer to a bowl. Pour ½ cup (125 mL) water into blender and whiz 2 seconds to incorporate remainder in blender. Pour into another bowl and set aside.

2. In a small bowl, soak saffron in ¼ cup (50 mL) very hot water. Set aside.

3. In a bowl, stir together yogurt and cornstarch to a creamy consistency. Set aside.

4. In a saucepan, heat oil over medium-high heat. Add cinnamon, cloves, cardamom pods and seeds, mace and bay leaves and sauté until fragrant, about 1 minute. Add onions and mix well. Sauté until onions are golden brown, about 20 minutes, adjusting heat as onions brown, but maintaining an audible sizzle.

5. Return heat to medium-high. Add ginger, garlic and lamb, breaking up lumps to brown evenly. Mix well with onion mixture. Cook until juices have been absorbed and meat is well browned, about 20 minutes. Reduce heat to medium and continue cooking until meat is dark brown, 10 to 12 minutes. Add coriander, salt, cumin and cayenne and cook for 2 minutes. If necessary, deglaze pan with reserved blender water.

6. Add 2½ cups (625 mL) water to pan and stir in nut paste. Add yogurt and saffron with liquid and mix well. Cover and bring to a boil. Reduce heat to medium-low and simmer, stirring periodically, until gravy is thick, 15 to 20 minutes. Serve hot with rice or an Indian bread.

Tips

Mace flakes refer to the lacy outer covering of nutmeg in its natural form.

The lengthy browning of lamb is necessary to achieve the rich flavor of the dish.

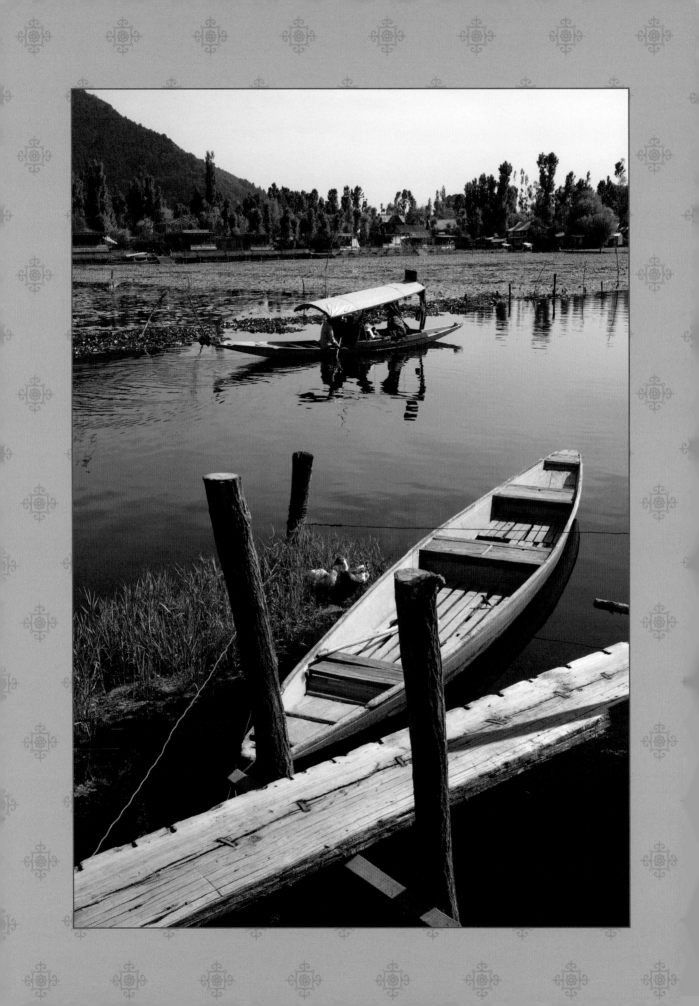

Bhoona Gosht

Lamb Nuggets in Spiced Yogurt

2½ tbsp	oil, divided	32 mL
10	cashews	10
1½ cups	plain nonfat yogurt, at room temperature	375 mL
1½ tsp	cornstarch	7 mL
1½ tsp	salt or to taste	7 mL
1 tsp	cayenne pepper	5 mL
½ tsp	turmeric	2 mL
1½ lbs	boneless lamb, cut into 1½-inch (4 cm) cubes	750 g
1½ tsp	Indian poppy seeds (see Tip, page 219)	7 mL
2 cups	thinly sliced onions (lengthwise slices)	500 mL
15	cloves garlic, puréed	15
1 tbsp	minced peeled gingerroot	15 mL
2	sticks cinnamon, each 2 inches (5 cm) long	2
1½ tsp	coriander powder	7 mL
¾ tsp	ground cardamom	4 mL
4	whole cloves, crushed	4
1 tsp	garam masala	5 mL

Serves 4 to 6

Bhoona *refers to the technique of browning an ingredient by sautéing it slowly to achieve a concentrated flavor. After lamb becomes fork-tender, it is browned to develop a complexity that is essential to the finished dish.*

1. In a small skillet, heat ½ tbsp (7 mL) oil over medium heat. Add cashews and sauté until golden, about 1 minute. Transfer to a bowl.

2. In a large bowl, stir together yogurt, cornstarch, salt, cayenne and turmeric. Add lamb and mix well. Set aside for 15 minutes.

3. In a smooth mortar, soak poppy seeds in 2 tsp (10 mL) water for 15 minutes. Grind to a paste with a pestle. Set aside.

4. In a saucepan, heat remaining oil over medium-high heat. Add onions and sauté until golden brown, about 10 minutes. Reduce heat to medium. Add garlic, ginger, poppy seed paste, cinnamon, coriander, cardamom and cloves and mix well. Cook, stirring continuously, until masala is darker and begins to form a thick mass, 2 minutes. If necessary, add 1 tbsp (15 mL) water to prevent sticking.

5. Add lamb with marinade to pan and mix well. Increase heat to medium-high and bring to a boil, stirring periodically. Reduce heat to medium-low. Cover and cook, stirring frequently, to ensure masala does not burn on bottom of pan, about 45 minutes. When gravy thickens, uncover, reduce heat to medium-low and cook to reduce further. At this point, stir almost continuously. The total cooking process should take about 1 hour.

6. Remove from heat. Sprinkle with garam masala and let rest, covered, for 5 minutes. Mix gently. Mound lamb mixture on platter and garnish with cashews before serving.

Desi Gosht
Braised Goat

See Tip, page 218

Serves 6 to 8

HOT

Cabrito (young goat) is the meat of choice in India. Lean and flavorful, it is available in Middle Eastern butcher shops and specialty meat markets throughout North America.

20	dried Indian red chiles, broken into pieces, most of the seeds removed	20
5	star anise (badian)	5
2 tsp	each cardamom seeds and whole cloves	10 mL
1 tsp	black peppercorns	5 mL
1 tsp	black cumin (shah jeera)	5 mL
3	sticks cinnamon, each about 3 inches (7.5 cm) long, broken into pieces	3
2 tbsp	each minced gingerroot and minced garlic	25 mL
1 tbsp	salt or to taste	15 mL
5 lbs	cabrito (young goat) or lamb shanks, each cut in half	2.5 kg
6 tbsp	oil, divided	90 mL
4	black cardamom pods, cracked open	4
2 lbs	potatoes, cut into 1-inch (2.5 cm) wide wedges	1 kg
1 cup	cilantro leaves, chopped	250 mL
1/2 cup	crispy fried onions (see Tip, page 218)	125 mL

1. In a spice grinder, grind chiles, star anise, cardamom seeds, cloves, peppercorns, black cumin and cinnamon to a powder.

2. In a blender, combine ginger, garlic, chile spice powder, salt and 1/4 cup (50 mL) water and blend to make a paste.

3. Rinse cabrito and pat dry. In a large wide saucepan, heat 1/4 cup (50 mL) of the oil over medium-high heat. Add black cardamom and sauté until fragrant, 30 seconds. Add meat, in batches as necessary, and brown, turning once, adding a little water periodically to prevent sticking and to deglaze, 8 to 10 minutes per batch.

4. Remove meat with slotted spoon. After removing last batch, add remaining oil to pan. Reduce heat to medium. Add spice paste and sauté until fragrant and a little darker, 4 to 5 minutes, adding 2 tbsp (25 mL) water to deglaze pan periodically. Return meat to pan and mix well. Add enough water to cover meat. Cover, increase heat to high and bring to a boil. Reduce heat to medium-low and cook, stirring periodically, for 1 hour.

5. Arrange potatoes over meat and continue to cook until meat is fork-tender, gravy is reduced and potatoes are soft, 30 minutes.

6. Remove from heat and sprinkle with chopped cilantro. Transfer meat to a serving dish. Garnish with crispy fried onions. Serve with rice or an Indian bread.

Grilled Cabrito Chops

5 lbs	small single cabrito chops (young goat)	2.5 kg
¾ cup	plain yogurt, excess moisture drained	175 mL
¾ cup	cilantro, chopped	175 mL
¼ cup	freshly squeezed lime or lemon juice	50 mL
2 tbsp	ginger paste (see Tips, page 207)	25 mL
2 tbsp	garlic paste	25 mL
1 tbsp	coriander powder	15 mL
2½ tsp	salt or to taste	12 mL
1½ tsp	cumin powder	7 mL
1 tsp	cayenne pepper	5 mL
2 tbsp	oil	25 mL
	Oil for barbecue	

Marinated Red Onions, optional

1	red onion	1
⅓ cup	white vinegar	75 mL

Serves 8

Tiny chops, delicately perfumed with spices and grilled to succulent perfection, are a specialty in North India.

1. Rinse chops and pat dry thoroughly.

2. In a large shallow nonreactive pan, mix together yogurt, cilantro, lime juice, ginger, garlic, coriander, salt, cumin, cayenne and oil. Add chops and coat with marinade. Cover and refrigerate for at least 8 hours or preferably for 24 hours.

3. *Marinated Red Onions, if using:* Slice red onion into thin rings. Place in a bowl and add vinegar. Soak for 2 to 3 hours.

4. When ready to grill, preheat barbecue to medium. Brush generously with oil. Add chops and cook, covered, 5 to 6 minutes per side. Discard marinade.

5. Serve with marinated red onions scattered over top of chops on serving platter, if desired.

Assamese Poached Egg Curry

Serves 3 to 6

A simple but delicious dish from Assam, where eggs are popular.

Tips

Cayenne pepper is not as fiery as you might expect, but if you prefer, substitute paprika and increase to 1 tsp (5 mL).

Mustard oil is made from cold-pressed mustard seeds and is not an infusion. It has a distinctive taste and is the preferred oil in Bengal and other eastern states. However, it has an element that can be toxic to some. Heating it to smoking point neutralizes this and makes it safe for cooking.

1 lb	medium all-purpose potatoes (about 4)	500 g
2 tbsp	mustard oil	25 mL
3/4 tsp	cumin seeds	4 mL
3/4 tsp	fenugreek seeds (methi)	4 mL
1 cup	minced onions	250 mL
2	large cloves garlic, smashed	2
2 tsp	minced peeled gingerroot	10 mL
1 1/2 tsp	minced green chiles, preferably serranos	7 mL
1 tbsp	coriander powder	15 mL
3/4 tsp	turmeric	4 mL
1 1/4 tsp	salt	6 mL
6	eggs	6
3/4 tsp	cayenne pepper (see Tips, left)	4 mL

1. Peel potatoes and slice crosswise into 1/2-inch (1 cm) thick disks. Set aside in a bowl of water.

2. In a shallow saucepan, heat oil over medium-high heat until just beginning to smoke. Remove from heat and let cool for 1 minute (see Tips, left). Return to medium heat. Add cumin and sauté for 20 seconds. Add fenugreek and sauté for 10 seconds.

3. Add onions and sauté for 5 minutes. Add garlic, ginger and chiles and sauté until onions are golden, about 5 minutes. Reduce heat to medium-low if mixture begins to burn before onions are golden. Add coriander and turmeric and sauté for 2 minutes.

4. Add 1 1/2 cups (375 mL) water and salt. Return to a gentle boil. Drain potatoes and layer in pan, making sure they are covered with liquid. Cover and cook until potatoes are tender, 6 to 8 minutes.

5. Break eggs carefully over top of potatoes. Cover and cook until eggs are just set, 5 to 6 minutes. Sprinkle cayenne over top. Serve over rice.

Poora Kukura

Assamese Roast Chicken

- *Roasting pan*

3 to 3½ lbs	whole chicken	1.5 to 1.75 kg
¼ cup	freshly squeezed lime or lemon juice	50 mL
2 tsp	salt or to taste	10 mL
2	dried Indian red chiles broken into pieces, or 2 tsp (10 mL) hot pepper flakes	2
1 tsp	fenugreek seeds (methi)	5 mL
½ tsp	cumin seeds	2 mL
1 tsp	coriander powder	5 mL
4 tsp	minced peeled gingerroot	20 mL
4 tsp	minced garlic	20 mL
4 tsp	minced green chiles, preferably serranos	20 mL
1 tbsp	cider vinegar	15 mL
2 tbsp	oil	25 mL

1. Skin chicken and rinse and pat dry thoroughly. Make long deep slits on the breast and legs. Mix lime juice with salt until salt is dissolved. Rub all over chicken, including inside the cavity and in slits.

2. In a spice grinder, grind red chiles, fenugreek and cumin to a powder. Transfer to a bowl and mix in coriander powder.

3. In a mortar, mix together ginger, garlic, green chiles and vinegar. Add spice mix and grind to a paste with a pestle. Mix oil into paste.

4. Coat chicken, inside and out, with paste. Cover and refrigerate for at least 4 hours or for up to 12 hours.

5. Preheat oven to 350°F (180°C). Reserving marinade, place chicken, breast side up, in roasting pan. Roast for 30 minutes. Pour reserved marinade over chicken. Increase heat to 400°F (200°C) and cook until joint at thigh moves easily and juices run clear when the thigh is pierced, about 30 minutes.

Serves 4 to 6

Roast chicken with a difference! Removing the skin and making deep gashes allows flavors to get down to the bone.

Murgi Jhol

Bengali Chicken Stew

Serves 6 to 8

This stew is typical of everyday Bengali food — lightly spiced, with a broth-like gravy. It is served with steamed rice, which absorbs the thin gravy admirably.

Tip

Panch phoran is a mix of equal proportions of five aromatic seeds, including mustard, cumin, fennel, fenugreek and nigella. It can be premixed and stored indefinitely.

12	skinless bone-in chicken thighs	12
3½ tbsp	oil, divided	52 mL
1 tbsp	panch phoran (see Tip, left)	15 mL
2	bay leaves	2
1 tbsp	minced peeled gingerroot	15 mL
1 tbsp	minced garlic	15 mL
3	plum (Roma) tomatoes, cut into 1-inch (2.5 cm) wedges	3
1 tbsp	coriander powder	15 mL
1 tbsp	cumin powder	15 mL
2 tsp	turmeric	10 mL
2 tsp	salt	10 mL
8 oz	all-purpose potatoes, peeled and cut into chunks (about 2)	250 g
6 to 8	large cauliflower florets (about half a small head)	6 to 8

1. Rinse chicken and pat dry thoroughly.

2. In a large saucepan, heat 2 tbsp (25 mL) of the oil over medium heat. Brown chicken, in 2 batches, 6 to 8 minutes per batch. Remove with tongs and set aside.

3. Remove from heat. Scrape up any bits and pieces that may be stuck to the pan and add to chicken.

4. Add remaining oil to pan and heat over medium-high heat. Add panch phoran. When the seeds stop popping, in a few seconds, reduce heat to medium. Immediately add bay leaves, ginger, garlic and tomatoes and stir to mix. Add coriander, cumin and turmeric and sauté for 1 minute.

5. Add 4 cups (1 L) water. Increase heat to medium-high. Add chicken, making sure all pieces are submerged. Add salt. Cover and bring to a boil. Reduce heat to low and simmer for 35 minutes.

6. Add potatoes and cauliflower. Cook, stirring occasionally, until vegetables are tender and chicken is no longer pink inside, 12 to 14 minutes.

Murgi Kalia
Bengali Muslim-Style Chicken

Serves 6 to 8

Bengali Muslim food has its roots in Moghlai cuisine, which is evident in this well-recognized dish.

Tip

Crispy fried onions are available in Indian and Middle Eastern markets. They can be stored in the refrigerator for up to 1 year after opening.

12	skinless bone-in chicken thighs	12
½ tsp	saffron threads	2 mL
¼ cup	very hot milk	50 mL
½ cup	plain nonfat yogurt	125 mL
½ tsp	cornstarch	2 mL
1 cup	drained canned tomatoes, puréed	250 mL
3 to 4	whole green chiles, preferably serranos	3 to 4
2 tsp	salt or to taste	10 mL
1 tsp	minced peeled gingerroot	5 mL
1 tsp	minced garlic	5 mL
1 tsp	cumin seeds	5 mL
1 tsp	cayenne pepper	5 mL
½ tsp	turmeric	2 mL
1	stick cinnamon, about 3 inches (7.5 cm) long	1
6	green cardamom pods, cracked open	6
8	whole cloves	8
10	black peppercorns	10
2 tbsp	oil	25 mL
1 cup	crispy fried onions (see Tip, left)	250 mL
½ cup	mint leaves, coarsely chopped	125 mL
½ cup	cilantro leaves, coarsely chopped	125 mL

1. Rinse chicken and pat dry thoroughly.

2. In a small bowl, soak saffron in hot milk for 15 minutes.

3. In a large nonreactive bowl, stir together yogurt and cornstarch to a creamy consistency. Mix in tomatoes, green chiles, salt, ginger, garlic, cumin, cayenne, turmeric, cinnamon, cardamom, cloves and peppercorns. Add chicken and coat pieces well with mixture. Marinate for 30 minutes at room temperature.

4. In a large saucepan, heat oil over medium-high heat. Add chicken with marinade, pour in saffron with soaking liquid and scatter onions over top. Sprinkle with half each of the mint and cilantro. Cover and cook for 10 minutes. Shake pan to loosen chicken pieces. Reduce heat to low and cook, gently stirring occasionally, until chicken is no longer pink inside, about 40 minutes. Garnish with remaining mint and cilantro.

Murgi Posto

Chicken with Poppy Seeds

- *Saucepan with tight-fitting lid*

4 tsp	Indian poppy seeds (see Tip, right)	20 mL
12	skinless bone-in chicken thighs (about 3 lbs/1.5 kg)	12
1 cup	plain nonfat yogurt, at room temperature	250 mL
1 tsp	cornstarch	5 mL
1 cup	puréed onion	250 mL
1 tbsp	minced peeled gingerroot	15 mL
1 tsp	minced garlic	5 mL
2 tsp	coriander powder	10 mL
2 tsp	cumin powder	10 mL
2 tsp	cayenne pepper	10 mL
2 tsp	salt or to taste	10 mL
¾ tsp	fennel seeds (saunf), ground to a coarse powder	4 mL
¾ tsp	powdered mace (javitri)	4 mL
3 tbsp	oil	45 mL
5 tbsp	slivered or sliced blanched almonds, divided	75 mL
2 tbsp	raisins	25 mL

1. In a smooth mortar, soak poppy seeds in 2 tbsp (25 mL) water for 30 minutes or several hours. Grind to a paste with a pestle, periodically scraping sides of mortar and end of pestle. (This will take about 6 to 8 minutes and a strong arm.) Set aside.

2. Rinse chicken and pat dry thoroughly.

3. In a saucepan, mix together yogurt and cornstarch until creamy. Add onion, ginger, garlic, poppy seed paste (posto), coriander, cumin, cayenne, salt, fennel, mace, oil and chicken.

4. Cover with a tight-fitting lid and bring to a boil over medium-high heat. Reduce heat to medium-low and cook, stirring occasionally, until chicken is almost tender, 40 to 45 minutes. (At this point there will be a lot of liquid in the pan.)

5. Add 3 tbsp (45 mL) of the almonds and raisins. Continue to cook, uncovered, maintaining a gentle boil until chicken is no longer pink inside and liquid is reduced to about 1 cup (250 mL), 15 to 20 minutes. Sauté gently, until lightly browned and thick masala coats chicken, 6 to 8 minutes. Garnish with remaining almonds. Serve with rice.

Serves 6 to 8

Poppy seeds, known as posto, *feature prominently in Bengali food. Indian poppy seeds, like all poppy seeds, are free of opium and are a pale ivory color. Poppy seed paste, which is considered a delicacy, is the primary seasoning in this dish.*

Tip

Indian poppy seeds are pale-colored and are preferred as they do not discolor the dish as dark poppy seeds tend to do. However, if you only have dark ones, they can be substituted.

Ghoogni

Lamb with Brown Chickpeas

Serves 6

Traditionally, this Bengali dish would be cooked until there is no moisture and then served in bowls as a snack. Since it is a substantial dish, I prefer to leave in a little more liquid and serve it with rice or an Indian bread. Either way it's delicious.

1/2 cup	dried brown chickpeas (kala channa)	125 mL
1 1/2 tsp	salt or to taste, divided	7 mL
1/2 cup	finely diced fresh coconut	125 mL
3 tbsp	oil, divided	45 mL
2 cups	peeled cubed (1/2 inch/1 cm) potatoes	500 mL
3 1/2 cups	thinly sliced onions (lengthwise slices)	875 mL
1/4 cup	sliced garlic	50 mL
8 oz	ground lamb	250 g
1 1/2 tsp	minced peeled gingerroot	7 mL
1/2 tsp	turmeric	2 mL
2 tsp	coriander powder	10 mL
1 tsp	cumin powder	5 mL
1/2 tsp	freshly ground black pepper	2 mL
1/2 cup	cilantro, chopped, divided	125 mL
1 tsp	garam masala	5 mL

1. Rinse chickpeas and transfer to a bowl. Add water to cover by 4 inches (10 cm) and soak at room temperature for 6 hours or overnight. Drain chickpeas and place in a saucepan with 4 cups (1 L) water. Bring to a boil over high heat. Reduce heat to medium-low, cover partially and cook until chickpeas are soft, 20 to 25 minutes. Add 1 tsp (5 mL) of the salt and remove from heat.

2. In a dry skillet over medium heat, toast coconut, stirring until lightly browned, 3 to 4 minutes. Remove and set aside.

3. In same skillet, heat 1 1/2 tbsp (22 mL) of the oil. Add potatoes and sauté until lightly browned, 6 to 7 minutes. Set aside.

4. In a saucepan, heat remaining oil over medium heat. Add onions and sauté until golden, 10 to 12 minutes. Add garlic and sauté for 5 minutes.

5. Add lamb, ginger, turmeric and remaining salt and mix well, breaking up all lumps. Sauté, stirring frequently, until well browned, 12 to 15 minutes. If necessary, deglaze periodically with 2 tbsp (25 mL) water to prevent sticking.

6. Pour chickpeas including liquid into pan. Add coriander, cumin and black pepper. Add potatoes and most of the cilantro, saving a little for garnish, and mix well. Bring to a gentle boil and reduce heat to medium-low. Cover and simmer, stirring occasionally, until gravy is thick, 10 to 12 minutes. Add garam masala. Garnish with remaining cilantro and serve with steamed rice.

Coorg Egg and Potato Curry

1 lb	potatoes (any variety) (about 4)	500 g
½ tsp	black peppercorns	2 mL
4	dried Indian red chiles	4
2 tsp	coriander seeds	10 mL
½ tsp	cumin seeds	2 mL
1	stick cinnamon, about 2 inches (5 cm) long, broken into pieces	1
6	whole cloves	6
¼ tsp	cardamom seeds	1 mL
½ tsp	turmeric	2 mL
½ cup	grated coconut, fresh or frozen, thawed	125 mL
2 tbsp	oil	25 mL
2 to 3	green chiles, cut in half lengthwise	2 to 3
2 cups	thinly sliced onions (lengthwise slices)	500 mL
2 tbsp	julienned peeled gingerroot	25 mL
2 tbsp	thinly sliced garlic	25 mL
1	sprig curry leaf, stripped (12 to 15 leaves)	1
1½ tsp	salt or to taste	7 mL
2 tbsp	freshly squeezed lime or lemon juice	25 mL
6	hard-cooked eggs, peeled and cut in half horizontally	6

1. Peel potatoes and cut into 2-inch (5 cm) pieces. Set aside.

2. Heat a skillet over medium heat for 3 minutes. Add peppercorns and stir for 20 seconds. Add red chiles and stir for 20 seconds. Add coriander, cumin, cinnamon, cloves and cardamom. Stir mixture until fragrant, 20 seconds. Transfer to a bowl and let cool. Grind to a powder in a spice grinder. Transfer to a bowl and stir in turmeric.

3. In a blender, blend together coconut and ½ cup (125 mL) water to make a smooth purée.

4. In a saucepan, heat oil over medium heat. Add green chiles, onions, ginger, garlic and curry leaves and sauté until golden, 6 to 8 minutes. Add spice powder and sauté for 3 minutes.

5. Add 3 cups (750 mL) water and coconut purée. Increase heat to medium-high and bring to a boil. Add potatoes and salt and mix. Cover pan and return to a boil. Reduce heat to medium-low and cook until potatoes are soft, 8 to 10 minutes. Stir in lime juice.

6. Arrange eggs in a single layer on a shallow serving dish. Spoon potatoes and coconut gravy over eggs. Serve hot with rice.

Serves 4 to 6

HOT

Coorg is a small area in the southern part of the Western Ghats, bordering on Kerala. It is a district in Karnataka, populated by a diverse mix of people from various surrounding areas. At one time, there were lush forests, home to a large variety of animals, including tigers, panthers and wild pigs. Coorgis' traditional cuisine is based on local produce, including bananas, bamboo shoots, coconuts, wild mushrooms and, of course, rice. Pork is the preferred meat.

Tip
In Step 5, if gravy is too thin, mash a couple of pieces of potato to thicken.

Eggs in Hyderabadi Tomato Gravy

Serves 8

Shahnaz, a friend of mine whose family is from Hyderabad, is an accomplished cook. She served this dish as part of a wonderful Hyderabadi feast at her home. The table was laden with several dishes, but this was my favorite.

1 ½ tbsp	oil	22 mL
¾ tsp	dark mustard seeds	4 mL
¼ tsp	asafetida (hing)	1 mL
2	dried Indian red chiles	2
¾ tsp	cumin seeds	4 mL
¾ tsp	nigella seeds (kalaunji)	4 mL
½ tsp	fenugreek seeds	2 mL
2	sprigs fresh curry leaves, stripped (20 to 25 leaves)	2
1 tbsp	chopped garlic	15 mL
1	can (28 oz/796 mL) diced tomatoes, including juice	1
2 cups	tomato sauce	500 mL
1 tbsp	minced peeled gingerroot	15 mL
2 tsp	minced garlic	10 mL
2 tsp	minced green chiles, preferably serranos	10 mL
1 tsp	cayenne pepper	5 mL
1 tsp	salt or to taste	5 mL
½ tsp	turmeric	2 mL
8	hard-cooked eggs, peeled and cut in half horizontally	8

1. In a saucepan, heat oil over high heat until a couple of mustard seeds thrown in start to sputter. Add all the mustard seeds and cover quickly. When the seeds stop popping, in a few seconds, uncover and reduce heat to medium. Add asafetida and sauté for 10 seconds. Add red chiles, cumin, nigella, fenugreek, curry leaves and chopped garlic and sauté for 30 seconds.

2. Add tomatoes with juice, tomato sauce, ginger, minced garlic, green chiles, cayenne, salt and turmeric and mix well. Reduce heat to low and simmer, stirring periodically, until sauce reduces and tomatoes are soft, about 30 minutes. Mash tomatoes with back of spoon.

3. Slowly pour in ½ cup (125 mL) hot water and stir to mix. Cook until heated through, 3 to 4 minutes. Pour mixture into a serving dish and place eggs in gravy. Serve with an Indian bread.

Andhra Country Chicken Curry

Serves 4 to 6

"Country chicken" refers to free-range chicken. Although in the larger cities commercially raised chicken — known simply as "broiler chicken" — is the norm, in small towns, free-range chicken is still the order of the day. If you use free-range chicken for this recipe, you might need to adjust the cooking time. This is a home-style dish, with a typically thin curry, as Indians prefer to soak their rice with it.

Tip

Andhra Pradesh uses garam masala freely, the result of Moghlai influence on Hyderabadi cuisine. It is different than the North Indian garam masala blends because the main ingredient is a distinctive local variety of black cumin (*shah jeera*). It is readily available in Indian markets and is a distinctive feature of Andhra cuisine. Regular garam masala is acceptable to use.

2 lbs	skinless bone-in chicken thighs	1 kg
½ cup	plain nonfat yogurt, at room temperature	125 mL
½ tsp	cornstarch	2 mL
2 tbsp	oil	25 mL
2 cups	finely chopped onions	500 mL
6	whole cloves	6
4	green cardamom pods, cracked open	4
1 tbsp	minced peeled gingerroot	15 mL
1 tbsp	minced garlic	15 mL
2 tsp	coriander powder	10 mL
1 tsp	cayenne pepper	5 mL
1 tsp	salt or to taste	5 mL
1½ tsp	Andhra garam masala (see Tip, left)	7 mL
3 tbsp	cilantro, chopped	45 mL

1. Rinse chicken and pat dry thoroughly.

2. In a bowl, stir together yogurt and cornstarch to a creamy consistency. Set aside.

3. In a saucepan, heat oil over medium heat. Add onions, cloves and cardamom and sauté until golden, 8 to 10 minutes. Add ginger and garlic and sauté for 2 minutes. Add chicken and mix well. Sauté until chicken is browned on both sides, 6 to 8 minutes.

4. Add coriander and cayenne and sauté for 2 minutes.

5. Add 1½ cups (375 mL) water. Add yogurt and salt. Cover and bring to a boil. Reduce heat to low. Cook, stirring occasionally, until chicken is no longer pink inside and gravy is thickened, 20 to 25 minutes. Sprinkle garam masala over top. Garnish with cilantro. Serve over steamed rice.

Achari Murg
Chicken with Pickling Spices

12	skinless bone-in chicken thighs (or thighs and drumsticks)	12
4 tsp	coriander seeds	20 mL
2 tbsp	cumin seeds, divided	25 mL
2 tbsp	ginger paste (see Tips, page 207)	25 mL
2 tbsp	garlic paste	25 mL
2 tbsp	cayenne pepper	25 mL
10	green chiles, preferably serranos, cut in half vertically	10
5 to 6	sprigs fresh curry leaves, stripped (about 60 to 70 leaves)	5 to 6
¾ cup	freshly squeezed lime or lemon juice	175 mL
2 tsp	salt or to taste	10 mL
3 tbsp	oil	45 mL
2 tsp	dark mustard seeds	10 mL
10	dried Indian red chiles	10
2 tsp	fenugreek seeds (methi)	10 mL
1 tsp	nigella seeds (kalaunji)	5 mL

1. Rinse chicken and pat dry thoroughly. Place in a nonreactive saucepan.

2. In a spice grinder, grind coriander and 2 tsp (10 mL) of the cumin seeds to a powder. Transfer to a bowl. Mix in ginger, garlic, cayenne, green chiles, curry leaves, lime juice and salt. Pour marinade over chicken and mix well. Cover and marinate for 30 minutes at room temperature.

3. In a small saucepan, heat oil over high heat until a couple of mustard seeds thrown in start to sputter. Add all the mustard seeds and cover quickly. When the seeds stop popping, in a few seconds, uncover, reduce heat to medium and add red chiles and remaining cumin seeds. Sauté for 30 seconds. Add fenugreek and nigella seeds and sauté for 10 seconds. Pour mixture over chicken.

4. Cover immediately. Place saucepan over medium-high heat and bring to a boil. Reduce heat to medium-low and cook, stirring occasionally, until chicken is no longer pink inside, about 45 minutes. Adjust heat to allow chicken to cook without additional liquid. When cooked, chicken should be enveloped in the thick spice mixture (masala) and there should be no liquid left.

Serves 8

HOT

This is a recipe from Hyderabad, where a pocket of Moghlai cuisine with South Indian overtones has resulted in a unique style known as Hyderabadi cuisine. Nigella and fenugreek seeds are used extensively in spicy oil-based pickles, hence the name. This dish is best served with simple dal and rice, and accompanied by a raita or a lightly seasoned vegetable.

Tip
The whole dried red chiles are to flavor the oil and should not be eaten. If you prefer, remove chiles before serving.

Chicken Curry in Yogurt Gravy

Serves 6

The yogurt gravy makes this dish from Tamil Nadu taste ultra-rich. Enhanced with a little cashew meal and coconut milk, it is a delicious dish for entertaining.

4 lbs	skinless bone-in chicken thighs	2 kg
1 ½ cups	plain nonfat yogurt, at room temperature	375 mL
1 ½ tsp	cornstarch	7 mL
2 cups	coarsely chopped onions	500 mL
⅓ cup	coarsely chopped garlic	75 mL
¼ cup	coarsely chopped peeled gingerroot	50 mL
2 tbsp	chopped green chiles, preferably serranos	25 mL
2 tbsp	oil, divided (approx.)	25 mL
1 ½ tsp	coriander seeds	7 mL
1 ½ tsp	cumin seeds	7 mL
1 tsp	fennel seeds (saunf)	5 mL
2	sticks cinnamon, each about 3 inches (7.5 cm) long, broken into pieces, divided	2
9	whole cloves, divided	9
¼ tsp	cardamom seeds	1 mL
¼ tsp	ground white pepper	1 mL
2 tsp	salt	10 mL
2	bay leaves	2
1 cup	thinly sliced shallots	250 mL
3 tbsp	raw cashews, ground into meal	45 mL
2 tbsp	freshly squeezed lime or lemon juice	25 mL
1 cup	coconut milk	250 mL
½ cup	cilantro, chopped	125 mL

1. Rinse chicken and pat dry thoroughly.

2. In a large bowl, stir together yogurt and cornstarch to a creamy consistency. Set aside.

3. In a food processor, purée onions, garlic, ginger and green chiles. Add to yogurt.

4. In a skillet, heat 1 tsp (5 mL) of the oil over medium heat. Add coriander, cumin, fennel, 1 stick cinnamon, 6 cloves, cardamom and white pepper and sauté until fragrant, about 2 minutes. Let cool.

5. Transfer to a spice grinder and grind to a powder. Add to yogurt mixture. Add salt and mix well. Add chicken to yogurt marinade. Cover and marinate for 30 minutes at room temperature or for up to 8 hours in the refrigerator.

6. In a saucepan, heat remaining oil over medium heat. Add bay leaves, remaining cloves and cinnamon and sauté for 1 minute. Add shallots and sauté for 2 minutes.

7. Add chicken and marinade and mix well. Cover and bring to a boil. Cook for 5 minutes. Reduce heat to low and cook, stirring periodically, for 30 minutes. Stir in cashew meal and lime juice. Cover and cook for 10 minutes. Stir, scraping bottom of pan to make sure chicken is not sticking to pan.

8. Stir in coconut milk. Simmer, uncovered, stirring periodically, until chicken is no longer pink inside and gravy is thickened, 8 to 10 minutes. Garnish with cilantro. Serve hot with rice.

Vasu's Chicken Curry

Serves 6 to 8

HOT

My friend Vasu shared this typical home-style Andhra recipe, emphasizing that the Andhra garam masala makes a difference here. The distinctive Andhra black cumin (shah jeera) is the main component of their garam masala, which is used in meat and poultry dishes only.

Tip

Dry unsweetened coconut powder is available in Indian markets. Refrigerate in a resealable freezer bag for up to 2 years.

3 to 3½ lbs	skinless bone-in chicken thighs	1.5 to 1.75 kg
1 cup	plain nonfat yogurt	250 mL
1 tsp	cornstarch	5 mL
2½ tbsp	minced peeled gingerroot, divided	32 mL
2½ tbsp	minced garlic, divided	32 mL
2 tsp	cayenne pepper	10 mL
1½ tsp	salt	7 mL
1 tsp	freshly ground black pepper	5 mL
1 tsp	turmeric	5 mL
2 tbsp	oil	25 mL
1½ tsp	black cumin (shah jeera)	7 mL
4 cups	chopped onions	1 L
¼ cup	dry unsweetened coconut powder (see Tip, left)	50 mL
2 tbsp	Indian poppy seeds (see Tip, page 219)	25 mL
2 tsp	coriander powder	10 mL
2 tsp	Andhra garam masala, divided (see Tip, page 224)	10 mL

1. Rinse chicken and pat dry thoroughly.

2. In a large bowl, stir together yogurt and cornstarch to a creamy consistency. Stir in 2 tbsp (25 mL) ginger, 2 tbsp (25 mL) garlic, cayenne, salt, black pepper and turmeric. Add chicken and mix well with marinade. Cover and marinate for 30 minutes at room temperature or for up to 8 hours in refrigerator.

3. In a saucepan, heat oil over medium-high heat. Add black cumin and sauté for 1 minute. Add onions and sauté until light golden, for 10 minutes.

4. Add remaining ginger and garlic and sauté until onions are brown, 6 to 8 minutes.

5. Add chicken with marinade and mix well. Cover and bring to a boil. Reduce heat to low and cook, stirring occasionally, until chicken is no longer pink, 35 to 40 minutes.

6. Meanwhile, in a skillet over medium heat, toast coconut, stirring continuously, until fragrant, about 3 minutes. Transfer to a bowl. Add poppy seeds, coriander and 1 tsp (5 mL) of the Andhra garam masala.

7. When chicken is cooked, stir in coconut mixture and simmer for 5 minutes. Remove from heat. Sprinkle remaining garam masala over top and cover. Let rest for 5 minutes. Stir garam masala into chicken. Serve hot.

Kerala Chicken Curry

12	skinless bone-in chicken thighs (about 4 lbs/2 kg)	12
2 tbsp	coriander powder	25 mL
1½ tsp	cayenne pepper	7 mL
¾ tsp	turmeric	4 mL
2 tbsp	oil	25 mL
4 cups	chopped onions	1 L
3 to 4	sprigs fresh curry leaves, stripped (35 to 45 leaves)	3 to 4
2 tbsp	minced peeled gingerroot	25 mL
2 tbsp	minced garlic	25 mL
1 tbsp	minced green chiles, preferably serranos	15 mL
8	plum (Roma) tomatoes, each cut into 6 wedges	8
2 tsp	salt or to taste	10 mL
1 tsp	freshly ground black pepper	5 mL
1	can (14 oz/400 mL) coconut milk	1

Serves 8

This mild chicken curry is best with plain steamed rice.

1. Rinse chicken and pat dry thoroughly. Set aside.

2. In a small bowl, mix together coriander, cayenne and turmeric. Stir in ¼ cup (50 mL) water to make a paste.

3. In a large saucepan that can accommodate chicken in a single layer, heat oil over medium heat. Add onions and sauté until golden, 8 to 10 minutes.

4. Add curry leaves, ginger, garlic and chiles and sauté for 2 minutes. Add tomatoes and cook until slightly soft, 4 to 5 minutes.

5. Scrape mixture (masala) to side of pan and arrange chicken in a single layer. Spoon masala over top of chicken. Sprinkle with salt and pepper and cook until chicken is lightly browned, 6 to 8 minutes. Turn pieces and cook until golden, 4 to 5 minutes. (There will be chicken juices in the pan.) Mix well with masala, cover and reduce heat to low. Cook, stirring periodically, until chicken is half-cooked, 20 to 25 minutes.

6. Pour in coconut milk and mix well. Cover and simmer until chicken is no longer pink inside, 10 to 15 minutes.

Koshi Ishtu
Kerala Chicken Stew

Serves 4 to 6

This is a recipe from the Syrian Christian community of Kerala.

Variation
Substitute beef or lamb, if you prefer, for the chicken.

2 lbs	skinless boneless chicken thighs	1 kg
2 tbsp	oil	25 mL
6	green cardamom pods, cracked open	6
6	whole cloves	6
1	stick cinnamon, about 2 inches (5 cm) long	1
¼ tsp	black peppercorns	1 mL
2	bay leaves	2
2½ cups	finely chopped onions	625 mL
2 tbsp	minced green chiles, preferably serranos	25 mL
1 tbsp	minced peeled gingerroot	15 mL
1 tsp	fennel seeds (saunf), powdered	5 mL
¼ tsp	turmeric	1 mL
1½ tsp	salt	7 mL
6	small potatoes, halved (about 12 oz/375 g)	6
1 cup	chopped green beans (2-inch/5 cm pieces)	250 mL
1 cup	chopped carrot (2-inch/5 cm pieces)	250 mL
20	fresh curry leaves	20
2 tbsp	julienned peeled gingerroot	25 mL
2 tbsp	thinly sliced garlic	25 mL
1	can (14 oz/400 mL) coconut milk	1
½ cup	frozen peas, thawed	125 mL

1. Rinse chicken and pat dry thoroughly. Set aside. In a saucepan, heat oil over medium heat. Add cardamom, cloves, cinnamon, peppercorns and bay leaves. Sauté until fragrant, about 40 seconds.

2. Add onions and sauté until golden, 10 to 12 minutes. Add chiles, ginger, fennel and turmeric and sauté for 2 minutes.

3. Push masala to side of pan. Add chicken, folding each piece to double the thickness. Spoon masala over top and brown for 5 minutes. Flip chicken to brown other side, 3 minutes. Stir chicken to mix well with masala.

4. Add 1 cup (250 mL) water and salt. Bring to a boil. Reduce heat to medium-low, cover and simmer until chicken is partially cooked, about 15 minutes.

5. Add potatoes, green beans, carrot, curry leaves, ginger and garlic. Increase heat to medium and return to a boil. Reduce heat to medium-low, cover and simmer for 10 minutes.

6. Add coconut milk and peas. Continue to simmer until vegetables are tender, 6 to 8 minutes. Serve hot over rice.

Chettinad Chicken

The Ultimate Black Pepper Chicken

Serves 8

HOT

This fiery chicken is a favorite from South India, the home of peppercorns. The rajas of Chettinad were known for their refined palates, and this recipe has been attributed to their palace kitchens.

12	skinless bone-in chicken thighs (or thighs and drumsticks)	12
½ cup	plain nonfat yogurt	125 mL
½ tsp	cornstarch	2 mL
2 tbsp	black peppercorns, pounded coarsely	25 mL
3 tbsp	minced peeled gingerroot, divided	45 mL
2 tbsp	minced garlic, divided	25 mL
2 tbsp	freshly squeezed lime or lemon juice	25 mL
3½ tsp	salt or to taste, divided	17 mL
2 tbsp	oil	25 mL
2 cups	chopped onions	500 mL
1 cup	chopped tomatoes	250 mL
1 tsp	garam masala	5 mL

1. Rinse chicken and pat dry thoroughly.

2. In a large nonreactive bowl, stir together yogurt, cornstarch, peppercorns, 1½ tbsp (22 mL) of the ginger, 1½ tbsp (22 mL) of the garlic, lime juice and 1½ tsp (7 mL) of the salt. Add chicken and coat all the pieces well. Cover and marinate for 30 minutes at room temperature.

3. In a saucepan, heat oil over medium-high heat. Add onions and sauté until golden, 8 to 10 minutes. Add remaining ginger and garlic and sauté until onions are brown, 8 to 10 minutes.

4. Add tomatoes, 2 tsp (10 mL) of salt, and chicken with marinade and sauté until masala turns darker, 6 to 8 minutes. Add 1 cup (250 mL) water and bring to a boil.

5. Reduce heat to medium-low. Cover and simmer, stirring occasionally, until chicken is no longer pink inside, 35 to 40 minutes. Stir in garam masala. (There should be a thick gravy when chicken is ready. If too dry, add ½ cup/125 mL hot water to return to a coating consistency.) Serve with rice or bread.

Kori Kachpoo
Mangalorean Chicken Masala

15	dried Indian red chiles, broken into pieces, seeds removed from 7 of them	15
1 1/2 tsp	cumin seeds	7 mL
1/2 tsp	black peppercorns	2 mL
4 cups	coarsely chopped onions	1 L
10	cloves garlic	10
1/4 cup	unsalted Thai tamarind purée	50 mL
1 tsp	turmeric	5 mL
2 tbsp	oil	25 mL
3 cups	finely chopped onions	750 mL
16	skinless boneless chicken thighs	16
2 tsp	salt or to taste	10 mL
1 1/2 cups	grated coconut, preferably fresh (or frozen, thawed)	375 mL

Serves 6 to 8

HOT

The food of Mangalore is spicy and rich with coconut, and the dishes are made with customized spice pastes.

1. In a spice grinder, grind chiles, cumin and peppercorns to a powder.

2. In a food processor, purée 4 cups (1 L) onions, garlic, tamarind, turmeric and powdered spices. Set aside.

3. In a saucepan, heat oil over medium-high heat. Add 3 cups (750 mL) onions and sauté until light brown, reducing heat to medium halfway through, about 15 minutes. Adjust heat to allow browning without burning.

4. Increase heat to medium-high and add chicken, onion purée and salt. Mix well and cook, stirring periodically, until chicken and masala begin to brown, about 15 minutes. Reduce heat to low and continue to brown until it turns a rich brown color. Stir more frequently, scraping bottom of pan to prevent masala from burning. If necessary, deglaze pan with water, 2 tbsp (25 mL) at a time, to allow even browning and prevent burning. The chicken should have been cooking about 30 minutes by this time. Test to see if it is cooked through. Cook in this manner until chicken is no longer pink inside.

5. Stir in coconut and cook for 5 minutes. Serve hot.

Beef and Vegetable Thoran

Serves 8

HOT

This is a dish from the Syrian Christian community of Kerala, where three distinct ethnic groups live, each with its particular cuisine. These groups are the Muslims, descendants of Arab traders who married local women, and are known as Mophlas, the Christians, who were early converts to Christianity, and the Hindus. All except the Hindus eat beef.

3	dried Indian red chiles, broken into pieces	3
1 tsp	cumin seeds	5 mL
3	shallots, cut into chunks	3
1 cup	grated coconut, preferably fresh (or frozen, thawed)	250 mL
½ tsp	turmeric	2 mL
1½ lbs	stewing beef, cut into 2-inch (5 cm) pieces	750 g
2 tbsp	cider or wine vinegar	25 mL
2 tbsp	minced peeled gingerroot	25 mL
2	sticks cinnamon, each about 3 inches (7.5 cm) long	2
6	whole cloves	6
2 tsp	salt, divided	10 mL
1 cup	thinly sliced cabbage	250 mL
1 cup	chopped peeled carrots, ½-inch (1 cm) cubes (about 3 medium)	250 mL
1 cup	chopped green beans (½-inch/1 cm pieces)	250 mL
3 tbsp	oil	45 mL
1 tsp	dark mustard seeds	5 mL
1 cup	finely chopped onion	250 mL
2 tbsp	thinly sliced green chiles, preferably serranos	25 mL
2 tbsp	chopped peeled gingerroot	25 mL
3	sprigs fresh curry leaves, stripped (25 to 30 leaves)	3

1. In a blender, combine red chiles, cumin and shallots and purée for 30 seconds. Add coconut, turmeric and 5 tbsp (70 mL) water. Blend to a smooth paste, scraping down sides of blender periodically. Set aside.

2. In a large saucepan, combine beef, vinegar, ginger, cinnamon, cloves, 1½ tsp (7 mL) of the salt and 5 cups (1.25 L) water. Bring to a boil over high heat. Reduce heat to medium and cook for 5 minutes, skimming scum off the top as it forms. Reduce heat to medium-low. Cover and cook, maintaining a gentle boil, until beef is fork-tender, about 1 hour. (If necessary, add an additional 1 cup/250 mL hot water.) When beef is cooked, there should be about ¾ to 1 cup (175 to 250 mL) water remaining in pan. Transfer beef with a slotted spoon to a dish and let cool. When cool enough to handle, tear beef into large shreds with fingers.

3. Add cabbage, carrots and green beans to remaining liquid in pan. Cover and cook over medium-low heat until vegetables are partially cooked, about 5 minutes. (There should still be some liquid in the pan.) Push vegetables to side of pan. Pour coconut-spice mixture into middle of pan. Cover mixture with vegetables and shredded beef. Cover and cook over gentle heat to "steam" coconut masala for 5 minutes. Uncover and mix well, stirring continuously, until there is no more liquid in pan. Remove from heat.

4. In another saucepan, heat oil over high heat until a couple of mustard seeds thrown in start to sputter. Add all the mustard seeds and cover quickly. When the seeds stop popping, in a few seconds, uncover, reduce heat to medium and add onion, chiles, ginger and curry leaves. Sauté until onions are golden, 3 to 4 minutes. Add to saucepan with beef mixture. Add salt and mix well. Return to medium heat and sauté to brown beef and blend flavors, 5 to 6 minutes. Serve hot.

Lamb with Green Peppercorns and Fennel

Serves 6 to 8

HOT

This spice-rich dish hails from South India, where peppercorns and cardamom grow in abundance.

2 cups	plain nonfat yogurt, at room temperature	500 mL
2 tsp	cornstarch	10 mL
4 tsp	coriander seeds	20 mL
1 tbsp	cumin seeds	15 mL
1 3/4 tsp	black cumin (shah jeera)	9 mL
1 1/2 tsp	black peppercorns	7 mL
2 tsp	salt or to taste	10 mL
2 1/2 lbs	boneless leg of lamb, cut into 1 1/2-inch (4 cm) pieces	1.25 kg
1 tsp	saffron threads	5 mL
2 1/2 tbsp	oil	32 mL
5	green cardamom pods, cracked open	5
1	black cardamom pod, cracked open	1
5	whole cloves	5
1	piece cinnamon, about 1 inch (2.5 cm) long	1
1	bay leaf	1
1/4 tsp	powdered mace (javitri)	1 mL
2 cups	thinly sliced onions (lengthwise slices)	500 mL
2 tbsp	minced peeled gingerroot	25 mL
2 tbsp	minced green chiles, preferably serranos	25 mL
1 tbsp	green peppercorns in brine, drained	15 mL
3/4 cup	half-and-half (10%) cream or table (18%) cream	175 mL
2 tsp	crushed fennel seeds (saunf)	10 mL

1. In a large bowl, stir together yogurt and cornstarch to a creamy consistency. Set aside.

2. In a spice grinder, grind coriander, cumin, black cumin and black peppercorns to a powder. Stir spice powder and salt into yogurt. Add lamb and mix well. Cover and marinate for 1 hour or for up to several hours in refrigerator.

3. In a small bowl, soak saffron in 2 tbsp (25 mL) very hot water. Set aside.

4. In a large saucepan, heat oil over medium-high heat. Add green and black cardamom pods, cloves, cinnamon, bay leaf and mace. Sauté until fragrant, 30 to 40 seconds. Add onions and sauté until golden brown, reducing heat to medium halfway through, 10 to 15 minutes.

5. Add ginger, chiles and green peppercorns and sauté for 2 minutes.

6. Stir in lamb with marinade. Add 3 cups (750 mL) water and mix well. Cover and bring to a boil. Reduce heat to low and simmer, stirring occasionally, until meat is fork-tender, about 1 hour. If liquid begins to dry, stir in $\frac{1}{2}$ cup (125 mL) hot water.

7. Add saffron with liquid and cream and simmer until gravy thickens, about 5 minutes. Sprinkle fennel over top and remove from heat. Cover and let rest for 5 minutes. Stir fennel into gravy before serving.

Variation

You can substitute stewing beef for lamb if you prefer.

Mutabak
Indian Lasagna

S

Serves 10 to 12

- *Preheat oven to 375°F (190°C)*
- *13-by 9-inch (3 L) glass baking dish, sprayed with vegetable spray*

6 tbsp	oil, divided	90 mL
4 cups	chopped onions	1 L
2 tbsp	minced peeled gingerroot	25 mL
2 tbsp	minced garlic	25 mL
1 1/2 lbs	lean ground beef, lamb or chicken	750 g
2 1/2 tsp	salt or to taste, divided	12 mL
1 tsp	garam masala	5 mL
3/4 tsp	freshly ground pepper	4 mL
14	large eggs	14
2 cups	milk	500 mL
1/2 cup	freshly squeezed lime or lemon juice	125 mL
4 tbsp	minced green chiles, preferably serranos	60 mL
1 1/2 cups	cilantro leaves and soft stems, chopped	375 mL
1 1/2 cups	mint leaves, chopped	375 mL
10	whole wheat chapatis or Whole Wheat Griddle Bread (see recipe, page 144) (see Tip, right)	10

This delicious Muslim dish is rich party food that's so good. I like to serve it as part of an elaborate buffet for a special celebration. However, you can also serve it as a lunch entrée with a salad.

Variation
Store-bought whole wheat tortillas can be substituted for the chapatis.

1. In a saucepan, heat 2 tbsp (25 mL) of the oil over medium-high heat. Add onions and sauté until golden, 12 to 15 minutes. Add ginger and garlic and sauté for 2 minutes.

2. Add ground meat and brown well, breaking up all clumps, about 10 minutes.

3. Remove from heat and fold in 1 tsp (5 mL) of the salt, garam masala and pepper.

4. In a large bowl, beat together eggs, milk, lime juice and remaining salt. Stir in chiles, cilantro and mint.

5. Arrange 5 chapatis on bottom of prepared dish to cover completely, overlapping where necessary. Spread half of the ground meat mixture over top. Layer with remaining chapatis. Spread remaining ground meat mixture over to cover. Pour egg mixture over top. Drizzle remaining oil evenly over top. Bake in preheated oven until lightly browned and set, 35 to 40 minutes. Cut into squares to serve.

Kerala Pork Uluruthu

S

Serves 4 to 6

HOT

In Kerala, pork is eaten by the Christians and is usually heavily spiced.

Variation
Use stewing beef instead of pork.

8 to 10	dried Indian red chiles, broken into pieces, half with seeds removed	8 to 10
2 tbsp	coriander seeds	25 mL
1/4 tsp	black peppercorns	1 mL
1/4 tsp	fennel seeds (saunf)	1 mL
4	whole cloves	4
1	stick cinnamon, about 2 inches (5 cm) long, broken in half	1
2 cups	coarsely chopped red onions	500 mL
2 tbsp	cider vinegar	25 mL
1 tsp	chopped peeled gingerroot	5 mL
1 tsp	turmeric	5 mL
1 tsp	salt	5 mL
2 lbs	boneless pork loin, all fat removed, cut into 1-inch (2.5 cm) pieces	1 kg
1 tbsp	julienned peeled gingerroot	15 mL
2 tbsp	thinly sliced garlic	25 mL
2 tbsp	oil	25 mL
1 tsp	dark mustard seeds	5 mL
2 cups	thinly sliced red onions (lengthwise slices)	500 mL

1. In a spice grinder, grind chiles, coriander, peppercorns, fennel, cloves and cinnamon to a powder.

2. In a blender, purée chopped onions, vinegar, chopped ginger, turmeric, salt and spice mix. Transfer to a large nonreactive saucepan. Add pork, julienned ginger and garlic and mix well. Add pork. Cover and marinate at room temperature for 30 minutes.

3. Add ¾ cup (175 mL) water and bring to a boil over medium heat. Reduce to medium-low. Cover and simmer, stirring periodically, until pork is fork-tender, 45 minutes to 1 hour. There should be a very thick gravy.

4. In another saucepan, heat oil over high heat until a couple of mustard seeds thrown in start to sputter. Add all the mustard seeds and cover quickly. When the seeds stop popping, in a few seconds, uncover and reduce heat to medium. Add thinly sliced onions and sauté until golden, 6 to 8 minutes. Add to saucepan with pork and masala gravy and mix well. Cook over medium heat, stirring often, until there is no liquid left and thick gravy envelops pork, 6 to 8 minutes.

Coorgi Pepper Pork

1 lb	boneless pork loin, fat removed, cut into 1-inch (2.5 cm) pieces	500 g
¾ tsp	salt or to taste	4 mL
½ tsp	turmeric	2 mL
2 tbsp	oil	25 mL
2 cups	thinly sliced onions (lengthwise slices)	500 mL
2½ tbsp	thinly sliced garlic	32 mL
2 tbsp	julienned peeled gingerroot	25 mL
2	green chiles, preferably serranos, halved lengthwise	2
2 tbsp	unsalted Thai tamarind purée	25 mL
1 tsp	coarsely ground black pepper	5 mL

Serves 4

HOT

This recipe is from Coorg in South India, where pork is relished. The people of Coorg are amongst the few in India who eat pork. Pepper and tamarind add a punch to this tasty dish.

1. In a saucepan, combine pork, salt and turmeric. Add ¾ cup (175 mL) water and bring to a boil over medium heat. Reduce heat to medium-low. Cover and simmer until pork is fork-tender and water has been absorbed, 30 to 40 minutes.

2. In another saucepan, heat oil over medium heat. Add onions and sauté until golden, 6 to 8 minutes. Add garlic, ginger and chiles and sauté until chiles are softened, 6 to 8 minutes.

3. Add pork and tamarind and mix well. Sauté until thick masala enrobes pork, about 5 minutes. Stir in pepper and mix well. Serve hot.

Maharashtrian Masala Eggs

Serves 2 to 4

HOT

These eggs are perfect with a simple dal and rice meal — they're spicy and complement the flavors of a mild-tasting dal. Serve a simple salad to round out the meal.

4	hard-cooked eggs	4
3	dried Indian red chiles, broken into pieces	3
4	whole cloves	4
1	piece cinnamon, about 1 inch (2.5 cm) long	1
2	cloves garlic, cut into pieces	2
½ tsp	salt, divided	2 mL
¼ tsp	turmeric	1 mL
¼ cup	grated coconut, preferably fresh (or frozen, thawed)	50 mL
1 tbsp	oil	15 mL
1 cup	thinly sliced red onion (lengthwise slices)	250 mL
3 tbsp	unsalted Thai tamarind purée	45 mL
3 to 4 tbsp	cilantro, chopped	45 to 60 mL

1. Peel eggs and make three or four ½-inch (1 cm) long slashes in each with tip of knife.

2. In a spice grinder, grind chiles, cloves and cinnamon to a powder.

3. In a smooth mortar, using a pestle, mash garlic and ¼ tsp (1 mL) of the salt into a paste. Add turmeric, powdered spices and 2 tsp (10 mL) water and mix into a paste. Transfer to a large bowl. Add eggs and coat with paste. Set aside.

4. In a blender, combine coconut and ½ cup (125 mL) water and blend until smooth.

5. In a saucepan, heat oil over medium heat. Add onion and sauté until golden, 4 to 5 minutes. Add eggs and sauté for 3 to 4 minutes to cook masala. Pour coconut paste into pan. Add tamarind and remaining salt and mix well. Bring to a boil. Reduce heat to low. Cover and cook until a thick masala coats eggs, 6 to 8 minutes. Garnish with cilantro.

Chicken with Star Anise

3 to 3½ lbs	chicken drumsticks, about 12 (see Tip, right)	1.5 to 1.75 kg
2 tbsp	ginger paste (see Tip, page 207)	25 mL
4 cups	coarsely chopped onions	1 L
¼ cup	coarsely chopped garlic	50 mL
20	dried Indian red chiles, half with seeds removed, broken in two, or 1 tbsp (15 mL) hot pepper flakes	20
2 to 3 tbsp	oil	25 to 45 mL
1 tsp	freshly ground black pepper	5 mL
4	star anise (badian), each broken into 2 pieces	4
1½ tsp	salt or to taste	7 mL
1 tsp	coriander powder	5 mL

1. Pull skin off drumsticks with paper towel. Rinse chicken and pat dry thoroughly. Make 2 deep slits diagonally in the thickest part of each piece. Rub ginger paste into chicken, pressing into slits. Cover and refrigerate for at least 1 hour or for up to 8 hours.

2. In a food processor, purée onions, garlic and chiles. Set aside.

3. In a wide-bottomed pan large enough to hold chicken in a single layer, heat oil over medium heat. Arrange drumsticks in a single layer and shake pan to ensure pieces are not sticking to pan. Sprinkle pepper over chicken and brown, turning pieces, 10 to 12 minutes.

4. Pour in onion purée and add star anise and salt. Mix well. Cover and bring to a boil. Reduce heat to low and simmer, gently stirring occasionally, until juices run clear when chicken is pierced, for 30 minutes. (When chicken is cooked, there will be some gravy in the pan.) Uncover and simmer, shaking pan periodically, until gravy is reduced to a thick paste. Sprinkle with coriander and cook, stirring gently, for 5 minutes. Chicken should have a thick masala paste coating each piece. Serve hot with any Indian bread.

Serves 6 to 8

HOT

A stunningly simple preparation, the flavor of star anise makes this dish memorable.

Tip

Use bone-in chicken thighs if you prefer. If thighs are large, cut each in half through the bone. Do not make slits if cutting in half.

Chicken Temperado

12	skinless bone-in chicken thighs	12
2 tsp	salt or to taste	10 mL
½ tsp	black peppercorns	2 mL
2	sticks cinnamon, each about 2 inches (5 cm) long	2
4	green cardamom pods, cracked open	4
2 tbsp	oil	25 mL
4 cups	thinly sliced onions (lengthwise slices)	1 L
¼ cup	unsalted Thai tamarind purée	50 mL
2 tsp	cumin seeds, crushed	10 mL
8	whole cloves, crushed	8
6	large cloves garlic, crushed	6
2 tsp	minced peeled gingerroot	10 mL
Scant 1 tsp	turmeric	5 mL
8	dried Indian red chiles, broken into pieces	8
¼ cup	cider vinegar	50 mL
1 tbsp	granulated sugar	15 mL

Serves 8

HOT

The cuisine of Goa is replete with garlic and vinegar, the influence of 461 years of Portuguese presence. Dried red chiles are often ground to a paste with garlic and vinegar to form the base of many Goan dishes.

1. Rinse chicken and pat dry thoroughly. Rub well with salt and set aside.

2. In a spice grinder, grind peppercorns, cinnamon and cardamom to a powder. Set aside.

3. In a saucepan large enough to hold chicken in a single layer, heat oil over medium-high heat. Add onions and sauté until moisture evaporates, 6 to 8 minutes. Continue to sauté until golden, about 15 minutes, reducing heat to medium as onions begin to brown.

4. Push onions to side of pan. Add chicken in a single layer. Spoon onions over top. Cover and increase heat to medium-high. Cook until chicken is brown, 3 to 4 minutes. Turn and brown other side, 3 to 4 minutes. Spoon onions on top again.

5. Add tamarind purée. Cover and reduce heat to medium. Cook, stirring once, for 10 minutes.

6. Add cumin, cloves, garlic, ginger, turmeric, powdered spices and chiles. Mix well and add 1¼ cups (300 mL) water. Cover and cook for 5 minutes. Reduce heat to low and simmer until chicken is no longer pink inside, about 15 minutes. If necessary, add ¼ cup (50 mL) additional water to make a thick masala that coats chicken.

7. In a small bowl, combine vinegar and sugar. Pour over chicken and cook for 5 minutes. Serve hot with an Indian bread.

Chicken Bafat

East Indian Chicken Stew

Serves 8

This dish is from the East Indian community, the indigenous Hindus of Bombay. They converted to Christianity after the arrival of the Portuguese and continue to live in small neighborhoods around the city and its environs.

Tip

Gram (*channa*) is a form of small chickpea. Roasted, it is a popular snack eaten out of hand and is available in Indian groceries. Unroasted gram is often used as a thickening agent in cooking. You can substitute 1 tbsp (15 mL) chickpea flour instead.

12	skinless bone-in chicken thighs (or thighs and drumsticks)	12
¾ cup	grated coconut, fresh or frozen, thawed	175 mL
12 to 15	large cloves garlic	12 to 15
1	piece (1-inch/2.5 cm square) peeled gingerroot	1
10 to 12	dried Indian red chiles, broken into pieces, half with seeds removed	10 to 12
1 tbsp	sesame seeds	15 mL
1 tbsp	unroasted skinned gram (see Tip, left)	15 mL
1 tbsp	skinned peanuts	15 mL
2 tsp	cumin seeds	10 mL
½ tsp	turmeric	2 mL
3 tbsp	oil	45 mL
3 cups	thinly sliced onions (lengthwise slices)	750 mL
2 tsp	salt or to taste	10 mL
12	small potatoes (1 ½ lbs/750 g), halved	12
3 cups	chopped carrots (½-inch/1 cm pieces)	750 mL
¾ cup	frozen peas, thawed	175 mL
3 tbsp	unsalted Thai tamarind purée	45 mL
1 ½ tbsp	jaggery (gur) or brown sugar	22 mL
12	cherry tomatoes, halved	12

1. Rinse chicken and pat dry thoroughly.

2. In a blender, combine coconut, garlic, ginger, chiles, sesame seeds, gram, peanuts, cumin and turmeric. Blend as fine as possible. Add 5 to 6 tbsp (75 to 90 mL) water and blend to a paste.

3. In a large saucepan, heat oil over medium-high heat. Add onions and sauté until golden, 10 to 12 minutes. Reduce heat to medium. Add paste and sauté, stirring continuously, to prevent burning. Add 2 tbsp (25 mL) water to deglaze if masala begins to stick to pan. Continue in this manner until masala is several shades darker, about 10 minutes.

4. Add chicken and brown with masala for about 10 minutes, deglazing pan as required with a little water. Add salt and enough water to cover chicken and cook for 20 minutes.

5. Add potatoes, carrots and peas. Bring to a boil. Reduce heat to low and cook, covered, until chicken is no longer pink inside and vegetables are tender, about 30 minutes. Add more water if required to prevent drying. Stir in tamarind and jaggery and simmer for 5 minutes. Add tomatoes and heat through. Serve with rice.

Chicken Chile Fry

2 tbsp	oil	25 mL
2 cups	thinly sliced onions (lengthwise slices)	500 mL
1 ½ tbsp	minced peeled gingerroot	22 mL
1 tbsp	minced garlic	15 mL
2 tsp	minced green chiles, preferably serranos	10 mL
2	tomatoes, cut into 1-inch (2.5 cm) wedges	2
½ cup	½-inch (1 cm) thick slices green bell pepper	125 mL
½ cup	½-inch (1 cm) thick slices red or yellow bell pepper	125 mL
1 ½ tsp	coriander powder	7 mL
1 tsp	cumin powder	5 mL
1 tsp	salt or to taste	5 mL
½ tsp	cayenne pepper	2 mL
¼ tsp	turmeric	1 mL
½ cup	cider vinegar	125 mL
2 tsp	granulated sugar	10 mL
4 cups	cooked shredded chicken	1 L
½ cup	cilantro, chopped	125 mL

Serves 8

Leftover cooked chicken is not uncommon, and here is a new way to put it to good use.

Tip

Use as a filling for a wrap or stuff into a whole wheat pita half for a delicious sandwich.

1. In a skillet, heat oil over medium heat. Add onions and sauté until lightly golden, 8 to 12 minutes.

2. Add ginger, garlic and chiles and sauté for 2 minutes.

3. Add tomatoes and green and red bell peppers and sauté until tomatoes are slightly soft, about 5 minutes.

4. Add coriander, cumin, salt, cayenne and turmeric and sauté for 2 minutes. Add vinegar and sugar and mix well.

5. Add chicken and toss to mix. Cover, remove from heat and let stand to allow flavors to blend for 5 minutes. Stir in cilantro. Serve hot.

Parsi Chicken Curry

Serves 8

Ava, a young Parsi friend and cooking enthusiast, brought this dish to my house when she was visiting. My family tucked into it with such gusto, I begged for the recipe. Since then, I have cooked it for many a party, and it has always drawn raves.

12	skinless bone-in chicken thighs	12
1/2 cup	plain nonfat yogurt, at room temperature	125 mL
1/2 tsp	cornstarch	2 mL
3 tbsp	coriander seeds	45 mL
3 tbsp	Indian poppy seeds (see Tip, page 219)	45 mL
3 tbsp	unroasted skinned gram (channa) (see Tips, right)	45 mL
3 tbsp	skinned raw peanuts	45 mL
2 tsp	cumin seeds	10 mL
10	dried Indian red chiles, broken into pieces, some seeds removed	10
1/2 cup	oil	125 mL
1 1/2 cups	thinly sliced onions (lengthwise slices)	375 mL
2 tsp	minced peeled gingerroot	10 mL
2 tsp	minced garlic	10 mL
1 tsp	turmeric	5 mL
1/2 tsp	ground cardamom	2 mL
1/4 cup	tomato paste	50 mL
2 1/2 tsp	salt or to taste	12 mL
1	sprig fresh curry leaves, stripped (12 to 15 leaves)	1
1	can (14 oz/400 mL) coconut milk	1
3 to 4 tbsp	freshly squeezed lime or lemon juice	45 to 60 mL

1. Rinse chicken and pat dry thoroughly.

2. In a bowl, stir together yogurt and cornstarch to a creamy consistency. Set aside.

3. In a small dry skillet over medium heat, separately toast coriander, poppy seeds, channa, peanuts and cumin seeds until each is a shade darker and aromatic. Transfer all to a blender. Add chiles and grind to a fine powder. Scrape sides of blender frequently. Add 1/2 cup (125 mL) water and blend to a smooth, thick paste. Transfer to a bowl and set aside.

4. In a large saucepan, heat oil over medium heat. Add onions and sauté until golden, 6 to 8 minutes. Add ginger and garlic and sauté for 1 minute.

5. Add reserved paste, turmeric and cardamom and sauté for 6 to 8 minutes. (The oil will be absorbed by the paste and you may have to add water, 1 tbsp (15 mL) at a time, to deglaze pan and prevent masala from burning.)

6. Add chicken and mix with masala. Sauté for 3 minutes.

7. Pour yogurt over chicken. Mix tomato paste with 2 cups (500 mL) water and add to pan. Add salt and mix well. Add curry leaves and simmer, stirring frequently to prevent masala from sticking to bottom of pan, until chicken is no longer pink inside, for 40 minutes. Stir in more hot water if gravy seems too thick.

8. Add coconut milk and return to a gentle boil. Cook for 5 minutes. Add lime juice. Serve hot with plain rice.

Tip

Gram (*channa*) is a form of small chickpea (not a powder). Roasted, it is a popular snack eaten out of hand and is available in Indian groceries. Unroasted gram is often used as a thickening agent in cooking. If unavailable, increase peanuts to 5 tbsp (75 mL).

Variation

The same curry, omitting ginger, can be used for fish. Follow same method, but then simmer 20 minutes instead of 40 minutes. Add 2 lbs (1 kg) fish of your choice, cut into about 4-by 3-inch (10 by 7.5 cm) pieces, at the very end, after curry is ready, and allow fish to cook through, about 6 to 8 minutes.

Haldi Chicken
Turmeric Chicken

3 lbs	skinless boneless chicken thighs	1.5 kg
1¼ tsp	turmeric	6 mL
1 tsp	salt or to taste	5 mL
2 tbsp	freshly squeezed lime or lemon juice	25 mL
3 tbsp	oil	45 mL
8	dried Indian red chiles	8
3	sprigs fresh curry leaves, stripped (30 to 35 leaves)	3
12 oz	shallots, finely chopped	375 g
1½ cups	chopped tomatoes	375 mL
3 to 4 tbsp	cilantro, coarsely chopped	45 to 60 mL

Serves 6 to 8

Turmeric, one of the most-used spices in Indian cooking, is a well-known antiseptic. Recently, it has been recognized by the medical community as an anti-inflammatory and anti-carcinogenic and is even available as a supplement in capsule form. This healthy dish is a delicious way to get your turmeric boost.

1. Rinse chicken and pat dry thoroughly.

2. In a large bowl, combine turmeric, salt and lime juice and rub into chicken. Cover and marinate for 30 minutes at room temperature or for up to 24 hours in refrigerator.

3. In a large saucepan, heat oil over medium-high heat. Add chiles and curry leaves and sauté until fragrant, about 1 minute. Stir in shallots and sauté until golden, 6 to 8 minutes.

4. Reduce heat to medium. Add tomatoes and sauté until soft, 5 to 7 minutes.

5. Add chicken and mix well. Cook until masala thickens and chicken is browned, 10 to 12 minutes. If chicken sticks to pan, deglaze with 1 tbsp (15 mL) water periodically while browning.

6. Add 1 cup (250 mL) water. Bring to a boil. Reduce heat to medium-low. Cover and simmer until chicken is no longer pink inside and there is a thick masala coating the chicken, 6 to 8 minutes. Garnish with cilantro. Serve hot with any Indian bread.

Preeti's Chicken Frankies

Makes 16

Frankies are a popular Bombay wrap made with boneless pieces of baby goat meat. They tend to be rather greasy, but they are nevertheless delicious! This is my daughter-in-law Preeti's cleaned up version, one that was an instant winner with the family.

Masala Paste

5 to 6	dried Indian red chiles, broken into pieces, some seeds removed	5 to 6
¼ cup	white vinegar	50 mL
2 tbsp	cumin seeds	25 mL
4	black peppercorns	4
8 to 10	cloves garlic	8 to 10

Topping

¾ cup	chopped red onions	175 mL
½ cup	white vinegar	125 mL
¼ cup	cilantro leaves, chopped	50 mL
1 tbsp	minced green chiles, preferably serranos	15 mL

Chicken

2 lbs	chicken breast tenders or filets (see Tip, right)	1 kg
3 tbsp	oil, divided	45 mL
1½	medium onions, puréed	1½
⅓ cup	tomato paste	75 mL
2 tbsp	white vinegar	25 mL
1 tsp	salt or to taste	5 mL
¼ tsp	cayenne pepper, optional	1 mL
½ cup	cilantro leaves	125 mL
	Vegetable spray	
16	10-inch (25 cm) flour tortillas	16
3	eggs, beaten	3

1. *Masala Paste:* In a small bowl, soak chiles in vinegar for 15 minutes.

2. In a dry skillet over medium-high heat, toast cumin seeds until fragrant, 2 to 3 minutes. In a blender, combine cumin and peppercorns and blend to a powder. Add garlic and chile mixture and blend to a smooth paste. (This makes more than needed for this recipe. Masala can be refrigerated for up to 3 months. It can be used on fish.)

3. *Topping:* In a bowl, combine onions, vinegar, cilantro and chiles. Cover and marinate for 1 hour or for up to 2 days in the refrigerator.

4. *Chicken:* Marinate chicken in 1 tbsp (15 mL) of the masala paste for 15 minutes.

5. In a large skillet, heat 2 tbsp (25 mL) of the oil over medium heat. Add onions and sauté until well browned, 6 to 8 minutes. Set aside.

6. Reheat skillet and add remaining oil. Add chicken mixture and sauté for 2 minutes. Add browned onions and 1 tbsp (15 mL) of the remaining masala paste and sauté for 2 to 3 minutes. Add tomato paste, vinegar, salt and cayenne, if using, and mix well. Simmer until chicken is no longer pink inside, about 5 minutes. Set aside.

7. *To assemble:* Spray a clean skillet with vegetable spray. Add tortillas, one at a time, and heat for 30 seconds. Brush top generously with beaten egg and flip to cook for 30 seconds more. Transfer to a plate. Continue with remaining tortillas. Place chicken filling off-center on egg-coated tortilla. Top with some onion-vinegar topping. Fold one side of tortilla over to cover filling. Fold over both sides and roll up like a wrap. Secure with toothpick. Continue with the remaining tortillas and topping. Serve immediately.

Tip

If chicken breast tenders or filets are not available, substitute skinless boneless chicken breasts cut crosswise into $\frac{1}{2}$-inch (1 cm) thick strips.

Minted Baked Chicken

Serves 8

Baked dishes were introduced by the British and became the symbol of "elegant" dining. True to form, Indian seasonings were added to enhance the chicken, and dishes of this kind were thought of as Anglo-Indian food.

⁓

- *13-by 9-inch (3 L) baking pan, sprayed with vegetable spray*

12	skinless bone-in chicken thighs	12
1¼ cup	tomato sauce	300 mL
6 tbsp	crumbled dried mint, divided	90 mL
2 tbsp	freshly squeezed lime or lemon juice	25 mL
1 tbsp	minced peeled gingerroot	15 mL
1 tbsp	minced garlic	15 mL
1 tbsp	cumin powder	15 mL
1½ tsp	cracked black peppercorns	7 mL
1 tsp	hot pepper flakes	5 mL
1 tsp	ground cardamom	5 mL
2 tsp	salt or to taste	10 mL
1	egg, slightly beaten	1
1½ cups	dry bread crumbs	375 mL
3 tbsp	oil	45 mL

1. Rinse chicken and pat dry thoroughly.

2. In a large bowl, mix together tomato sauce, 2 tbsp (25 mL) of the mint, lime juice, ginger, garlic, cumin, black pepper, hot pepper flakes, cardamom, salt and egg. Add chicken pieces and coat well with marinade.

3. Mix bread crumbs with remaining mint. Coat chicken with crumbs and place in the prepared pan. Cover and refrigerate for 2 hours or for up to 4 hours longer.

4. Preheat oven to 375°F (190°C). Drizzle chicken with oil. Cover tightly with foil and bake in a preheated oven for 45 minutes. Remove foil and cook for 10 minutes until chicken is no longer pink inside and coating is brown.

Tash Kabab
Layered Beef

- *Large saucepan with tight-fitting lid*

2½ tbsp	ginger paste (see Tips, page 207)	32 mL
2 lbs	boneless sirloin tip or round steaks, each ½ inch (1 cm) thick, trimmed of all fat	1 kg
1 cup	plain nonfat yogurt, at room temperature	250 mL
2 tsp	salt or to taste	10 mL
1 tsp	cornstarch	5 mL
2 tbsp	coriander seeds	25 mL
2 tbsp	cumin seeds	25 mL
1 tsp	powdered mace (javitri)	5 mL
½ tsp	black peppercorns	2 mL
4	whole cloves	4
4	green cardamom pods, seeds only	4
5	dried Indian red chiles, broken into pieces and seeds removed	5
20	cloves garlic, crushed	20
2½ cups	thinly sliced onions (lengthwise slices)	625 mL
2 cups	crispy fried onions (see Tip, page 193)	500 mL
3 tbsp	oil	45 mL

Serves 6

Thin beef steaks are layered with two types of onion in this unusual Muslim recipe.

1. Rub ginger into meat in a shallow dish and marinate for 30 minutes at room temperature.

2. In a large bowl, stir together yogurt, salt and cornstarch to a creamy consistency. Set aside.

3. In a skillet over medium heat, toast coriander and cumin, shaking skillet to ensure even browning, until lightly browned, 3 to 4 minutes.

4. In a small blender, grind toasted coriander and cumin, mace, peppercorns, cloves, cardamom and chiles to a powder. Add garlic and 2 tbsp (25 mL) of the yogurt mixture and blend to a paste. Stir paste into remaining yogurt mixture.

5. Transfer one-quarter of the yogurt mixture to a bowl. Mix in onions.

6. Coat meat with remaining yogurt mixture.

7. In a large saucepan, arrange half the meat in a layer. Cover with half of the yogurt-onion mixture. Top with half of the fried onions. Repeat process with remaining meat and onions. Drizzle oil over top and around sides of pan. Cover with a tight-fitting lid and bring to a boil over medium-high heat. Reduce heat to low and simmer, shaking pan periodically, until meat is fork-tender, about 1 hour.

Chutney Gosht ke Kabab

Lacy Beef Skewers

Serves 8

These are traditionally made with cabrito (young goat) in India, but beef or lamb is equally suitable. I like to serve these as finger food, but they are elegant on a banquet table as well.

- Twenty 6-inch (15 cm) bamboo skewers, soaked in water for 30 minutes
- Wok or deep-fryer
- Candy/deep-fry thermometer

2 lbs	boneless stewing beef, cut into 1-inch (2.5 cm) pieces	1 kg
1½ tbsp	minced garlic	22 mL
1½ tbsp	minced peeled gingerroot	22 mL
2 tsp	salt or to taste	10 mL
1 tsp	turmeric	5 mL
1 tsp	cumin powder	5 mL
1 tsp	coriander powder	5 mL
½ tsp	cayenne pepper	2 mL
¼ tsp	freshly ground black pepper	1 mL
3	bay leaves	3
1 cup	Cilantro Mint Chutney (see recipe, page 417) or store-bought coriander chutney	250 mL
1 cup	dry bread crumbs (approx.)	250 mL
4	eggs, lightly beaten	4
	Oil for deep-frying	

1. In a saucepan, combine beef, garlic, ginger, salt, turmeric, cumin, coriander, cayenne, pepper and bay leaves. Add enough water to cover. Bring to a boil over high heat. Reduce heat to low and simmer until beef is tender, 45 minutes to 1 hour. (There should be no liquid left in the pan.) Do not mix with spoon while boiling. Instead, shake pan periodically to prevent sticking. Transfer to a bowl. Let cool.

2. Add chutney to beef. Mix gently to coat, taking care not to break any pieces.

3. Thread 3 to 4 pieces of beef onto each skewer. Roll in bread crumbs. Coat generously in beaten egg.

4. In a wok or deep-fryer, heat oil to 350°F (180°C). Add beef skewers, in batches, without crowding, and deep-fry until egg forms a lacy fringe on edges, 3 to 4 minutes. Remove with tongs and drain on paper towels. Bamboo skewers will be cool enough to handle in a few minutes. Eat as satay skewer or slide gently off skewer onto plate.

Haleem

Serves 6

Healthy and filling, this one-dish meal is a Muslim classic. The porridge-like consistency is pure comfort food, customized with a variety of garnishes to add additional flavor and zing.

2 tbsp	plain nonfat yogurt	25 mL
1 ½ tbsp	ginger paste (see Tips, page 207)	22 mL
1 ½ tbsp	garlic paste	22 mL
1 ½ tsp	salt or to taste	7 mL
1 ½ lbs	boneless lamb or cabrito (young goat), preferably leg, cut into 1-inch (2.5 cm) pieces	750 g
1 cup	wheat berries (haleem wheat)	250 mL
2 tbsp	grated coconut, preferably fresh (or frozen, thawed)	25 mL
2 tbsp	raw cashews	25 mL
2 tbsp	oil	25 mL
6	green cardamom pods, cracked open	6
6	whole cloves	6
1	stick cinnamon, about 3 inches (7.5 cm) long, broken in half	1
1 ½ tsp	cayenne pepper or to taste	7 mL
3 cups	thinly sliced onions (lengthwise slices)	750 mL
1 ½ tsp	salt or to taste	7 mL
¼ cup	freshly squeezed lime or lemon juice	50 mL

Garnishes

1 cup	crispy fried onions (see Tip, page 193)	250 mL
1 cup	cilantro, coarsely chopped	250 mL
1 cup	mint, coarsely chopped	250 mL
4 to 5	minced green chiles, preferably serranos	4 to 5
	Lemon wedges	

1. In a large bowl, combine yogurt, ginger, garlic and salt. Add lamb and mix well. Cover and marinate for 30 minutes at room temperature or for up to 24 hours in refrigerator.

2. In a saucepan, soak wheat berries in 5 cups (1.25 L) water for 10 minutes. Bring to a boil over medium-high heat. Reduce heat to low and simmer, partially covered, until berries are soft, about 30 minutes. Mash with potato masher. Stir in hot water, if necessary, to make a porridge-like consistency.

3. Meanwhile, in a blender, blend coconut, cashews and 3 tbsp (45 mL) water to make a smooth paste.

4. In a large saucepan, heat oil over medium-high heat. Toss in cardamom, cloves and cinnamon and sauté for 30 seconds. Stir in cayenne and sauté for 10 seconds. Add onions and sauté until almost caramelized, about 15 minutes, adjusting heat as you go along to prevent burning.

5. Add lamb with marinade and mix well. Cover, reduce heat to medium and cook until meat releases juices, 6 to 8 minutes. Reduce heat to low and simmer, stirring periodically, until liquid is absorbed, 10 to 12 minutes. Continue to brown meat well, adding water, 1 tbsp (15 mL) at a time, to deglaze pan as necessary, about 10 minutes.

6. Stir in cashew paste and sauté for 2 minutes.

7. Pour in 2 cups (500 mL) water. Increase heat to medium and return to a boil. Reduce heat to low. Cover and simmer until meat is fork-tender, 45 minutes to 1 hour.

8. Remove half the meat and reserve. Mash remaining meat in pan. Stir in mashed wheat berries. Pour in enough hot water to restore porridge consistency and then an additional $\frac{1}{2}$ cup (125 mL) more water to allow for additional simmering. Add salt. Cover and simmer to blend flavors and restore to a porridge consistency, 8 to 10 minutes. Stir in reserved meat and lime juice.

9. *Garnishes:* Spoon into pasta bowls and mound 2 tbsp (25 mL) crispy onions in center of each bowl. Sprinkle some of the cilantro and mint around them. Serve hot. Pass around remaining garnishes and lemon wedges.

Badami Gosht

Lamb in Almond Sauce

Serves 6 to 8

In this sensuous dish, puréed almonds, enhanced with coconut milk, create a rich creamy gravy for succulent pieces of lamb. Best served with steamed basmati rice.

1 tsp	saffron threads	5 mL
2 cups	plain nonfat yogurt, at room temperature	500 mL
2 tsp	cornstarch	10 mL
2 tsp	cumin seeds	10 mL
2 tsp	salt or to taste	10 mL
2 lbs	boneless lamb, preferably leg or shoulder, cut into 1 1/2-inch (4 cm) pieces	1 kg
1/2 cup	blanched almonds	125 mL
2 tbsp	oil	25 mL
1	stick cinnamon, about 2 inches (5 cm) long	1
12	green cardamom pods, cracked open	12
6	whole cloves	6
2 cups	finely chopped onions	500 mL
1 1/2 tbsp	minced garlic	22 mL
1 1/2 tbsp	minced peeled gingerroot	22 mL
1 tsp	cayenne pepper	5 mL
1	can (14 oz/400 mL) coconut milk	1
2 tbsp	sliced or slivered almonds, toasted	25 mL

1. In a small bowl, soak saffron threads in 1/4 cup (50 mL) very hot water for 10 minutes.

2. In a large bowl, stir together yogurt, cornstarch, cumin and salt. Stir in saffron with soaking liquid. Add lamb and mix well. Cover and marinate for 30 minutes at room temperature or refrigerate for up to 24 hours.

3. In a bowl, soak almonds in 1/2 cup (125 mL) very hot water for 10 minutes. Transfer almonds and water to blender and blend to a smooth purée. Set aside.

4. In a saucepan, heat oil over medium-high heat. Add cinnamon, cardamom pods and cloves and sauté for 30 seconds. Add onions and sauté until soft and golden, 8 to 10 minutes. Add garlic and ginger and sauté for 2 minutes.

5. Stir in meat with marinade. Add cayenne, almond purée and coconut milk and mix well. Reduce heat to medium. Cover and bring to a boil, stirring occasionally, to prevent sticking to bottom.

6. Reduce heat to low. Cover and cook gently, stirring periodically and scraping bottom to prevent burning, until lamb is tender and the sauce is thickened, 25 to 30 minutes. Garnish with toasted almonds before serving.

Masoor ma Gosht
Lamb with Lentils

1 ½ cups	brown lentils (sabat masoor)	375 mL
2 tbsp	oil	25 mL
5 cups	thinly sliced onions (lengthwise slices)	1.25 L
2 tbsp	minced garlic	25 mL
1 ½ tbsp	sambhar powder (see page 28) or garam masala	22 mL
1 tbsp	cumin seeds	15 mL
1 tbsp	coriander seeds	15 mL
1 tsp	cayenne pepper	5 mL
1 tsp	turmeric	5 mL
3 to 4 tbsp	freshly squeezed lime or lemon juice	45 to 60 mL
1 lb	boneless lamb, preferably leg or shoulder, cut into 1 ½-inch (4 cm) cubes	500 g
1 cup	cilantro, chopped	250 mL
3 cups	chopped tomatoes	750 mL
1 ½ tbsp	minced green chiles, preferably serranos	22 mL
2 tsp	salt or to taste	10 mL

Serves 8

This substantial dish is a classic of the Parsi community and is both delicious and nutritious. Rice and a vegetable side dish or salad complete the meal.

1. Clean and pick through lentils for any small stones and grit. Rinse several times in cold water. Soak in 6 cups (1.5 L) water in a bowl at room temperature for 1 hour.

2. In a large saucepan, heat oil over medium-high heat. Add onions and garlic and sauté until golden brown, 10 to 12 minutes.

3. Add sambhar powder, cumin, coriander, cayenne, turmeric and lime juice. Reduce heat to medium-low and sauté for 4 minutes.

4. Increase heat to medium. Add lamb and cook until meat is brown, 10 to 15 minutes.

5. Drain lentils and add to meat. Add cilantro, tomatoes, chiles and salt. Add 2 cups (500 mL) water and mix well. Bring to a boil. Cover, reduce heat and simmer, stirring periodically, until meat is tender and lentils are cooked, 45 minutes to 1 hour. If mixture becomes too dry, add additional hot water to make a thick, creamy consistency.

Kacha Aam ka Gosht

Lamb with Green Mango

Serves 6 to 8

Green mangoes are a summer treat in India. They are very hard, unripe and sour. In North America, they are now available in Asian markets almost year-round.

Tip

Dried coconut flakes are available in packages in Indian stores or in bulk bins in health food stores and specialty markets. The flakes are about ¾-by ½-inch (2 by 1 cm) pieces.

Variation

Lamb with Green Mango and Spinach: Heat 1 tbsp (15 mL) oil in a skillet. Sauté ½ tsp (2 mL) cumin seeds until fragrant for 30 seconds. Add ¼ tsp (1 mL) fenugreek seeds and sauté for 15 seconds. Add 8 cups (2 L) loosely packed baby spinach leaves and sauté until just wilted. Place in a serving dish and spoon lamb over top without covering spinach entirely.

2 tbsp	Indian poppy seeds (see Tip, page 219)	25 mL
½ cup	granulated sugar	75 mL
1 ½ lbs	green mangoes, peeled and cut into ¼-inch (0.5 cm) thick slices (approx.)	750 mL
3 tbsp	oil, divided	45 mL
1 tbsp	cashews	15 mL
1 tbsp	slivered almonds	15 mL
1 tbsp	dried coconut flakes (see Tip, left)	15 mL
8	whole cloves	8
12	green cardamom pods, cracked open	12
3	sticks cinnamon, each about 2 inches (5 cm) long	3
3	bay leaves	3
2 lbs	boneless lamb, preferably leg or shoulder, cut into 1 ½-inch (4 cm) pieces	1 kg
2 tbsp	dry unsweetened coconut powder (see Tip, page 228)	25 mL
2 tsp	salt or to taste	10 mL
1 ½ tsp	cayenne pepper	7 mL
½ tsp	turmeric	2 mL

1. In a smooth mortar, soak poppy seeds in 2 tbsp (25 mL) water for 15 minutes. Grind to a paste with pestle. Set aside.

2. In a saucepan, melt sugar in ¾ cup (175 mL) water over medium heat. Add mangoes and cook gently for 3 minutes. Set aside.

3. In a large saucepan, heat 1 tbsp (15 mL) of the oil over medium heat. Add cashews, almonds and coconut flakes and sauté until lightly browned, 1 to 2 minutes. Transfer to a bowl and set aside.

4. Add remaining oil to saucepan and return to medium-high heat. Add cloves, cardamom, cinnamon and bay leaves and sauté until fragrant, for 30 seconds. Add lamb and sauté until brown, 8 to 10 minutes.

5. Add poppy seed paste and coconut powder. Reduce heat to medium. Cook, stirring continuously, until mixture is dark brown, 3 to 4 minutes. Add salt, cayenne and turmeric and sauté for 2 minutes.

6. Add 2 cups (500 mL) water and bring to a boil. Reduce heat to low. Cover and simmer, stirring periodically, until lamb is fork-tender, about 1 to 1½ hours.

7. Stir mangoes with syrup into meat and cook for 5 minutes. Serve hot, garnished with fried nut mixture.

Shredded Lamb with Fresh Curry Leaves

W

Serves 8

The goodness of ginger and garlic and the heady aroma of fresh curry leaves make this a standout dish. It would be outstanding served with a tasty rice, such as South Indian Vegetable Rice (see recipe, page 162) and a dal dish. I also like to wrap it in a chapati and serve with a side of raita.

Tip

In this recipe, it is not necessary to stabilize the yogurt with cornstarch because it is used to keep the meat moist and not to create a creamy consistency.

4 to 4 1/2 lbs	leg of lamb, cut across the bone into 2-inch (5 cm) slices	2 to 2.25 kg
1 cup	plain nonfat yogurt, at room temperature, stirred to creamy consistency	250 mL
1 1/2 cups	chopped onions	375 mL
1/3 cup	chopped peeled gingerroot	75 mL
18 to 20	cloves garlic, smashed	18 to 20
2	bay leaves	2
3	sticks cinnamon, each about 2 inches (5 cm) long	3
10	whole cloves	10
2 tsp	salt or to taste	10 mL
1/2 tsp	black peppercorns	2 mL
4 1/2 tbsp	oil, divided	67 mL
5 cups	thinly sliced onions (lengthwise slices), divided	1.25 L
1 cup	julienned peeled gingerroot, divided	250 mL
1 cup	fresh curry leaves, divided	250 mL
6	2-inch (5 cm) long green chiles, preferably serranos, slivered, divided	6

1. Place lamb in a large saucepan. Add yogurt, chopped onions, chopped ginger, garlic, bay leaves, cinnamon, cloves, salt and peppercorns. Add enough water to cover meat. Bring to a boil over medium heat. Skim scum off the top. Reduce heat to low. Cover and simmer until meat falls off the bone, 1 1/2 to 2 hours.

2. Strain and reserve stock for another use. Shred lamb into bite-size pieces, discarding bones.

3. Reserve 1/4 cup (50 mL) julienned ginger, 1/4 cup (50 mL) curry leaves and 1/4 cup (50 mL) slivered green chiles.

4. In a large wok, heat 1 1/2 tbsp (22 mL) of the oil over medium heat. Add half of the sliced onions and stir-fry until golden, 8 to 10 minutes. Add half of remaining ginger, curry leaves and chiles. Toss with onions and sauté for 2 minutes. Add half of the meat and sauté until meat is lightly browned and slightly crispy, 6 to 8 minutes. Transfer to a bowl and keep warm. Repeat process with remaining onions, ginger, curry leaves, chiles and meat.

5. In another small pan, heat remaining 1 1/2 tbsp (22 mL) oil over medium heat. Toss in reserved ginger, curry leaves and chiles and sauté until crisp. Pour over meat as garnish.

Talela Gosht
Spicy Fried Meat

W

¼ cup	oil, divided	50 mL
4 cups	finely chopped onions	1 L
2 lbs	boneless lamb, preferably leg, cut into 1½-inch (4 cm) cubes	1 kg
1½ tbsp	minced peeled gingerroot	22 mL
1 tbsp	minced garlic	15 mL
¾ tsp	turmeric	4 mL
1½ tsp	salt or to taste	7 mL
1	onion, unpeeled and cut into 1-inch (2.5 cm) pieces	1
1½ tbsp	dry unsweetened coconut powder (see Tip, page 228)	22 mL
1½ tbsp	coriander seeds	22 mL
1 tbsp	fennel seeds (saunf)	15 mL
1 tbsp	cayenne pepper	15 mL
1½ tsp	Indian poppy seeds (see Tip, page 219)	7 mL
5 tbsp	freshly squeezed lime or lemon juice, divided	75 mL
1 tsp	garam masala	5 mL

1. In a large saucepan, heat 2 tbsp (25 mL) of the oil over medium heat. Add 4 cups (1 L) onions and sauté until deep brown, about 20 minutes.

2. Add lamb, ginger, garlic, salt, turmeric and 1 cup (250 mL) water. Cover and bring to a boil. Reduce heat to low and, maintaining a gentle boil, cook until lamb is tender, about 1 hour. Gently stir or shake pan every 15 minutes. If water dries before lamb is cooked, add ½ cup (125 mL) hot water and continue to simmer. When lamb is fork-tender and there is no water left, increase heat to medium-low and sauté until meat is browned, 6 to 8 minutes.

3. While lamb is cooking, prepare spice mixture. In a heavy skillet, heat remaining oil over medium heat. Add onion, coconut, coriander, fennel, cayenne and poppy seeds and sauté, stirring constantly, until aromatic, 8 to 10 minutes. Remove from heat. Add 3 tbsp (45 mL) lime juice and let cool slightly. Transfer to a blender and purée mixture as fine as possible. Set aside.

4. After meat is browned, add spice mixture and mix well. Cover and simmer until spices are cooked and a thick coating of masala envelops lamb, 5 to 8 minutes. Add garam masala and remove from heat. Sprinkle with additional lime juice before serving.

Serves 6 to 8
HOT

This assertively spiced dish reflects the nature of the Maratha people, respected warriors who fought the Muslims and also thwarted British attempts to subjugate them. They come from the interior of Maharashtra and are known for their fiery cuisine.

Tip
This is a "dry" dish (see Tip, page 358) and should be served with an Indian bread or naan. If you prefer, you can make a gravy by adding 1 cup (250 mL) hot water after the last step. Cover and simmer for 5 minutes. Serve with rice or bread.

Fish and Seafood

IN NORTH AMERICA, NORTH INDIAN FOOD is synonymous with Indian food, and very little, if anything, is known about the cuisine of the rest of the country. Therefore, it is not surprising that few are familiar with the fish and seafood dishes so enjoyed by the people of the coastal areas. The long coastline of India — from Gujarat in the west to the tip of India, where the Arabian Sea, the Indian Ocean and the Bay of Bengal meet, and up the east coast to Orissa and Bengal — is rich with marine life. It is augmented in the Bay of Bengal by the delta of the mighty Ganges and Brahmaputra rivers, providing Bengalis with a wealth of freshwater fish and shellfish. Is it any wonder that in Bengal, freshly caught fish is on the menu every day? In a country where perishables, particularly seafood, were not shipped long distances and where refrigeration facilities were minimal (this is changing), the north had no access to fish, except for the limited varieties found in local rivers, and thus seafood was never a big part of the diet. Those of us who were raised in coastal cities, where seafood was almost more desirable than meat and poultry, understand well how delicious fresh fish can be.

I was born and raised in Mumbai, and we spent many weekends at a beach house several hours outside the city. It was on the outskirts of a small fishing village, and the local catch came in early in the morning. Some of the smaller craft even pulled up on our beach, and we would run down to meet the boat and bargain for fresh crab, sardines and whatever else was the catch of the day.

OUR COOK WAS FROM KERALA AND WAS as happy to prepare the fresh catch as we were to eat it. Even today my mouth waters at the memory of the crispy masala sardines he whipped up in minutes as a snack. Try as I might, I have not been able to duplicate them in my kitchen, and I've decided that it was the flavor of the just-caught fish that made the difference.

The most popular fish in Mumbai is pomfret — a flat flounderlike fish that's either silvery or dark gray. Silver pomfret is sweet and mild, while advocates of the dark gray variety claim it is more flavorful. It can be prepared in curries, pan-fried or deep-fried. Sadly, pomfret is so popular that much is exported, and the rest is snapped up by the hospitality industry. What is available in the market is so small and the price so inflated that few housewives buy it anymore. There is also great demand for local salmon and mackerel, shrimp and langoustine. Crab is also a favorite. Today seafood restaurants serving specialties from different coastal regions are the rage.

Further down the west coast, there are a number of micro-coastal communities, each with its own special ingredients and masalas.

Thatched-roof eateries dot the coast, and if you are fearless enough to abandon your ideas of health department guidelines, you will most likely eat the freshest, most astonishing seafood dishes anywhere in India.

GOA IS A MAJOR TOURIST DESTINATION and a paradise for seafood lovers. Chiles and cumin, along with liberal amounts of garlic and vinegar, are the classic Goan seasonings. The local dried red chiles pack a lot of heat, and the famous Goa fish curry is not for the fainthearted. In western India, most people believe that a touch of tang enhances the flavors of fish and seafood. There are several options, such as lime or lemon juice, tamarind and an ingredient that is not well known in North America: *kokum*. This is the soft leathery skin of a sour tropical fruit, and it is thrown into curries to impart a delicate tang. It is popular in Goa. Coconut — ground into a masala paste with chiles and spices — and coconut milk, too, are used freely. Eating in Goa is a favorite pastime, and there are a number of shacks along the beaches that serve up some incredible seafood dishes.

Fish and Seafood

——————————— ❧ ———————————

Kerala, where the three distinct cuisines of the state — Muslim (Mophla), Syrian Christian and Hindu — share prominence, has a wide variety of seafood dishes. Coconut is without doubt the most common ingredient, and coconut oil is also used.

TRAVELING TO THE SOUTHERN TIP in Tamil Nadu, you'll find that, in addition to fresh fish and seafood, dried fish is also popular. Shark from the local waters is relished, too. Coconut is used, but in limited quantities, and the tang in their dishes comes from tamarind and lime juice.

Andhra Pradesh in the southeast has a large repertoire of seafood dishes. Unlike Kerala on the opposite coast, the use of coconut is minimal. Instead, tomatoes and tamarind are signature seasonings along with spices.

AS WE MOVE FARTHER UP THE EAST coast to Orissa and Bengal, seasonings change substantially. Mustard seeds and mustard oil are the defining flavors. The Bengali daily diet of rice and fish is well known, and river fish from the delta are preferred over seafood from the Bay of Bengal. Finding the freshest fish is a preoccupation of Bengalis, and it was traditionally the man of the house who was the delegated buyer. There are a minuscule number of Bengali recipes for meat and chicken but a large variety for seafood. Perhaps the most recognized of their dishes is the flavorful mustard fish *(shorshe maach),* made with ground mustard seeds and seasoned with slivered green chiles. The most prized fish are *hilsa* and *bekti* from local rivers, but halibut, red snapper, catfish and tilapia are good substitutes in most dishes. Coconut is used sparingly. It is, however, the defining flavor in the gravy for Shrimp in Coconut Milk *(Chingri Maacher Malai),* a classic rich shrimp curry. Orissa has its own lesser-known version of mustard fish, which, in fact, is my personal favorite.

IN THE NORTHEASTERN STATES, THERE is no seafood apart from local river fish. Assamese Fish Pitika is a delicious salad that is the essence of simplicity and another of my favorite recipes. As with other dishes from the area, there is minimal use of oil and spices, making the food light yet surprisingly tasty.

Amritsari Fish

- *Wok or deep-fryer*
- *Candy/deep-fry thermometer*

4 lbs	fish steaks, such as halibut or any other firm fish (½ inch/1 cm thick)	2 kg
⅓ cup	cider vinegar	75 mL
4 tsp	salt or to taste, divided	20 mL
1¼ cups	chickpea flour (besan)	300 mL
3 tbsp	minced peeled gingerroot	45 mL
3 tbsp	minced garlic	45 mL
3 tbsp	carom seeds (ajwain)	45 mL
1 tsp	cayenne pepper	5 mL
1 tsp	freshly ground black pepper	5 mL
½ tsp	turmeric	2 mL
	Few drops orange food coloring, optional	
	Oil for deep-frying	
3 to 4 tbsp	chaat masala (see Tip, right)	45 to 60 mL
	Lemon wedges	

1. Rinse fish and pat dry thoroughly.

2. In a shallow dish, combine vinegar with 2 tsp (mL) of the salt. Add fish, turning to coat, and marinate for 30 minutes in refrigerator.

3. Meanwhile, in a bowl, mix chickpea flour with enough water, 6 to 8 tbsp (90 to 125 mL), to make a thick smooth paste to coat and adhere to fish. Stir in ginger, garlic, carom seeds, cayenne, pepper, turmeric, remaining salt and food coloring, if using.

4. Drain fish and wipe dry. Coat fish with chickpea flour paste and set aside for 20 minutes.

5. In a wok or deep-fryer, heat oil to 350°F (180°C). Add fish and deep-fry, in batches, without crowding, until crisp and cooked through, 6 to 8 minutes per batch. Remove with a large-holed strainer. Drain on paper towels.

6. Sprinkle fish generously with chaat masala while still warm. Serve with lemon wedges.

Serves 6 to 8

This is arguably the most well-known fish dish from Punjab, using local river fish. Carom seed (ajwain) *is the distinctive flavor here. The orange hue of the fish is traditional and purely cosmetic, so feel free to omit it if you prefer.*

Tip

Chaat masala is a mixture of slightly spicy, salty and sour ingredients, including mango powder, pepper, cayenne and black salt. It is readily available in Indian markets.

Macha Jhol
Garhwali Fish Curry

Serves 4

This recipe from Garhwal in Uttarakhand uses local river fish. Jhol is a very light broth-like gravy and is the choice for everyday dishes. Indians pour it over rice and it adds flavor while keeping the rice moist. If you prefer, cut the amount of water to suit your preference.

2 lbs	skinless fish fillets (any variety)	1 kg
2 cups	loosely packed mint leaves	500 mL
1	piece (1 inch/2.5 cm square) peeled gingerroot, coarsely chopped	1
3	cloves garlic, coarsely chopped	3
1 to 2	2-inch (5 cm) long green chiles, preferably serranos, coarsely chopped	1 to 2
1 tsp	dark mustard seeds	5 mL
2 tbsp	oil	25 mL
1 tsp	coriander powder	5 mL
½ tsp	cayenne pepper	2 mL
½ tsp	turmeric	2 mL
1 tsp	salt or to taste	5 mL
2 tbsp	unsalted Thai tamarind purée	25 mL

1. Rinse fish and pat dry thoroughly. Cut into 4-inch (10 cm) pieces.

2. In a small food processor or blender, process mint, ginger, garlic and chiles as fine as possible. If using a blender, add 2 tbsp (25 mL) water to facilitate blending. Set aside.

3. In a spice grinder or in a mortar and pestle, powder mustard seeds. Transfer to a small bowl and stir in 1½ tbsp (22 mL) water to make a paste.

4. In a skillet large enough to accommodate fish in a single layer, heat oil over medium heat. Add mint paste and sauté for 2 minutes. Add coriander, cayenne and turmeric and sauté for 2 minutes.

5. Stir in mustard paste. Add 2 cups (500 mL) water and salt. Bring to a boil. Reduce heat to medium-low and cook until reduced by half, about 5 minutes.

6. Stir in tamarind. Arrange fish in a single layer and spoon some of the gravy over top. Cover and cook until fish flakes easily with the tip of a paring knife. Serve hot over rice.

Grilled Fish Skewers

- *Bamboo skewers, soaked in water for 30 minutes*

2 lbs	skinless firm fish fillets, such as catfish, snapper, redfish, halibut or cod	1 kg

Marinade

1 cup	plain nonfat yogurt	250 mL
3 tbsp	chickpea flour (besan)	45 mL
2 tsp	minced garlic	10 mL
2 tsp	coriander powder	10 mL
1 1/2 tsp	salt or to taste	7 mL
1 tsp	cumin powder	5 mL
1 tsp	turmeric	5 mL
1 tsp	cayenne pepper	5 mL
3/4 tsp	carom seeds (ajwain)	4 mL
1/2 tsp	garam masala	2 mL
3 tbsp	freshly squeezed lime or lemon juice	45 mL
1 tbsp	oil	15 mL

Additional oil for broiler pan or grill
Lemon wedges
Mint sprig

Serves 8

Fish recipes are limited in the land-locked northern states. Traditionally, local river fish would be used for this recipe, but any firm-fleshed fish will be suitable.

1. Rinse fish and pat dry thoroughly. Cut into 1 1/2-inch (4 cm) pieces.

2. *Marinade:* In a large nonreactive bowl, whisk together yogurt, chickpea flour, garlic, coriander, salt, cumin, turmeric, cayenne, carom seeds and garam masala. Add lime juice and oil. Add fish and stir to coat with mixture. Set aside at room temperature for 15 minutes or refrigerate for up to 2 hours.

3. Thread 2 to 3 pieces on each skewer. Thread another skewer parallel to first, through pieces, so fish does not rotate on skewers. Discard remaining marinade.

4. Preheat broiler. Line broiler pan with foil and brush liberally with oil. Arrange skewers on pan and broil, turning once, 3 to 4 minutes. Alternatively, cook on a well-oiled preheated grill, turning once, 3 to 4 minutes. Garnish with lemon wedges and mint sprig.

Fish Pitika

Serves 4 to 6

When I first came across this recipe, I was intrigued by its utter simplicity. I was a little skeptical about the taste but curious enough to try it. At the first mouthful, there was sheer delight written on the faces of my family, and it has been voted one of the tastiest fish recipes. Pitika translates as "mash." My Assamese friend Rakhi tells me pitikas are served at room temperature and are eaten as a first course mixed with warm rice. A word of caution — use only fresh, not frozen, fish to taste the delicate flavors.

- *Steamer*

2 tsp	dark mustard seeds	10 mL
1 lb	skinless fish fillets, such as catfish, tilapia or red snapper	500 g
1 tbsp	mustard oil	15 mL
1 tsp	minced garlic	5 mL
2 tsp	minced green chiles, preferably serranos	10 mL
2 to 3 tbsp	freshly squeezed lime or lemon juice	25 to 45 mL
1 tsp	salt or to taste	5 mL

1. In a spice grinder, grind mustard seeds to a powder. Transfer to a small bowl and stir in 2 tbsp (25 mL) water. Set aside for at least 20 minutes or for up to 2 hours for flavor to develop.

2. Place fish on a dish to fit steamer. Set up the steamer or place a rack in a pot of water to hold the dish above the level of the water. Bring water to a boil over high heat and carefully place dish inside. Steam fish until it flakes easily with a fork. Time will depend on thickness of fish. Transfer to a bowl. Flake with fork.

3. In a small skillet, heat oil over high heat until smoking. Remove from heat and let cool for 1 minute (see Tip, page 281). Return to low heat. Add garlic and sauté for 1 minute. Add mustard paste and cook for 30 seconds. Add mixture to fish.

4. Add chiles, lime juice and salt and mix well. Serve at room temperature with warm steamed rice or as a first course with a green salad.

Shorshe Maach

Mustard Fish

1 tbsp	dark mustard seeds	15 mL
2 lbs	skinless catfish or snapper fillets	1 kg
1 ½ tsp	salt or to taste	7 mL
Scant ½ tsp	turmeric	2 mL
3 tbsp	mustard oil, divided	45 mL
15	fresh curry leaves, cut into strips	15
4 tsp	minced green chiles, preferably serranos	20 mL
2	2-inch (5 cm) long green chiles, preferably serranos, slivered	2

Serves 4 to 6

The Bengali penchant for mustard and fresh fish come together beautifully in this classic dish.

1. In a small bowl, soak mustard seeds in 2 tbsp (25 mL) water for 30 minutes.

2. Rinse fish and pat dry thoroughly. Cut into 4-by 2-inch (10 by 5 cm) pieces.

3. In a large bowl, combine salt and turmeric. Add fish and rub in mixture. Set aside for 10 minutes.

4. In a mortar, using a pestle, grind soaked mustard seeds into as smooth a paste as possible. Mix with ½ cup (125 mL) water and set aside.

5. In a saucepan, heat oil over high heat until almost smoking. Remove from heat and let cool for 1 minute (see Tip, page 281). Transfer 1 tbsp (15 mL) to a small pan. Set aside. Return pan to medium heat. Add minced chiles and sauté for 1 minute. Add fish and sauté briefly, gently turning pieces to seal all sides but not cooked through.

6. Pour mustard seed paste over fish. Sprinkle curry leaves and minced chiles over top. Reduce heat to medium-low. Cook gently, uncovered, until liquid is reduced by half, about 10 minutes. Cover and simmer on very low heat, 3 to 4 minutes more.

7. Heat the small pan of reserved oil over medium heat. Add slivered chiles and sauté until crisp. Transfer fish to serving dish and pour oil with chiles over top. Serve with steamed rice.

Orissa Mustard Fish

Serves 4 to 6

Mustard fish is a staple in the east, with many variations. Although in this recipe the mustard flavor is predominant, tomatoes give it a different texture and taste.

1½ tsp	salt or to taste, divided	7 mL
1 tsp	turmeric, divided	5 mL
2 lbs	skinless fish fillets, such as catfish, snapper	1 kg
3 tbsp	dark mustard seeds	45 mL
2 tsp	Indian poppy seeds (see Tip, page 219)	10 mL
1½ tsp	cumin powder	7 mL
1 tsp	cayenne pepper	5 mL
5	large cloves garlic, coarsely chopped, or 2 tbsp (25 mL) garlic paste	5
¼ cup	mustard oil	50 mL
1 cup	finely chopped tomato	250 mL
2	2-inch (5 cm) long green chiles, julienned	2
3 tbsp	cilantro, chopped	45 mL

1. In a large dish, combine ¾ tsp (4 mL) of the salt and ½ tsp (2 mL) of the turmeric. Add 2 tbsp (25 mL) water to make a paste.

2. Rinse fish and pat dry. Cut into approximately 4-inch (10 cm) pieces. Rub paste on fish and marinate for 15 minutes at room temperature or for up to 6 hours in refrigerator.

3. In a spice grinder, grind mustard and poppy seeds into a powder. Transfer to a bowl. Stir in remaining turmeric, cumin and cayenne.

4. In a mortar, using a pestle, make a paste with garlic and remaining salt. Stir paste into spice mixture. Add ¼ cup (50 mL) water and stir into a smooth paste. Set aside.

5. In a skillet large enough to accommodate fish in a single layer, heat oil over high heat until smoking. Remove from heat and let cool for 1 minute (see Tip, page 281). Return to medium heat. Add fish in a single layer and fry until fish is opaque but not cooked through, 2 to 4 minutes. Using a slotted spatula, transfer fish to a flat dish. Drain all but 1 tbsp (15 mL) of the oil from skillet.

6. Return skillet to medium heat. Add tomato and chiles and sauté until tomatoes soften and can be mashed with the back of a spoon, about 5 minutes.

7. Add spice paste and sauté until masala looks well mixed and a shade darker, 3 to 4 minutes.

8. Return fish and accumulated juices to skillet. Spoon masala over top of fish. Cover, reduce heat to low and cook until fish flakes easily with tip of paring knife. Cooking time will depend on thickness of fish. If necessary, add 2 to 3 tbsp (25 to 45 mL) water to facilitate cooking. Garnish with cilantro. Serve hot.

Fish and Spinach Tenga

Serves 3 to 4

Throughout the east and northeast, fish curries abound. Freshwater fish from the mighty rivers of India, the Ganges and the Brahmaputra and hundreds of smaller tributaries, provide a large variety of fish. Tenga is a slightly sour, broth-like Assamese dish, minimally spiced but surprisingly flavorful. It is served with plain rice.

1 lb	skinless fish fillets, such as catfish, snapper, tilapia or cod	500 g
1¼ tsp	salt, divided	6 mL
1 tsp	turmeric	5 mL
¼ cup	mustard oil	50 mL
1 tsp	fenugreek seeds (methi)	5 mL
12 oz to 1 lb	fresh spinach, coarsely chopped	375 to 500 g
2 tbsp	freshly squeezed lime or lemon juice	25 mL

1. Rinse fish and pat dry thoroughly. Cut into 3- to 4-inch (7.5 to 10 cm) pieces.

2. In a bowl, mix together 1 tsp (5 mL) salt and turmeric. Add fish and coat all over with mixture. Set aside for 15 minutes at room temperature or for up to 2 hours in refrigerator.

3. In a wide saucepan, heat oil over high heat until smoking. Remove from heat and let cool for 1 minute (see Tip, page 281). Return to medium heat. Add fish and sauté for 2 minutes. Flip pieces and cook just until opaque but not cooked through. Using a slotted spoon, transfer fish to a dish, draining off all but 1 tbsp (15 mL) of the oil.

4. Return saucepan to medium heat. Add fenugreek and sauté for 10 seconds. Add spinach and sauté until spinach is wilted.

5. Add 1 cup (250 mL) water and remaining salt. Bring to a gentle boil. Add fish to pan along with any accumulated juices. Return to a gentle boil. Reduce heat to medium-low, cover and cook until fish flakes easily with tip of knife. Add lime juice. Serve hot with steamed rice.

Monjula's Prawn Curry

2 lbs	prawns or large shrimp, peeled and deveined	1 kg
2 tbsp	oil	25 mL
4 cups	thinly sliced onions (lengthwise slices)	1 L
2	cloves garlic, crushed	2
2 tsp	minced green chiles, preferably serranos	10 mL
2 tsp	jaggery (gur) or brown sugar	10 mL
1½ tsp	ground cloves	7 mL
1½ tbsp	all-purpose flour	22 mL
1½ tsp	ground cinnamon	7 mL
1 tsp	cayenne pepper	5 mL
½ tsp	turmeric	2 mL
2 cups	fish stock or water	500 mL
1 cup	coconut milk	250 mL
2 tsp	salt or to taste	10 mL
2 tbsp	freshly squeezed lime or lemon juice	25 mL

Serves 8

My Bengali friend Monjula shared this recipe with me many years ago, and I was intrigued with the addition of jaggery. Although it is used in dal and vegetable dishes on the west coast, I had never encountered it in a seafood dish before.

1. Rinse prawns and pat dry thoroughly. Set aside.

2. In a saucepan, heat oil over medium heat. Add onions, garlic and chiles and sauté until beginning to color, 8 to 10 minutes.

3. Add jaggery and cloves and sauté for 1 minute. Sprinkle with flour and add cinnamon, cayenne and turmeric. Mix well and sauté for 1 minute. Slowly add stock, stirring vigorously to mix. Add coconut milk. Bring to a boil, stirring constantly. Cook, uncovered, stirring frequently, for 5 minutes.

4. Add prawns and increase heat to medium. Bring to a gentle boil. Reduce heat to low. Cover and simmer until prawns are pink and opaque, 6 to 8 minutes.

5. Remove from heat and add lime juice. Serve hot with rice.

Chingri Maacher Malai

Shrimp in Coconut Milk

1 ½ lbs	large shrimp, peeled and deveined	750 g
¾ tsp	salt	4 mL
1 tsp	turmeric	5 mL
1 tsp	cayenne pepper	5 mL
1 ½ cups	coarsely chopped onions	375 mL
2 ½ tbsp	oil, divided	32 mL
6	whole cloves	6
6	green cardamom pods, cracked open	6
1	stick cinnamon, about 3 inches (7.5 cm) long	1
2	bay leaves	2
2 tsp	minced peeled gingerroot	10 mL
1	can (14 oz/400 mL) coconut milk	1

1. Rinse shrimp and pat dry thoroughly. Toss with salt.

2. In a small bowl, mix together turmeric and cayenne. Add ¼ cup (50 mL) water and stir to dissolve. Set aside.

3. In a food processor, pulse onion just until finely chopped, for 30 seconds. (Do not allow onion juices to exude.)

4. In a wok, heat 1 ½ tbsp (22 mL) of the oil over medium-high heat. Add shrimp and sauté just until pink but not cooked through, about 2 minutes. Transfer to a bowl and set aside.

5. In the same wok, heat remaining oil over medium-high heat. Add cloves, cardamom, cinnamon and bay leaves and sauté until fragrant, for 1 minute. Reduce heat to medium. Add spice mixture and sauté, stirring vigorously, until moisture evaporates and spices are cooked, 1 to 2 minutes.

6. Add onions and sauté, stirring gently, until beginning to color, 4 to 5 minutes. Add ginger. Continue to sauté, until purée begins to brown. Add water, 1 tbsp (15 mL) at a time, to deglaze pan and prevent burning. Sauté until mixture is deep gold and forms a semi-solid mass, about 10 minutes.

7. Slowly pour half of the coconut milk around edges. Mix well with masala. Add remaining coconut milk and mix well. Bring to a gentle boil over medium-low heat, stirring periodically.

8. Add shrimp and any accumulated juices. Stir to mix. Simmer until shrimp are pink and opaque, 3 to 4 minutes. Do not overcook.

Serves 6 to 8

In a Bengali household, a son-in-law occupies an exalted position, and special dishes are prepared to honor him. This traditional dish is a must on the occasion of a son-in-law's visit.

Tip

If you are planning to serve the dish later, remove from heat just as it comes to a boil. Cover and set aside for up to 30 minutes. The residual heat will cook the shrimp further and they will be perfect when reheated over low heat until steaming hot.

Bhapa Chingri
Mustard Steamed Shrimp

Serves 4 to 6

In this delicate dish from Bengal, melt-in-your mouth shrimp, aromatic with crushed mustard seeds, are ethereal. I like to use jumbo shrimp and serve these as a first course with salad.

Tip
Although not traditional, leftover shrimp can be served cold, and they taste equally good.

- *Steamer*

2 tbsp	dark mustard seeds	25 mL
1/4 tsp	turmeric	1 mL
1 tbsp	mustard oil	15 mL
2 tbsp	slivered peeled gingerroot	25 mL
1 tbsp	slivered green chiles, preferably serranos	15 mL
1 1/4 tsp	salt or to taste	6 mL
2 lbs	jumbo shrimp, peeled and deveined, tails left on	1 kg

1. In a spice grinder, grind mustard seeds to a powder. Transfer to a large bowl. Add turmeric and 2 tbsp (25 mL) water. Stir into a paste and set aside for 15 minutes.

2. In a small skillet, heat oil over high heat until smoking. Let cool and pour over mustard paste. Add ginger, chiles and salt and mix well.

3. Rinse shrimp and pat dry. Mix thoroughly with mustard mixture. Transfer to a container that is suitable for steaming, such as a glass pie dish. Cover tightly with foil.

4. Set up the steamer. When water comes to a boil, place foil-covered dish inside and steam until shrimp turn pink, 20 to 25 minutes. Serve immediately.

Lau Chingri
Bengali Shrimp and Long Squash

2 lbs	medium shrimp, peeled and deveined	1 kg
1 1/2 tsp	salt or to taste	7 mL
Scant 1 tsp	turmeric, divided	5 mL
2 tbsp	mustard oil, divided	25 mL
2	bay leaves	2
1 tsp	panch phoran (see Tip, page 216)	5 mL
1 1/2 lbs	long squash, peeled and cut into 1/2-inch (1 cm) cubes	750 g
4	green chiles, preferably serranos, slit lengthwise, but keeping stem end intact	4
1 tsp	cayenne pepper	5 mL
1 tsp	cumin powder	5 mL
2 to 3 tbsp	cilantro, chopped	25 to 45 mL

Serves 4 to 6

This is a classic dish in Bengal, where seafood is often cooked with vegetables. Long squash, also know as opo squash in markets in North America, is mild flavored, a little like zucchini, which can be substituted.

Tip
Mustard oil is made from cold-pressed mustard seeds and is not an infusion. It has a distinctive taste and is the preferred oil in Bengal and other eastern states. However, it has an element that can be toxic to some. Heating it to smoking point neutralizes this and makes it safe for cooking.

1. Rinse shrimp and pat dry thoroughly.

2. In a large bowl, combine 1 tsp (5 mL) of the salt and 1/2 tsp (2 mL) of the turmeric. Add shrimp and marinate at room temperature for 20 minutes.

3. In a wok, heat 1 tbsp (15 mL) of the oil over high heat until smoking. Remove from heat for 1 minute (see Tip, right). Return to medium-high heat. Add shrimp mixture and sauté just until pink, about 2 minutes. Transfer shrimp to a bowl and set aside.

4. Wipe wok and add remaining oil to pan and repeat heating and cooling process. Add bay leaves and panch phoran. As soon as the mustard seeds in the panch phoran stop popping, add squash. Reduce heat to medium. Mix well and add 1/2 cup (125 mL) water and remaining salt. Cover and bring to a boil. Reduce heat to low and simmer until vegetables are almost tender, 12 to 15 minutes. If necessary, add additional water, a little at a time, to prevent burning.

5. Stir in the remaining turmeric, chiles, cayenne and cumin. Cover and cook for 3 to 4 minutes.

6. Add shrimp and 1/2 cup (125 mL) water and increase heat to medium. Cook, uncovered, stirring occasionally, until there is a thick gravy and shrimp are pink and opaque. Sprinkle with cilantro. Serve hot with rice.

Chapa Pulusu
Andhra Fish Curry

Serves 6

This is a simple but delicious curry from coastal Andhra, where tamarind is an essential ingredient. Unlike in Kerala, coconut is noticeably absent from coastal Andhra cooking.

2 lbs	sturdy fish fillets, such as catfish or cod	1 kg
1 ½ tsp	cumin seeds	7 mL
¾ tsp	fenugreek seeds (methi)	4 mL
2 tbsp	oil	25 mL
2 cups	puréed onions	500 mL
2 tsp	minced peeled gingerroot	10 mL
2 tsp	minced garlic	10 mL
2	2-inch (5 cm) long green chiles, preferably serranos, chopped	2
1 tbsp	coriander powder	15 mL
1 ¼ tsp	salt or to taste	6 mL
½ tsp	cayenne pepper	2 mL
½ tsp	turmeric	2 mL
6 tbsp	unsalted Thai tamarind purée, stirred into 1 ½ cups (375 mL) water	90 mL
2 tbsp	cilantro, chopped	25 mL

1. Rinse fish and pat dry thoroughly. Cut into 3- to 4-inch (7.5 to 10 cm) pieces. Set aside.

2. In a small dry skillet over medium heat, toast cumin seeds, shaking pan constantly, until seeds become aromatic and a shade darker, 2 to 3 minutes. Transfer to a small bowl. Add fenugreek seeds to skillet and toast until slightly darker, 30 to 40 seconds. Add to cumin seeds. Let cool slightly and grind to a powder in a spice grinder or in a mortar and pestle. Set aside.

3. In a deep skillet or a saucepan large enough to accommodate fish in a single layer, heat oil over medium heat. Add onions, ginger, garlic and chiles and sauté until onions begin to brown. Reduce heat to medium-low and continue to cook, stirring often, until onions are golden brown, about 10 minutes. Add water, 2 tbsp (25 mL) at a time, to prevent burning and continue to sauté until mixture is dark brown, 12 to 14 minutes.

4. Add coriander, salt, cayenne and turmeric and sauté for 2 minutes. Add tamarind water and bring to a gentle boil. Simmer for 5 minutes.

5. Add fish to saucepan in a single layer. Spoon gravy over fish. Cover and simmer until fish flakes easily with tip of paring knife, 10 to 15 minutes, depending on type and thickness of fish. Garnish with cilantro. Serve hot over steamed rice.

Fish Moilee

1 cup	coarsely chopped onion	250 mL
10	cloves garlic, coarsely chopped (about 3 tbsp/45 mL)	10
1	piece (1-by ¼-inch/2.5 by 0.5 cm) peeled gingerroot	1
2 tsp	chopped green chiles, preferably serranos	10 mL
1 tsp	coriander powder	5 mL
½ tsp	cumin powder	2 mL
½ tsp	turmeric	2 mL
2 tbsp	coconut oil or other preferred oil	25 mL
¾ tsp	dark mustard seeds	4 mL
2	sprigs fresh curry leaves, stripped (20 to 25 leaves)	2
1 cup	coconut milk	250 mL
3 to 4 tbsp	unsalted Thai tamarind purée	45 to 60 mL
2 tsp	jaggery (gur)	10 mL
1½ tsp	salt or to taste	7 mL
2 lbs	skinless fish filets, such as catfish, tilapia or red snapper	1 kg

Serves 6

A classic dish from Kerala, it is popular on restaurant menus in North America. The subtle flavors and sensual creamy gravy appeal to even the most timid palates.

1. In a food processor, purée onion, garlic, ginger, chiles, coriander, cumin and turmeric.

2. In a saucepan, heat oil over high heat until a couple of mustard seeds thrown in start to sputter. Add all the mustard seeds and cover quickly. When the seeds stop popping, in a few seconds, uncover, reduce heat to medium and add curry leaves. Sauté for 20 seconds.

3. Add onion purée and reduce heat to medium-low. Sauté mixture, (masala) stirring gently, until fragrant, 6 to 8 minutes. Do not allow to brown.

4. Add coconut milk, tamarind, jaggery and salt. Mix well and bring to a gentle boil. Simmer, stirring periodically, for 8 minutes.

5. Meanwhile, rinse fish and pat dry thoroughly.

6. Slip fish into curry and return to a gentle boil. Simmer until fish flakes easily with tip of paring knife, 10 to 15 minutes, depending on thickness of fish. Serve hot with steamed rice.

Meen Varuval
Pan-Fried Masala Fish

2 lbs	skinless fish fillets, such as catfish, flounder, red snapper or tilapia	1 kg
5 tbsp	oil, divided (approx.)	75 mL
1/2 cup	coarsely chopped onion	125 mL
1	sprig fresh curry leaves, stripped (12 to 15 leaves)	1
3 to 4	cloves garlic, cut into large pieces	3 to 4
4 tsp	unsalted Thai tamarind purée	20 mL
1 tbsp	coriander powder	15 mL
1 1/2 tsp	salt or to taste	7 mL
1 tsp	cayenne pepper	5 mL
1/2 tsp	turmeric	2 mL
1/2 tsp	freshly ground black pepper	2 mL
2 to 3 tbsp	cilantro, coarsely chopped	25 to 45 mL

Serves 4 to 6

This simple recipe from Tamil Nadu is truly mouthwatering — the spices are a perfect foil for the fish. The freshness of the fish is paramount, and I would recommend that you use fish that has not been previously frozen.

1. Rinse fish and pat dry thoroughly. Cut each fillet into about 4-inch (10 cm) pieces and transfer to a bowl.

2. In a skillet, heat 2 tsp (10 mL) of the oil over medium heat. Add onion, curry leaves and garlic and sauté until onions are translucent, 5 to 6 minutes. Let cool.

3. Transfer onion mixture to small food processor and process to a paste. Transfer to a bowl. Add tamarind, coriander, salt, cayenne, turmeric and pepper. Mix well.

4. Spread mixture evenly on both sides of fish fillets. Cover and refrigerate for 1 to 2 hours.

5. In a large nonstick skillet, heat 1/4 cup (50 mL) of the remaining oil over medium heat. Add fish and fry, in 2 batches, turning pieces once, to brown both sides until fish flakes easily with tip of paring knife, 4 to 5 minutes. Using a slotted spatula, transfer fish to a dish and keep warm. Add more oil, if necessary, to fry second batch. Garnish with cilantro. Serve hot.

Sardines with Green Mango

S

Serves 4

This is an updated version of an old Kerala recipe using dried fish. My friend Sushila recommended I use fresh sardines or any other small fish, such as smelt or whitebait, instead.

¾ cup	grated coconut, preferably fresh (or frozen, thawed)	175 mL
8 oz	fresh or frozen sardines, thawed if frozen	250 g
1	large clove garlic	1
¾ tsp	salt	4 mL
3 tbsp	thinly sliced onion (lengthwise slices), divided	45 mL
1 tbsp	chopped green chiles, preferably serranos	15 mL
2 tsp	chopped peeled gingerroot	10 mL
1	sprig fresh curry leaves, leaves stripped (12 to 15)	1
1 tbsp	coriander powder	15 mL
1½ tsp	cayenne pepper	7 mL
¼ tsp	turmeric	1 mL
½ cup	peeled chopped green mango (½-inch/1 cm cubes)	125 mL
1 tbsp	oil	15 mL
¼ tsp	dark mustard seeds	1 mL
2	dried Indian red chiles, broken in half	2

1. In a blender, purée coconut with ½ cup (125 mL) water to a paste. Set aside.

2. Rinse fish, pat dry thoroughly and place in a saucepan.

3. In a mortar, using a pestle, crush garlic and salt to a paste. Add to fish. Add 2 tbsp (25 mL) of the onion, green chiles, ginger, curry leaves, coriander, cayenne and turmeric. Mix well. Add 1 cup (250 mL) water and bring to a boil over medium-high heat. Reduce heat to low. Cover and cook for 5 minutes.

4. Add green mango. Cover and simmer for 10 minutes.

5. Add coconut paste and mix well. Cook, uncovered, stirring periodically, until curry thickens, 6 to 8 minutes.

6. In a small pan, heat oil over high heat until a couple of mustard seeds thrown in start to sputter. Add all the mustard seeds and cover quickly. When the seeds stop popping, in a few seconds, uncover, reduce heat to medium and add red chiles and remaining 1 tbsp (15 mL) onion. Sauté until onion begins to color, 2 to 3 minutes. Pour into curry. Mix well and serve hot with rice.

Spicy Coastal Shrimp

4	dried Indian red chiles, seeds removed	4
2 lbs	large shrimp, peeled and deveined	1 kg
1 tsp	salt, divided	5 mL
½ tsp	turmeric	2 mL
3	large onions, cut into chunks	3
4	2-inch (5 cm) long green chiles, preferably serranos, coarsely chopped	4
1	piece (1-by ½-inch/2.5 by 1 cm) peeled gingerroot, coarsely chopped	1
3	cloves garlic	3
1 tbsp	coriander seeds	15 mL
1 tsp	dark mustard seeds	5 mL
¾ tsp	fenugreek seeds (methi)	4 mL
2 tbsp	oil	25 mL
½ cup	fresh curry leaves	125 mL
3 to 4 tbsp	freshly squeezed lime or lemon juice	45 to 60 mL

1. In a bowl, soak chiles in ½ cup (125 mL) hot water for 10 minutes.

2. Rinse shrimp and pat dry thoroughly. In a bowl, rub ½ tsp (2 mL) of the salt and turmeric into shrimp and set aside.

3. Drain red chiles. In a food processor, combine onions, red and green chiles, ginger and garlic and process into a coarse mixture. Set aside.

4. In a dry skillet over medium heat, toast coriander and mustard seeds, stirring, for 1 minute. Add fenugreek and toast until seeds are fragrant and a shade darker, about 20 seconds. Take care not to burn. Let cool. Transfer to a spice grinder and grind to a fine powder.

5. In a skillet or wok, heat oil over medium heat. Add curry leaves and sauté for 1 minute. Increase heat to medium-high. Add onion mixture and sauté until golden, 6 to 8 minutes.

6. Add powdered spices and remaining salt and sauté for 3 minutes.

7. Add shrimp and mix well with masala. Increase heat to high. Stir-fry until shrimp turn pink, 3 to 4 minutes. Do not overcook. Remove from heat and mix in lime juice. Serve immediately.

Serves 6 to 8

HOT

This is one of the few coastal recipes that does not use coconut. It has great flavor. The heat of chiles is balanced by the onions, resulting in a delicious masala, finished with lime juice.

Tip

This dish should be prepared just before serving, as the shrimp will exude moisture if left to sit for too long. However, shrimp can be marinated and refrigerated for several hours, and Steps 2 and 3 can also be done several hours ahead. Proceed with remainder of recipe just before serving.

Mangalore Crab Curry

Serves 6 to 8

HOT

Mangalore, a city on the Konkan coast on the west coast of India, is renowned for its distinctive cuisine. The area is populated by distinct communities, each with its well-recognized specialties. Meat, poultry and seafood are all relished and cooked with quantities of coconut and spices. Kokum is a popular ingredient.

Tip

Kokum (*Garcinia indica*) is the soft leathery skin of a deep purple, sour tropical fruit grown and used on the west coast of India. If unavailable, substitute 2 tbsp (25 mL) unsalted Thai tamarind purée.

2 cups	grated coconut, fresh or frozen, thawed	500 mL
3 tbsp	coriander seeds	45 mL
1½ tbsp	cumin seeds	22 mL
24	dried Indian red chiles, broken in half, 12 with seeds removed	24
10	green cardamom pods, cracked open	10
1	stick cinnamon, about 2 inches (5 cm) long	1
24	cloves garlic	24
70	fresh curry leaves, divided (about 6 sprigs)	70
1¼ tsp	turmeric	6 mL
¼ cup	oil	50 mL
4 lbs	dressed crabs or 3 to 3½ lbs (1.5 to 1.75 kg) crab claws	2 kg
2	cans (each 14 oz/400 mL) coconut milk	2
1½ tsp	salt or to taste	7 mL
20	kokum (see Tip, left)	20

1. In a dry skillet over medium heat, toast coconut in a single layer, stirring constantly, until golden and aromatic, 5 to 6 minutes. Watch it carefully, as coconut can burn easily. Transfer to a bowl.

2. In the same skillet, toast separately coriander, cumin, chiles, cardamom and cinnamon in that order until each is fragrant. The time will vary from a few seconds to up to 2 minutes. Take care not to burn. Add each to bowl with coconut.

3. Transfer coconut and spices to a blender and grind to a fine powder. Add garlic, 30 curry leaves and turmeric. Pour in ½ cup (125 mL) water and blend. Continue to add more water as needed, to make a smooth thick paste, scraping down sides of blender occasionally.

4. In a wide-bottomed saucepan, heat oil over medium heat. Add coconut paste and remaining curry leaves. Sauté, stirring continuously, until masala (mixture) turns a few shades darker and aromatic, 5 to 6 minutes. If necessary, deglaze pan with 1 tbsp (15 mL) water periodically while sautéing to prevent burning. Add crab and mix well. Sauté until crab is well seasoned with masala, 3 to 4 minutes.

5. Pour coconut milk into pan. Add salt and kokum. Shake pan to settle crab. Cover and bring to a gentle boil over medium heat. Cook, stirring periodically, until gravy is thickened, about 10 minutes. Serve hot over rice or with South Indian Rice and Lentil Crêpes (see recipe, page 166).

Prawn Ghassi

Serves 8

This traditional and well-known dish from Mangalore is very popular in the seafood restaurants that have sprung up in Mumbai in the past decade.

Tip

In the tradition of Indian curries, there should be a fair amount of liquid (gravy). If you prefer less, reduce water to 1 cup (250 mL). Leftover gravy can be frozen in an airtight container for up to 3 months. Reheat in a saucepan over low heat and proceed with Steps 1 and 6.

Variation

Shrimp or "prawns" as they are known in India can be substituted with fish. Use 2 lbs (1 kg) skinless fish fillets, such as catfish or red snapper, cut into 4-by 3-inch (10 by 7.5 cm) pieces.

2 lbs	medium prawns or shrimp, shelled and deveined	1 kg
1 1/2 tsp	salt or to taste	7 mL
4	dried Indian red chiles, 2 with seeds removed	4
2 tsp	coriander seeds	10 mL
1 tsp	cumin seeds	5 mL
1/2 tsp	black peppercorns	2 mL
1/4 tsp	fenugreek seeds (methi)	1 mL
1 1/2 cups	finely chopped onions, divided	375 mL
3/4 cup	grated coconut, preferably fresh (or frozen, thawed)	175 mL
4 tsp	minced garlic	20 mL
2 tbsp	unsalted Thai tamarind purée	25 mL
1/2 tsp	turmeric	2 mL
2 tbsp	oil	25 mL

1. Rinse prawns and pat dry thoroughly. In a bowl, rub salt into prawns. Cover and refrigerate for 1 hour.

2. In a dry skillet over medium heat, toast red chiles until dark, about 1 minute. Break into pieces and transfer to a spice grinder. Add coriander, cumin, peppercorns and fenugreek to grinder and grind to a powder.

3. In a blender, combine 3/4 cup (175 mL) of the onions, coconut, spice powder, garlic, tamarind and turmeric. Add 1/4 cup (50 mL) water and blend to a smooth paste. If necessary, add more water to make a paste of thick pouring consistency. Set aside.

4. In a saucepan, heat oil over medium heat. Add remaining onions and sauté until golden, 5 to 6 minutes.

5. Add paste and sauté until a shade darker and aromatic, 3 to 4 minutes. Deglaze pan with 1 tbsp (15 mL) water if necessary to prevent burning. Add 1 1/2 cups (375 mL) water, mix well and bring to a boil.

6. Add prawns. Return to a boil and reduce heat to medium-low. Cover and simmer until prawns are pink and opaque, about 5 minutes. Serve hot over steamed rice.

Goan Fish Recheado

3	whole scaled tilapia or pompano, each about 1 1/2 to 1 3/4 lbs (750 to 875 g)	3
1 1/2 tsp	salt	7 mL
3/4 tsp	turmeric	4 mL
2	lemons, cut in half	2

Masala

24	dried Indian red chiles, 12 with seeds removed	24
1 1/2 tsp	cumin seeds	7 mL
1 tsp	black peppercorns	5 mL
3/4 tsp	coriander seeds	4 mL
8	whole cloves	8
1	stick cinnamon, about 2 inches (5 cm) long	1
3 tbsp	minced garlic	45 mL
1/3 cup	white vinegar	75 mL
1 tbsp	balsamic vinegar	15 mL
2 1/2 cups	oil (approx.)	625 mL
1	onion, thinly sliced into rings	1
2	lemons, cut into wedges	2

Serves 6

HOT

The spice paste for this dish is hot and very tasty. It can be made in a larger quantity and refrigerated in an airtight container for up to one year. Goan vinegar is distinctive and not available commercially outside of Goa. I have used white and balsamic vinegars to simulate the authentic Goan vinegar.

1. Remove fins from fish. Rinse and pat dry thoroughly. Cut slits on both sides of fish, about 1 1/2 inches (4 cm) apart, and place in a large dish. In a bowl, mix together salt, turmeric and juice of 1 lemon. Dip remaining 2 lemon halves in mixture and rub into fish, squeezing gently to release more juice. Cover and refrigerate for 30 minutes.

2. *Masala:* Meanwhile, in a spice grinder, grind together red chiles, cumin, peppercorns, coriander, cloves and cinnamon. Transfer to blender. Add garlic and white and balsamic vinegars and purée to a smooth paste.

3. Spread paste evenly over fish, pressing into slits. Set aside for 15 minutes.

4. In a large skillet, heat 3/4 cup (175 mL) of the oil over medium heat. Add one fish at a time to hot oil and fry for 8 minutes, spooning oil in skillet periodically over top of fish to "set" masala. Carefully flip fish and fry other side, until fish flakes easily with tip of a paring knife, 6 to 8 minutes. Transfer to a platter and keep warm. Repeat with remaining fish, adding more oil as necessary. Garnish with onion rings and lemon wedges before serving.

Fish with Green Mango

Serves 6 to 8

Green mangoes are used in Indian cooking for their wonderful tartness. Here they are used as a souring substitute for tamarind, which is often used in fish dishes of the west coast.

Tips

Look for green mangoes with the vegetables in the produce section, not in the fruit aisle. Buy a rock-hard, dark green mango for the sourest flavor.

One large mango will yield the 2 cups (500 mL) batons needed for this recipe.

3 lbs	skinless fish fillets, such as catfish, snapper or any other similar fish	1.5 kg
2 tbsp	freshly squeezed lime or lemon juice	25 mL
2½ tsp	salt, divided	12 mL
1 tsp	turmeric	5 mL
4 cups	loosely packed cilantro	1 L
3 tbsp	grated coconut, preferably fresh (or frozen, thawed)	45 mL
3 to 4	2-inch (5 cm) long green chiles, preferably serranos, cut into pieces	3 to 4
1	piece (1 inch/2.5 cm square) chopped peeled gingerroot	1
6	cloves garlic	6
2 tbsp	oil	25 mL
2 cups	green mango batons (3 by ½ inch/7.5 by 1 cm) (see Tips, left)	500 mL
1 tsp	granulated sugar	5 mL
½ tsp	garam masala	2 mL

1. Rinse fish and pat dry thoroughly. Cut into 3- to 4-inch (7.5 to 10 cm) pieces and place in a bowl.

2. In a small bowl, mix together lime juice, 1½ tsp (7 mL) of the salt and turmeric. Rub into both sides of fish. Set aside for 15 minutes.

3. In a blender, combine cilantro, coconut, chiles, ginger and garlic. Add 4 to 5 tbsp (60 to 75 mL) water and blend to a paste.

4. In a saucepan large enough to accommodate fish in a single layer, heat oil over medium heat. Add cilantro paste and sauté until slightly darker, 2 to 3 minutes. Add 1 cup (250 mL) water and bring to a boil.

5. Add fish in a single layer and top with mango. Sprinkle with sugar and remaining salt. Cover and cook for 5 minutes. Reduce heat to low and simmer until fish flakes easily with tip of a paring knife, 6 to 8 minutes. Shake pan to allow mango to settle in between fish as it cooks.

6. Remove from heat. Sprinkle with garam masala and cover for 2 minutes. Serve with steamed rice.

Konkani Fish Curry

1 lb	fish, such as pomfret, cut into ½-inch (1 cm) thick steaks (see Tip, right)	500 g
1 tsp	turmeric, divided	5 mL
1 tsp	salt, divided	5 mL
1 tsp	each coriander seeds and cumin seeds	5 mL
4	dried Indian red chiles	4
½ cup	grated coconut, fresh or frozen, thawed	125 mL
2 tbsp	oil	25 mL
2 cups	thinly sliced onions (lengthwise slices)	500 mL
2 tbsp	minced green chiles, preferably serranos	25 mL
1	can (14 oz/400 g) chopped tomatoes, including juice	1
3 tbsp	unsalted Thai tamarind purée	45 mL
2	sprigs fresh curry leaves (20 to 25 leaves), stripped and coarsely chopped	2

Serves 3 to 4

The Konkan coast, south of Mumbai is famous for its seafood dishes. The prized pomfret, a flat flounder-like fish, would be first choice for this recipe.

Tip

You can use any flatfish, such as flounder, preferably cut into steaks, or use any firm fillet of fish.

1. Rinse fish and pat dry thoroughly. In a bowl, mix together ½ tsp (2 mL) turmeric and ½ tsp (2 mL) salt. Add fish and rub on both sides with salt mixture. Cover and refrigerate for up to 3 hours.

2. In a dry skillet over medium heat, toast coriander, cumin and red chiles, shaking pan constantly, until fragrant, about 3 minutes. Transfer to a bowl and let cool slightly. Grind to a powder in a spice grinder.

3. In a blender, combine coconut, spice powder and remaining turmeric. Blend to a paste with ¼ cup (50 mL) water. Transfer to a bowl. Swirl ¼ cup (50 mL) water in blender jar and pour into another bowl.

4. In a saucepan that can accommodate fish in a single layer, heat oil over medium heat. Add onions and green chiles and sauté until onions are soft, about 5 minutes.

5. Add coconut paste and sauté until masala is a little darker and fragrant, 8 to 10 minutes. Deglaze pan periodically with reserved water from blender, 1 tbsp (15 mL) at a time and adjust heat to allow masala to brown without burning.

6. Add tomatoes with juice, tamarind and remaining salt and mix well. Reduce heat to medium-low. Cover and cook for 5 minutes to allow tomatoes to soften. Mash with back of spoon.

7. Carefully place fish in masala, spooning masala over fish. Cover and simmer until fish flakes easily with tip of a paring knife, about 10 minutes, depending on thickness of fish. Sprinkle with curry leaves before serving.

Fish Biriyani

Serves 6 to 8

This elaborate layered dish is worth the effort. Serve it with a yogurt salad or a simple side dish of your favorite vegetable and papadums.

* *Large casserole dish, sprayed with vegetable spray*

Fish and Potato Layer

3	dried Indian red chiles	3
½ tsp	saffron threads	2 mL
2 lbs	skinless fish fillets, such as cod, halibut, snapper or catfish	1 kg
3	green chiles, preferably serranos	3
1	head garlic, about 25 cloves	1
1	piece (2 by 1 inch/5 by 2.5 cm) peeled minced gingerroot	1
2 tbsp	oil	25 mL
3	pieces cinnamon, each about 1 inch (2.5 cm) long	3
3	green cardamom pods, cracked open	3
4	whole cloves	4
10	black peppercorns	10
8 oz	all-purpose potatoes, cut into 2-inch (5 cm) pieces (about 2)	250 g
8	dried apricot halves	8
½ cup	plain lowfat yogurt, at room temperature, stirred to a creamy consistency	125 mL
1 tbsp	salt, divided	15 mL
1 tbsp	coriander powder	15 mL
½ tsp	turmeric	2 mL
½ tsp	garam masala	2 mL
¼ cup	freshly squeezed lime or lemon juice	50 mL
½ cup	cilantro leaves	125 mL
10 to 12	mint leaves or 1 tsp (5 mL) dried mint	10 to 12

Rice Layer

1¼ cups	Indian basmati rice (see Tip, page 134)	300 mL
2 tsp	salt or to taste	10 mL
½ cup	crispy fried onions (birishta)	125 mL
2 tbsp	oil	25 mL
1	stick cinnamon, about 2 inches (5 cm) long	1
3	whole cloves	3
3	green cardamom pods, cracked open	3

1. *Fish and Potato Layer:* In a bowl, soak red chiles in ½ cup (125 mL) very hot water for 15 minutes. In a separate bowl, soak saffron in ¼ cup (50 mL) hot water for at least 10 minutes. Set both aside.

2. Rinse fish and pat dry thoroughly. Cut into 2-inch (5 cm) square pieces. Set aside.

3. In a blender, combine red chiles and soaking water, green chiles, garlic and ginger. Blend to a paste. Set aside.

4. In a large saucepan, heat 2 tbsp (25 mL) oil over medium heat. Add cinnamon, cardamom, cloves and peppercorns and sauté for 1 minute. Add potatoes and sauté until golden on all sides, 6 to 8 minutes. Remove potatoes and set aside. In the same pan, add chile paste and sauté until mixture is fragrant and almost dry, 2 to 3 minutes.

5. Add apricots, yogurt, coriander, 2 tsp (10 mL) salt, turmeric and garam masala. Cook, stirring continuously, until almost dry, 3 to 4 minutes. Return potatoes to pan and mix well. Reduce heat to low. Cover and cook until potatoes are half-cooked, about 5 minutes.

6. Carefully arrange fish in pan. Sprinkle with remaining salt. Drizzle lime juice and saffron and soaking water over top. Spoon masala on top of fish. Sprinkle with cilantro and mint. Increase heat to medium. Cover and cook for 5 minutes. Uncover and cook until liquid is reduced by half. There should be a fairly thick gravy in the pan. Set aside.

7. *Rice Layer:* Place rice in a large bowl with plenty of cold water and swish vigorously with fingers. Drain. Repeat 4 to 5 times until water is fairly clear. Cover with 3 to 4 inches (7.5 to 10 cm) cold water and set aside to soak for 10 minutes.

8. Fill a large saucepan three-quarters full of water. Add 2 tsp (10 mL) salt. Bring to a boil over high heat. Drain rice and add to saucepan. Return to a boil and cook until rice is cooked on the outside but uncooked in the center, 2 to 3 minutes. Do not overcook. Drain immediately and spread in a shallow pan to cool.

9. Preheat oven to 300°F (150°C). Spread a thin layer of rice on bottom of prepared casserole dish. Carefully spread fish and potato mixture on rice. Spoon remaining rice on top. Sprinkle fried onions on top.

10. Heat 2 tbsp (25 mL) oil in a small pan. Add cinnamon, cloves and cardamom and sauté until fragrant, about 30 seconds. Pour on top of rice. Cover dish tightly with foil and bake in preheated oven for 30 minutes. Let rest for 5 minutes before serving.

11. *To serve:* Carefully spoon rice into a mound on a large platter, taking care not to break up fish. Place some fish and potatoes carefully on top of rice.

Macchi no Saas
Parsi Fish in Egg Sauce

7 tbsp	vinegar, divided	105 mL
4 tsp	salt, divided	20 mL
2 lbs	flounder steaks or any firm fish fillets, 1 1/2 inches (4 cm) thick	1 kg
2 tbsp	oil	25 mL
1/2 tsp	cumin seeds	2 mL
1 cup	thinly sliced onion (lengthwise slices)	250 mL
2 tbsp	minced garlic	25 mL
1 tbsp	minced peeled gingerroot	15 mL
1 tbsp	minced green chiles, preferably serranos	15 mL
1/4 tsp	turmeric	1 mL
2	eggs	2
2 tbsp	all-purpose flour	25 mL
2 tbsp	granulated sugar	25 mL
3 tbsp	cilantro, chopped	45 mL

Serves 6 to 8

A Parsi favorite, this sweet-and-sour egg sauce is smooth and rich. On the west coast of India, the fish of choice would be the delicate pomfret, a shiny silvery flatfish, similar in appearance to flounder, which is a good substitute.

Tip

Typically, there should be a lot of egg sauce in this dish. If you prefer less, reduce water to 3 cups (750 mL) in Step 4.

1. In a shallow dish, mix together 1 tbsp (15 mL) of the vinegar and 2 tsp (10 mL) of the salt.

2. Rinse fish and pat dry thoroughly. Add to vinegar mixture and turn to coat evenly. Set aside.

3. In a shallow saucepan large enough to accommodate fish in a single layer, heat oil over medium heat. Add cumin and sauté until fragrant, for 30 seconds. Add onion and sauté until golden, 6 to 7 minutes. Add garlic, ginger, chile and turmeric and sauté for 2 minutes.

4. Add 4 cups (1 L) water and bring to a boil. Reduce heat to medium-low and gently boil for 5 minutes.

5. Add fish in a single layer and shake pan gently to settle fish. Increase heat to medium. Cover and return to a gentle boil. Reduce heat to medium-low. Cook for 5 minutes.

6. Meanwhile, in a bowl, beat eggs lightly. In another bowl, whisk together remaining vinegar, flour, sugar and remaining salt until smooth and lump-free. Whisk into beaten eggs.

7. Gradually add 1/2 cup (125 mL) liquid from saucepan into egg mixture.

8. Slowly pour mixture over fish. Shake pan to mix. Reduce heat to low. Simmer, uncovered, until fish flakes easily with tip of a paring knife, about 5 minutes. Sprinkle with cilantro. Serve with steamed rice or chapati.

Thum Methi Macchi

Sindhi Fish with Fenugreek and Garlic

Serves 6 to 8

My aunt taught me this classic Sindhi recipe shortly after we moved to the United States in the 1970s. I had always loved the strong and very distinctive taste of the signature mixture (masala) made with green garlic and fresh fenugreek. At that time I had to compromise by using regular garlic and dried fenugreek, but now frozen chopped green garlic and frozen fenugreek leaves are available in most Indian markets.

Tip

To freeze masala, pack in an airtight container and freeze for up to 1 year.

3 lbs	skinless catfish fillets or other similar fish, such as red snapper, redfish or halibut	1.5 kg
3 tbsp	freshly squeezed lime or lemon juice	45 mL
1¾ tsp	salt, divided	9 mL
1½ tsp	cayenne pepper	7 mL
½ tsp	turmeric	2 mL
Masala		
6	green onions	6
⅓ cup	thawed frozen green garlic or 10 medium cloves garlic	75 mL
4	3-inch (7.5 cm) long green chiles, preferably serranos, cut into pieces	4
4 cups	loosely packed spinach	4
2	bunches fresh fenugreek (methi) (about 7 to 8 cups), loosely packed, or 4 cubes frozen fenugreek, thawed (see Tip, page 336)	2
2 tbsp	oil	25 mL
2	sprigs fresh curry leaves (20 to 25 leaves), stripped	2
2 cups	chopped tomatoes	500 mL
2 tsp	coriander powder	10 mL
1 tsp	cumin powder	5 mL
½ tsp	turmeric	2 mL

1. Rinse fish and pat dry thoroughly. Cut into 3-inch (7.5 cm) pieces.

2. In a bowl, mix together lime juice, ¾ tsp (4 mL) of the salt, cayenne and turmeric into a paste. Coat fish on both sides with paste and set aside.

3. *Masala:* In a food processor, combine green onions, garlic and chiles. Add spinach and fenugreek by the handfuls and process as fine as possible.

4. In a skillet large enough to hold fish in a single layer, heat oil over medium heat. Add masala and sauté for 3 to 4 minutes. Add curry leaves, tomatoes, coriander, cumin, turmeric and remaining salt. Continue to sauté until tomatoes are softened, about 5 minutes. Mash tomatoes with back of spoon as they soften. Add 1½ cups (375 mL) water and cover. Bring to a boil. Reduce heat to medium-low and cook until masala looks soft and homogenized, about 10 minutes.

5. Add fish in a single layer. Spoon masala over top of fish. Cover and simmer until fish flakes easily with tip of a paring knife, 6 to 8 minutes. Adjust thickness of gravy by reducing, uncovered, if there is too much liquid. If too thick, drizzle a little hot water around the edges. When ready, there should be a fairly thick masala gravy coating the fish. Serve with rice or an Indian bread.

Variations

This masala can be used for many other dishes. Among my favorites are shrimp, following the same procedure for coating the fish.

Omit fish and add 1 recipe Lower-Fat Panir (see recipe, page 312), cubed, and mix into masala to make a vegetarian entrée.

You can also use a combination of potato and baby corn. Use 1 lb (500 g) any variety of peeled potatoes, cut into 4-by 1½-inch (10 by 4 cm) pieces and 1 can (5 oz/150 g) drained baby corn. Cook until potatoes are tender and masala thickens, 6 to 8 minutes.

Bombay Shrimp

Serves 6 to 8

This dish is the essence of simplicity. Garlic and shrimp are always great together, and in this case the shower of fresh cilantro raises the dish to another level.

Tip

The chile sauce balances the sweetness of the almost caramelized onions. You can substitute 1 tbsp (15 mL) white vinegar and 2 tsp (10 mL) hot pepper flakes.

2 lbs	medium shrimp, peeled and deveined	1 kg
3 to 4 tbsp	oil	45 to 60 mL
¼ cup	coarsely chopped garlic	50 mL
8 cups	chopped onions (about 4)	2 L
½ cup	tomato paste	125 mL
2 to 3 tbsp	Asian chile sauce (sambal oelek)	25 to 45 mL
2 cups	cilantro, chopped	500 mL

1. Rinse shrimp and pat dry thoroughly. Set aside.

2. In a large saucepan, heat oil over medium heat. Add garlic and sauté until golden, 2 to 3 minutes. Remove with slotted spoon and place in a bowl. Set aside.

3. Increase heat to medium-high. Add shrimp and sauté, in 2 batches, just until pink but not cooked through, about 2 minutes per batch. Remove with slotted spoon and add to garlic in bowl.

4. Add onions to pan and sauté until dark golden, 10 to 12 minutes. Stir in tomato paste and chile sauce.

5. Return garlic and shrimp with any accumulated juices to pan. Add all but 2 tbsp (25 mL) of the cilantro and mix well. Cook until shrimp turn pink and opaque, 4 to 5 minutes.

6. Sprinkle remaining cilantro over top. Serve immediately with an Indian bread.

Prawn Caldeen

2 lbs	medium prawns or shrimp, peeled and deveined	1 kg
1 tbsp	coriander seeds	15 mL
1 tsp	cumin seeds	5 mL
1/2 tsp	black peppercorns	2 mL
3	dried Indian red chiles, some seeds removed	3
4 tbsp	grated coconut, preferably fresh (or frozen, thawed)	60 mL
2 tsp	minced garlic	10 mL
1/2 tsp	turmeric	2 mL
2 tbsp	oil	25 mL
2 cups	thinly sliced onions (lengthwise slices)	500 mL
4 to 5 tbsp	unsalted Thai tamarind purée	60 to 75 mL
8 oz	okra, cut into 1/2-inch (1 cm) pieces	250 g
1 3/4 tsp	salt or to taste	9 mL
1/2 cup	coconut milk	125 mL
3	2-inch (5 cm) long green chiles, preferably serranos, slivered	3

Serves 6 to 8

This is a popular Goan dish, best made with fresh okra in the summer. In India, okra is a year-round vegetable, much loved across the country. In North America, this humble vegetable is regarded as slimy — except, of course, in the south, where it is a staple in gumbo. Even if you are not fond of the vegetable, do give this recipe a try. You will change your mind.

1. Rinse prawns and pat dry thoroughly. Set aside.

2. In a spice grinder, grind coriander, cumin, peppercorns and chiles to a powder.

3. In a blender, combine coconut, ground spices, garlic and turmeric. Add 3 to 4 tbsp (45 to 60 mL) water and blend to a smooth paste. Set aside in a bowl.

4. In a saucepan, heat oil over medium-high heat. Add onions and sauté until deep golden, 10 to 12 minutes.

5. Add prawns and sauté until almost dry, 3 to 4 minutes. Add spice paste and continue to cook until mixture looks a little darker, 3 to 4 minutes.

6. Stir in tamarind and 1/2 cup (125 mL) water. Add okra and salt. Reduce heat to medium-low. Cover and cook until okra is soft, 10 to 12 minutes

7. Stir in coconut milk and green chiles. Serve over hot rice.

Shrimp with Green Chiles and Coconut

2 lbs	large shrimp, peeled and deveined	1 kg
2 tbsp	freshly squeezed lime or lemon juice	25 mL
1 ½ tsp	salt or to taste	7 mL
½ tsp	cayenne pepper	2 mL
3 tbsp	oil, divided	45 mL
1 ¼ tsp	cumin seeds	6 mL
⅓ cup	chopped green garlic (see Tip, left), 2 tbsp (25 mL) chopped garlic or ½ cup (125 mL) chopped garlic chives	75 mL
6 to 8	green chiles, preferably serranos, cut in half	6 to 8
1 cup	grated coconut, preferably fresh or frozen, thawed	250 mL
2 cups	cilantro, coarsely chopped	500 mL

1. Rinse shrimp and pat dry thoroughly. Place in a large bowl and toss with lime juice, salt and cayenne. Marinate at room temperature for 10 minutes or for up to 30 minutes.

2. In a large wok or saucepan, heat 1 tbsp (15 mL) of the oil over medium-high heat. Add half the shrimp and toss to cook just until pink but not cooked through, about 2 minutes. Transfer to a bowl. Add 1 tbsp (15 mL) of oil and repeat with remaining shrimp. Set aside.

3. Add remaining oil to wok and return to medium-high heat. Add cumin and sauté for 30 seconds. Add garlic and green chiles and sauté until chiles begin to blister, about 2 minutes.

4. Return shrimp and any accumulated juices to wok. Toss to cook through, 3 to 4 minutes.

5. Remove from heat and sprinkle with coconut and cilantro. Toss to coat. Serve immediately.

Shrimp Baked in Banana Leaves

Serves 4

It is best to use jumbo shrimp for this dish, because there is no gravy to smother the shrimp and the presentation is impressive.

Tips

Shrimp can be refrigerated in leaves for 5 to 6 hours. Bake just before serving.

If increasing recipe, it is a good idea to wrap no more than 1½ lbs (750 g) shrimp in each banana leaf package for even cooking. Increase baking time to 30 minutes.

Variation

You may substitute fish fillets for the shrimp if you prefer. Adjust the baking time according to the thickness of the fish.

- *Preheat oven to 375ºF (190ºC)*
- *Baking sheet, lined with foil*

1 lb	jumbo shrimp, cleaned and deveined	500 g
4 tsp	dark mustard seeds, divided	20 mL
1	piece (1 inch/2.5 cm square) peeled gingerroot	1
4 tsp	coarsely chopped green chiles, preferably serranos	20 mL
1 tsp	salt or to taste	5 mL
½ tsp	cayenne pepper	2 mL
Scant ½ tsp	turmeric	2 mL
1 tsp	fennel seeds (saunf)	5 mL
1 tsp	cumin seeds	5 mL
¾ tsp	fenugreek seeds (methi)	4 mL
1 tbsp	oil	15 mL
2	banana leaves	2

1. Rinse shrimp and pat dry thoroughly. Place in a bowl and set aside.

2. In a spice grinder or in a mortar with a pestle, grind mustard seeds to a powder.

3. In a food processor, process ginger, chiles and three-quarters of the mustard seed powder as fine as possible. Add 2 to 3 tbsp (25 to 45 mL) water to make a paste. Transfer to a bowl. Stir in salt, cayenne and turmeric.

4. In a spice grinder or in a mortar with a pestle, grind fennel, cumin and fenugreek seeds to a powder. Stir in remaining mustard powder.

5. In a small skillet, heat oil over medium heat. Add powdered spices and sauté until fragrant, for 1 minute. Pour over ginger paste and mix well. Add to shrimp and mix well to coat with paste.

6. Cut banana leaves into 2 large squares. Place 1 banana leaf, glossy side down, on prepared baking sheet. Place shrimp in center of leaf. Do not pile high. Cover with second leaf. Bring sides of foil up to loosely enclose leaves. It is not necessary to completely enclose top. Bake in preheated oven for 25 minutes.

7. *To serve:* Place "package" on serving platter. Fold foil back and remove covering leaf.

Tandoori Shrimp

- *Preheat barbecue to medium-high or preheat oven broiler*
- *Bamboo skewers, soaked in water for 30 minutes*

2 lbs	large shrimp, peeled and deveined	1 kg
½ cup	well-drained thick yogurt	125 mL
¼ cup	freshly squeezed lime or lemon juice	50 mL
1 tsp	ginger paste (see Tip, right)	5 mL
1 tsp	garlic paste	5 mL
1 tsp	coriander powder	5 mL
1 tsp	garam masala	5 mL
½ tsp	cumin powder	2 mL
½ tsp	cayenne pepper	2 mL
½ tsp	paprika	2 mL
1½ tsp	salt or to taste	7 mL
3 to 4	drops red food coloring, optional	3 to 4
2 to 3 tbsp	melted butter for basting	25 to 45 mL
	Juice of 1 lime or lemon	

1. Rinse shrimp and pat dry thoroughly.

2. In a nonreactive bowl, mix together yogurt, lime juice, salt, ginger, garlic, coriander, garam masala, cumin, cayenne, paprika and food coloring, if using. Add shrimp to bowl and mix well. Set aside for 15 minutes.

3. Thread 3 to 4 shrimp on 2 parallel skewers to prevent shrimp from rotating. Brush with melted butter and grill or broil, turning once, just until shrimp are firm and opaque, 3 to 4 minutes. Do not overcook.

4. Squeeze more lime or lemon juice over top and serve.

Serves 8

Although tandoori food is associated with the north, tandoori marinade is popular in many parts of the west coast. Tandoori fish and shrimp are popular in restaurants in Mumbai.

Tip
Ginger and garlic pastes are available in jars in Indian and Asian markets. Making your own is a simple matter of grating peeled gingerroot or garlic cloves on a Microplane grater.

Mussels in Coconut Milk

Serves 8

The west coast of India abounds in a variety of clams. Mussels are easier to find in North America and are a very good substitute. This dish is inspired by Goan seasonings.

Tips

After adding mussels in Step 7, you can cool and refrigerate for up to 8 hours. Return to room temperature before continuing with recipe.

If using frozen mussels, omit Step 2.

10	dried Indian red chiles	10
4 lbs	mussels, fresh or frozen New Zealand green mussels, thawed if frozen	2 kg
1 tsp	fennel seeds (saunf)	5 mL
1 tsp	cumin seeds	5 mL
1/2 tsp	cardamom seeds	2 mL
1/2 tsp	black peppercorns	2 mL
10	cloves garlic	10
1 cup	chopped onion	250 mL
1 cup	grated coconut, preferably fresh (or frozen, thawed)	250 mL
2 tbsp	oil	25 mL
4 cups	mussel broth or clam juice (see Tip, left)	1 L
2 cups	coconut milk	500 mL
6 to 8 tbsp	unsalted Thai tamarind purée or to taste	90 to 120 mL
1/2 tsp	salt or to taste	2 mL

1. In a bowl, soak chiles in 1 cup (250 mL) hot water for 15 minutes.

2. If using fresh mussels, scrub thoroughly and soak in cold water for 15 minutes. Remove beards and rinse well in 2 to 3 changes of water. Discard any that are open and do not close when tapped. Place mussels in a large pot and pour in 5 cups (1.25 mL) water. Cover and bring to a boil over medium-high heat. Cook until mussels open, about 2 minutes. Remove mussels from pot and strain liquid through a cheesecloth-lined strainer into a bowl. Set mussels and broth aside. Discard any mussels that did not open.

3. In a spice grinder, grind fennel, cumin, cardamom and peppercorns to a powder. Set aside.

4. Drain red chiles and cut into pieces. Place in a blender with garlic and blend for 30 seconds. Add onion, coconut, reserved spice powder and 1/3 cup (75 mL) reserved mussel broth and blend into a paste, adding a little more broth if needed. Blend to a smooth thick paste, scraping down sides of blender as necessary.

5. In a large Dutch oven or saucepan, heat oil over medium heat. Pour paste into pan and sauté, gently stirring continuously for 5 minutes. At this time, you will need to deglaze pan with 2 tbsp (25 mL) of mussel broth. Continue sautéing masala paste and deglazing pan until color changes to light tan, 10 to 12 minutes.

6. Pour in remaining broth. Add salt and stir to mix. Reduce heat to low. Cover and simmer for 10 minutes.

7. Stir in coconut milk and tamarind and return mussels to pan. Shake pan to settle mussels in the gravy and simmer for 10 minutes. Or, if you are planning to serve later, cover and remove from heat after replacing mussels. Set aside for up to 30 minutes. Fifteen minutes before serving, return to medium-low heat and bring to a gentle boil, making sure all mussels are immersed in gravy. Simmer until heated through, 6 to 8 minutes. Serve immediately in shallow bowls with steamed rice.

Hot Mussels

6 lbs	mussels	3 kg
2 tbsp	oil	25 mL
¼ cup	minced peeled gingerroot	50 mL
2 tbsp	finely chopped green chiles (approx.)	25 mL
6 cups	very thinly sliced onions (lengthwise slices)	1.5 L
¼ cup	coriander powder	50 mL
2½ tsp	salt or to taste	12 mL
1½ tsp	turmeric	7 mL
3 to 4	sprigs fresh curry leaves, stripped	3 to 4
1½ cups	chopped tomato, preferably plum (Roma)	375 mL
1½ cups	cilantro, coarsely chopped	375 mL
¾ cup	freshly grated coconut	175 mL

Serves 6

HOT

The west coast of India, between Mumbai and Karnataka, is known as the Konkan coast, and seafood dishes reign supreme. There are distinct styles of cooking and specific spice blends and pastes, but the common denominator is coconut.

1. Scrub mussels thoroughly, removing beards if attached. Discard any that are open and do not close when tapped.

2. In a large stockpot, heat oil over medium-high heat. Add ginger and chiles and sauté until fragrant, about 2 minutes. Stir in onions and sauté until they begin to color, 10 to 12 minutes. Reduce heat to medium and sauté until onions are deep gold, 10 to 12 minutes. Adjust heat if necessary, to prevent burning but maintain a sizzle.

3. Add coriander, salt and turmeric and sauté for 2 minutes. Add 3 cups (750 mL) water. Increase heat to medium-high and bring to a boil. Cook for 2 minutes.

4. Stir in mussels. Scatter curry leaves over top. Cover and steam for 5 minutes. Discard any mussels that have not opened. Remove from heat. Add tomato, cilantro and coconut. Toss to coat mussels. Spoon into bowls and serve with crusty bread.

Vegetables

THE SYMBIOTIC RELATIONSHIP BETWEEN Indian cuisine and vegetables is well recognized. If beans and lentils form the base of the diet, then vegetables are a close second. It would not be an exaggeration to say that Indians are passionate about vegetables. Throughout the country, they play a major role in the diet, and Indians' creativity reaches new heights in their vegetable dishes.

Indians love leafy greens, and spinach is a particular favorite. It is always fresh and never eaten uncooked.

INDIAN CUISINE AS WE KNOW IT TODAY would not exist without the tomato. It may surprise you to learn that tomatoes arrived with the Europeans in the 16th century but did not make much headway until the British demonstrated their use in the late 1800s. In India, tomatoes are used as a souring agent and are not expected to be sweet. I was astonished to find that tomatoes in North America are quite the opposite. As a result, I have had to make a few adjustments in traditional recipes that expect tart tomatoes.

Peas, beloved by most Indians, were introduced by the British and even today are considered an "English vegetable." When I was growing up in India, a dish containing peas was mandatory when you entertained, as they were pricier than most vegetables and considered elegant for company.

KASHMIR IS THE LAND OF PLENTY. Kashmiris enjoy everything from fruits, such as apples, almonds and walnuts, to vegetables, such as *kak* — a local green that is their signature leafy vegetable — to lotus roots, which abound in their lakes. The precious morel mushroom (known as *gucchi*), a wild mushroom that grows at higher altitudes,

Vegetables

has resisted cultivation and is a prized ingredient in *gucchi pulao,* a rice dish cooked for weddings and special occasions. The growing season in Kashmir is short and the winters long. The blanket of snow lingers for many months, and through those bleak months Kashmiris depend on the stock of dried vegetables and fruits they put away in the fall. Everything from greens to lotus roots are carefully prepared for drying, and in the fall every home is festooned with garlands of sliced vegetables, bunches of herbs and strings of red chiles hanging from the eaves.

ONE OF THE SIGNATURE DISHES IN the north, particularly Punjab, is mustard greens (*sarson ka saag*). It is a cool-weather green, and Punjabis look forward to its arrival in the market with anticipation. Other popular vegetables in the north are cauliflower (also best in the cooler months), a special winter carrot (a very sweet and juicy pinkish variety that is particular to the area), turnips and daikon radish. The latter is very popular as a stuffing for whole wheat griddle-fried bread (*mooli paratha*). Lotus root (*bhee nadru*) is another exotic vegetable that is prized in the north. Sindhis are very fond of it and cook it with meat, as a side dish seasoned with fenugreek, or as a chaat dish, smothered in yogurt and tamarind chutney.

Rajasthan is a desert state, and fresh vegetables are hard to come by. There are no greens to speak of, and their signature "vegetable" dish is made of a type of dried berry and dried bean (*ker sangri*). Potatoes and tomatoes, however, are used freely.

SEVERAL DIFFERENT TRIBES INHABIT the seven northeastern states. A multitude of local greens are grown, and there are many different types of local chiles. Bamboo shoots are perhaps the most popular vegetable, and assorted wild mushrooms and colocasia, or taro root (*arvi*), a starchy root vegetable, are also popular.

Bengal and Orissa have a veritable cornucopia of vegetables and fruits. Apart from the large variety of greens, eggplant and *potol,* a long torpedo-shaped vegetable, are very popular. A Bengali meal usually includes two or three vegetable dishes and begins with a mixed vegetable dish that includes a bitter vegetable, such as bitter melon. This is believed to be a digestive aid. Banana flower, the heart of the banana tree, and unripe bananas are chopped and used as vegetables. Pineapples, several varieties of bananas and mangos are the most common fruits. Pineapple and mango are used to make the traditional sweet-and-sour relish *tauk,* which is served in small bowls at the end of the meal as a digestive.

IN THE WEST, GUJARAT HAS, WITHOUT a doubt, the most creative vegetarian cuisine. Their use of vegetables is supreme — lightly cooked, with minimal spices and maximum flavors. Growing up, I was fortunate to be included in many a family meal at the home of my Gujarati Jain friends, and my memories of those family meals are still vibrant. The Gujarati Jains are almost pious about everything they eat and are very particular about the preparation of fresh vegetables. Some Gujaratis eat all vegetables, while others, for religious reasons, shun anything grown underground, including onions, garlic, potatoes and carrots.

Maharashtrians relish all vegetables. Eggplant is a favorite, and many varieties of squash are available. Pumpkin is a year-round vegetable and is cooked as a sweet and also with spices. In Maharashtra, stuffed vegetables are popular, and small eggplants are stuffed with many different mixtures. Peanuts and coconut are used freely, often combined with vegetables, usually ground and mixed into stuffings or sprinkled on top of dishes.

Vegetables play a relatively minor role in the food of Goa. Cabbage is enjoyed, both as a substitute for lettuce, which doesn't do well in the Indian climate, and also cooked as a vegetable with spices. Pumpkin and many varieties of squash are also enjoyed. Many different types of bananas are also grown year-round and are a popular fruit. Coconuts and coconut oil are synonymous with Goan cuisine.

IN THE SOUTH, THE PICTURE CHANGES dramatically. Bananas and plantains are perhaps the most important fruit and vegetable, respectively, and there are countless varieties. They are made into chips fried in coconut oil, used in vegetable dishes, and made into fritters and desserts. Jackfruit, a huge knobby green tropical fruit with a strong aroma when ripe, is also very popular. It is eaten as is and cooked. A much-loved vegetable is the drumstick, a strange-looking ridged green pod about $\frac{1}{2}$ inch (1 cm) around and 15 to 18 inches (37.5 to 45 cm) long that grows on a large tropical tree. Not shaped like a chicken drumstick as you might imagine, it actually resembles a stick used to play drums. Drumsticks are particularly delicious in the all-important lentil-and-vegetable stew *sambhar*. They are eaten in other parts of India, too, but nowhere else are they as prized as in the south. Cashews, which came from Brazil with the Portuguese, are popular in cooking, often eaten as a snack, and an important export crop. Coconuts are used extensively, and coconut oil is also used as a cooking medium.

Lower-Fat Panir

Makes 2¾ to 3 cups (675 to 750 mL) 12 oz (375 g)

Panir, the only form of cheese indigenous to India, is very popular in Punjab. This recipe is one I developed when I was looking for a lower-fat version that was still as good as the original full-fat one. I have taught this recipe for more than 25 years and have always received raves. Panir can be grated and used as a stuffing for vegetables and patties, diced and simmered with vegetables, and cut into batons and stir-fried with vegetables.

Tip

Panir can be wrapped in plastic wrap and refrigerated for up to 4 days or frozen, tightly wrapped, for up to 3 months.

- *Double layer of fine cheesecloth*

8 cups	2% milk	2 L
4 cups	buttermilk	1 L

1. Line a large strainer with a double layer of cheesecloth.

2. In a large saucepan or enamel pot over medium heat, bring milk to a boil. (Do not use a nonstick pan.)

3. Pour in buttermilk and stir. When liquid separates from the solids in about 1 minute, remove from heat. Stir until solids are completely separated.

4. Pour contents of pan into cheesecloth-lined strainer. Discard liquid or save for another use.

5. Gather up cheesecloth, twist to form a ball and tie with string. Tie the ends loosely on kitchen faucet and let drain over sink for 5 minutes. Open cheesecloth, flatten panir with hand and enclose again.

6. Place a tray at edge of sink. Place wrapped panir on edge of tray and twist ends of cheesecloth arranging both ends to drip over the edge into sink. Place a weight on top of panir. (You can use the pot in which panir was made and fill three-quarters full of water.) Let drain for 30 minutes or longer. (Panir will be solid at this point. The range in time is just to indicate that it is not critical to remove at 30 minutes, but okay to leave longer.) Remove and use as required.

Matar Panir
Curried Peas and Cheese

2 tbsp	oil	25 mL
1	can (28 oz/796 mL) tomatoes, including juice, chopped	1
1¼ tsp	salt or to taste	6 mL
¾ tsp	turmeric	4 mL
½ tsp	freshly ground black pepper	2 mL
⅓ cup	cilantro, chopped	75 mL
2	packages (each 10 oz/300 g) frozen peas	2
1	recipe Lower-Fat Panir, cut into ½-inch (1 cm) cubes (see recipe, page 312)	1

Serves 8

I love the combination of panir with peas and tomatoes. It is no wonder that this is probably the second most popular panir recipe, after Saag Panir *(Curried Spinach and Cheese, see recipe, page 314).*

There are several versions of this dish, but I grew up eating this one and still find it the best.

1. In a saucepan, heat oil over medium heat. Add tomatoes with juice, salt, turmeric, pepper and cilantro. Bring to a boil. Reduce heat to medium-low. Cover and simmer for 5 minutes.

2. Add peas and panir. Increase heat to medium and return to a boil. Reduce heat to maintain a gentle boil. Cover and cook, stirring occasionally, until gravy is slightly thicker, 12 to 15 minutes. Serve with rice or any Indian bread.

Saag Panir
Curried Spinach and Cheese

Serves 8

This recipe is an amazingly successful light version of a very popular North Indian classic. This creamy dish seems sinfully rich but is instead guilt-free.

~❧~

Tip

The spinach mixture should be creamy. If too dry, add a little more yogurt. This dish freezes well. Reheat in a microwave on Medium (50%), or on the stove over low heat.

2 tbsp	oil	25 mL
1 ½ cups	chopped onions	375 mL
1 tbsp	minced peeled gingerroot	15 mL
2 tbsp	minced green chiles, preferably serranos	25 mL
2 tsp	coriander powder	10 mL
1 tsp	turmeric	5 mL
2	packages (each 10 oz/300 g) frozen spinach, thawed	2
1 ½ tsp	salt or to taste	7 mL
1 cup	nonfat milk	250 mL
2 cups	plain nonfat yogurt, at room temperature	500 mL
2 tsp	cornstarch	10 mL
1	recipe Lower-Fat Panir, cut into ½-inch (1 cm) cubes (see recipe, page 312)	1

1. In a large saucepan, heat oil over medium heat. Add onions, ginger and chiles and sauté until softened and pale golden, 5 to 8 minutes.

2. Reduce heat to medium. Stir in coriander and turmeric and sauté, stirring well, 2 to 3 minutes.

3. Mix in spinach and salt. Cover and simmer for 5 minutes. Remove from heat.

4. In a blender, purée spinach with milk.

5. Reduce heat to low and return mixture to stove. Stir together yogurt and cornstarch to creamy consistency. Stir into spinach mixture. Add panir and mix thoroughly but gently. Cover and simmer until heated through, 10 to 12 minutes. Serve with any Indian bread.

Corn and Spinach Curry

3 tbsp	raw unsalted cashews	45 mL
1½ cups	loose frozen spinach or one-third of 10-oz (300 g) block frozen spinach, thawed	375 mL
1½ tbsp	oil	22 mL
¾ cup	chopped onion	175 mL
1 tsp	chopped peeled gingerroot	5 mL
1 tsp	minced garlic	5 mL
1 cup	chopped tomatoes, preferably plum (Roma)	250 mL
¾ tsp	salt or to taste	4 mL
½ tsp	garam masala	2 mL
½ tsp	cayenne pepper	2 mL
2 cups	fresh or frozen corn	500 mL
2 tsp	oil	10 mL
½ tsp	cumin seeds	2 mL
1 tbsp	slivered peeled gingerroot	15 mL

Serves 6 to 8

This is a tasty and healthy vegetarian entrée from North India, enriched and thickened with cashew meal. Serve it with paratha or rice.

1. In a blender or spice grinder, grind cashews to a fine powder. Transfer to a small bowl and add ½ cup (125 mL) water. Stir until smooth. Set aside.

2. In a saucepan, combine spinach and 1½ cups (375 mL) water. Cover and cook over medium heat for 5 minutes. Pour into a blender and purée. Set aside.

3. In same saucepan, heat 1½ tbsp (22 mL) oil over medium heat. Add onion and sauté until golden, 6 to 7 minutes. Add chopped ginger and garlic and sauté for 2 minutes.

4. Add tomatoes, salt, garam masala and cayenne and mix well. Cover and cook until tomatoes are soft, about 5 minutes. Mash with back of a spoon.

5. Add corn and spinach purée. Stir in ¾ to 1 cup (175 to 250 mL) hot water. Cover and cook for 5 minutes.

6. Stir in cashew paste. Reduce heat to low. Simmer, stirring once to prevent sticking to bottom of pan, for 5 minutes.

7. In a small skillet, heat 2 tsp (10 mL) oil over medium heat. Add cumin and slivered ginger and sauté for 1 minute. Pour over top of spinach.

Mushroom Keema

Serves 6 to 8

Keema *refers to a ground or finely chopped ingredient. Mushroom keema is extremely versatile. It can be served as a side dish, used as a stuffing for tomatoes, bell peppers or any other suitable vegetable, or as a stuffing for pan-fried potato patties. I also like to serve it as an appetizer with pita chips.*

Tip

Chopping mushrooms in a processor discolors them and they exude juices, which changes the taste.

2 tbsp	oil	25 mL
2 cups	finely chopped onions	500 mL
1 tbsp	minced peeled gingerroot	15 mL
1 tsp	minced garlic	5 mL
2 tsp	minced green chiles, preferably serranos	10 mL
2 cups	chopped tomatoes	500 mL
2 tsp	coriander powder	10 mL
1 ¼ tsp	salt or to taste	6 mL
1 tsp	cumin powder	5 mL
1 tsp	turmeric	5 mL
½ tsp	cayenne pepper	2 mL
2 lbs	button mushrooms, finely chopped by hand (see Tip, left)	1 kg
¾ tsp	garam masala	4 mL
⅓ cup	cilantro, chopped	75 mL

1. In a saucepan, heat oil over medium-high heat. Add onions and sauté until deep gold, about 10 minutes.

2. Reduce heat to medium. Add ginger, garlic and chiles and sauté until onions are dark brown, 8 to 10 minutes more.

3. Add tomatoes, coriander, salt, cumin, turmeric and cayenne and mix well. Reduce heat to medium-low. Cover and cook until tomatoes are soft and can be mashed with the back of a spoon, 6 to 8 minutes. Uncover and cook until mixture is thick, about 2 minutes more.

4. Increase heat to medium. Add mushrooms and mix well. Cook, stirring occasionally, 5 to 6 minutes. Do not overcook or mushrooms will exude juices. Remove from heat. Sprinkle with garam masala and cilantro.

Rai jo Teevan
Mustard-Flavored Vegetable Curry

2 tbsp	oil	25 mL
1 1/2 tbsp	dark mustard seeds	22 mL
1	sprig fresh curry leaves, stripped (12 to 15 leaves)	1
2	green chiles, preferably serranos, partially slit tip to stem, keeping ends intact	2
2	plum (Roma) tomatoes, cut into wedges	2
1 1/2 tsp	salt or to taste	7 mL
1 tsp	coriander powder	5 mL
1/2 tsp	turmeric	2 mL
3 tbsp	whole wheat flour	45 mL
6	green beans, cut into 2-inch (5 cm) lengths	6
1	carrot, cut into 2-inch (5 cm) lengths	1
1	potato, cut into 1 1/2-inch (4 cm) cubes	1
1 cup	fresh or frozen boiling onions, peeled	250 mL

Serves 6 to 8

This is a Sindhi classic, easy to prepare and very tasty. The strong mustard flavor comes through, but it is not pungent. It is unusual because it is always served with chapati — whole wheat flatbread — and not with rice.

1. In a large saucepan, heat oil over high heat until a couple of mustard seeds thrown in start to sputter. Add all the mustard seeds and cover quickly. When the seeds stop popping, in a few seconds, uncover, reduce heat to medium and add curry leaves, chiles and tomatoes. Sauté for 1 minute.

2. Add 3 cups (750 mL) water, salt, coriander and turmeric. Increase heat to medium-high. Cover and bring to a boil.

3. Reduce heat to medium. In a bowl, mix together flour and 1/2 cup (125 mL) water to make a smooth paste. Gradually drizzle into boiling liquid, stirring continuously. Cook, uncovered, stirring until curry thickens, 4 to 5 minutes.

4. Add beans, carrot, potato and onions. Return to a boil. Reduce heat to low. Cover and simmer until vegetables are tender, 15 to 18 minutes. Serve with an Indian bread or, if you prefer, with rice.

Sarson ka Saag

Punjabi
Mustard Greens

12 oz	mustard greens, fresh or frozen	375 g
4 oz	spinach, fresh or frozen	125 g
1 tbsp	chopped green chiles, preferably serranos	15 mL
1 tbsp	cornmeal	15 mL
2 tbsp	oil	25 mL
1 cup	thinly sliced onion (lengthwise slices)	250 mL
1 tbsp	minced peeled gingerroot	15 mL
1 tbsp	minced garlic	15 mL
1 cup	chopped tomatoes	250 mL
³⁄₄ tsp	salt	4 mL
1 tbsp	unsalted butter	15 mL

Serves 4 to 6

Mustard greens are arguably the signature greens of Punjab. Mustard greens and griddle-baked corn bread are a marriage made in heaven and relished with gusto by all Punjabis.

1. In a saucepan over medium heat, cook mustard greens, spinach, chiles and 3¹⁄₂ cups (875 mL) water for 20 minutes. Purée in a blender, in 2 batches, with cornmeal and set aside.

2. In another saucepan, heat oil over medium heat. Add onion and sauté until golden, 7 to 8 minutes. Add ginger and garlic and sauté for 2 minutes.

3. Add tomatoes and salt. Cook until tomatoes are soft and can be mashed with the back of a spoon, about 5 minutes.

4. Add greens mixture and mix well. Cover, reduce heat to medium-low and simmer, stirring periodically, for 10 minutes. Transfer to a serving dish and place butter on top. When melted, stir to mix. Serve with griddle-baked corn bread or any other Indian bread.

Sial Bhindi

Sindhi-Style Okra in Green Masala

Serves 8

This is one of my favorite okra recipes, which goes back to my childhood. The basic green purée, with slight variations, is used as a base for several dishes.

- *Saucepan with tight-fitting lid*

4 cups	cilantro leaves	1 L
2 cups	chopped onions	500 mL
4	2-inch (5 cm) long green chiles, preferably serranos, cut into pieces	4
1	piece (1 inch/2.5 cm square) peeled gingerroot, cut into pieces	1
10	cloves garlic	10
2 tbsp	oil	25 mL
2 cups	chopped tomatoes	500 mL
2 tsp	coriander powder	10 mL
1 1/2 tsp	salt or to taste	7 mL
1/2 tsp	cayenne pepper	2 mL
1/2 tsp	turmeric	2 mL
2 lbs	okra, tops and ends trimmed	1 kg
2	medium potatoes (any variety), peeled and sliced 1/4-inch (0.5) thick (about 8 oz/250 g)	2

1. In a food processor, purée cilantro, onions, chiles, ginger and garlic until smooth.

2. In a saucepan, heat oil over medium heat. Add cilantro purée and sauté until it begins to dry a little, 6 to 8 minutes.

3. Add tomatoes, coriander, salt, cayenne and turmeric and mix well. Cover with a tight-fitting lid and cook over low heat until tomatoes are soft enough to be mashed with the back of a spoon, about 10 minutes.

4. Stir in 1 1/2 cups (375 mL) water. Cover and bring to a boil.

5. Add okra and potatoes to "masala" and mix gently. Cover and simmer until vegetables are cooked, 12 to 15 minutes. Add a little additional hot water if vegetables are not tender and the masala dries out. There should be a thick masala covering the vegetables when the dish is ready. Serve with any Indian bread.

Besan ke Gatte
Chickpea Flour Dumplings

1 cup	plain nonfat yogurt, at room temperature	250 mL
1 tsp	cornstarch	5 mL
Gatte		
3 cups	chickpea flour (besan)	750 mL
1 tbsp	salt or to taste	15 mL
2 tsp	minced peeled gingerroot	10 mL
2 tsp	cayenne pepper	10 mL
1 tsp	garam masala	5 mL
7 tbsp	oil, divided	105 mL
¼ tsp	asafetida (hing)	1 mL
1 tsp	cumin seeds	5 mL
1 tbsp	minced green chiles, preferably serranos	15 mL
2 tsp	coriander powder	10 mL
1 tsp	cayenne pepper	5 mL
¾ tsp	turmeric	4 mL
½ tsp	garam masala	2 mL
1 tsp	each salt and mango powder (amchur)	5 mL
½ cup	cilantro leaves, chopped	125 mL

Serves 6 to 8

This is one of the signature dishes of Rajasthan, where fresh vegetables are scarce. Chickpea flour (besan) is used extensively in a variety of dishes, and this type of dumpling is typical.

1. Stir yogurt and cornstarch together until smooth. Set aside.

2. *Gatte:* In a large bowl, mix together chickpea flour, 1½ tsp (7 mL) of the salt, ginger, cayenne and garam masala.

3. In a small pan, heat 5 tbsp (75 mL) of the oil over medium heat. Make a well in center of flour mixture and pour in hot oil. Mix to incorporate. Drizzle in 2 to 3 tbsp (25 to 45 mL) water and mix to make a stiff dough. (Dough will be sticky at first.) Rinse hands and divide into 10 equal portions. Roll each into a ½-inch (1 cm) thick rope. Cut each rope into 3 equal pieces

4. In a saucepan, bring 4 cups (1 L) salted water to a boil over high heat. Drop pieces into water all at once and cook until pale and firm, 15 to 20 minutes. Remove carefully with slotted spoon onto a cutting board, reserving water. When cool, cut into ¾-inch (2 cm) pieces.

5. In a saucepan, heat remaining oil over high heat. Add asafetida and sauté for 30 seconds. Reduce heat to medium. Add cumin and green chiles and sauté for 30 seconds. Reduce heat to low. Stir in coriander, cayenne, turmeric and garam masala and sauté, stirring briskly, for 30 seconds. Stir in yogurt and salt. Add 2 cups (500 mL) reserved water. Cover and simmer until gravy thickens slightly, 6 to 8 minutes.

6. Add dumplings and mango powder and simmer for 5 to 6 minutes. Garnish with cilantro. Serve with rice.

Drumsticks with Potatoes

Serves 6

This Sindhi dish is typical of the cuisine — made with a little onion, a good dose of tomatoes and light on the spices. Drumsticks, not chicken drumsticks as you might imagine, but a much-loved vegetable, are a Sindhi favorite and now that frozen ones are readily available, I prepare this dish often.

Tip

Drumstick is a long strange-looking ridged green pod that resembles sticks used to play drums. Frozen drumsticks, cut into 3-inch (7.5 cm) pieces, are available in Indian markets. They can be added frozen to the dish. Do not overcook, as they fall apart. To eat, hold a piece between thumb and finger and pull drumstick between teeth, like an artichoke leaf, leaving the soft flesh in the mouth and discarding the fibrous outer skin.

1 ½ tbsp	oil	22 mL
1 cup	chopped onion	250 mL
2 tsp	minced green chiles, preferably serranos	10 mL
1 cup	chopped tomatoes	250 mL
2 tsp	coriander powder	10 mL
1 tsp	cayenne pepper	5 mL
1 tsp	salt or to taste	5 mL
¼ tsp	turmeric	1 mL
12 oz	all-purpose potatoes, peeled and cut into 1 ½ to 2-inch (4 to 5 cm) pieces (about 3)	375 g
1	package (12 oz/375 g) frozen drumsticks (see Tip, left)	1

1. In a saucepan, heat oil over medium heat. Add onion and chiles and sauté until onion is golden, 7 to 8 minutes.

2. Add tomatoes, coriander, cayenne, salt and turmeric. Cook until tomatoes are soft and can be mashed with the back of a spoon, about 5 minutes. Add potatoes and 2 ½ cups (625 mL) water and bring to a boil. Cover, reduce heat to low and cook until potatoes are semi-soft but not cooked all the way through, 10 to 12 minutes.

3. Add drumsticks. Increase heat to medium and return to a boil. Reduce heat to low, cover and simmer until vegetables are tender and gravy is thicker, about 10 minutes. If gravy is too thin, mash one or two pieces of potato with back of spoon and simmer a few minutes more. Serve with an Indian bread.

Masala Aloo
Fiery Yogurt Potatoes

2 lbs	potatoes (any variety), peeled and cut into 1-inch (2.5 cm) pieces	1 kg
1¼ cups	plain nonfat yogurt, at room temperature	300 mL
1 tsp	cornstarch	5 mL
2 tbsp	oil	25 mL
1½ tsp	cumin seeds	7 mL
2	dried Indian red chiles, broken in half	2
2	sprigs fresh curry leaves, stripped (20 to 25 leaves)	2
2 cups	coarsely chopped onions	500 mL
3 to 4 tsp	minced green chiles, preferably serranos	15 to 20 mL
2 tbsp	minced peeled gingerroot	25 mL
1 tbsp	minced garlic	15 mL
½ tsp	turmeric	2 mL
2 tsp	salt or to taste	10 mL
1 tsp	crushed black peppercorns	5 mL
¾ tsp	hot pepper flakes	4 mL
2 tsp	mango powder (amchur)	10 mL
1 tsp	cumin powder	5 mL
¼ cup	cilantro leaves, chopped	50 mL

Serves 6 to 8

HOT

This recipe can be modified to suit individual tastes. To make it milder, reduce green chiles and hot pepper flakes. The dried red chiles can be removed before serving.

1. Fill a saucepan three-quarters full of water. Bring to a boil over high heat. Add potatoes and return to a boil. Reduce heat to medium and cook until potatoes are tender but not cooked all the way, 10 to 12 minutes. Drain.

2. Stir yogurt and cornstarch together until smooth. Set aside.

3. In a saucepan, heat oil over medium heat. Add cumin seeds and sauté for 1 minute. Add red chiles and curry leaves and sauté for 30 seconds. Add onions, green chiles, ginger and garlic and sauté until onions are soft, 5 to 6 minutes.

4. Add turmeric and stir for 1 minute. Add potatoes, salt and yogurt mixture to pan and mix well. Cover and simmer over low heat until potatoes are soft, 6 to 8 minutes.

5. Fold in crushed peppercorns and hot pepper flakes. Remove from heat. Sprinkle with mango and cumin powders. Cover and let rest for 5 minutes before transferring to a serving dish. Garnish with cilantro before serving.

Aloo Tuk

Heavenly Sindhi Potatoes

Serves 6 to 8

A classic Sindhi dish, these potatoes are truly heavenly! The essence of simplicity, they are crispy on the outside and soft on the inside, with a subtle spicy touch.

Tip

It is important to fry potatoes very slowly the first time around over moderate heat. The second frying over high heat makes the potatoes crispy on the outside and soft on the inside, making them silky soft in the mouth.

- *Wok or deep-fryer*
- *Candy/deep-fry thermometer*

12	medium all-purpose potatoes, each about 3-inches (7.5 cm) long and 2-inches (5 cm) wide	12
2½ tsp	salt or to taste	12 mL
2 tsp	cayenne pepper or to taste	10 mL
1½ tsp	mango powder (amchur)	7 mL
1 tsp	coriander powder	5 mL
	Oil for deep-frying	

1. Peel and cut potatoes in half horizontally. Mix with salt and set aside.

2. In a small bowl, mix together cayenne, mango and coriander powders.

3. In a wok or deep-fryer, heat oil to 325°F (160°C). Add potatoes to oil slowly, in batches, and fry, turning occasionally, 20 to 25 minutes. Do not crowd. Test for doneness with tip of knife. Drain on paper towels. While still warm but cool enough to handle, gently press each piece between palms of hands to "smash" slightly. Take care not to let the potatoes fall apart. This is a tricky operation. (Potatoes can be prepared up to this point and set aside for up to 2 hours).

4. Just before serving, heat oil to 400°F (200°C). Refry potatoes in batches, until golden, 2 to 3 minutes. Remove with a large-holed strainer. Drain on paper towels. Sprinkle with powdered spices while still warm. Serve immediately.

Achari Aloo
Potatoes in Pickling Spices

2 lbs	all-purpose or Yukon Gold potatoes, peeled and cut into 1-inch (2.5 cm) pieces (about 8)	1 kg
3½ tbsp	oil, divided	52 mL
3 cups	puréed onions	750 mL
2 tsp	minced peeled gingerroot	10 mL
2 tsp	puréed garlic	10 mL
1 tbsp	cayenne pepper	15 mL
¾ tsp	turmeric	4 mL
2 tsp	salt or to taste	10 mL
2 tsp	granulated sugar	10 mL
½ cup	white vinegar	125 mL
1 tsp	dark mustard seeds	5 mL
2	dried Indian red chiles	2
2 tsp	cumin seeds	10 mL
1 tsp	nigella seeds (kalaunji)	5 mL

Serves 6 to 8

Sweet, sour and spicy, these potatoes are a delicious accompaniment to any chicken or meat preparation. Mustard, cumin and nigella seeds feature in most pickles, hence the name.

1. Fill a large saucepan three-quarters full of water. Bring to a boil over high heat. Add potatoes and cook until partially cooked, 6 to 8 minutes. Drain and set aside.

2. In a large wok or saucepan, heat 2 tbsp (25 mL) of the oil over medium-high heat. Add onions and sauté until golden, 6 to 8 minutes.

3. Add ginger and garlic and sauté for 2 minutes. Reduce heat to medium. Add cayenne and turmeric and sauté for 2 minutes.

4. Add potatoes and salt and mix well. Add 1 cup (250 mL) water. Cover, reduce heat to low and simmer until potatoes are soft and there is a thick gravy, about 5 minutes.

5. Dissolve sugar in vinegar and stir into potatoes. Transfer to a serving dish immediately and keep warm.

6. In a skillet, heat 1½ tbsp (22 mL) oil over high heat until a couple of mustard seeds thrown in start to sputter. Add all of the mustard seeds and cover quickly. When the seeds stop popping, in a few seconds, uncover, reduce heat to medium and add red chiles, cumin and nigella. Sauté for 30 seconds and pour over potatoes. Spread lightly with a fork on surface. Serve with an Indian bread.

Kalay Tilwalle Aloo
Crushed Potatoes with Black Sesame Seeds

Serves 6 to 8

Not only do these potatoes taste fabulous, they also look exotic with black sesame seeds. They can be served hot or at room temperature. Take them on a picnic to replace potato salad and you'll win kudos.

❧

Tip

Mustard oil is made from cold-pressed mustard seeds and is not an infusion. It has a distinctive taste. However, it has an element that can be toxic to some. Heating it to smoking point neutralizes this and makes it safe for cooking.

2½ lbs	small red or white new potatoes	1.25 kg
3 tbsp	mustard oil	45 mL
2½ tsp	black sesame seeds	12 mL
2 tsp	hot pepper flakes	10 mL
¾ tsp	turmeric	4 mL
2 tsp	salt or to taste	10 mL
¼ cup	freshly squeezed lime or lemon juice	50 mL
2 tbsp	cilantro, chopped	25 mL

1. Place potatoes in a large saucepan filled three-quarters full of water. Bring to a boil over high heat. Reduce heat to medium and cook just until tender, 12 to 14 minutes.

2. Drain and let cool slightly. Press each potato between palms to "crush," by applying gentle pressure, keeping potato intact. This exposes parts of the inside of the potato to the spices and creates a crusty potato.

3. In a large skillet, heat oil over high heat until almost smoking. Remove from heat and let cool for 1 minute (see Tip, left). Return skillet to medium heat. Add sesame seeds, hot pepper flakes and turmeric and sauté for 1 minute.

4. Add potatoes and salt and mix well. Drizzle 1 tbsp (15 mL) water around edges of pan. Cover, reduce heat to low and cook for about 10 minutes, stirring every 3 to 4 minutes. Shake pan periodically. Potatoes should be slightly crusty and coated in masala.

5. Remove from heat and pour lime juice over top. Stir to mix. Garnish with cilantro. Serve with an Indian bread.

Pahari Aloo
Sesame Seed Potatoes

Serves 8

Pahari *literally means "from the hills," and we refer to the people who live in the proximity of the Himalayan range as paharis. These sesame seed potatoes are a staple food for these people in the north. Vendors sell them along well-traveled routes, and travelers rely on them for long journeys.*

Tips

The gravy can be increased by adding a little more water, but it is best served as a semi-dry dish. The masala should be thick and cling to the potatoes.

Sesame seeds burn quickly and turn bitter if toasted too long.

4 lbs	all-purpose potatoes (12 to 16)	2 kg
1/2 cup	sesame seeds (see Tips, left)	125 mL
18	cloves garlic	18
3 cups	cilantro, loosely packed	750 mL
2 tsp	turmeric	10 mL
3 tbsp	oil	45 mL
2 1/2 tsp	salt or to taste	12 mL
2 tbsp	mango powder (amchur)	25 mL

1. In a saucepan of boiling water, cook whole potatoes until tender, 20 to 25 minutes. Drain. When cool enough to handle but still warm, peel and cut into 1 1/2-inch (4 cm) cubes.

2. In a dry heavy skillet over medium heat, toast sesame seeds, shaking pan frequently, until slightly darker, about 3 minutes. Take care not to burn seeds. Let cool. Reserve 3 tbsp (45 mL). In a spice grinder, grind remaining seeds into a fine powder. Reserve 2 tbsp (25 mL) powder. Add 2 to 3 tbsp (25 to 45 mL) water to remaining powder to make a fine paste. Set aside.

3. In a food processor, process garlic, cilantro, turmeric and 2 to 3 tbsp (25 to 45 mL) water to a fine paste. Set aside.

4. In a large wok or saucepan, heat oil over medium heat. Add cilantro paste and sauté for 3 to 4 minutes, adding a spoonful of water if masala starts to stick to the pan. Add potatoes, reserved sesame seed paste and salt. Mix well. Reduce heat to low and cook, stirring periodically, 3 to 4 minutes. Add mango powder and reserved sesame seeds. Mix well. Add 3 cups (750 mL) water and mix again. Cover and simmer until gravy thickens, for 5 minutes. Garnish with reserved sesame seed powder. Serve with an Indian bread.

Kashmiri Saag

Kashmiri Spinach

2 tbsp	mustard oil	25 mL
1 tsp	fenugreek seeds (methi)	5 mL
2	dried Indian red chiles	2
4 tsp	coarsely chopped garlic	20 mL
1½ lbs	spinach, trimmed and coarsely chopped (18 to 20 cups/4.5 to 5 L)	750 g
8 oz	mushrooms, cut into quarters	250 g
1 tsp	salt or to taste	5 mL

1. In a large wok or skillet, heat mustard oil until very hot. Remove from heat and let cool for 1 minute (see Tip, page 326). Reheat oil over medium heat and add fenugreek seeds, chiles and garlic. Sauté until seeds turn a little darker and aromatic, about 45 seconds. (Take care not to burn the seeds or they will be very bitter.)

2. Increase heat to high. Add spinach, in large batches, along with mushrooms, tossing well to mix with seasonings. Continue to sauté over high heat, until spinach and mushrooms are cooked, about 5 minutes. Sprinkle with salt before removing from heat.

Serves 6 to 8

This classic dish made with pure mustard oil is simplicity itself.

Tip
There will be some natural juices from spinach and mushrooms. Do not try to cook off the juices, as the vegetables will become overcooked and will continue to exude more juices.

Kashmiri Turnips

1 lb	turnips	500 g
2 tbsp	oil	25 mL
1½ tsp	fenugreek seeds (methi)	7 mL
1 tsp	crushed coriander seeds	5 mL
1 cup	chopped tomatoes	250 mL
½ tsp	granulated sugar	2 mL
½ tsp	salt or to taste	2 mL

1. Peel turnips. Cut in half and slice thinly. If turnips are large, cut in quarters, then slice.

2. In a saucepan, heat oil over medium heat. Add fenugreek and coriander seeds and sauté for 1 minute. Add turnip and sauté for 2 minutes.

3. Add tomatoes, sugar, ½ cup (125 mL) water and salt and mix well. Cover and reduce heat to medium-low. Simmer until tomatoes are soft and mashed and turnips are tender, 8 to 10 minutes. When ready, there will be a little broth-like gravy.

Serves 8

My daughter-in-law Preeti introduced me to turnips, an extremely popular vegetable in Punjab. This simple dish shines with a lightly spiced and flavorful broth. It came from her grandmother, who was from Kashmir.

Beets with Asafetida

Serves 6

Kashmiris relish beets. When I first ate this dish, I was struck by the unusual combination with potatoes. It is a colorful addition to a buffet table and adds a festive touch to a holiday menu.

½ cup	plain nonfat yogurt, at room temperature	125 mL
½ tsp	cornstarch	2 mL
5	beets, peeled and cut into ½-inch (1 cm) cubes (about 6 cups/1.5 L)	5
3 cups	peeled and diced potatoes (any variety), ½-inch (1 cm) cubes	750 mL
2 tbsp	coriander powder	25 mL
2 tsp	cayenne pepper	10 mL
1 tsp	turmeric	5 mL
1½ tsp	salt or to taste	7 mL
1½ tbsp	oil	22 mL
¾ tsp	fenugreek seeds (methi)	4 mL
¾ tsp	fennel seeds (saunf)	4 mL
¾ tsp	carom seeds (ajwain)	4 mL
¼ tsp	asafetida (hing)	1 mL
3 to 4 tbsp	freshly squeezed lime or lemon juice	45 to 60 mL
1 tsp	powdered carom seeds (ajwain)	5 mL
2 tsp	minced green chiles, preferably serranos	10 mL

1. Stir yogurt and cornstarch together until smooth. Set aside.

2. In a saucepan, combine beets and potatoes. Stir coriander powder, cayenne and turmeric into 4 cups (1 L) water. Pour over vegetables and bring to a boil over high heat. Reduce heat to medium. Cook until vegetables are tender and water is reduced to barely cover vegetables, 12 to 15 minutes. Remove from heat.

3. Add salt and yogurt and stir into vegetables. Return to low heat and simmer for 5 minutes.

4. In a small pan, heat oil over medium heat. Add fenugreek, fennel, carom seeds and asafetida and sauté until fragrant and slightly darker in color, for 30 seconds. Pour over vegetables. Cover and simmer for 2 minutes.

5. Just before serving, stir in lime juice. Top with powdered carom seeds and minced chiles. Serve hot with rice or an Indian bread.

Panir with Caramelized Tomatoes

3 to 4 tbsp	oil	45 to 60 mL
½ tsp	fenugreek seeds (methi)	2 mL
3	bay leaves	3
20	whole cloves	20
3 to 4	green chiles, preferably serranos, cut into large pieces	3 to 4
¾ tsp	cayenne pepper	4 mL
8 cups	chopped tomatoes, preferably plum (Roma)	2 L
1½ tsp	salt or to taste	7 mL
1	recipe Lower-Fat Panir with 1 cup (250 mL) reserved whey (see recipe, page 312)	1
½ cup	cilantro leaves, chopped	125 mL

Serves 6 to 8

Flavorful summer tomatoes are best for this recipe. I like to serve it with a simple dal and rice or a "dry" meat preparation, such as Nina's Broiled Chicken or Grilled Cabrito Chops (see recipes, pages 197 and 213).

1. In a saucepan, heat oil over medium heat. Add fenugreek and sauté for 30 seconds. Add bay leaves, cloves, green chiles and cayenne and sauté for 1 minute.

2. Add tomatoes and salt. Increase heat to high and cook, stirring frequently, until moisture evaporates. Reduce heat to medium and continue to cook, stirring periodically, until mixture is considerably darkened and reduced to a thickish mass, about 30 minutes. (This prolonged cooking concentrates and caramelizes the tomatoes and ultimately gives this dish its unique richness.)

3. Cut panir into 1½-inch (4 cm) squares, each ¼ inch (0.5 cm) thick. Add ¾ cup (175 mL) of the reserved whey to saucepan and stir to make a gravy. Add panir and cover pieces with gravy. Cover and simmer until heated through. Add remaining whey if needed. Garnish with cilantro before serving.

Panir Bhari Lauki

Panir-Stuffed Long Squash

Serves 6 to 8

Stuffed vegetables are popular in North India and make an excellent vegetarian entrée. Grated panir adds texture and flavor to the stuffing mixture. The same stuffing can be used to stuff halved blanched bell peppers.

- Preheat oven to 375°F (190°C)
- Baking dish, lightly greased

2 lbs	long (opo) squash (lauki)	1 kg
Stuffing		
1 ½ tbsp	oil	22 mL
1 ¼ cups	chopped onions	300 mL
1 tbsp	minced green chiles, preferably serranos	15 mL
1 tsp	minced peeled gingerroot	5 mL
1 tsp	minced garlic	5 mL
1 tsp	cayenne pepper	5 mL
1 tsp	cumin powder	5 mL
8 oz	boiled potato, mashed (about 1 potato)	250 g
½	recipe Lower-Fat Panir, grated (see recipe, page 312), grated	½
3 tbsp	cilantro, chopped	45 mL
1 ½ tsp	salt	7 mL
Gravy		
2 tbsp	oil	25 mL
1 tsp	cumin seeds	5 mL
¼ tsp	fenugreek seeds (methi)	1 mL
3 cups	finely chopped onions	750 mL
1 tbsp	minced green chiles, preferably serranos	15 mL
2 tsp	minced peeled gingerroot	10 mL
2 tsp	minced garlic	10 mL
¾ tsp	cayenne pepper	4 mL
½ tsp	turmeric	2 mL
3 cups	canned chopped tomatoes, including liquid	750 mL

1. Peel squash and halve lengthwise. Scoop out flesh, leaving a ½-inch (1 cm) thick wall. Reserve flesh for other use.

2. *Stuffing:* In a large skillet, heat oil over medium heat. Add onions and sauté until soft, about 5 minutes. Add chiles, ginger and garlic and sauté until onions are pale gold, about 5 minutes. Stir in cayenne and cumin and sauté for 1 minute.

3. Remove from heat and add potato, panir, cilantro and salt to skillet. Mix together thoroughly. Let cool and divide mixture in two. Stuff each squash half with mixture.

4. *Gravy:* In a saucepan, heat oil over medium heat. Add cumin and sauté for 30 seconds. Add fenugreek and sauté until seeds are a little darker and aromatic, 15 seconds.

Continued on next page…

Continued from page 332...

5. Add onions and sauté until golden brown, about 10 minutes. Add chiles, ginger, garlic, cayenne and turmeric and sauté for 2 minutes.

6. Pour in tomatoes with juice and mix well. Increase heat to medium-high. Cover and bring to a boil. Cook for 5 minutes after gravy comes to a boil. Remove from heat. Mash tomatoes with back of spoon to thicken gravy.

7. Place stuffed squash in prepared baking dish. Pour gravy over squash. Cover tightly with foil. Bake in preheated oven until squash is soft, 1 hour.

Lauki Sabzi

Indian Long Squash

Serves 6 to 8

This is a simple home-style recipe that could be used with any soft squash, such as zucchini. Lauki is very popular in India and is highly nutritious and mild flavored.

Tip

Look for small or medium-size squash as they have better flavor than very large ones. Also known as opo squash in Asian markets.

1 tbsp	oil	15 mL
1 ½ tsp	cumin seeds	7 mL
2	dried Indian red chiles	2
1 tsp	fenugreek seeds (methi)	5 mL
2	long squash, each about 1 ½ lbs (750 g), peeled and diced, about 8 cups (2 L) (see Tip, left)	2
2 tsp	minced green chiles, preferably serranos	10 mL
¼ cup	cilantro, chopped	50 mL
4 cups	diced tomatoes	1 L
1 ¼ tsp	salt or to taste	6 mL
¾ tsp	turmeric	4 mL

1. In a saucepan, heat oil over medium heat. Add cumin seeds and sauté for 30 seconds. Add red chiles and fenugreek seeds and sauté for 30 seconds.

2. Add squash, green chiles and cilantro and sauté for 2 minutes.

3. Add tomatoes, salt and turmeric and mix well. Sauté for 2 to 3 minutes. Cover, reduce heat to low and cook until vegetables are soft, about 20 minutes. If there is too much liquid, uncover and cook to reduce. Serve with rice or an Indian bread.

Baigan Bharta
Smoky Eggplant Purée

- *Preheat broiler*

2 to 2½ lbs	eggplant (about 2)	1 to 1.25 kg
¼ cup	oil	50 mL
2 cups	chopped onions	500 mL
5 to 6	green chiles, preferably serranos	5 to 6
4 cups	chopped tomatoes	1 L
1¼ tsp	salt or to taste	6 mL
1 cup	cilantro, coarsely chopped, divided	250 mL

1. Place eggplant on a broiler pan. Place under preheated broiler, about 3 to 4 inches (7.5 to 10 cm) from heat. Cook until skin is charred, 8 to 10 minutes. Turn and cook other side for 5 minutes. Turn again to evenly crisp all sides, about 5 minutes more. Remove and let cool to room temperature.

2. Holding eggplant over a bowl, remove charred skin and discard. Cut off top. Juices will collect in bowl. Mash eggplant and juices to a purée with a fork or potato masher. Set aside.

3. In a wok or large skillet, heat oil over medium-high heat. Add onions and chiles and sauté until onions are deep gold, 6 to 8 minutes.

4. Add tomatoes and salt. Cook until mushy, 6 to 8 minutes. Add eggplant and mix well. Stir in ¾ cup (175 mL) of the cilantro and remove from heat. Garnish with remaining cilantro just before serving with an Indian bread.

Serves 6 to 8

A simple but very traditional dish from Punjab. I tasted this version at my cousin's home in Delhi. It is by far the best recipe I have found. The eggplant can be cooked in the spent fire of a charcoal grill, puréed and refrigerated for several days, or even frozen. In summer, I serve it chilled, as a salad or as a dip with pita chips. It is particularly good with grilled foods.

Methi Gajar Matar
Carrots and Peas with Fenugreek

Serves 6 to 8

This was a favorite dish in our family when I was growing up, and it was particularly good made with juicy, salmon-colored winter carrots. The sweet carrots and the slightly bitter flavor of fenugreek is a marriage made in heaven.

Tip
Fenugreek leaves are sold frozen in portions slightly larger than ice cubes in Indian markets.

- *Large skillet with tight-fitting lid*

2 tbsp	oil	25 mL
3 tbsp	coarsely chopped garlic	45 mL
4 cups	fresh fenugreek leaves (methi), chopped, or 4 cubes frozen fenugreek, thawed (see Tip, left)	1 L
1 1/2 lbs	carrots, peeled and diagonally sliced 1/4 inch (1 cm) thick	750 g
1 1/2 cups	frozen peas, thawed	375 mL
1 tsp	salt or to taste	5 mL
1/2 tsp	turmeric	2 mL

1. In a large skillet, heat oil over medium heat. Toss in garlic and sauté until it begins to color, about 2 minutes.

2. Add fenugreek all at once and sauté until there is no more moisture and masala is cooked, 3 to 4 minutes.

3. Add carrots, peas, salt and turmeric. Mix well with masala. Drizzle 1 tbsp (15 mL) water around edges of pan. Cover immediately with a tight-fitting lid and cook for 2 minutes to build steam, then reduce heat to low but maintain an audible sizzle. Cook for 3 to 4 minutes.

4. Stir to mix. Add another 1 tbsp (15 mL) water if masala is sticking to pan. Continue to cook in this manner until carrots are tender, 6 to 8 minutes.

Cauliflower Peas Pancake

N

- *12-inch (30 cm) nonstick skillet with tight-fitting lid*

1 ½ lbs	cauliflower, cut into ½-inch (1 cm) pieces (about 5 cups/1.25 L)	750 g
½ cup	frozen peas, thawed	125 mL
⅓ cup	cilantro, chopped	75 mL

Batter

1 cup	chickpea flour (besan)	250 mL
1 ¼ cups	buttermilk	300 mL
2 tbsp	freshly squeezed lime or lemon juice	25 mL
1 tbsp	granulated sugar	15 mL
2 tsp	coriander powder	10 mL
2 tsp	cumin powder	10 mL
2 tsp	cayenne pepper	10 mL
1 ¾ tsp	salt or to taste	9 mL
1 tsp	garam masala	5 mL
¾ tsp	turmeric	4 mL
3 tbsp	oil, divided	15 mL
2 to 3	sprigs cilantro	2 to 3

1. In a large bowl, mix cauliflower, peas and cilantro.

2. *Batter:* In another bowl, whisk together chickpea flour, buttermilk, lime juice, sugar, coriander, cumin, cayenne, salt, garam masala and turmeric. Whisk in 1 tbsp (15 mL) of the oil. Pour batter onto vegetables and mix well.

3. In skillet, heat remaining oil over medium heat. Swirl to coat bottom and sides. Pour in mixture and spread evenly. Cover with a tight-fitting lid and cook until mixture begins to steam, 6 to 8 minutes. Reduce heat to low and cook until batter is set and pancake slides in skillet, about 30 minutes. If necessary, loosen with a wide spatula.

4. Slide onto a serving platter and garnish with cilantro. Cut into pie-shaped wedges and serve with an Indian bread.

Serves 6 to 8

An eggless frittata is a better description of this most unusual dish. A simple concept, it lends itself to wonderful flavors limited only by your imagination and creativity. It's a recipe from my cousin Gita's repertoire — who claims she's not a cook!

Tips

Make sure that the vegetable mixture is spread evenly and is no thicker than approximately 1 inch (2.5 cm), otherwise it will not cook in the center.

This is a wonderful side dish with scrambled eggs or a great sandwich filling. It's also excellent for picnics because it can be served at room temperature.

Wadi Matar Aloo ki Sabzi
Dried Bean Nuggets with Potatoes and Peas

½ cup	plain nonfat yogurt, at room temperature	125 mL
½ tsp	cornstarch	2 mL
1 cup	chopped tomatoes, preferably plum (Roma)	250 mL
2 tbsp	chopped green chiles, preferably serranos	25 mL
2 tsp	minced peeled gingerroot	10 mL
2 tsp	minced garlic	10 mL
2 tbsp	oil, divided	25 mL
½ cup	small bean nuggets (wadis)	125 mL
1 cup	diced peeled potato, ½-inch (1 cm) cubes	250 mL
½ cup	frozen peas, thawed	125 mL
¾ tsp	cumin seeds	4 mL
¼ tsp	asafetida (hing)	1 mL
¾ tsp	salt	4 mL
½ tsp	cayenne pepper	2 mL
¼ tsp	turmeric	1 mL
½ tsp	garam masala	2 mL
3 tbsp	cilantro, coarsely chopped	45 mL

Serves 4

Rajasthani cuisine makes extensive use of dried bean nuggets (wadis)*, which are made from a variety of beans. Some are spicier than others, so be sure you select the ones that suit your heat quotient. Any variety will be fine in this recipe.*

1. Stir yogurt and cornstarch together until creamy. Set aside.

2. In a food processor or blender, purée tomatoes, chiles, ginger and garlic. Set aside.

3. In a skillet, heat 1½ tbsp (22 mL) of the oil over medium heat. Add bean nuggets and sauté, stirring continuously, until golden brown, 3 to 4 minutes.

4. Add potato and peas and sauté for 2 minutes. Remove from heat and set aside.

5. In a saucepan, heat remaining oil over medium heat. Add cumin and sauté for 30 seconds. Add asafetida and sauté until mixture is fragrant, about 30 seconds. Add tomato mixture and yogurt. Add salt, cayenne and turmeric and mix well. When mixture begins to boil, reduce heat to medium-low and cook until thick and bubbly, about 10 minutes.

6. Add vegetables and bean nuggets and mix gently. Add 1½ cups (375 mL) water. Cover and return to a boil. Reduce heat to low and simmer until gravy thickens, 10 to 12 minutes.

7. Remove from heat. Sprinkle with garam masala. Cover and let rest for 2 minutes. Stir to mix. Garnish with cilantro. Serve hot.

Soy Chips with Peas

Soy products were introduced in the middle of the last century as an inexpensive source of protein. Vegetarians particularly have embraced its many forms, and today it is available as flour, nuggets, chips and other forms. It is well suited to Indian recipes, as you can tell from the recipe that follows.

Tip

If serving with rice, allow gravy to be a little runny, or a little thicker to eat with bread.

1 ½ tbsp	oil	22 mL
¾ tsp	dark mustard seeds	4 mL
¾ tsp	cumin seeds	4 mL
2 tbsp	minced green chiles, preferably serranos	25 mL
1 tbsp	minced peeled gingerroot	15 mL
2	sprigs fresh curry leaves, stripped (20 to 25 leaves)	2
Scant ½ tsp	turmeric	2 mL
1	can (14 oz/ 398 mL) diced tomatoes, including juice	1
1 tsp	salt or to taste	5 mL
1 cup	soy chips	250 mL
½ cup	cilantro, chopped, divided	125 mL
1 cup	frozen peas, thawed	250 mL

1. In a saucepan, heat oil over high heat until a couple of mustard seeds thrown in start to sputter. Add all the mustard seeds and cover quickly. When the seeds stop popping, in a few seconds, uncover, reduce heat to medium and add cumin, chiles, ginger and curry leaves. Sauté for 20 seconds. Add turmeric and sauté for 20 seconds. Add tomatoes with juice and salt and mix well. Bring to a boil. Reduce heat to low and simmer until tomatoes are soft, 6 to 8 minutes. Mash with back of a spoon.

2. Add 1½ cups (375 mL) water and mix. Increase heat to medium and return to a boil. Add soy chips and ¼ cup (50 mL) of the cilantro and stir well. Reduce heat to low. Cover and simmer, stirring periodically, until chips are soft, 20 to 30 minutes. Add a little more water if gravy gets absorbed.

3. Add peas and mix well. Cover and cook for 5 minutes. Garnish with remaining cilantro. Serve hot with rice or an Indian bread.

Bhee Gajru
Lotus Root and Carrots

8 oz	fresh, canned or frozen lotus root (bhee) (see Tip, right)	250 g
8 oz	carrots	250 g
1 ½ tbsp	oil	22 mL
¼ cup	finely chopped onion	50 mL
2 tbsp	chopped garlic	25 mL
1 tsp	minced green chiles, preferably serranos	5 mL
1 cup	loosely packed fresh fenugreek leaves (methi) or ½ cup (125 mL) frozen fenugreek, thawed	250 mL
1 tsp	salt or to taste	5 mL
¾ tsp	coriander powder	4 mL

Serves 6

This is another traditional dish from Sindh, where lotus root features prominently in the cuisine. Although lotus root itself is fairly bland, the texture is exciting, and, of course, visually it is most intriguing.

Tip
Asian markets sell vacuum-packed sliced lotus root. It is packed in brine and should be rinsed and soaked in 2 to 3 fresh changes of water to remove the excess brine. Some of the larger Asian markets sell fresh lotus root imported from China. Sliced frozen lotus root is available in many Indian markets.

1. If using fresh lotus root, peel off thin outer skin. Rinse well under running water and wipe dry. Cut into diagonal ¼-inch (0.5 cm) thick slices. Place in a saucepan with water to cover by 2 inches (5 cm) and bring to a boil over medium-high heat. Cover, reduce heat to medium and cook until soft, 20 to 25 minutes. Drain and set aside. (If using canned, slice but omit peeling, and do not boil.)

2. Peel carrots and cut into diagonal ¼-inch (0.5 cm) slices. Set aside.

3. In a skillet, heat oil over medium-high heat. Add onion and sauté until soft, about 3 minutes. Add garlic and chiles and sauté until garlic is soft, 2 minutes.

4. Add fenugreek and reduce heat to medium. Sauté until mixture (masala) is aromatic, 4 to 5 minutes. If masala begins to stick to pan, deglaze with water, 1 tbsp (15 mL) at a time.

5. Add salt and coriander and cook for 2 minutes. Stir in carrots and mix well. Pour in ½ cup (125 mL) water. Cover and cook for 3 minutes. Reduce heat to low and cook until carrots are almost cooked through, 6 to 8 minutes, adding more water if necessary.

6. Stir in lotus root and add ½ cup (125 mL) hot water and mix well. Cover and cook until liquid has been absorbed and vegetables are tender, 5 to 8 minutes.

Orissa Greens

In this recipe from Orissa, I have replaced their local greens called kosala saga *with fresh collard greens.*

———❧———

Tip
Orissa, the state adjacent to Bengal has its own version of panch phoran, the seed mixture that defines Bengali cuisine. In the Oriya version, nigella is replaced with hot pepper flakes and the proportions are not the same.

Variation
Instead of collard greens, you can use fresh mustard greens or spinach, if you prefer. Adjust timing if using spinach. Cook for 4 to 5 minutes.

½ tsp	cumin seeds	2 mL
½ tsp	dark mustard seeds	2 mL
¼ tsp	fennel seeds (saunf)	1 mL
¼ tsp	fenugreek seeds (methi)	1 mL
¼ tsp	hot pepper flakes	1 mL
1 lb	fresh collard greens	500 g
1 cup	cubed peeled potato	250 mL
1 cup	chopped onion	250 mL
1 cup	cubed eggplant	250 mL
1 tsp	salt or to taste	5 mL
2 tsp	oil	10 mL
2	large cloves garlic, crushed	2
1	dried Indian red chile	1

1. In a small bowl, mix together cumin, mustard, fennel, fenugreek and hot pepper flakes. Set aside.

2. Trim collard green stalks and chop leaves. Set aside.

3. In a saucepan, combine potato, onion, eggplant and ¾ cup (175 mL) water. Cover and bring to a boil over medium heat. Reduce heat to low and simmer until vegetables are soft, 6 to 8 minutes.

4. Add greens to pan. Cover and cook until greens are cooked through and most of the water has been absorbed, 8 to 10 minutes.

5. In a small pan, heat oil over medium-high heat. Add garlic and red chile and sauté for 20 seconds. Add mixed spices. When seeds start sputtering, in a few seconds, pour contents of pan into greens. Mix well and serve with rice.

Phulkopir Dalna
Bengali Cauliflower Curry

3 tbsp	oil, divided	45 mL
½	large head cauliflower, cut into 1½-inch (4 cm) pieces	½
1	medium potato, cut into 1½-inch (4 cm) pieces	1
½ tsp	turmeric	2 mL
½ tsp	cayenne pepper	2 mL
½ tsp	cumin seeds	2 mL
2	bay leaves	2
1	piece cinnamon, about 1 inch (2.5 cm) long	1
6	whole cloves	6
4	green cardamom pods, cracked open	4
1½ tsp	coriander powder	7 mL
¾ tsp	cumin powder	4 mL
2 tsp	minced peeled gingerroot	10 mL
1 cup	chopped tomato	250 mL
1 tsp	salt	5 mL
½ tsp	granulated sugar	2 mL
1 tsp	ghee, melted	5 mL

Serves 4 to 6

Vegetable dishes in Bengal are lightly spiced and seldom use onions and garlic. The addition of a little sugar is typical.

1. In a skillet, heat 1 tbsp (15 mL) of the oil over medium heat. Add cauliflower and sauté, turning pieces to cook evenly, 6 to 8 minutes. Set aside.

2. In the same skillet, heat 2 tsp (10 mL) of oil over medium heat. Add potato and sauté, turning pieces to color evenly, 5 to 6 minutes. Set aside.

3. In a small bowl, mix together turmeric and cayenne. Stir in 3 tbsp (45 mL) water. Set aside.

4. In a saucepan, heat remaining oil over medium heat. Add cumin seeds, bay leaves, cinnamon, cloves and cardamom. Sauté for 2 minutes. Add turmeric mixture and sauté for 30 seconds. Add coriander, cumin powder and ginger and sauté vigorously for 30 seconds.

5. Add cauliflower and potatoes and mix well. Reduce heat to medium-low. Continue to sauté vegetables, adding water, 1 tbsp (15 mL) at a time, to prevent burning, until vegetables are semi-cooked, 6 to 8 minutes.

6. Add tomato, salt and sugar and mix well. Cover and cook until tomatoes are soft, about 5 minutes. Mash tomatoes with back of spoon.

7. Add 1 cup (250 mL) water. Cover and cook until vegetables are soft and a little liquid gravy remains, 8 to 10 minutes. Drizzle ghee over top. Serve hot with any Indian bread.

Cabbage and Cauliflower with Panch Phoran

Serves 8

Panch phoran, a mixture of five seeds, is the signature of Bengali cooking. This is the simplest of dishes, but it has tremendous flavor.

Tip
This dish can be served hot or at room temperature and is a good addition to a buffet table or a patio party.

¾ tsp	dark mustard seeds	4 mL
¾ tsp	cumin seeds	4 mL
¾ tsp	fennel seeds (saunf)	4 mL
¾ tsp	fenugreek seeds (methi)	4 mL
¾ tsp	nigella seeds (kalaunji)	4 mL
3 to 4 tbsp	oil	45 to 60 mL
1	medium cauliflower, separated into florets, about 4 cups (1 L)	1
½	medium cabbage, sliced, about 4 cups (1 L)	½
1 tsp	salt or to taste	5 mL
¾ tsp	turmeric	4 mL

1. In a bowl, mix together mustard, cumin, fennel, fenugreek and nigella seeds.

2. In a large skillet, heat oil over high heat until almost smoking.

3. Add seed mixture and cover immediately. When seeds stop popping, in a few seconds, add cauliflower, cabbage, salt and turmeric. Mix thoroughly. Reduce heat to medium. Sauté, stirring and tossing, until vegetables are cooked, 6 to 8 minutes. Serve immediately.

Green Beans in Mustard Poppy Seed Sauce

2 tbsp	Indian poppy seeds (see Tip, page 219)	25 mL
1 tsp	dark mustard seeds	5 mL
1 ½ tbsp	oil	22 mL
½ tsp	panch phoran (see Tip, right)	2 mL
2 tsp	minced green chiles, preferably serranos	10 mL
1 tsp	granulated sugar	5 mL
1 tsp	salt or to taste	5 mL
¼ tsp	turmeric	1 mL
1 lb	green beans, cut into 1 ½-inch (4 cm) pieces	500 g

1. In a small bowl, soak poppy seeds in 3 tbsp (45 mL) water for 30 minutes. In a separate bowl, soak mustard seeds in 2 tsp (10 mL) water for 30 minutes.

2. In a smooth mortar, separately grind poppy seeds and mustard seeds with a pestle into as smooth a paste as possible. Set both aside.

3. In a skillet, heat oil over medium heat. Add panch phoran. When seeds stop popping in a few seconds, add chiles, sugar, salt and turmeric. Sauté for 20 seconds.

4. Add green beans, mustard paste and ¼ cup (50 mL) water and mix well. Reduce heat to low. Cover and cook until beans are tender-crisp, 6 to 8 minutes.

5. Add poppy seed paste and 2 tbsp (25 mL) water and mix well. Cover and cook until beans are tender, 6 to 7 minutes. Remove from heat. Let stand for 5 minutes for flavors to develop before serving.

Serves 4 to 6

This flavorful dish is from Bengal, using its signature seasoning, panch phoran. Poppy seeds and additional mustard seeds are made into a paste adding extra flavor.

Tip

Panch phoran is a mix of equal proportions of five aromatic seeds: mustard, cumin, fennel, fenugreek and nigella. It can be premixed and stored indefinitely.

Panch Phoran Tarkari

Indian Ratatouille with Five Spices

Serves 8

Panch phoran, the signature five-seed blend used in Bengali food, is magical. Versatile and easy to use, its distinctive flavor is perfect in both Indian and non-Indian dishes.

2	dried Indian red chiles, broken in half	2
2	bay leaves	2
1 tsp	panch phoran (see Tip, page 345)	5 mL
2 tbsp	oil	25 mL
1 lb	eggplant, cut into 2-inch (5 cm) pieces	500 g
1 lb	potatoes, peeled and cut into 1 1/2-inch (4 cm) pieces	500 g
8 oz	butternut squash, cut into 2-inch (5 cm) pieces	250 g
2 to 3 tsp	chopped green chiles, preferably serranos	10 to 15 mL
1 tbsp	milk	15 mL
1 tsp	salt or to taste	5 mL
1/2 tsp	granulated sugar	2 mL
1 cup	frozen peas	250 mL

1. In a small dish, combine red chiles, bay leaves and panch phoran.

2. In a large saucepan, heat oil over medium-high heat until very hot. Stir spices into hot oil and sauté until seeds stop popping, 30 to 40 seconds. Immediately add eggplant, potatoes and squash and mix well.

3. Add green chiles, milk, salt, sugar and 3/4 cup (175 mL) water. When mixture comes to a boil, reduce heat to medium. Cover and simmer until vegetables are tender, 10 to 12 minutes. Add peas and simmer until water is absorbed, 2 to 3 minutes. Serve hot with an Indian bread.

Jhinge Posto

Ridged Gourd with Poppy Seeds

Serves 6 to 8

Ridged gourd is available year-round in India and is a favorite with northerners. Known as turai *in Hindi, it is called* jhinge *in Bengali. In North America, it is readily available in Asian markets and is sometimes known as Chinese okra, although it bears no resemblance whatsoever to okra.*

Tips

Ridged gourd is 12 to 14 inches (30 to 35 cm) long, about 2 inches (5 cm) around and about 3 inches (7.5 cm) at the tip. The skin is thickish, rough and grayish green, and ridges run up and down the length of the vegetable. It is always peeled before cooking. The white flesh is mild flavored.

Poppy seed paste is called *posto* (pronounced posht-o).

Variation
Zucchini is a good substitute for ridged gourd.

½ cup	Indian poppy seeds (see Tip, page 219)	125 mL
2 tbsp	mustard oil	25 mL
1 tsp	nigella seeds (kalaunji)	5 mL
3 cups	chopped onions	750 mL
2 tsp	chopped green chiles, preferably serranos	10 mL
2 lbs	ridged gourd, peeled and cut into 1-inch (2.5 cm) pieces (see Tips, left)	1 kg
1 tsp	turmeric	5 mL
1 tsp	salt or to taste	5 mL

1. In a bowl, soak poppy seeds in hot water to just cover for at least 2 hours.

2. In a smooth mortar, grind poppy seeds including water with a pestle into a smooth paste. (This will need a strong arm and may take several minutes.)

3. In a saucepan, heat oil over high heat until very hot. Remove from heat and let cool for 1 minute (see Tip, page 326). Return pan to medium-high heat. Add nigella and sauté for 30 seconds. Add onions and chiles and sauté until onion is soft and transparent, 5 to 6 minutes.

4. Add poppy seed paste and sauté for 3 to 4 minutes.

5. Add gourd, turmeric and salt and mix well. Cover and simmer until vegetables are very soft, 25 to 30 minutes. If necessary add 2 to 3 tbsp (25 to 45 mL) water to prevent sticking.

Roasted Winter Vegetables

- *Preheat oven to 400°F (200°C)*
- *Roasting pan*

1 lb	acorn squash	500 g
1 lb	butternut squash	500 g
1 lb	hard yellow squash (see Tip, right)	500 g
1 lb	turnips	500 g
3 tbsp	oil, divided	45 mL
1 ½ tsp	salt or to taste	7 mL
1 tbsp	jaggery (gur) or brown sugar	15 mL
1 tsp	hot pepper flakes	5 mL
2 tsp	panch phoran (see Tip, page 345)	10 mL

1. Peel and cut vegetables into 1½-inch (4 cm) pieces. In a large bowl, toss with 2 tbsp (25 mL) of the oil and salt. Spread in a roasting pan and roast in preheated oven for 30 minutes. Remove from oven and mix well. Return to oven for 20 minutes.

2. Remove from oven. Sprinkle with jaggery and hot pepper flakes.

3. Heat 1 tbsp (15 mL) oil in a small pan. Toss in panch phoran. When seeds stop sizzling and popping, pour over vegetables. Toss to mix seasonings with vegetables. Return to oven for 10 minutes. Serve as a side dish or wrap in a tortilla and serve as a light lunch, accompanied by a raita.

Serves 6 to 8

This a delightful medley of vegetables lightly seasoned with the aromatic five-seed mixture panch phoran. Although this is not a traditional recipe, it is in the spirit of Bengali dishes, using their signature spice mix and a little sugar, which is traditional in the food of West Bengal. I love it with non-Indian meat or poultry entrées.

Tip

If unable to find hard squash, increase others to make a total of 4 lbs (2 kg). I like to use at least three to four varieties for their different flavors and textures.

Chettinad-Style Spinach

Serves 6 to 8

Many dishes from Tamil Nadu claim to be from Chettinad, a town known for its refined cuisine. I particularly enjoy this recipe, because mustard seeds marry beautifully with spinach.

2	large bunches spinach (about 20 cups/5 L loosely packed)	2
3 tbsp	oil	45 mL
1 tsp	dark mustard seeds	5 mL
1 tbsp	split white lentils (urad dal)	15 mL
¼ tsp	asafetida (hing)	1 mL
2	dried Indian red chiles	2
1	sprig curry leaves, stripped (12 to 15 leaves)	1
8 to 10	cloves garlic, thinly sliced	8 to 10
3	slit green chiles, preferably serranos	3
3 tbsp	unsalted Thai tamarind purée	45 mL
1 tbsp	rice flour	15 mL
1 tsp	salt or to taste	5 mL

1. Rinse and drain spinach. Chop coarsely and set aside.

2. In a large wok, heat oil over high heat until a couple of mustard seeds thrown in start to sputter. Add all the mustard seeds and cover quickly. When the seeds stop popping, in a few seconds, uncover, reduce heat to medium and add urad dal, asafetida, red chiles and curry leaves. Sauté for 1 minute.

3. Add garlic and green chiles and sauté until garlic is pale gold and fragrant, about 2 minutes.

4. Add spinach and tamarind and mix well. Cook, stirring frequently, until wilted, 3 to 4 minutes.

5. In a bowl, combine rice flour with ¼ cup (50 mL) water and stir into a paste. Add to spinach mixture along with salt and mix well. Cook until thickened, about 2 minutes. Serve hot with an Indian bread.

Potatoes with Two Onions

2 tsp	salt or to taste	10 mL
¾ tsp	turmeric	4 mL
2 lbs	all-purpose potatoes, peeled and cut into 1-inch (2.5 cm) cubes	1 kg
2 tbsp	oil	25 mL
1 tsp	dark mustard seeds	5 mL
1 tsp	cumin seeds	5 mL
1 tsp	split white lentils (urad dal)	5 mL
2½ cups	chopped onions	625 mL
1½ tbsp	slivered peeled gingerroot	22 mL
2	sprigs fresh curry leaves, stripped (20 to 25 leaves)	2
4	2-inch (5 cm) long green chiles, preferably serranos, slivered	4
¾ tsp	cayenne pepper	4 mL
1 cup	chopped tomatoes	250 mL
¼ cup	finely sliced green onions, with some green	50 mL

Serves 6 to 8

These make a wonderful picnic dish, as they are equally good at room temperature. They're also excellent topped with grilled fish or poached eggs.

1. Fill a saucepan three-quarters full of water. Add salt and turmeric and bring to a boil over high heat. Add potatoes and cook until tender, about 12 minutes. Drain and set aside.

2. In a wok or large skillet, heat oil over high heat until a couple of mustard seeds thrown in start to sputter. Add all the mustard seeds and cover quickly. When the seeds stop popping, in a few seconds, uncover, reduce heat to medium and add cumin and urad dal. Sauté for 30 seconds. Add onions, ginger, curry leaves and chiles. Sauté until onions are golden, 5 to 6 minutes.

3. Add potatoes, cayenne and tomatoes. Add ¼ cup (50 mL) water. Cover and reduce heat to medium-low. Cook until tomatoes soften slightly and flavors blend, for 5 minutes. Potatoes should be soft and semi-dry. Garnish with green onions before serving.

Fiery Tamarind Potatoes

Serves 6 to 8

HOT

This is not a dish for the faint of heart. The red chiles provide a kick to otherwise bland potatoes, and tamarind purée adds the essential sour balance.

2 lbs	all-purpose or Yukon gold potatoes (about 8)	1 kg
20	dried Indian red chiles, most seeds removed, broken into pieces	20
20	cloves garlic	20
4 tsp	cumin seeds	20 mL
3 tbsp	oil	45 mL
2	sprigs fresh curry leaves, stripped (20 to 25 leaves)	2
1 tsp	cumin powder	5 mL
2 tsp	salt or to taste	10 mL
1 cup	unsalted Thai tamarind purée	250 mL
1 cup	cilantro leaves, coarsely chopped	250 mL

1. Fill a saucepan three-quarters full of water. Bring to a boil over high heat. Add potatoes and return to a boil. Reduce heat to medium and cook until potatoes are tender, about 20 minutes. Drain. Let cool, peel and cut into largish chunks. Set aside.

2. Meanwhile, in a blender, combine chiles, garlic and cumin seeds and blend to a chunky mix. Set aside.

3. In a wok or large skillet, heat oil over medium heat. Add curry leaves and sauté for 30 seconds. Add cumin powder and sauté for 10 seconds. Add chile mixture and sauté until masala is a few shades darker and aromatic, 3 to 4 minutes. Add 1 tbsp (15 mL) water, if necessary, to prevent burning.

4. Add potatoes and salt and mix well. Sauté for 2 to 3 minutes.

5. Add tamarind purée and ¾ cup (175 mL) water and stir to mix. Cover and simmer for 3 to 4 minutes. Remove from heat. Stir in cilantro. Serve hot with any Indian bread.

Baigan Tarkari
Braised Eggplant

S

1 tsp	dark mustard seeds	5 mL
1 tsp	cumin seeds	5 mL
1	eggplant (about 1 ½ lbs/750 g)	1
2 tbsp	oil	25 mL
3	dried Indian red chiles	3
1 tsp	fenugreek seeds (methi)	5 mL
2 cups	plain nonfat yogurt, at room temperature	500 mL
2 tsp	cornstarch	10 mL
¾ tsp	granulated sugar	4 mL
¾ tsp	salt or to taste	4 mL
3	green chiles, preferably serranos, cut lengthwise halfway, leaving stem end intact	3
2 tbsp	cilantro, chopped	25 mL

Serves 6 to 8

Eggplant, easily available year-round throughout the country, is versatile and easy to prepare. This braised version makes an excellent side dish.

1. In a dry heavy skillet over medium heat, toast mustard and cumin seeds, shaking pan constantly, until fragrant, 3 to 4 minutes. Let cool and grind to a powder in a spice grinder. Set aside.

2. Halve eggplant lengthwise. Cut each half crosswise into ½-inch (1 cm) thick slices.

3. In a saucepan, heat oil over medium heat. Add red chiles and sauté for 30 seconds. Add fenugreek seeds and sauté until seeds turn darker, about 30 seconds. Add eggplant and mix well.

4. Stir together yogurt, cornstarch, sugar, salt and ½ cup (125 mL) water. Pour over eggplant. Add green chiles and stir to mix. Reduce heat to medium-low, cover and cook, stirring gently occasionally, until eggplant is tender and gravy has thickened, 10 to 12 minutes. Add powdered spices and mix well. Garnish with cilantro. Serve hot.

Kotmir Vangaia

Eggplant in Cilantro Masala

1½ lbs	small Indian eggplants, about 20 (see Tip, right)	750 g
3 tbsp	oil, divided	45 mL
2¼ tsp	cumin seeds, divided	11 mL
2 tbsp	minced green chiles, preferably serranos	25 mL
2 tbsp	minced garlic	25 mL
1 tbsp	peeled minced gingerroot	15 mL
6 cups	loosely packed cilantro, including soft stems, coarsely chopped	1.5 L
1 tsp	dark mustard seeds	5 mL
2	sprigs fresh curry leaves, stripped (20 to 25 leaves)	2
¼ tsp	asafetida (hing)	1 mL
2 cups	finely chopped onions	500 mL
1½ tsp	salt or to taste	7 mL
3 to 4 tbsp	freshly squeezed lime or lemon juice	45 to 60 mL

1. Make 4 slits in each eggplant, to look like +, from stem to base, keeping the stem end intact. Set aside.

2. In a skillet, heat 1 tbsp (15 mL) of the oil over medium heat. Add 1½ tsp (7 mL) of the cumin seeds and sauté until fragrant, about 30 seconds. Add chiles, garlic and ginger and sauté for 2 minutes. Remove from heat and mix in cilantro.

3. Transfer mixture to a blender. Add ¼ cup (50 mL) water and blend to a paste. Set aside.

4. In a large skillet with a lid, heat remaining oil over high heat until a couple of mustard seeds thrown in start to sputter. Add all the mustard seeds and cover quickly. When the seeds stop popping, in a few seconds, uncover, reduce heat to medium and add remaining cumin seeds, curry leaves and asafetida. Sauté for 30 seconds.

5. Add onions and sauté until golden, 10 to 12 minutes. Mix in cilantro paste and sauté until fragrant, 3 to 4 minutes.

6. Add 1½ cups (375 mL) water and salt. Bring to a boil and reduce heat to medium-low. Simmer for 2 minutes.

7. Arrange eggplant in pan, in a single layer, spooning masala into cuts and over top of eggplant. Cover and cook until eggplant is tender, 15 to 20 minutes. While cooking, periodically spoon masala into eggplant and over top. Drizzle lime juice over top. Serve with any Indian bread.

Serves 6 to 8

In this recipe from Andhra Pradesh, small eggplant smothered in a cilantro masala makes a perfect side dish with a rich meat curry.

Tip

Small Indian eggplants are deep purple, egg-shaped and vary in size from 1½ to 2½ inches (4 to 6 cm). They can be cooked whole or stuffed with spices in the cut sections and are available year-round in Indian and Asian markets. Don't confuse them with small pale Thai eggplant, which are not suitable for Indian recipes.

Baghare Baigan
Hyderabadi Stuffed Eggplant

Serves 8

This is a classic dish from Hyderabad, known for its rich, complex, highly spiced cuisine.

Tip

The tamarind pod is knobby and flatish, about 4 to 5 inches (10 to 12.5 cm) long and tan. When the pod is ripe, the papery outer skin splits, revealing a soft dark brown pulp on the inside that covers 4 to 5 large shiny brown seeds. The pods are processed commercially, where the outer skin and seeds are removed and the flesh compressed into a brick about 8 inches (20 cm) long and 4 inches (10 cm) wide.

- *Preheat broiler*
- *Large skillet with tight-fitting lid*

1	1-inch (2.5 cm) wide piece brick tamarind (see Tip, left)	1
2 tbsp	grated jaggery (gur) or brown sugar	25 mL

Masala One

3	medium onions	3
3 tbsp	dry unsweetened coconut powder (see Tip, right)	45 mL
2½ tbsp	coriander seeds	32 mL
2 tbsp	sesame seeds	25 mL
2 tbsp	raw skinned peanuts	25 mL
2 tbsp	Indian poppy seeds (see Tip, page 219)	25 mL
1½ tbsp	cumin seeds	22 mL

Masala Two

1	piece (2 by 1 inch/5 by 2.5 cm) peeled gingerroot	1
16	cloves garlic	16
4	dried Indian red chiles	4
4	green chiles, preferably serranos	4
½ cup	cilantro leaves	125 mL
1½ tsp	salt or to taste	7 mL
2 lbs	Japanese eggplant or baby Indian eggplant (6 Japanese or 18 to 20 Indian)	1 kg
¼ cup	oil	50 mL
1½ tsp	cumin seeds	7 mL

1. Break tamarind into pieces and soak in 2 cups (500 mL) very hot water for 30 minutes. Rub with fingers to soften further. Strain the liquid through a coarse sieve into a saucepan, pressing down with back of spoon to extract as much thick pulp as possible. Discard fibrous residue. Add jaggery to the strained liquid and stir over low heat to dissolve. Set aside.

2. *Masala One:* Place onions, with skins on, under preheated broiler and broil, turning periodically with tongs, until evenly charred, 5 to 8 minutes. Let cool. Peel and discard charred layers. Purée onions in a food processor.

3. In a dry heavy skillet over medium heat, toast coconut, shaking pan constantly, until pinkish and aromatic, 3 to 4 minutes. Transfer to a bowl. Follow same procedure and separately toast coriander, sesame seeds, peanuts, poppy seeds and cumin seeds until each is fragrant. Add to bowl. (Some ingredients will need less time.) In a spice grinder, grind all toasted ingredients together as fine as possible. Add to onion purée and process to blend.

4. *Masala Two:* In a blender, combine ginger, garlic, red and green chiles, cilantro and ¼ cup (50 mL) water and blend to make a smooth thick paste. Add to Masala One. Add salt and process to mix well. Set aside.

5. If using baby Indian eggplant, do not remove stems. Make a cross-shaped slit (like a +) down the middle of each eggplant, stopping about 1 inch (2.5 cm) from stem end. If using Japanese eggplant, cut crosswise into about 4-inch (10 cm) sections. In each piece, make a cross-shaped slit (like a +) part of the way through, for stuffing. Stuff eggplant with processed mixture.

6. In a large skillet, heat oil over medium heat. Add cumin seeds and sauté for 1 minute. Add eggplant, in a single layer, and cook, turning to brown skin evenly, 5 to 7 minutes.

7. Pour tamarind liquid evenly over top. Increase heat to medium-high and cook, uncovered, about 5 minutes. Cover with a tight-fitting lid, reduce heat to low and cook until eggplant is tender and a thick gravy coats eggplant.

Tip

Dry unsweetened coconut powder is available in Indian markets. Refrigerate in a resealable freezer bag for up to 2 years.

Green Bean Poriyal

Serves 8

Poriyals are lightly seasoned "dry" vegetable dishes from the south. They emphasize the fresh flavors of the vegetable cooked in their own moisture, the technique being similar to North Indian "dum," or steam, cooking. Poriyals add the textural contrast to the distinctly soupy curries of the south.

Tip

Indian meals are comprised of both "wet" and "dry" dishes for balance. Wet refers to dishes with a gravy (sauce) or a soupy dal. Dry dishes are those cooked without the addition of liquid (or just a little liquid, which creates a thick masala with the other ingredients), usually seasoned with spices and then covered tightly to allow steaming in their own inherent moisture. The balance of wet and dry dishes is very important in the food of every region.

- *Large skillet with tight-fitting lid*

2 tbsp	oil	25 mL
2 tsp	dark mustard seeds	10 mL
2 tsp	cumin seeds	10 mL
2 tsp	split white lentils (urad dal), rinsed	10 mL
2 tsp	split yellow peas (channa dal), rinsed	10 mL
2	dried Indian red chiles, broken in half	2
½ tsp	asafetida (hing)	2 mL
2	sprigs fresh curry leaves, stripped (20 to 25 leaves), optional	2
2 lbs	green beans, cut into ¼-inch (0.5 cm) pieces	1 kg
¾ tsp	salt or to taste	4 mL
2 tbsp	grated coconut, preferably fresh (or frozen, thawed, or dry unsweetened coconut powder)	25 mL

1. In a large skillet, heat oil over high heat until a couple of mustard seeds thrown in start to sputter. Add all the mustard seeds and cover quickly. When the seeds stop popping, in a few seconds, uncover, reduce heat to medium and add cumin seeds, urad and channa dals, chiles, asafetida and curry leaves, if using. Sauté for 30 seconds.

2. Add beans and salt and mix well. Sprinkle with 2 tbsp (25 mL) water and cover with a tight-fitting lid. Reduce heat to medium-low and cook, stirring periodically, until beans are barely tender, 5 to 7 minutes. Avoid overcooking, as beans will lose their bright color. Sprinkle with grated coconut. Serve hot or at room temperature.

Mirchi ka Salan
Peppers in Sesame Seed Sauce

½ cup	sesame seeds	125 mL
2 tbsp	raw cashews	25 mL
1 lb	mild banana peppers or any mild peppers	500 g
6 to 8	hot green chiles, preferably serranos, optional	6 to 8
½ cup	oil (see Tip, right)	125 mL
1 tsp	dark mustard seeds	5 mL
½ tsp	nigella seeds (kalaunji)	2 mL
2 cups	finely chopped onions	500 mL
2 tsp	cumin powder	10 mL
1½ tsp	salt or to taste	7 mL
3 to 4 tbsp	freshly squeezed lime or lemon juice	45 to 60 mL

Serves 8

HOT

A specialty of Hyderabad, this is typical of the style of cooking known as Hyderabadi food — complex and spicy, with unusual flavors and rich sauces. In Hyderabad, this dish would be made with hot peppers, but I prefer to use milder ones. You can use any peppers of your choice.

Tip

The unusually large quantity of oil in this dish is necessary to fry the paste correctly. Skim it off the top before serving the dish so it will not seem so greasy.

1. In a spice grinder, grind sesame seeds and cashews together as fine as possible. Transfer to a bowl. Mix with 3 to 4 tbsp (45 to 60 mL) water to make a thick paste. Set aside.

2. Halve banana peppers lengthwise. With the tip of a very small spoon, scoop out seeds and membranes. Halve the green chiles, leaving seeds intact.

3. In a saucepan, heat oil over medium heat. Add banana peppers and serrano chiles and sauté until slightly soft, 3 to 4 minutes. Remove with a slotted spoon.

4. Reheat oil over high heat until a couple of mustard seeds thrown in start to sputter. Add all the mustard seeds and cover quickly. When the seeds stop popping, in a few seconds, uncover, reduce heat to medium and add nigella. Sauté for 30 seconds. Add onions and cook until softened and golden, 5 to 7 minutes.

5. Add sesame paste, cumin and salt. Mix well with onions and sauté for 4 to 5 minutes.

6. Add 1½ cups (375 mL) water and let gravy come to a gentle boil. Return peppers to saucepan. Cover and cook until oil rises to the top, for 5 minutes. Skim extra oil off the top and stir in lime juice. Serve hot.

Avial
Kerala-Style Mixed Vegetables

Serves 6 to 8

This is the signature dish of the Nairs of Kerala. It is both a popular home-style dish and one served at weddings.

Tip

Coconut oil is available in Indian markets. If unavailable, use any oil you prefer.

1 cup	plain nonfat yogurt, at room temperature	250 mL
1 tsp	cornstarch	5 mL
¾ cup	grated coconut, preferably fresh (or frozen, thawed, or dry unsweetened coconut powder)	175 mL
2 tbsp	minced green chiles, preferably serranos	25 mL
1 tsp	cumin seeds	5 mL
1	green plantain	1
1	chayote squash (mirliton) or 2 cucumbers, thinly sliced	1
2	carrots, cut into 2-by ¼-inch (5 by 0.5 cm) batons	2
10	green beans, preferably slender, cut into 2-inch (5 cm) lengths	10
1¼ tsp	salt or to taste	6 mL
¼ tsp	turmeric	1 mL
2 tbsp	coconut oil (see Tip, left)	25 mL
1	sprig fresh curry leaves, stripped (12 to 15 leaves)	1

1. Stir yogurt and cornstarch together until creamy. Set aside.

2. In a blender, combine coconut, chiles, cumin seeds and ¼ cup (50 mL) of the yogurt mixture. Grind coarsely. Set aside.

3. Cut plantain, unpeeled, into ¼-inch (0.5 cm) thick disks. Cut each disk into ¼-inch (0.5 cm) strips, so that there is some skin on each piece.

4. Place plantains in a saucepan. Top with layers of chayote, carrots and green beans. Stir salt and turmeric into 1½ cups (375 mL) water. Pour over vegetables. Cover and bring to a boil over medium-high heat. Reduce heat to medium-low and simmer until vegetables are half-cooked, 5 to 8 minutes.

5. Stir remaining yogurt and coconut mixture into vegetables and simmer until vegetables are tender, 8 to 10 minutes. The sauce should be fairly thick.

6. Remove from heat. Stir in coconut oil and curry leaves. Serve over steamed rice.

Kummu Kari

Coorg Mushroom Curry

Serves 6

Wild mushrooms abound in the forests of Coorg, a small district in Karnataka, and there are many preparations using them. In this recipe, easier-to-find button mushrooms are used as a substitute.

1 lb	button mushrooms or a mix of mushrooms of your choice	500 g
4	dried Indian red chiles, 2 with seeds removed, broken into pieces	4
1 tbsp	coriander seeds	15 mL
½ tsp	cumin seeds	2 mL
½ tsp	black peppercorns	2 mL
½ cup	grated coconut, preferably fresh (or frozen, thawed)	125 mL
2 tbsp	oil	25 mL
2	sprigs fresh curry leaves, stripped (about 20 to 25 leaves)	2
2	green chiles, preferably serranos, cut in half lengthwise	2
2 cups	thinly sliced onions (lengthwise slices)	500 mL
1½ cups	chopped tomatoes	375 mL
1 tsp	salt or to taste	5 mL
2 tbsp	freshly squeezed lime or lemon juice	25 mL

1. If mushrooms are medium-size, cut each in half. If large, cut in quarters and put in a bowl.

2. In a spice grinder, grind together red chiles, coriander, cumin and peppercorns. Add to mushrooms and toss. Set aside.

3. In a blender, purée coconut with ⅓ cup (75 mL) water until smooth. Set aside.

4. In a saucepan, heat oil over medium heat. Add curry leaves, green chiles and onions and sauté until onions are golden, 4 to 5 minutes.

5. Add mushroom mixture and mix well. Sauté until partially cooked, 3 to 4 minutes.

6. Add coconut paste and sauté for 2 minutes. Rinse blender with 2 tbsp (25 mL) water and pour into pan. Mix well. Add 1½ cups (375 mL) water and bring to a boil. Reduce heat to medium-low and cook for 5 minutes.

7. Add tomatoes and salt. Cover and cook until tomatoes are soft, 5 minutes. Drizzle with lime juice and mix. Serve hot with rice.

Bananas in Fenugreek Masala

4 cups	fresh fenugreek leaves, or 4 cubes frozen chopped fenugreek, thawed, or ¼ cup (50 mL) dried fenugreek (kasuri methi)	1 L
2 tbsp	oil	25 mL
½ tsp	dark mustard seeds	2 mL
½ cup	finely chopped onion	125 mL
2 tbsp	minced green chiles, preferably serranos	25 mL
1 tbsp	minced peeled gingerroot	15 mL
½ tsp	turmeric	2 mL
2 tsp	coriander powder	10 mL
2 tsp	cumin powder	10 mL
1 tsp	salt or to taste	5 mL
3 to 4	firm but ripe bananas, unpeeled, sliced into 1-inch (2.5 cm) sections (about 30 pieces)	3 to 4

1. If using fresh fenugreek leaves, wash, dry and chop. If using frozen, thaw and drain before using. If using dried, soak in warm water for 5 minutes. Skim off leaves from the surface, discarding the residue at the bottom of the bowl.

2. In a skillet, heat oil over high heat until a couple of mustard seeds thrown in start to sputter. Add all the mustard seeds and cover quickly. When the seeds stop popping, in a few seconds, uncover, reduce heat to medium and add onion. Sauté until translucent, 3 to 4 minutes.

3. Add fenugreek and sauté until mixture is aromatic, about 5 minutes. Add chiles, ginger and turmeric and sauté for 2 to 3 minutes.

4. Add coriander, cumin and salt and mix well. Sauté for 2 to 3 minutes.

5. Add bananas and mix well. Cover and cook for 3 to 4 minutes. Stir, reduce heat to low and cook until skins are softened and bananas are cooked but not mushy, 4 to 5 minutes. Serve hot with an Indian bread.

Serves 6

The herb fenugreek has a strong flavor and you either love it or you don't. After cilantro, it is without doubt the most-loved herb in Indian cooking. I love fresh fenugreek (methi), and it is wonderful in this dish, where the bitter herb is well balanced by the sweetness of ripe bananas.

Tip

When cooked, banana skins are edible and are traditionally eaten.

Corn Curry in Coconut Milk

Serves 6 to 8

Many years ago I came across this dish in Mumbai (Bombay) at a friend's home. She knew little about its background, suggesting that it was more likely a Mumbai hybrid. The arrival of fresh corn is much anticipated when the monsoon rains drench the west coast and vendors appear on the streets of Mumbai carrying baskets of corn on their heads and a small charcoal brazier alongside.

1	medium onion, cut into chunks	1
3 to 4	2-inch (5 cm) long green chiles, cut into pieces, preferably serranos	3 to 4
1 cup	cilantro, coarsely chopped	250 mL
3	plum (Roma) tomatoes	3
4 tsp	minced peeled gingerroot	20 mL
4 tsp	minced garlic	20 mL
3 tbsp	freshly squeezed lime or lemon juice	45 mL
1 ½ tsp	salt or to taste	7 mL
¾ tsp	granulated sugar	4 mL
2 tbsp	oil	25 mL
1 tsp	dark mustard seeds	5 mL
2 to 3	sprigs fresh curry leaves, stripped (25 to 30 leaves)	2 to 3
1 ½ cups	chopped onion	375 mL
1	package (16 oz/500 g) frozen corn, thawed, or 4 to 5 ears fresh corn, kernels scraped off the cobs	1
1	can (14 oz/400 mL) coconut milk	1
3 tbsp	cilantro, chopped	45 mL

1. In a food processor, process onion chunks, chiles, 1 cup (250 mL) cilantro, tomatoes, ginger, garlic, lime juice, salt and sugar to a paste.

2. In a saucepan, heat oil over high heat until a couple of mustard seeds thrown in start to sputter. Add all the mustard seeds and cover quickly. When the seeds stop popping, in a few seconds, uncover, reduce heat to medium and add curry leaves. Sauté for 30 seconds. Add chopped onion and sauté until soft, about 5 minutes.

3. Stir in paste. Increase heat to medium-high and cook until reduced by about one-third and color is darker, 6 to 8 minutes.

4. Add corn and coconut milk and mix well. Simmer, uncovered, for 8 minutes. Garnish with chopped cilantro. Serve hot with rice.

Hot-and-Sour Vegetable Curry

¾ cup	white vinegar	175 mL
1½ tsp	granulated sugar	7 mL
3 tbsp	oil, divided	45 mL
1½ cups	½-inch (1 cm) cubes peeled sweet potato	375 mL
1 cup	½-inch (1 cm) cubes peeled potato	250 mL
1 cup	½-inch (1 cm) cubes peeled carrots	250 mL
1 cup	green beans, cut into 1-inch (2.5 cm) pieces	250 mL
1 cup	frozen peas, thawed	250 mL
¼ cup	coarsely chopped garlic	50 mL
2 tbsp	coarsely chopped peeled gingerroot	25 mL
2 cups	finely chopped onions	500 mL
1½ cups	chopped tomatoes	375 mL
1 tbsp	cumin powder	15 mL
1½ tsp	cayenne pepper	7 mL
1 tsp	turmeric	5 mL
1 tsp	salt or to taste	5 mL
1 cup	cilantro, coarsely chopped, divided	250 mL

Serves 6 to 8

HOT

This versatile curry is delicious over rice, which is traditional, but it's equally good over couscous. It is a wonderful vegetarian entrée and a marvelous way to get a boost of healthy vegetables.

1. In a bowl, stir sugar into vinegar to dissolve. Set aside.

2. In a nonstick skillet, heat 1 tsp (5 mL) of the oil over medium heat. Add sweet potato and sauté until pieces start to brown lightly, about 2 minutes. Transfer to a bowl. Repeat process separately with potato, carrots and green beans, adding each to bowl with sweet potatoes. Toss peas into mixture and set aside.

3. In a blender, blend garlic, ginger and 3 tbsp (45 mL) water into a paste. Set aside.

4. In a saucepan, heat remaining oil over medium-high heat. Add onion and sauté until golden, 6 to 8 minutes.

5. Reduce heat to medium-low. Stir in paste, tomatoes, cumin, cayenne, turmeric and salt. Mix well. Cover and cook until tomatoes are soft and can be mashed with the back of a spoon, 6 to 8 minutes.

6. Stir in vegetables and ¾ cup (175 mL) of the cilantro. Pour vinegar mixture and ½ cup (125 mL) water over top and cook until vegetables are tender, 5 to 8 minutes. Garnish with remaining cilantro before serving.

Pumpkin Potato Curry

3 to 4 tbsp	freshly squeezed lime or lemon juice	45 to 60 mL
½ tsp	granulated sugar	2 mL
2 tbsp	plain nonfat yogurt, at room temperature	25 mL
1 ½ tsp	coriander powder	7 mL
1 tsp	salt or to taste	5 mL
¾ tsp	cumin powder	4 mL
½ tsp	cayenne pepper	2 mL
½ tsp	turmeric	2 mL
2 tbsp	oil	25 mL
½ tsp	dark mustard seeds	2 mL
1 tsp	nigella seeds (kalaunji)	5 mL
½ tsp	fenugreek seeds (methi)	2 mL
2	green cardamom pods, seeds only	2
2	whole cloves	2
2	pieces cinnamon, each about 1 inch (2.5 cm) long	2
2	bay leaves	2
¼ tsp	asafetida (hing)	1 mL
1 cup	chopped tomato	250 mL
1 lb	all-purpose potatoes, cut into 1 ½-inch (4 cm) pieces (about 3 ½ cups/825 mL)	500 g
3 ½ to 4 cups	½-inch (1 cm) pieces pumpkin or butternut squash (about 1 lb/500 g)	875 mL to 1 L

1. In a small bowl, stir sugar into lime juice to dissolve. Set aside.

2. In a bowl, mix together yogurt, coriander, salt, cumin, cayenne and turmeric. Set aside.

3. In a saucepan, heat oil over high heat until a couple of mustard seeds thrown in start to sputter. Add all the mustard seeds and cover quickly. When the seeds stop popping, in a few seconds, uncover, reduce heat to medium and add nigella, fenugreek, cardamom, cloves, cinnamon, bay leaves and asafetida. Sauté for 30 seconds.

4. Add yogurt mixture and cook, stirring continuously, for 2 minutes. Add tomato and cook for 2 minutes.

5. Add potatoes, pumpkin and 1 cup (250 mL) water. Cover and simmer until vegetables are tender and liquid is reduced to a gravy, about 20 minutes. Remove from heat. Fold lime juice mixture into vegetables. Serve hot with rice or bread.

Serves 8

Pumpkin is available all year in India and is widely used in savory dishes and also to make a sweet halva, a generic word that refers to any sweet that has the texture of corn pudding.

Variation
Butternut squash is an excellent substitute for the pumpkin.

Khati Mithi Sabzi
Sweet-and-Sour Vegetables

Serves 6 to 8

A mélange of vegetables enriched with panir makes for a substantial dish. Ideal as a vegetarian entrée.

Tip
The whey that results from making panir is very flavorful. I like to freeze it in batches and use it to make soups. It can be frozen for up to 6 months.

1	recipe Lower-Fat Panir (see recipe, page 312), cut into 1-inch (2.5 cm) cubes with 1¼ cups (300 mL) reserved whey (see Tip, left)	1
2 tbsp	oil	25 mL
1 tsp	cumin seeds	5 mL
2 tbsp	minced peeled gingerroot	25 mL
2 tsp	minced green chiles, preferably serranos	10 mL
½ tsp	freshly ground black pepper	2 mL
¼ tsp	asafetida (hing)	1 mL
¾ cup	unsalted Thai tamarind purée	175 mL
½ cup	jaggery (gur) or brown sugar	125 mL
2 cups	sliced carrots	500 mL
2 tsp	coriander powder	10 mL
2 tsp	mango powder (amchur)	10 mL
2 tsp	paprika	10 mL
1 tsp	cayenne pepper	5 mL
3 cups	cubed zucchini	750 mL
3 cups	quartered tomatoes (3 to 4 tomatoes)	750 mL
2 cups	diced celery	500 mL
2 cups	sliced peeled plantains, ¾-inch (2 cm) slices	500 mL
1½ tsp	salt or to taste	7 mL

1. In a large saucepan, heat oil over medium heat. Add cumin and sauté for 30 seconds. Add ginger and green chiles and sauté for 30 seconds. Add pepper and asafetida and sauté for a few more seconds.

2. Pour in reserved whey and cook for 3 to 4 minutes.

3. Add tamarind purée and jaggery and stir until jaggery is dissolved.

4. Add carrots, coriander, mango powder, paprika and cayenne. Bring to a boil. Cook, stirring periodically, until slightly thickened, about 5 minutes.

5. Add panir, zucchini, tomatoes, celery, plantain and salt and mix well. Cover and cook until vegetables are tender and vegetable juices form a gravy, 8 to 10 minutes. Serve with rice or any Indian bread.

Garlic Tindli

- *Saucepan with tight-fitting lid*

2 lbs	tindli	1 kg
40	cloves garlic, divided	40
2 tbsp	peeled minced gingerroot	25 mL
2 tbsp	oil	25 mL
1 tsp	cumin seeds	5 mL
6	dried Indian red chiles	6
2 tbsp	coriander powder	25 mL
1½ tsp	salt or to taste	7 mL
1 tsp	turmeric	5 mL
3 to 4 tbsp	cilantro, chopped	45 to 60 mL

1. Rinse tindli and wipe dry. Trim ends from each and cut lengthwise in half.

2. Coarsely chop 20 cloves of the garlic. In a blender, combine chopped garlic and ginger with 3 to 4 tbsp (45 to 60 mL) water and blend into a paste. Thinly slice remaining garlic.

3. In a saucepan, heat oil over medium heat. Add cumin and red chiles and sauté until cumin is fragrant, about 1 minute. Stir in garlic paste and sauté for 30 seconds. Add thinly sliced garlic and sauté for 1 minute.

4. Add tindli and mix well. Sauté for 3 to 4 minutes, deglazing pan with 1 to 2 tbsp (15 to 25 mL) water, if necessary, to prevent burning.

5. Add coriander, salt and turmeric. Reduce heat to medium-low and sauté for 2 minutes. Drizzle 2 tbsp (25 mL) water around edge of pan. Cover with a tight-fitting lid and cook, stirring once, until vegetables are tender, 8 to 10 minutes. Garnish with cilantro. Serve with any Indian bread.

Serves 8

Tindli *resembles a gherkin and is a popular vegetable in Western India. With a taste somewhat similar to that of zucchini, it is, however, a little crisper. Also known as* tindora, *it is now available year-round in Indian markets. Select smaller tindli, as they have better flavor.*

Variation
Chayote squash (mirliton) instead of the tindli would be just as good in this recipe. Peel squash and cut in half. Remove pit. Slice into 1-inch (2.5 cm) pieces.

Lasooni Aloo
Garlic Potatoes

2 lbs	thin-skinned potatoes (about 8)	1 kg
4 to 6	dried Indian red chiles (see Tip, left)	4 to 6
6	cloves garlic, chopped	6
1 ½ tsp	salt, divided	7 mL
2 tsp	granulated sugar	10 mL
¼ cup	freshly squeezed lime or lemon juice	50 mL
3 tbsp	oil	45 mL
2 tsp	cumin seeds	10 mL
¼ tsp	asafetida (hing)	1 mL
½ tsp	turmeric	2 mL
¼ cup	cilantro leaves, chopped	50 mL

Serves 8

HOT

Garlic and chiles are a marriage made in heaven. This recipe is hot, but you can certainly tone it down to suit your palate.

Tip

To make the dish milder, break 3 red chiles in half and shake out seeds. Discard seeds.

1. Place potatoes in a saucepan with enough water to cover by 3 to 4 inches (7.5 to 10 cm). Bring to a boil over high heat. Reduce heat to low and simmer until potatoes are tender, 20 to 25 minutes. Drain and set aside until cool enough to handle. Cut potatoes, without peeling, into 1-inch (2.5 cm) cubes.

2. In a bowl, soak red chiles in hot water for 10 minutes. Drain and tear into pieces. In a mortar and using a pestle, crush chiles, garlic and ½ tsp (2 mL) of the salt to form a paste.

3. In a small bowl, dissolve sugar in lime juice. Set aside.

4. In wok or skillet, heat oil over medium heat. Add cumin and asafetida and sauté for 1 minute. Add chile paste and turmeric and sauté for 2 minutes.

5. Add potatoes, remaining salt and lime juice mixture. Toss until potatoes are well coated with spices and heated through.

6. Remove from heat and toss with cilantro just before serving with your choice of Indian bread.

Okra Crisps

- *Wok or deep-fryer*
- *Candy/deep-fry thermometer*

2 lbs	okra	1 kg
	Oil for deep-frying	
	Salt and freshly ground pepper to taste	
1 tsp	mango powder (amchur)	5 mL

1. Rinse okra and pat dry. With a sharp knife, slice paper-thin diagonally.

2. In a wok or deep-fryer, heat oil to 350°F (180°C).

3. Add okra, in batches, and fry until very crisp, 8 to 10 minutes per batch.

4. Remove with a large-holed strainer and drain on paper towels. Sprinkle salt, pepper and mango powder and toss to mix. Serve as a side dish or in bowls for cocktails.

Serves 4 to 6

These ethereal slivers of crispy okra are addictive. They were made weekly in our home because my father adored them, and he could go through a pound of okra himself. Fortunately, it was not my mother who was in the kitchen but the family cook.

Garlicky Okra

2 lbs	okra	1 kg
3 tbsp	oil	45 mL
16	cloves garlic, sliced and crushed	16
¼ tsp	asafetida (hing)	1 mL
2 cups	chopped onions	500 mL
4	2-inch (5 cm) long green chiles, preferably serranos, halved lengthwise	4
18	kokum, optional (see Tip, left)	18
1 tsp	salt or to taste	5 mL
1 tsp	mango powder (amchur)	5 mL

Serves 6 to 8

If cooked correctly, okra is a tasty vegetable, much loved by Indians. The trick to removing the sliminess is simply to sauté them, stirring gently. This simple recipe is both tasty and healthy. Always look for young tender okra, as the bigger pods are tough.

Tip

Kokum is the thick black skin of a sour tropical plum-like fruit, used to add an element of tartness. If not using kokum, add additional 1 tsp (5 mL) mango powder.

1. Rinse okra and pat dry. Cut into ½-inch (1 cm) pieces. Set aside.

2. In a skillet, heat oil over medium heat. Add garlic and asafetida and sauté until garlic is golden, about 2 minutes.

3. Add onions and sauté until golden, 7 to 8 minutes.

4. Add chiles and sauté for 2 minutes. Add kokum, if using, and sauté for 1 minute.

5. Add okra and mix well. Sauté, stirring frequently, until there is no more sliminess, 10 to 15 minutes. Adjust heat to prevent burning but maintain a gentle sizzle at all times. If okra is not completely cooked, add 1 tbsp (15 mL) water. Reduce heat to low. Cover and cook until tender. Shake pan periodically to prevent burning.

6. Remove from heat, sprinkle with salt and mix. Sprinkle mango powder over top. Serve as a side dish.

Grilled Corn Pockets

Makes 10 to 12

Here's corn pudding in a glamorous guise. Fun to make and fun to eat, they can be folded several hours ahead and held at room temperature. Grill just before serving.

Variation

For a variation, omit cilantro stuffing. Make corn pockets without stuffing and serve with a chutney of your choice.

2	ears corn	2
1 tbsp	oil	15 mL
1/4 tsp	asafetida (hing)	1 mL
3/4 tsp	cumin seeds	4 mL
1 cup	whole or 2% milk	250 mL
1 cup	cooked rice	250 mL
3 tbsp	freshly squeezed lime or lemon juice	45 mL
2 tsp	minced green chiles, preferably serranos	10 mL
1 tsp	salt or to taste	5 mL
1/2 tsp	granulated sugar	2 mL

Stuffing

1 cup	cilantro	250 mL
1	2-inch (5 cm) long green chile, preferably serrano, cut into large pieces	1
1/2 tsp	minced peeled gingerroot	2 mL
1/2 tsp	granulated sugar	2 mL
2 tbsp	freshly squeezed lime or lemon juice	25 mL
	Vegetable spray	

1. Carefully remove corn husks from corn. Rinse and dry husks and save 15 of the freshest ones.

2. Scrape corn off the cobs and purée in a food processor.

3. In a saucepan, heat oil over medium-high heat. Add asafetida and sauté until it stops sizzling, about 20 seconds. Add cumin seeds and sauté for 30 seconds. Add corn purée and sauté for 2 minutes.

4. Add milk and reduce heat to medium. Cook, stirring periodically, until mixture is almost dry, 5 to 6 minutes. Remove from heat and fold in rice, lime juice, chiles, salt and sugar. Mix well. (Mixture should be able to hold its shape. If it doesn't, cook a little longer to stiffen.)

5. *Stuffing:* In a food processor, process cilantro, chile, ginger, sugar and lime juice to a paste.

6. Spray one side of each corn husk with vegetable spray. Place about 1 1/2 tbsp (22 mL) of the corn mixture 2 inches (5 cm) from bottom of husk on sprayed side. Make a depression in center of mixture and spoon 1 tsp (5 mL) cilantro mixture into it. Scrape corn mixture over stuffing. Fold husk over corn like a flag to make triangular pockets. Secure with a toothpick if necessary. Repeat process until all the husks and mixture are used.

7. Cook pockets on preheated grill on both sides until grill marks appear.

Cabbage and Peppers with Mustard Seeds

2 tbsp	oil	25 mL
2 tsp	dark mustard seeds	10 mL
1	dried Indian red chile	1
¼ tsp	asafetida (hing) (see Tip, right)	1 mL
1 tbsp	minced peeled gingerroot	15 mL
1	large head cabbage, finely sliced (5 to 6 cups/1.25 to 1.5 L)	1
1	green bell pepper, sliced thinly lengthwise	1
1 tsp	coriander powder	5 mL
1 tsp	granulated sugar	5 mL
1 tsp	salt or to taste	5 mL
¾ tsp	turmeric	4 mL
½ tsp	cayenne pepper	2 mL

1. In a large wok or skillet, heat oil over high heat until a couple of mustard seeds thrown in start to sputter. Add all the mustard seeds and cover quickly. When the seeds stop popping, in a few seconds, uncover, reduce heat to medium and add red chile, asafetida and ginger. Sauté for 1 minute.

2. Add cabbage, bell pepper, coriander, sugar, salt, turmeric and cayenne. Mix well. Increase heat to medium-high. Stir-fry briskly just until cooked, about 5 minutes. (Do not overcook, as it will become mushy.)

Serves 6 to 8

This simple dish is delicious with any non-Indian entrée. I sometimes use it in a wrap, where it replaces lettuce. Use red bell pepper, if desired, or a mix of red and green.

Tip

Asafetida makes vegetables of the cruciferous family, such as cauliflower, cabbage and Brussels sprouts, more digestible besides adding a garlicky flavor.

Gujarati Stuffed Bananas

Serves 6 to 8

The Gujarati penchant for combining sweet and spicy is clearly evident in this extraordinary dish. Be sure to use only very ripe bananas, as the sugar is concentrated and they are "juicy," which is critical to the success of this dish.

❦

Tip

You can make bananas a day ahead. Cover and refrigerate. Reheat in microwave and serve warm or at room temperature.

6	firm very ripe bananas, preferably with little black spots	6

Stuffing

1 cup	chickpea flour (besan)	250 mL
1 1/2 tsp	coriander powder	7 mL
1 tsp	cayenne pepper	5 mL
3/4 tsp	cumin powder	4 mL
3/4 tsp	turmeric	4 mL
2 1/2 tbsp	finely chopped green chiles, preferably serranos	32 mL
1 tsp	granulated sugar	5 mL
3/4 tsp	salt or to taste	4 mL
3 to 4 tbsp	freshly squeezed lime or lemon juice	45 to 60 mL
2 tbsp	oil	25 ml

1. Trim ends off unpeeled bananas. Cut in half crosswise. Cut each half in 2, crosswise. You will now have 4 pieces. Slit each piece in half, lengthwise, but do not separate, like a book.

2. *Stuffing:* In a bowl, mix together chickpea flour, coriander, cayenne, cumin and turmeric. Add green chiles, sugar and salt and mix well. Reserve 1/4 cup (50 mL) of the mixture. Stir lime juice into remaining mixture and mix to make a dough-like consistency. You may need to add 1 to 2 tbsp (15 to 25 mL) water. Place about 1 tbsp (15 mL) stuffing into each slit banana piece, pressing both sides gently together between palms to "glue" the sides together.

3. In a large skillet, heat oil over medium-high heat. Arrange bananas in single layer, not on cut side. Cover and cook for until a little soft, 6 to 8 minutes. Carefully turn bananas to brown evenly. Reduce heat to medium-low but maintain a sizzle at all times. Cover and cook until skins are evenly browned and tender, about 5 minutes more.

4. At this point, there should be banana juices in the skillet. Sprinkle reserved chickpea flour evenly over bananas. Shake pan to mix gently. Cook for 2 minutes more. The pan juices should have mixed with the spiced flour to make a thickish coating. Serve hot or at room temperature, eating the skin along with the banana.

Malu's Stuffed Baby Eggplant

- *12-inch (30 cm) skillet with lid*

1 lb	baby eggplant or Japanese eggplant, cut into 2½-inch (6 cm) sections (see Tip, right)	500 g
2½ cups	finely chopped onions	625 mL
½ cup	grated coconut, preferably fresh (or frozen, thawed, or dry unsweetened coconut powder)	125 mL
1½ tsp	coriander powder	7 mL
1½ tsp	cumin powder	7 mL
1½ tsp	cayenne pepper	7 mL
1½ tsp	salt or to taste	7 mL
½ tsp	turmeric	2 mL
2 cups	cilantro, chopped	500 mL
1½ cups	frozen peas, thawed	375 mL
¼ cup	oil, divided	50 mL
12 oz	baby new potatoes	375 g

1. Make 4 slits in each eggplant (like a +) from stem to base, keeping the stem end intact. Set aside.

2. In a bowl, mix together onions, coconut, coriander, cumin, cayenne, salt, turmeric, cilantro, peas and 1½ tbsp (22 mL) of the oil. Set aside one-third of the mixture. Stuff eggplant with remaining mixture, packing in as much as possible, without breaking eggplant apart. If there is stuffing leftover, combine with reserved mixture.

3. In a skillet, heat remaining oil. Arrange eggplant in a single layer. Arrange unpeeled potatoes in between. Sprinkle remaining onion masala on top. Cover and cook over medium heat until eggplant is partially cooked, about 15 minutes. Shake pan periodically to make sure vegetables do not burn. With tongs, rotate eggplant. Cover, reduce heat to medium-low and cook until eggplant is tender, 12 to 15 minutes. Shake pan periodically to make sure masala is not sticking. Serve with an Indian bread.

My friend Malu, who is an avid cook and collector of recipes, shared this with me on one of her visits. It has quickly become one of my favorites, both for family as well as for entertaining.

Tip

Japanese or Chinese eggplants are a suitable substitute if baby eggplant are unavailable. You will need about 10 to 12 baby Indian eggplants and about 3 Japanese eggplants, each 10 to 12 inches (25 to 30 cm). Cut into 2½-inch (6 cm) pieces and proceed with the cross slits as in Step 1, taking care not to cut all the way through.

Stuffed Okra

2 tbsp	coriander powder	25 mL
1 tbsp	cumin powder	15 mL
1 tbsp	garam masala	15 mL
1 tbsp	mango powder (amchur)	15 mL
1½ tsp	cayenne pepper	7 mL
1½ tsp	turmeric	7 mL
1 tsp	salt or to taste	5 mL
2 lbs	small okra	1 kg
3 tbsp	oil	45 mL

1. In a small bowl, mix together coriander, cumin, garam masala, mango powder, cayenne, turmeric and salt.

2. Remove stem end of okra and make a lengthwise slit on one side. With the tip of a small spoon, stuff with spice mixture.

3. In a large skillet, heat oil over medium heat. Arrange okra in a single layer. Drizzle 2 tbsp (25 mL) water around edges of skillet. Cover and shake pan to spread water. Reduce heat to low but maintaining an audible sizzle, cook until okra are tender, 20 to 25 minutes. Shake pan occasionally. If necessary, drizzle with water, 1 tbsp (15 mL) at a time, and continue cooking until okra is soft.

Serves 8

Okra lends itself to many different methods of cooking, but in India it is never breaded and fried. Pick out the smallest okra as they will be tender.

Stuffed Peppers

Serves 6

This is a substantial vegetarian dish. Vegetable fritters, crispy papadums and a tasty chutney round out the delicious meal.

Tip

Crispy fried onions are available in all Asian, Middle-Eastern and Indian markets. They can be stored in the refrigerator for up to 1 year after opening.

Stuffing

½ cup	yellow mung beans (yellow mung dal)	125 mL
½ cup	white rice (any variety)	125 mL
¾ cup	frozen peas	175 mL
1 tsp	salt	5 mL
¼ tsp	turmeric	1 mL
6	medium green bell peppers	6
2 tbsp	oil	25 mL
⅓ cup	peanuts	75 mL
3 tbsp	sambhar masala	45 mL

Gravy

1 cup	crisp fried onion (birishta) (see Tip, left)	250 mL
1 cup	plain nonfat yogurt	250 mL
1 tsp	cornstarch	5 mL
3	plum (Roma) tomatoes, chopped	3
2 tbsp	sambhar powder	25 mL
¾ tsp	salt or to taste	4 mL

1. *Stuffing:* Clean and pick through dal for any small stones and grit. Rinse several times in cold water until water is fairly clear. Mix in rice and soak in 2½ cups (625 mL) water in a saucepan for 10 minutes. Bring to a boil over medium-high heat and skim froth. Add peas, salt and turmeric. Reduce heat to low. Cover and simmer until mixture is very soft but all liquid has been absorbed, about 30 minutes. Uncover and let cool for 5 minutes.

2. In a skillet, heat oil over medium heat. Add peanuts and sauté for 1 minute. Sprinkle sambhar powder and sauté for 1 minute, adjusting heat so as not to burn. Remove from heat and stir into rice.

3. Slice ¼ inch (0.5 cm) to ½ inch (1 cm) from the top of each green pepper and discard. If bottom does not sit well, level it, taking care not to cut through. With a teaspoon, scoop out seeds and membranes. Scoop rice mixture into peppers. Set aside.

4. *Gravy:* In a blender, combine fried onions, yogurt, cornstarch, tomatoes, sambhar powder and salt. Blend to creamy consistency.

5. Pour into a Dutch oven. Bring to a gentle boil over medium heat, stirring frequently, for 8 minutes.

6. Arrange peppers in pan and spoon gravy over tops of peppers. Cover and return to gentle boil. Cook until peppers are soft, 15 to 20 minutes, scraping bottom of pan periodically to make sure gravy is not sticking to pan. Serve hot with rice or any Indian bread.

Peppers with Peanuts

4 tsp	oil, divided	20 mL
3 tbsp	grated coconut, preferably fresh (or frozen, thawed)	45 mL
1 tsp	coriander seeds	5 mL
1 tsp	sesame seeds	5 mL
¼ tsp	fenugreek seeds (methi)	1 mL
1 tsp	dark mustard seeds	5 mL
½ tsp	turmeric	2 mL
¼ tsp	asafetida (hing)	1 mL
6	bell peppers, green or mixed colors, cut into ½-inch (1 cm) cubes	6
1¼ tsp	salt or to taste	6 mL
¾ tsp	cayenne pepper	4 mL
3 tbsp	peanuts	45 mL
1½ tbsp	jaggery (gur) or 4 tsp (20 mL) brown sugar	22 mL

Serves 6 to 8

I love the versatility of bell peppers. In India, until recently only green peppers were available, but now red and sometimes yellow are being sold in upscale markets in big cities. I like to use different colors when possible, as the flavors work in harmony and the colors make the dish look festive.

1. In a small skillet, heat 1 tsp (5 mL) of the oil over medium heat. Add coconut, coriander, sesame and fenugreek and sauté until fragrant, 2 to 3 minutes. Let cool and transfer to a blender. Blend to a paste with ¼ cup (50 mL) water. Set aside.

2. In a saucepan, heat remaining oil over high heat until a couple of mustard seeds thrown in start to sputter. Add all the mustard seeds and cover quickly. When the seeds stop popping, in a few seconds, uncover, reduce heat to medium and add turmeric, asafetida and bell peppers. Mix well and sauté until peppers are soft, 6 to 8 minutes.

3. Add spice paste, salt, cayenne, peanuts and jaggery and mix well. Add ½ cup (125 mL) water. Cook until vegetables are mixed with seasonings and there is almost no liquid left, 8 to 9 minutes. Serve with any Indian bread.

Pitla

Savory Chickpea Flour Pudding

This recipe is from my friend Radhika, who makes it frequently for her family. A home-style dish from Maharashtra, it makes up in flavor and taste what it lacks in looks! Traditionally eaten with an Indian bread, I also like to serve it with a vegetable to round out the meal.

¼ cup	oil	50 mL
2 cups	finely chopped onions	500 mL
1 tsp	minced garlic	5 mL
2 cups	chickpea flour (besan)	500 mL
2 tsp	salt or to taste	10 mL
1 tsp	cayenne pepper	5 mL
½ tsp	turmeric	2 mL
1 cup	cilantro, chopped	250 mL

1. In a large wok, heat oil over medium heat. Add onions and sauté until translucent, 5 to 6 minutes. Add garlic and sauté for 2 minutes.

2. Add chickpea flour, salt, cayenne and turmeric. Increase heat to medium-high. Brown flour, stirring continuously, until golden and fragrant, 6 to 8 minutes. Do not allow to burn.

3. Reduce heat to medium. Pour 3½ to 4 cups (875 mL to 1 L) very hot water into wok, stirring vigorously to make a smooth paste.

4. Remove from heat and stir in cilantro. Serve immediately with chapati or pita bread.

Soy with Green Mango

½ cup	textured vegetable protein or soy granules	125 mL
½ cup	plain nonfat yogurt, at room temperature	125 mL
½ tsp	cornstarch	2 mL
1¼ tsp	salt or to taste, divided	6 mL
½	medium onion	½
1	piece (1 inch/2.5 cm square) peeled gingerroot	1
3	cloves garlic	3
2	2-inch (5 cm) long green chiles, preferably serranos, cut into pieces	2
2 cups	loosely packed cilantro	500 mL
½ cup	loosely packed mint	125 mL
¾ tsp	turmeric	4 mL
2 tbsp	oil	25 mL
1 cup	minced red onion	250 mL
1½ cups	chopped peeled green mango, ½-inch (1 cm) cubes	375 mL
2 tbsp	freshly squeezed lime or lemon juice	25 mL
3 tbsp	cilantro, chopped	45 mL

Serves 4 to 6

Soy is a high-protein addition to many Indian dishes. In this recipe, soy granules provide a wonderful textural contrast to green mango and absorb the flavors of the seasoned yogurt.

1. In a bowl, soak soy granules in 1½ cups (375 mL) hot water for at least 30 minutes.

2. In a bowl, stir together yogurt, cornstarch, 1 tsp (5 mL) of the salt and ½ cup (125 mL) water. Set aside.

3. In a blender, blend together onion, ginger, garlic, chiles and 2 tbsp (25 mL) water. Add cilantro, mint and turmeric. Add ¼ cup (50 mL) water and blend to a smooth paste. Set aside.

4. In a saucepan, heat oil over medium heat. Add red onion and sauté until golden, 8 to 10 minutes. Pour paste into onion. Continue to sauté over medium heat until paste begins to dry.

5. Add soy with any remaining water. Pour in yogurt mixture and ¼ tsp (1 mL) of salt and mix well. Stir in mango and bring to a boil over medium heat. Reduce heat to low. Cover and simmer, stirring occasionally, until gravy is thick and mangoes are soft, 12 to 15 minutes.

6. Stir in lime juice. Garnish with chopped cilantro. Serve hot with rice or an Indian bread.

Salads, Raitas and Chutneys

THE SALADS OF INDIA CONJURE UP IMAGES of cooked beans, fresh herbs, cubed potato, corn and many other ingredients mixed together. These are seasoned with spices, and the dressing is usually a healthy squeeze of lime or lemon juice. Seldom is there an oil-based dressing, and mayonnaise is used in only a couple of salads that are a legacy of the British. There are no mixed greens or raw spinach in a traditional Indian salad as there are in the West. There is however, the ubiquitous dish of sliced tomatoes, cucumbers and thinly sliced onion seasoned with salt and pepper that is often served with grilled foods in the north.

Yogurt salads — raitas — however, are an integral part of the cuisine. They help to cool the palate, soothe the stomach and generally balance a spicy meal. Traditionally, raitas are made with yogurt stirred until creamy, with a small amount of diced vegetable, cooked beans or pieces of fruits and nuts folded in. In the north, the seasonings are usually simple: salt, pepper and perhaps a little cayenne pepper or cumin powder. In the south, the word *raita* morphs into *pachadi*. Pachadis play an important role in southern cuisine and can be quite elaborate. They are generally topped with a mix of flash-fried ingredients such as mustard seeds, a tiny number of split yellow peas (*channa dal*), perhaps a pinch of asafetida and, usually, curry leaves. As a result, the flavors are more intense than in the north. Raitas and pachadis are always vegetarian.

THERE IS MUCH CONFUSION ABOUT chutney. To a non-Indian, chutney denotes a spicy-sweet condiment made of fruit. To an Indian, that is just the tip of the iceberg. The world of chutneys is vast and encompasses everything from spicy-sweet fruit-and-vegetable condiments to fresh herbs and seasonings blended into a purée. They also include complex mixes of powdered spices and nuts popular in the south, and the thick liquids used in many *chaat* dishes. Chutneys play as important a role in Indian cuisine as do spices and spice blends.

ANOTHER CATEGORY OF CONDIMENTS that are very popular are the oil-based pickles that line the shelves of Indian markets. Salty and spicy and totally submerged in oil, they add a unique dimension to Indian food. Almost any fruit or vegetable can be pickled, and there is also a shrimp pickle, a goat meat pickle and a chicken pickle! Ingredients are simmered in oil, heavily salted and doused with spices. The combination acts as a preservative, ensuring long storage. These highly seasoned pickles are not to be used as a

side dish but rather eaten in very tiny amounts with each mouthful. Their role is to tease the palate and enhance mild dishes.

IN THE NORTH, CHUTNEYS ARE usually made of fruit — mango is the most popular. But more popular are the oil-based pickles. Turnips and carrots are popular as brined pickles, and a mix of cauliflower, carrots and turnips is one of the favorite oil-based ones, always made in the cooler months, when these vegetables are at their best. Traditionally, pickle making was an important ritual in most homes, and several days would be devoted to putting up a variety of goodies for the year. Although my mother did not cook at all, she had somehow acquired the recipe for a superb Sindhi sweet mango chutney. Once a year, she took on the task of making this for several members of our extended family. Fresh spices would be bought, cleaned and spread on mats to dry in the sun before being ground. Several pounds of a particular variety of green mango would be purchased at the wholesale produce market, and then the kitchen would shift into high gear.

Salads, Raitas and Chutneys

❧

THE KITCHEN STAFF OF THREE WOULD spend the entire day preparing the mangoes under her watchful eye, being the master manager that she was. They stirred the huge pot and sterilized the enormous stoneware jar and lid to receive the year's supply of this wonderful chutney. It would be packed into the jar with a clean piece of muslin tied around the mouth, and the jar would be set out in the sun for several days of curing. Eventually, it would be portioned out to the lucky family members who had put in their bids in a timely fashion. After my mother passed away, while sorting through her possessions, I found her recipe, handwritten in Sindhi script on the back of an envelope. Here was a treasured keepsake from a woman who never saw a reason to spend hours in the kitchen and yet left behind a legacy that is valued even today. Nowadays, most families do not have full-time help, and at the same time the variety and quality of store-bought products has improved tremendously, so the art of pickle making is slowly disappearing.

And lastly, there are the brine-based pickles made seasonally in Indian homes. These are usually made with lemons or green chiles, fresh gingerroot, small boiling onions and carrots. They are cured in the sun for a few days, then refrigerated for a week or two.

IN THE EAST, PICKLES DO NOT PLAY AS important a role. Bengali food has a sweet-and-sour fruit or vegetable component eaten close to the end of the meal, but its role is to act as a digestive, not to enhance the food as in other parts of India. In the northeastern states, fresh chiles are ground into a paste, and vegetables mixed with small amounts of fermented soybeans, shredded dried or fermented fish, or dried meat are eaten as a condiment in small quantities.

THE SOUTH, OF COURSE, IS TOTALLY different. North Indian–style condiments are replaced by many that are coconut- or lentil-based. Coconut is unknown in the north and so is the concept of using lentils as a condiment. In the south, lentils are either soaked and ground into a paste with spices and seasonings, or toasted in a skillet, powdered and mixed with spices.

In Andhra Pradesh, toasting and grinding together different spices with toasted lentils and/or peanuts, garlic, etc. result in a dryish mixture. These dry mixes are called *podis*. They are stored in jars, and a tablespoon or two is mixed with rice or as an accompaniment to dishes such as rice crêpes (*dosa*) or rice cakes (*idli*).

IN THE WEST, THE TRADITION OF chutneys and pickles is alive and well. Gujaratis and Maharashtrians are addicted to these condiments. The ubiquitous "green chutney" comes into its own in the west with several variations, some including mint, others made with coconut and still others based on green onions. The common denominators are, of course, cilantro and chile. Tamarind chutney is very popular, drizzled on many appetizers or used as a dipping chutney, and its prized role is in the famous *bhel puri chaat* of Mumbai. Maharashtra has several specialties, but the pickled chiles and sweet-and-hot pickled eggplant are my favorite.

Goa has an assertive green chutney made with coconut, but its trademark is a fiery red coconut chutney, redolent of garlic and red chiles. My favorite from Goa, however, is *prawn balchow*, a spicy mixture of prawns, chiles and tomatoes, which I must confess I could eat by the fiery spoonful.

The recipes in this book are all suitable for home use, but some require more effort and time. Feel free to adjust the seasonings to your taste, because, after all, they are meant to enhance your meal.

Cucumber Raita

1 cup	plain nonfat yogurt	250 mL
2 cups	diced cucumber	500 mL
2 tbsp	cilantro, chopped	25 mL
½ tsp	cumin powder, preferably freshly toasted and ground (see Tips, page 198)	2 mL
	Salt and freshly ground black pepper to taste	

1. Stir yogurt in a bowl until smooth and creamy. Stir in cucumber, cilantro and cumin. Season with salt and pepper.

2. Cover and chill well before serving. (Raita can be refrigerated for up to 24 hours.)

Serves 8

This is arguably the most recognized raita, available on every restaurant menu. Its simplicity also makes it a favorite of home cooks.

Til ki Chutney

Sesame Chutney

¼ cup	sesame seeds	50 mL
2	large cloves garlic	2
2	2-inch (5 cm) long green chiles, preferably serranos	2
½ tsp	granulated sugar	2 mL
¼ tsp	salt	1 mL
¼ cup	plain nonfat yogurt	50 mL
2 cups	cilantro leaves and soft stems	500 mL
2 tbsp	freshly squeezed lime or lemon juice	25 mL

1. In a skillet, toast sesame seeds over medium heat, stirring continuously, until beginning to color, about 2 minutes. Do not overcook. Transfer to a bowl and let cool.

2. Transfer to a blender and add garlic, chiles, sugar, salt and yogurt. Add a handful of cilantro and blend to a purée. Add remaining cilantro, in 2 batches. Scrape down sides of blender periodically. When mixture is a smooth purée, transfer to a serving bowl. (Chutney can be refrigerated in an airtight container for up to 1 week.)

Makes ¾ cup (175 mL)

This chutney from Garhwal (Uttarakhand state) is a northern variation of the cilantro chutney that is popular throughout the country in many guises. The sesame adds flavor and acts as a thickener. It is used as a dipping chutney with appetizers, and I have also used it as a dressing for potato salad. Try it as a sandwich spread or smear it in a wrap.

Bhabiji's Tomato Chutney

Makes about 1½ cups (375 mL)

This is a recipe from my cousin Gita, whose mother-in-law was the source of not only this but also many other wonderful home-style dishes. Although regarded as a condiment, it can be served as a side dish as well. It's best made with flavorful summer tomatoes.

Tips

Chutney can be refrigerated in an airtight container for up to 2 weeks.

When spooning chutneys or pickles out of a jar, make sure the spoon is absolutely dry. If even a hint of moisture is introduced, the condiment will grow mold. Also, never return any unused chutney to the jar because once it has been removed, it is exposed to bacteria in the atmosphere. Instead, cover and refrigerate unused portion.

2 tsp	oil	10 mL
½ tsp	dark mustard seeds	2 mL
½ tsp	cumin seeds	2 mL
½ tsp	sesame seeds	2 mL
½ tsp	cayenne pepper	2 mL
1 lb	tomatoes, chopped	500 g
½ tsp	salt	2 mL
1 tbsp	jaggery (gur)	15 mL
2 tbsp	white vinegar	25 mL

1. In a saucepan, heat oil over high heat until a couple of mustard seeds thrown in start to sputter. Add all the mustard seeds and cover quickly. When the seeds stop popping, in a few seconds, uncover, reduce heat to medium and add cumin, sesame seeds and cayenne. Sauté for 20 seconds. Add tomatoes and salt and mix well.

2. Cover and cook until soft, 6 to 8 minutes. Mash with back of a spoon.

3. Stir in jaggery. Reduce heat to low. Cook until most of the juices are reduced to a thick jam-like consistency, 6 to 8 minutes.

4. Add vinegar and cook for 2 minutes. Serve as a dipping sauce with appetizers. If you prefer to serve it as a side dish, do not reduce as much.

Dahi Wada

Lentil Dumplings in Yogurt

Makes 18 to 20

This is a classic dish and is popular throughout India, with minor variations. It is laborious and a little tricky, but it helps that the dumplings can be made ahead and frozen.

Tip

Dumplings (*wadas*) can be made ahead and frozen in resealable freezer bags for up to 3 months. Do NOT soak after frying, but drain on paper towels. Let cool and freeze. To serve, thaw completely, then soak and continue with Step 5.

- Wok or deep-fryer
- Candy/deep-fry thermometer

1 cup	split white lentils (urad dal)	250 mL
6 tbsp	cilantro, chopped, divided	90 mL
2 tsp	minced green chiles, preferably serranos	10 mL
1 ½ tsp	minced peeled gingerroot	7 mL
1 tsp	toasted cumin seeds	5 mL
¾ tsp	salt	4 mL
	Oil for deep-frying	
4 cups	plain nonfat or low-fat yogurt	1 L
1 ½ tsp	granulated sugar	7 mL
¾ tsp	cumin powder	4 mL
½ tsp	each cayenne and freshly ground black pepper	2 mL
1 ½ tsp	chaat masala (see Tips, page 40)	7 mL
¼ cup	Sweet Tamarind Chutney (see recipe, page 424), optional	50 mL

1. Clean and pick through dal for any small stones and grit. Rinse several times in cold water until water is fairly clear. Soak overnight in water to cover by 3 to 4 inches (7.5 to 10 cm).

2. Next morning, drain dal, reserving liquid. In a blender, process dal in 3 batches, adding enough reserved liquid to make a thick batter, thicker than cake batter. Transfer to a bowl.

3. Whisk in 3 tbsp (45 mL) of the cilantro, chiles, ginger, cumin and salt. Whisk vigorously for 2 minutes to incorporate air and lighten batter. Set aside for 10 minutes.

4. In a wok or deep-fryer, heat oil to 350°F (180°C). Drop batter by spoonfuls into hot oil, forming walnut-size dumplings, and deep-fry, in batches, until golden brown, 3 to 4 minutes per batch.

5. Keep a bowl of very hot water handy and pop the balls into the water as soon as they are ready. Soak about 20 minutes. Remove carefully and squeeze each one gently between your palms to flatten and remove excess water. Arrange in a single layer in a shallow serving dish.

6. Stir yogurt until creamy. Add ½ cup (125 mL) water, sugar, cumin, cayenne and black pepper and mix well. Pour three-quarters of yogurt mixture over dumplings, covering them completely. Refrigerate, uncovered, for at least 3 hours. Before serving, pour remaining yogurt mixture over top. Sprinkle with chaat masala and remaining cilantro. Drizzle a little sweet tamarind chutney on top, if desired.

Dried Fruit Chutney

8 oz	dried apricots, preferably Afghani apricots (see Tip, right)	250 g
2 cups	granulated sugar	500 mL
¾ cup + 2 tbsp	freshly squeezed lime or lemon juice	200 mL
2 tbsp	coarsely chopped peeled gingerroot	25 mL
2 tbsp	chopped green chiles, preferably serranos	25 mL
2 cups	loosely packed mint leaves	500 mL
6	black cardamom pods, seeds only (about 1 tsp/5 mL)	6
1 tsp	seeds of green cardamom	5 mL
1 tsp	black peppercorns	5 mL
1 tsp	cayenne pepper	5 mL
2 tsp	salt	10 mL
½ cup	slivered or halved blanched almonds	125 mL
⅓ cup	raisins	75 mL

1. If using Afghani apricots, soak for 3 to 4 hours in water to soften. Drain and remove stones. If using deseeded Afghani apricots or any other apricots, omit this step.

2. In a large saucepan, mix together apricots, sugar and lime juice. Bring to a boil over medium heat.

3. In a blender, blend ginger, chiles, mint and 2 tbsp (25 mL) water into a paste. Add to pan.

4. In a spice grinder, grind together black and green cardamom seeds, peppercorns and cayenne. Add spices to pan. Stir in salt. Reduce heat to medium-low and cook for 5 minutes.

5. Add almonds and raisins. Cook, stirring periodically, until mixture thickens, 15 to 20 minutes. Transfer to sterilized jar or to serving dish. Let cool before serving.

Makes 4 cups (1 L)

Dried fruits are very expensive in India and hence are used mainly for special occasions. A condiment such as this would be served at a banquet and would not be a part of daily meals.

Tip
Afghani apricots are small, grayish, hard fruits with a stone containing a tiny almond. They are intensely sweet and have a completely different taste from the familiar Turkish apricots. Available in Indian and Middle Eastern stores in 8-oz (250 g) packages. Sometimes you can buy them with the seeds removed, in bulk bins in specialty stores. When sold this way, they are soft, dark brown and ready to eat or use in recipe.

Pickled Carrots

Makes 1 cup (250 mL)

This is a popular Sindhi condiment eaten with any meal. It is light (notice there is no oil), easy to make, and the slightly fermented liquid is considered to be a good digestive. It must be placed in a sunny spot to develop the tangy flavor.

Tip
Carrots should be consumed within 10 days, as they get mushy with longer storage.

• *3-cup (750 mL) glass jar*

1 cup	sliced (¼ inch/0.5 cm thick) peeled carrots (about 2 carrots)	250 mL
2 tbsp	chopped green garlic or 1 clove garlic, chopped	25 mL
1½ tsp	crushed dark mustard seeds	7 mL
1 tsp	whole dark mustard seeds	5 mL
¾ tsp	salt	4 mL
⅛ tsp	each turmeric and cayenne pepper	0.5 mL

1. In a small saucepan, combine carrots and 1½ cups (375 mL) water. Bring to a boil over high heat. Reduce heat to medium and cook for 2 minutes.

2. In a clean glass jar, combine garlic, crushed and whole mustard seeds, salt, turmeric and cayenne.

3. Pour carrots with liquid into jar. Add 1 cup (250 mL) additional water. Let cool and close jar. Shake well to mix things up and place on a sunny windowsill or patio. Shake jar twice a day. After 2 days, check to see if juice is tangy and carrots are slightly soft. Carrots should be soft but not mushy in 2 to 4 days. Store in the refrigerator.

Pickled Onions

Makes about 3 cups (750 mL)

Crushed mustard seeds add a tanginess to "water pickles," which are very popular in the north and west. Exposing the jar to the hot sun for several hours "cooks" the vegetable and accentuates the tang.

1	package (10 oz/300 g) pearl onions (16 to 18)	1
2 tbsp	crushed dark mustard seeds	25 mL
6	cloves garlic, partially smashed	6
4	2-inch (5 cm) long green chiles, preferably serranos, quartered lengthwise	4

1. Peel onions. Slit from the tip end thru the middle, almost to the bottom, without separating. Cut again at right angle to the first slit, again without separating so you have a plus + sign.

2. Layer onions in a 3- to 4-cup (750 mL to 1 L) glass jar with mustard seeds, garlic and chiles. Fill with enough water to cover onions and cover jar tightly. Place jar in the sun until onions are soft, shaking to mix once or twice a day, for 3 to 4 days. Store in the refrigerator. This pickle will keep for a month.

Anarosher Tok

Sweet-and-Sour Pineapple Relish

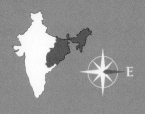

1 tbsp	oil	15 mL
1 tsp	dark mustard seeds	5 mL
¼ cup	minced peeled gingerroot	50 mL
1	cored and peeled pineapple, cut into 1-inch (2.5 cm) pieces	1
1 cup	granulated sugar (approx.) (see Tip, right)	250 mL
3 to 4 tbsp	raisins	45 to 60 mL
1 tsp	cayenne pepper	5 mL
Pinch	salt	Pinch

1. In a saucepan, heat oil over high heat until a couple of mustard seeds thrown in start to sputter. Add all the mustard seeds and cover quickly. When the seeds stop popping, in a few seconds, uncover, reduce heat to medium and add ginger, pineapple, sugar, raisins, cayenne and salt. Add 3 cups (750 mL) water and any juices from pineapple. Bring to a gentle boil. Reduce heat to low. Cover and cook until pineapple is very soft, about 15 minutes. There should be a fair amount of liquid in the dish when it is ready.

2. Serve in small bowls at the end of the meal but before dessert.

Serves 6 to 8

A typical sweet-and-sour relish served at the end of a meal in Bengal as a digestive. I confess I use it as a chutney to accompany a meal, and it is delicious.

Tip
You may need more or less sugar depending on the sweetness of the pineapple.

Kanchaoamer Tok
Sweet-and-Sour Mango Relish

Serves 4 to 6

Bengalis serve a sweet-sour relish such as this towards the end of a meal. It is served in individual small bowls and is believed to aid digestion. I usually serve it as a condiment, although that is not its true role.

2	medium unripe green mangoes, about 1 lb (500 g)	2
1 tbsp	mustard oil	15 mL
1	dried Indian red chile	1
1 tsp	panch phoran (see Tip, page 345)	5 mL
½ tsp	turmeric	2 mL
¼ tsp	salt	1 mL
3 to 4 tbsp	granulated sugar	45 to 60 mL
½ tsp	cayenne pepper	2 mL

1. Peel mangoes. Hold upright firmly, stem end up. With a sharp knife, cut close to the flat side of seed on both sides, resulting in 2 "cheeks." Cut each cheek lengthwise into ¼-inch (0.5 cm) thick slices. Cut sides around seed and slice. Discard seed.

2. In a saucepan, heat oil over high heat until very hot. Remove from heat and let cool for 1 minute (see Tip, page 326). Return pan to medium-high heat. Add chile and panch phoran and sauté until seeds stop popping, for 30 seconds. Do not allow seeds to burn.

3. Add turmeric and mango and mix well. Add salt. Reduce heat to medium. Sauté to allow spices to cook, 2 to 3 minutes. Add ¾ cup (175 mL) water and bring to a boil.

4. Add 3 tbsp (45 mL) of the sugar. Reduce heat to medium-low and simmer until mango is tender but not mushy, 4 to 5 minutes. Taste for sweet-sour balance and add more sugar if needed. Cook for another minute to dissolve sugar. Remove from heat and stir in cayenne pepper.

Bengali Eggplant Relish

1 lb	Japanese or Chinese eggplant, cut into $\frac{1}{2}$-inch (1 cm) cubes	500 g
$\frac{1}{2}$ tsp	sesame seeds	2 mL
1 tbsp	mustard oil	15 mL
1 tsp	cumin seeds	5 mL
$\frac{1}{2}$ tsp	fenugreek seeds	2 mL
3 tbsp	jaggery (gur)	45 mL
3 tbsp	unsalted Thai tamarind purée	45 mL
1 tsp	cayenne pepper	5 mL
$\frac{1}{2}$ tsp	salt or to taste	2 mL

1. In a saucepan over high heat, bring 1 cup (250 mL) water to a boil. Add eggplant and return to a boil. Cover and cook for 1 minute. Drain.

2. In a skillet over medium heat, toast sesame seeds until lightly colored, 3 to 4 minutes. Let cool, then crush in a mortar with a pestle.

3. In a saucepan, heat oil over high heat until almost smoking. Remove from heat and let cool for 1 minute (see Tip, page 326). Return to medium heat. Add cumin and sauté for 30 seconds. Add fenugreek and sauté for 20 seconds. Add eggplant and mix well. Add jaggery, tamarind, cayenne and salt. Mix well to melt jaggery. Remove from heat.

4. Stir in crushed sesame seeds and mix well. Let cool.

**Makes about
$1\frac{1}{2}$ cups (375 mL)**

This sweet-and-hot relish is delicious as a topping for crostini. Serve it warm or chilled. I like to serve it as a side dish with pork loin, too.

Tip
Relish can be stored in the refrigerator for up to 1 week.

Mango Salad

Serves 6 to 8

*Indians are passionate
about mangoes, and
hundreds of varieties
of the fruit are grown
throughout the country.
Not only are they
enjoyed as cut fruit, they
are also used extensively
in cooking.*

4	dried Indian red chiles, 2 with seeds removed	4
1½ cups	grated coconut, preferably fresh (or frozen, thawed)	375 mL
2 tbsp	jaggery (gur) or brown sugar	25 mL
3½ to 4 cups	cubed firm ripe mango, ½-inch (1 cm) pieces (2 large mangoes)	825 mL to 1 L
1½ tbsp	oil	22 mL
1 tsp	dark mustard seeds	5 mL
1 tsp	coriander seeds, smashed with pestle	5 mL
2	sprigs fresh curry leaves, stripped (20 to 25 leaves)	2
⅓ cup	toasted peanuts, coarsely chopped	75 mL

1. In a spice grinder, finely chop or grind red chiles. Transfer to a blender and add coconut and jaggery. Pour in ⅓ cup (75 mL) water and blend to a paste. If necessary, add 2 to 3 tbsp (25 to 45 mL) additional water to facilitate blending. Avoid making it too runny. Place mangoes in a large bowl and pour mixture over top.

2. In a small pan, heat oil over high heat until a couple of mustard seeds thrown in start to sputter. Add all the mustard seeds and cover quickly. When the seeds stop popping, in a few seconds, uncover, reduce heat to medium and add coriander and curry leaves. Sauté for 30 seconds and pour over mangoes. Sprinkle with peanuts and mix gently. Serve chilled or at room temperature.

Andhra-Style Fruit Salad

Serves 4 to 6

Split peas add an unexpected crunch to this fruit salad, which is further enhanced with jaggery. It's an exotic and tasty dish that is a great addition to a buffet table.

Tip

This salad is best served soon after it is made, as prolonged refrigeration toughens the dal. You can complete Step 2 early in the day and reserve at room temperature. Assemble up to 1 hour before serving and hold at room temperature.

1 cup	split yellow peas (channa dal)	250 mL
1/3 cup	jaggery (gur) or packed brown sugar	75 mL
3/4 tsp	salt	4 mL
1/2 tsp	fennel seeds (saunf), crushed	2 mL
1/4 tsp	cardamom seeds, powdered	1 mL
1 1/2 cups	chopped apples, 1/2-inch (1 cm) cubes, preferably Granny Smith	375 mL
1	can (11 oz/310 mL) mandarin oranges, drained, or 1 orange, peeled and sectioned	1
1/2 cup	seedless grapes	125 mL
1/4 cup	raisins	50 mL
1/4 cup	skinned raw peanuts, toasted	50 mL
1/2 cup	shredded coconut, preferably fresh (or frozen, thawed), divided	125 mL
3 tbsp	freshly squeezed lemon juice	45 mL

1. Clean and pick through dal for any small stones and grit. Rinse. Soak in water to cover by 2 inches (5 cm) for 3 to 4 hours. Drain.

2. In a saucepan over medium heat, melt jaggery in 3/4 cup (175 mL) water. Drain and add dal. Increase heat to medium-high. Cook, stirring frequently, until syrup is absorbed, 12 to 15 minutes. Add salt in the last few minutes of cooking. Remove from heat and stir in fennel and cardamom.

3. Transfer to a bowl and let cool to room temperature. Stir in apples, oranges, grapes, raisins, peanuts, 6 tbsp (90 mL) of the coconut and lemon juice. Mix well. Serve at room temperature garnished with remaining coconut.

Burrani
Eggplant Onion Yogurt Salad

¼ cup	oil, divided	50 mL
1 lb	eggplant, peeled and cut into 3-by ½-inch (7.5 by 1 cm) sticks	500 g
1 cup	thinly sliced onion (lengthwise slices)	250 mL
4 cups	plain nonfat yogurt	1 L
¾ tsp	salt or to taste	4 mL
½ tsp	freshly ground black pepper	2 mL
½ tsp	cayenne pepper	2 mL
1 tbsp	minced garlic	15 mL

Serves 8

This traditional accompaniment to meat pulaos *is typical of Muslim cuisine. It is both a side dish and a raita in one.*

1. In a large skillet, heat 1 tsp (5 mL) of the oil over medium heat. Add eggplant and sauté until soft, 6 to 8 minutes. Transfer to a bowl. Let cool to room temperature.

2. In same skillet, heat remaining oil over medium-high heat. Add onion and sauté until golden, 5 to 6 minutes. Add to eggplant.

3. In a large bowl, whisk yogurt to a creamy consistency. Add salt, black and cayenne peppers and garlic. Stir into eggplant-onion mixture. Mix well and chill for 2 hours for flavors to develop. Serve with biriyani or any meat pulao.

Mango Pachadi

Serves 6 to 8

Pachadi *is the South Indian equivalent of the northern raita-yogurt salad. Yogurt, either plain or as a salad, is a very important component of an Indian meal and allows for a lot of creativity. This recipe comes from Coorg.*

2 cups	plain yogurt	500 mL
¼ cup	grated coconut, preferably fresh (or frozen, thawed)	50 mL
2 tsp	minced peeled gingerroot	10 mL
1 tbsp	granulated sugar	15 mL
1 tsp	minced green chiles, preferably serranos	5 mL
½ tsp	salt or to taste	2 mL
2	ripe but firm mangoes, peeled and cut into ¾-inch (2 cm) pieces (about 2 cups/500 mL)	2
2 tbsp	oil	25 mL
1 tsp	dark mustard seeds	5 mL
2	sprigs fresh curry leaves, stripped (20 to 25 leaves)	2
1 tbsp	thinly sliced garlic	15 mL
¼ cup	minced shallot	50 mL

1. In a bowl, whisk together yogurt, coconut, ginger, sugar, chiles and salt until smooth. Mix in mangoes.

2. In a small pan, heat oil over high heat until a couple of mustard seeds thrown in start to sputter. Add all the mustard seeds and cover quickly. When the seeds stop popping, in a few seconds, uncover, reduce heat to medium and add curry leaves, garlic and shallots. Sauté until shallots are soft and lightly colored, 3 to 4 minutes.

3. Add to yogurt and stir well. Chill pachadi for at least 30 minutes before serving.

Andhra Tomato Chutney

2 tbsp	oil	25 mL
¾ tsp	dark mustard seeds	4 mL
1½ tsp	cumin seeds	7 mL
4	dried Indian red chiles	4
2 tbsp	minced garlic	25 mL
2 tbsp	minced green chiles, preferably serranos	25 mL
⅓ cup	minced onion	75 mL
3 tbsp	split yellow peas (channa dal), picked over and rinsed	45 mL
2 cups	chunky chopped tomatoes, preferably plum (Roma) (about 1 lb/500 g)	500 mL
½ tsp	granulated sugar	2 mL
¼ tsp	salt	1 mL
2 tsp	unsalted Thai tamarind purée	10 mL

1. In a saucepan, heat oil over high heat until a couple of mustard seeds thrown in start to sputter. Add all the mustard seeds and cover quickly. When the seeds stop popping, in a few seconds, uncover, reduce heat to medium and add cumin and red chiles. Sauté for 30 seconds. Add garlic and green chiles and sauté for 1 minute. Add onion and channa dal and sauté for 2 minutes.

2. Add tomatoes, sugar and salt. Reduce heat to medium-low. Cover and cook until tomatoes are soft, 6 to 8 minutes. Mash with back of a spoon. Let cool slightly and transfer to a blender. Add tamarind and 2 tbsp (25 mL) water. Blend until smooth.

3. Serve as a dipping chutney or to accompany rice crêpes (dosa).

Makes about 2 cups (500 mL)

Tomato chutney is a favorite condiment across the subcontinent, with many names and as many versions. This one from the southern state of Andhra Pradesh, uses split yellow peas for flavor and as a thickener. It is served with dosa, utthapam and other snacks. I have discovered it is also a tasty sandwich spread, particularly with chicken.

Tip
Chutney can be refrigerated in an airtight container for up to 1 week.

Bananas with Cardamom Yogurt

Serves 6 to 8

This is delicious as a raita or can be eaten as a light meal with a warm Indian bread.

3	large ripe bananas	3
6	green cardamom pods, seeds only, powdered	6
3 tbsp	grated or shaved jaggery (gur) or brown sugar	45 mL
4 cups	plain nonfat yogurt	1 L
3 tbsp	chopped walnuts	45 mL

1. Peel bananas, cut into pieces and place in a bowl. Mash. Add cardamom and jaggery and mix.

2. Fold in yogurt and walnuts. Chill well before serving.

Carrot Chutney

Makes 1½ cups (375 mL)

This simple everyday chutney is a great way to boost your daily vegetable intake.

2 tbsp	oil, divided	25 mL
½ tsp	asafetida (hing)	2 mL
2 tbsp	yellow lentils (toor dal), picked over and rinsed	25 mL
1 tbsp	split white lentils (urad dal), picked over and rinsed	15 mL
3	dried Indian red chiles	3
1½ cups	grated peeled carrots	375 mL
½ cup	chopped tomato	125 mL
2 tsp	minced green chiles, preferably serranos	10 mL
3 to 4 tbsp	cilantro, chopped	45 to 60 mL
½ tsp	salt or to taste	2 mL

1. In a skillet, heat 1 tbsp (1 mL) of the oil over medium heat. Add asafetida, toor and urad dals and red chiles. Sauté until dals turn golden, about 1 minute. Let cool slightly and transfer to a spice grinder. Grind to a fine powder and set aside.

2. In same skillet, heat remaining oil. Add carrots, tomato, green chiles and cilantro and sauté for 2 minutes. Transfer to a blender and purée. Add salt and powdered spice mix and blend to a smooth paste.

3. Serve with appetizers or as a dip for vegetables and pita crisps.

Brown Coconut Chutney

1 tbsp	oil	15 mL
2 tsp	dark mustard seeds	10 mL
4 tsp	split yellow peas (channa dal), picked over and rinsed	20 mL
1 tbsp	split white lentils (urad dal), picked over and rinsed	15 mL
2	dried Indian red chiles, broken in half	2
3	green chiles, preferably serranos, cut in half	3
½ tsp	asafetida (hing)	2 mL
¾ cup	grated coconut, preferably fresh (or frozen, thawed), or 1 cup (250 mL) dry unsweetened coconut powder (see Tip, right)	175 mL
1	piece (1 inch/2.5 cm square) tamarind brick, cut into 3 to 4 pieces, seeds removed	1
½ cup	cilantro, leaves and soft stems	125 mL
½ tsp	salt or to taste	2 mL

1. In a skillet, heat oil over high heat until a couple of mustard seeds thrown in start to sputter. Add all the mustard seeds and cover quickly. When the seeds stop popping, in a few seconds, uncover, reduce heat to medium and add channa and urad dals, red and green chiles and asafetida. Sauté until dals turn golden, 1 minute. Let cool slightly. Transfer mixture to a spice grinder and grind to a powder.

2. In a food processor, combine coconut, tamarind, cilantro and salt. Add powdered spices and process to mix well. Add just enough water to make a smooth paste.

3. Serve as a condiment with Indian snacks.

Makes about 1 cup (250 mL)

A classic coconut preparation from the south, this is a multipurpose condiment. Traditionally served with rice crêpes (dosas) and steamed rice cakes (idlis), I find it is a tasty accompaniment to all types of finger foods.

Tip

Dry unsweetened coconut powder is available in Indian markets. Refrigerate in a resealable freezer bag for up to 2 years.

Coconut Chutney

1 tbsp + ½ tsp	oil, divided	15 mL + 2 mL
1 tbsp	split yellow peas (channa dal), picked over and rinsed	15 mL
1 cup	dry unsweetened coconut powder (see Tip, page 403)	250 mL
2	dried Indian red chiles, 1 broken into pieces	2
¼ cup	freshly squeezed lime or lemon juice	50 mL
½ tsp	salt or to taste	2 mL
¾ tsp	dark mustard seeds	4 mL
¾ tsp	cumin seeds	4 mL
2 tsp	minced peeled gingerroot	10 mL
2	sprigs fresh curry leaves, stripped (20 to 25 leaves)	2

1. In a skillet, heat ½ tsp (2 mL) of the oil over medium heat. Add channa dal and sauté, 2 to 3 minutes. Set aside.

2. In same skillet, toast coconut and broken chile. Stir continuously to prevent burning. When coconut turns 2 or 3 shades darker, remove from heat. Let cool and transfer to a blender.

3. Add reserved channa dal, lime juice, salt and 1 cup (250 mL) water and blend to a smooth paste. Transfer to a bowl.

4. Heat remaining 1 tbsp (15 m) of oil over high heat until a couple of mustard seeds thrown in start to sputter. Add all the mustard seeds and cover quickly. When the seeds stop popping, in a few seconds, uncover, reduce heat to medium and add cumin seeds, remaining chile and ginger. Stir for 30 seconds and pour over top coconut mixture. Stir to mix well.

Servings 8

This is the classic condiment served with South Indian foods such as rice crêpes (dosas), steamed rice cakes (idlis) and lentil donuts (vadai).

Tip
Chutney can be refrigerated in an airtight container for up to 1 week. It can also be frozen for up to 3 months.

Sheela's Red Coconut Chutney

Makes about ³⁄₄ cup (175 mL)

This is a milder Mangalore version of the fiery red coconut chutney of Goa. The recipe comes from my dear friend and great cook Sheela, who is from Mangalore. You can increase the heat in this recipe by adding more dried red chiles.

½ tsp	oil	2 mL
3	dried Indian red chiles, broken into pieces	3
2 tsp	split yellow peas (channa dal), picked over and rinsed	10 mL
1	3-inch (7.5 cm) long green chile, preferably serrano, cut into pieces	1
³⁄₄ cup	grated coconut, preferably fresh (or frozen, thawed)	175 mL
3 tbsp	unsalted Thai tamarind purée	45 mL
¼ tsp	salt or to taste	1 mL

1. In a small skillet, heat oil over medium heat. Add red chiles and dal and sauté until dal is golden, 1 to 2 minutes.

2. Transfer to a blender and grind to a powder. Add green chile, coconut, tamarind and salt. Blend to a smooth paste, scraping down sides of blender as necessary.

Sheela's Green Coconut Chutney

Makes about ³⁄₄ cup (175 mL)

Coconut-based chutneys abound along the west coast. Most include dried red chiles ("red chutney") and/or fresh green chiles and cilantro ("green chutney"). Green chutney is mild, and the red tends to be hotter. You can adjust the heat to suit your taste.

3 to 4	green chiles, preferably serranos, cut into pieces	3 to 4
1	piece (1 inch/2.5 cm square) peeled gingerroot, cut into pieces	1
³⁄₄ cup	grated coconut, fresh or frozen, thawed	175 mL
2 to 3 tbsp	plain yogurt	25 to 45 mL
1½ cups	cilantro	375 mL
¼ tsp	salt	1 mL
2 to 3 tbsp	freshly squeezed lime or lemon juice	25 to 45 mL

1. In a blender, blend together chiles and ginger until minced. Add coconut, 2 tbsp (25 mL) of the yogurt, half of the cilantro, salt and 2 tbsp (25 mL) of the lime juice. Blend for 30 seconds. Add remaining cilantro. Blend to a smooth paste, scraping down sides of blender as necessary. If more liquid is required, add the remaining yogurt. Add remaining lime juice to taste. Use as a sandwich spread, serve with appetizers or use as a dip.

Red Bell Pepper Chutney

2 tsp	oil, divided	10 mL
1/3 cup	split yellow peas (channa dal), picked over and rinsed	75 mL
2	dried Indian red chiles	2
1	red bell pepper, chopped	1
2 tsp	chopped raw cashews	10 mL
2 tsp	unsalted Thai tamarind purée	10 mL
1/4 tsp	salt or to taste	1 mL

1. In a skillet, heat 1 tsp (5 mL) of the oil over medium heat. Add channa dal and chiles and sauté until dal is golden, about 2 minutes. Set aside.

2. In the same skillet, heat remaining oil over medium heat. Add bell pepper and sauté until soft, 3 to 4 minutes. Transfer to blender.

3. Add dal mixture, cashews, tamarind and salt and blend to a smooth paste. Serve with appetizers.

Makes 3/4 cup (175 mL)

Another one of my expert South Indian friends, Sudha, shared this fabulous chutney with me at a cooking session in her kitchen in Houston. It is extremely versatile. Aside from serving it as a dipping sauce, I have served it as a dressing for shrimp salad and drizzled it over deviled eggs. It is also delicious with grilled fish.

Tip

Chutney can be stored in an airtight container in the refrigerator for up to 10 days.

Usha's Onion Chutney

Makes 2 cups (500 mL)

My friend Usha is renowned for her South Indian specialties. This is her recipe for the onion chutney that is a traditional accompaniment to the signature South Indian rice crêpe (dosa).

Tip

When spooning chutney out of a jar, make sure the spoon is absolutely dry. If even a hint of moisture is introduced, the condiment will grow mold. Also, never return any unused chutney to the jar because once it has been removed, it is exposed to bacteria in the atmosphere. Instead, cover and refrigerate the unused portion.

3 tbsp	oil	45 mL
4 cups	chopped onions	1 L
1	sprig fresh curry leaves, stripped (12 to 15 leaves)	1
6	cloves garlic	6
6	dried Indian red chiles, broken in half	6
2 tbsp	roasted peanuts	25 mL
¼ cup	cilantro leaves	50 mL
1	piece (1½ by 1 inch/4 by 2.5 cm) tamarind brick, cut into 3 or 4 pieces, seeds removed	1
1 tsp	granulated sugar	5 mL
½ tsp	salt or to taste	2 mL

1. In a skillet, heat oil over medium heat. Add onions and sauté until golden, 12 to 15 minutes.

2. Add curry leaves, garlic and chiles and sauté until garlic is soft, 2 to 3 minutes. Transfer onion mixture to a large bowl and stir in peanuts, cilantro and tamarind.

3. Transfer part of mixture to blender and add sugar and salt. Blend with ½ cup (125 mL) water. Continue to add remaining mixture and about ¾ cup (175 mL) additional water until it is puréed to a smooth thick paste.

4. Serve immediately as a condiment or transfer to a jar and refrigerate for up to 10 days.

Ginger Chutney

- *Wok or deep-fryer*
- *Candy/deep-fry thermometer*

	Oil for deep-frying	
¾ cup	julienned peeled gingerroot	175 mL
3 tbsp + 1 tsp	split yellow peas (channa dal), picked over and rinsed, divided	45 mL + 5 mL
6	dried Indian red chiles, broken in half, divided	6
2 tsp	coriander seeds	10 mL
1½ tsp	dark mustard seeds, divided	7 mL
1 tsp	cumin seeds	5 mL
4 to 5	sprigs fresh curry leaves, stripped (about 40 leaves), divided	4 to 5
2 tbsp	jaggery (gur)	25 mL
1 tbsp	tomato paste	15 mL
½ tsp	salt or to taste	2 mL

1. In a wok or deep-fryer, heat oil to 350°F (180°C). Add ginger and deep-fry until crisp, 3 to 4 minutes. Remove with a large-holed strainer and drain on paper towels. Reserve oil.

2. Transfer 1 tsp (5 mL) of the deep-frying oil to a small skillet. Add 3 tbsp (45 mL) of the dal, 5 chiles, coriander, 1 tsp (5 mL) of the mustard seeds, cumin and 30 curry leaves and sauté until aromatic, 2 to 3 minutes. Transfer to a blender and blend to a fine powder.

3. Add jaggery, tomato paste, salt, fried ginger and ⅓ cup (75 mL) water and blend to a thick purée, scraping down sides of blender as you blend.

4. Transfer 1 tbsp (15 mL) of the deep-frying oil to a small pan over high heat until a couple of mustard seeds thrown in start to sputter. Add the remaining mustard seeds and cover quickly. When the seeds stop popping, in a few seconds, uncover, reduce heat to medium and add remaining chile, 1 tsp (5 mL) of the channa dal and remaining curry leaves. Sauté for 1 minute and pour into chutney. Stir to mix.

Makes 1 cup (250 mL)

HOT

An Andhra staple, this is a hot ginger chutney packed with flavor. If you prefer, you can reduce the number of chiles. I love to use it as a sandwich spread on a chicken or turkey sandwich. The recipe for this condiment varies from family to family, so tinker with it to suit your taste.

Tips

The chutney can be refrigerated in an airtight container for up to 3 weeks.

If using as a dipping sauce, add an additional 2 to 3 tbsp (25 to 45 mL) water when blending.

W

Gajar Chi Koshumbri

Maharashtrian Carrot Salad

Serves 4 to 6

This simple salad sparkles with flavor and crunch. The yogurt acts as a dressing, making this dish suitable to serve with grilled chicken or fish.

3 cups	grated peeled carrots	750 mL
½ cup	roasted peanuts, coarsely chopped	125 mL
1 cup	plain nonfat yogurt	250 mL
2 to 3 tsp	minced green chiles, preferably serranos	10 to 15 mL
1½ tsp	granulated sugar	7 mL
½ tsp	salt or to taste	2 mL
2 tsp	oil	10 mL
¼ tsp	asafetida (hing)	1 mL
1½ tsp	cumin seeds	7 mL
¼ cup	cilantro, coarsely chopped, divided	50 mL

1. In a large bowl, toss together carrots and peanuts.

2. In another bowl, stir together yogurt, chiles, sugar and salt. Pour over carrots.

3. In a small pan, heat oil over medium heat. Add asafetida and sizzle for 30 seconds. Add cumin and sauté until slightly darker and fragrant, 30 to 40 seconds. Pour over yogurt mixture. Add 3 tbsp (45 mL) of the cilantro. Toss to mix well.

4. Transfer to a serving dish. Garnish with remaining cilantro. Chill before serving.

Green Mango Kachumbar

2 cups	diced red onions	500 mL
2 cups	diced peeled green mangoes	500 mL
4 to 5 tsp	minced green chiles, preferably serranos	20 to 25 mL
1/2 cup	cilantro leaves, chopped	125 mL
2 tbsp	crushed dried mint	25 mL
1 cup	white vinegar	250 mL
	Granulated sugar to taste, optional	

Makes 5 cups (1.25 L)

Kachumbar or kosumbri (in Maharashtra) is a salad-like relish of finely chopped ingredients with a variety of textures and tastes that create harmony on the tongue.

1. In a bowl, mix together onions, mango, chiles, cilantro and mint. (If mango is too tart, add a little sugar to taste.)

2. In a small pan, bring vinegar to a boil over medium heat. Pour over mixture. Mix well and refrigerate several hours to combine flavors.

3. Serve as topping for fish or to accompany grilled chicken or meat.

Mango Citrus Chutney

1 cup	diced peeled ripe mango	250 mL
1/2 cup	cider vinegar	125 mL
1/3 cup	granulated sugar	75 mL
3 tbsp	minced shallots	45 mL
2 tsp	minced peeled gingerroot	10 mL
2 tsp	minced green chiles, preferably serranos	10 mL
1 tbsp	finely minced mixed citrus peel, such as lime, lemon or orange	15 mL
1/4 tsp	salt	1 mL
1 tbsp	oil	15 mL
1/2 tsp	nigella seeds (kalaunji)	2 mL
1/4 tsp	fenugreek seeds (methi)	2 mL

Makes 1 cup (250 mL)

I love the unusual citrusy note of this chutney and find it a perfect accompaniment to pork and grilled shrimp. Try to find a mango that is not fibrous and is fully ripened.

1. In a nonreactive pan, mix together mango, vinegar, sugar, shallots, ginger, chiles, citrus peel and salt. Bring to a boil over medium heat. Reduce heat slightly to maintain a gentle boil. Cook until reduced to a thick purée, about 15 minutes.

2. In a small pan, heat oil over medium heat. Add nigella and sauté until fragrant, 20 seconds. Add fenugreek and sauté for 10 seconds. Pour into chutney and mix. Transfer to a clean jar and let cool. Store tightly covered in the refrigerator for up to 10 days.

Kachumbar

Fresh Salad with Dhansak

1	medium-size cucumber, peeled	1
1 cup	chopped ripe tomatoes	250 mL
1/2 cup	chopped onion	125 mL
1/4 cup	cilantro leaves, chopped	50 mL
1/4 tsp	salt or to taste	1 mL
3 to 4 cups	shredded lettuce	750 mL to 1 L
3	radishes, sliced thin	3
	Lime or lemon wedges	

1. Cut cucumber in half lengthwise and scoop out seeds. Slice into half-moons.

2. In a bowl, mix together cucumber, tomatoes, onion, cilantro and salt.

3. Serve on a bed of shredded lettuce. Garnish with radish slices and lime wedges.

Serves 6 to 8

This salad is always a part of the Dhansak meal, which must include brown rice and Dhansak meatballs (see Parsi Meatballs, page 71).

Gor Amli ni Kachumbar

Special Relish for Dhansak

1/3 cup	jaggery (gur) or brown sugar	75 mL
1/4 cup	unsalted Thai tamarind purée	50 mL
1/4 cup	chopped onion	50 mL
1/4 cup	cilantro, chopped	50 mL
1 tsp	minced green chiles, preferably serranos	5 mL
1/4 tsp	salt or to taste	1 mL

1. In a small saucepan, mix together jaggery, tamarind and 1/3 cup (75 mL) hot water. Cook over medium-low heat until jaggery is dissolved.

2. Remove from heat and stir in onion, cilantro, chiles and salt.

Serves 8

This special relish can be substituted for the plain Kachumbar (see recipe, above) or served in addition to it when serving the Dhansak meal.

Boondi Kachumbar

Crunchy Chickpea Drops

Serves 8

This tangy, crunchy relish is delicious as an accompaniment to any meal. To retain the crunchy texture, assemble just before serving.

3 cups	boondi (see Tips, page 92)	750 mL
¼ cup	grated coconut, preferably fresh or frozen, thawed	50 mL
2 to 3 tbsp	minced green chiles, preferably serranos	25 to 45 mL
¼ cup	sliced green onions, with some green	50 mL
¼ cup	freshly squeezed lime or lemon juice	50 mL
½ tsp	salt to or to taste	2 mL

1. In a bowl, mix together boondi, coconut, chiles, green onions, lime juice and salt. Toss and serve immediately.

Dill Potato Raita

Serves 4 to 6

This is a winning combination. Cool and refreshing, it would make a wonderful accompaniment to a barbecue.

Variations

Double the potato and reduce the yogurt mixture. Serve as a potato salad.

Purée half the raita. Stir in the remaining chunky raita and serve as a chilled soup.

1 lb	all-purpose potatoes (about 4)	500 g
4 cups	plain nonfat yogurt	1 L
½ cup	chopped dill or 4 tsp (20 mL) dried dill	125 mL
1 tsp	salt	5 mL
1 tsp	granulated sugar	5 mL
1 tsp	freshly squeezed lime or lemon juice	5 mL
⅓ cup	toasted peanuts or walnuts, coarsely chopped	75 mL

1. In a saucepan of boiling water, cook whole potatoes until tender, 20 to 25 minutes. Drain and when cool enough to handle, peel and cut into ½-inch (1 cm) cubes.

2. In a large bowl, stir yogurt until smooth and creamy. Stir in dill, salt, sugar and lime juice. Mix in potatoes and peanuts. Chill well before serving.

Corn and Green Bean Raita

1 cup	blanched green beans, cut into ¼-inch (0.5 cm) pieces	250 mL
1 cup	corn kernels, fresh or frozen, thawed	250 mL
½ cup	boiled cubed (½ inch/1 cm) peeled potato, optional	125 mL
1½ cups	plain nonfat yogurt	375 mL
½ tsp	salt	2 mL
½ tsp	cayenne pepper	2 mL
½ tsp	granulated sugar	2 mL
1 tbsp	oil	15 mL
1 tsp	dark mustard seeds	5 mL
2	dried Indian red chiles	2
1 tsp	split yellow peas (channa dal), picked over and rinsed	5 mL
1 tsp	split white lentils (urad dal), picked over and rinsed	5 mL
Pinch	asafetida (hing)	Pinch
1	sprig fresh curry leaves, stripped (10 to 15 leaves)	1

Serves 6 to 8

Vegetables never tasted better. Summer corn and green beans, smothered in spiced yogurt seasoned with the traditional South Indian tempering spices, bursts with flavor. The best of the north and the south.

1. In a large bowl, mix together green beans, corn and potato, if using.

2. In another bowl, stir together yogurt, salt, cayenne and sugar. Pour over vegetables and mix.

3. In a small pan, heat oil over high heat until a couple of mustard seeds thrown in start to sputter. Add all the mustard seeds and cover quickly. When the seeds stop popping, in a few seconds, uncover, reduce heat to medium and add chiles, channa and urad dals, asafetida and curry leaves. Stir for 30 seconds and pour over yogurt mixture. Toss to mix thoroughly. Chill before serving.

Bhindi Raita

Okra Raita

1 ½ cups	plain nonfat yogurt, stirred to a creamy consistency	375 mL
¼ cup	grated coconut, preferably fresh or frozen, thawed	50 mL
2 to 3 tbsp	minced green chiles, preferably serranos	25 to 45 mL
1 tsp	dark mustard seeds, crushed	5 mL
2 lbs	okra	1 kg
	Oil for deep-frying	
	Salt and freshly ground black pepper to taste	

Serves 6 to 8

Perhaps a little more work than most raitas, it is nevertheless well worth the extra effort. The crunch of the okra is astonishing with the cool of the yogurt.

Tips

Do not mix yogurt with okra until ready to serve, as okra will become soggy.

Leftover raita is wonderful mixed with rice.

1. In a bowl, stir together yogurt, coconut, chiles and mustard seeds. Set aside for 30 minutes or refrigerate for up to 12 hours to allow flavors to develop.

2. Rinse okra and wipe dry. Cut into ¼-inch (0.5 cm) thick slices.

3. In a wok or skillet, heat 2 to 3 inches (5 to 7.5 cm) oil over medium-high heat. Add okra and fry, in 3 to 4 batches to avoid overcrowding, until crisp, 6 to 8 minutes per batch. Remove with a large-holed strainer and drain on paper towels. Transfer to large bowl and toss with salt and pepper. This can be done up to 1 hour ahead.

4. When ready to serve, pour yogurt over okra and serve immediately.

Hari Chutney
Cilantro Mint Chutney

4 cups	loosely packed cilantro leaves and soft stems	1 L
½ cup	mint leaves	125 mL
⅓ cup	freshly squeezed lime or lemon juice or more to taste	75 mL
3 to 4 tsp	minced green chiles, preferably serranos	15 to 20 mL
2 tsp	granulated sugar	10 mL
2 tsp	minced peeled gingerroot	10 mL
1 tsp	minced garlic	5 mL
1 tsp	cumin seeds	5 mL
½ tsp	salt	2 mL

Makes 1 cup (250 mL)

This chutney or a variation of it is a staple in most Indian homes. It is served as a dipping sauce with a multitude of Indian snacks and finger foods. It is also used as a sandwich spread.

1. In a blender, combine cilantro, mint, lime juice, chiles, sugar, ginger, garlic, cumin seeds, salt and 3 tbsp (45mL) water. Blend to a smooth paste, adding a little more water if necessary. Scrape sides of blender frequently to blend well. (For storing info, see page 405.)

Green Coconut Chutney

3 cups	grated coconut, preferably fresh (or frozen, thawed)	750 mL
12	cloves garlic	12
4	2-inch (5 cm) long green chiles, preferably serranos	4
2 tsp	cumin seeds	10 mL
1 tsp	granulated sugar	5 mL
1 tsp	salt or to taste	5 mL
3 to 4 tbsp	freshly squeezed lime or lemon juice	45 to 60 mL
4 cups	loosely packed cilantro leaves and soft stems	1 L

Makes about 3 cups (750 mL)

This fabulous chutney is served with a variety of Indian snacks, as a thick dipping sauce or as a sandwich spread. I have also used it with great success to stuff chicken breasts.

1. In a food processor, process coconut, garlic, chiles, cumin, sugar, and salt until coarse. Add lime juice. Add handfuls of cilantro and continue processing until fine. Scrape sides of bowl frequently to blend well. Transfer to a bowl. (For storing, info see page 405.)

Green Tomato Chutney

Makes 1 cup (250 mL)

There are no commercial tomato farms in India — tomatoes are grown in market gardens or small co-operatives. The tomatoes are far from perfect in shape and vary in taste depending on the weather. Green tomatoes are not uncommon, as they tend to be in North America. I like to use tomatillos as a substitute, as they are just as tart and have a wonderful flavor.

Tips

This is a "fresh chutney" and can be refrigerated, tightly covered, for up to 3 days. Fresh chutneys are those that are very lightly cooked, and the spices and other flavorings used are mainly for taste rather than for long-term preservation. Hence, storage life is usually just a few days.

Serve with Indian snacks or use as a dipping sauce with vegetables, chips or grilled chicken.

2 tbsp	dry unsweetened coconut powder (see Tip, page 403)	25 mL
1 tbsp	sesame seeds	15 mL
1 tbsp	oil, divided	15 mL
4	2-inch (5 cm) long green chiles, preferably serranos, cut into ½-inch (1 cm) pieces	4
8 oz	tomatillos, husks removed, or green tomatoes, chopped	250 g
½ tsp	dark mustard seeds	2 mL
Pinch	asafetida (hing)	Pinch
½ tsp	salt or to taste	2 mL

1. In a heavy skillet over medium-low heat, spread coconut powder and heat, stirring continuously, until pinkish golden, 2 to 3 minutes. Do not allow to burn. Tip into a bowl and set aside.

2. In the same skillet, toast sesame seeds until just beginning to color. Remove and set aside.

3. Heat 2 tsp (10 mL) of the oil in the same skillet. Add chiles and sauté for 1 minute. Add tomatillos and sauté until soft, 3 to 4 minutes.

4. Transfer chiles and tomatillos to a blender. Add coconut and sesame seeds and blend until smooth. Return to skillet.

5. In a small pan, heat remaining oil over high heat until a couple of mustard seeds thrown in start to sputter. Add all the mustard seeds and cover quickly. When the seeds stop popping, in a few seconds, uncover, reduce heat to medium and add asafetida. Stir and pour into tomatillo mixture. Add salt and mix well. Transfer to serving bowl.

Red Chile Garlic Chutney

30	dried Indian red chiles (see Tips, right)	30
1 tsp	oil	5 mL
6	cloves garlic, coarsely chopped	6
1 tbsp	dry unsweetened coconut powder, optional (see Tip, page 403)	15 mL
2 tsp	freshly squeezed lime or lemon juice	10 mL
¾ tsp	granulated sugar	4 mL
¼ tsp	salt	1 mL

1. Soak chiles in 1 cup (250 mL) very hot water for 30 minutes. Drain, reserving soaking water. Cut into pieces and transfer to a blender.

2. In a small skillet, heat oil over medium heat. Add garlic and sauté for 2 minutes. Do not allow to brown. Add to blender. Add coconut, if using, to blender. Add lime juice, sugar and salt. Add ¼ cup (50 mL) of the reserved soaking water and blend to a paste. If necessary, add a little more soaking water. Paste should be thick but puréed.

3. Transfer to jar and refrigerate for up to 1 month.

**Makes
⅓ cup (75 mL)**

HOT

This fiery chutney is an essential part of chaat dishes and is to be used with caution.

Tips

The Mexican arbol chile pepper can be substituted for Indian chiles. However, because they are twice as potent, remove seeds from half the chiles by breaking chile in half and shaking out the seeds. Do not touch seeds.

When spooning chutney out of a jar, make sure the spoon is absolutely dry. If even a hint of moisture is introduced, the condiment will grow mold. Also, never return any unused chutney to the jar because once it has been removed, it is exposed to bacteria in the atmosphere. Instead, cover and refrigerate the unused portion.

Lemon Chutney

10	thin-skinned lemons (see Tips, right)	10
3 tbsp	salt	45 mL
1 cup	granulated sugar	250 mL
1 cup	cider vinegar	250 mL
1 cup	untoasted sesame oil	250 mL
3 tbsp	paprika	45 mL
1 tbsp	cayenne pepper	15 mL
1	piece (2½ by 2 inches/6 by 5 cm) peeled gingerroot, thinly sliced and partially smashed	1
6	large cloves garlic, smashed	6
¼ cup	raisins, preferably golden	50 mL

1. Scrub lemons and wipe dry. Slice into ¼-inch (0.5 cm) rings, preferably on a nonporous board. Discard seeds. Place in a nonreactive bowl and rub salt into slices. Set aside for at least 2 hours.

2. In a nonreactive saucepan, combine sugar, vinegar and any juices collected from the lemons. Bring to a boil over medium heat, stirring until sugar is dissolved. Reduce heat to low and cook until a thin syrup forms, about 10 minutes.

3. Meanwhile, in a bowl, combine oil, paprika, cayenne, ginger and garlic. Stir into sugar syrup. Add lemon slices and raisins. Cook until mixture is slightly thicker, about 10 minutes.

4. Let cool and bottle in sterilized jars. When spooning chutney out of a jar, make sure the spoon is absolutely dry. If even a hint of moisture is introduced the condiment will grow mold. Also, never return any unused chutney to the jar because once it has been removed, it is exposed to bacteria in the atmosphere. Instead, cover and refrigerate the unused portion.

Makes about 6 cups (1.5 L)

This delicious condiment complements both Indian and non-Indian foods. Untoasted sesame oil is used extensively for making chutneys and pickles in the south and the western states. It is known as gingelly oil *and is available in Indian markets.*

Tips

Thin-skinned lemons have smooth skin and lack pores. They are also juicier. Do not buy by size because the largest and prettiest can be the driest.

Although it is typical in North America to suggest processing in a hot water canner, almost all Indian kitchens — including mine — have quite an assortment of homemade pickles and chutneys in their pantries that have not been in a hot water bath and that keep without refrigeration indefinitely at room temperature. Lemon will get softer with longer storage.

Orange Tamarind Chutney

**Makes 1 cup
(250 mL)**

*This assertive condiment
can double as a dressing
for a shredded chicken
salad, be combined with
garbanzos or top a
platter of boiled sliced
potatoes. Multipurpose
and so good!*

Tip

Chutney can be stored
in an airtight container
in the refrigerator for
up to 1 week.

½ cup	unsalted Thai tamarind purée	125 mL
½ cup	loosely packed jaggery (gur)	125 mL
1 tbsp	oil	15 mL
½ tsp	dark mustard seeds	2 mL
¼ tsp	asafetida (hing)	1 mL
2	dried Indian red chiles	2
1½ tsp	split white lentils (urad dal)	7 mL
1	sprig fresh curry leaves, stripped (12 to 15 leaves)	1
1 tbsp	minced green chiles, preferably serranos	15 mL
¼ tsp	fenugreek seeds (methi)	1 mL
	Zest of 1 orange, slivered	
2	oranges, peeled and sectioned	2
2 tbsp	chopped roasted peanuts	25 mL

1. In a nonreactive saucepan, mix together tamarind purée and jaggery. Cook over medium-low heat until mixture thickens like molasses, 6 to 8 minutes. Set aside.

2. In another saucepan or wok, heat oil over high heat until a couple of mustard seeds thrown in start to sputter. Add all the mustard seeds and cover quickly. When the seeds stop popping, in a few seconds, uncover, reduce heat to medium and add asafetida and red chiles. Sauté for 20 seconds. Add dal, curry leaves and green chiles. Sauté for 30 seconds. Add fenugreek seeds and orange zest slivers. Reduce heat to medium and sauté until zest begins to crisp, 2 to 3 minutes.

3. Add orange segments and sauté gently, 2 to 3 minutes.

4. Pour tamarind mixture into oranges and simmer until mixture thickens, 3 to 4 minutes. Stir in peanuts. Let cool and serve at room temperature.

Gor Keri

Diced Sweet Mango Chutney

W

2¼ lbs	unripe green mangoes	1.125 kg
2 tbsp	salt	25 mL
⅓ cup	untoasted sesame oil (see Tips, right)	75 mL
6	dried Indian red chiles	6
½ cup	cayenne pepper	125 mL
3 tbsp	crushed dark mustard seeds	45 mL
1½ tbsp	crushed fenugreek seeds (methi)	22 mL
1 tsp	asafetida (hing)	5 mL
1	stick cinnamon, about 3 inches (7.5 cm) long	1
1 lb	jaggery, chopped into small pieces or grated	500 g

1. Peel mangoes. Hold upright firmly, stem end up. With a sharp knife, cut close to the flat side of seed on both sides, resulting in 2 "cheeks." Cut each cheek lengthwise into ½-inch (1 cm) thick slices. Cut sides around seed and slice. Discard seed. Place in a nonreactive bowl and sprinkle with salt. Rub in well with fingers. Cover and let stand for 2 days at room temperature.

2. Drain on the third day. Line a baking sheet with double layer of paper towels. Spread mango on towels. Let dry for 24 hours.

3. The next day, in a saucepan, heat oil over medium heat. Add chiles and fry for 1 minute. Add cayenne, mustard and fenugreek seeds, asafetida, cinnamon and jaggery. Cook, stirring gently, until jaggery is melted, 6 to 8 minutes. Let cool slightly.

4. Stir in mango and mix well. Serve immediately.

5. Transfer chutney to a sterilized jar and store for up to 1 year.

**Makes
4 cups (1 L)**

HOT

This classic recipe is from Gujarat, where mango is revered. Look for the hardest green mangoes you can find. These are found in the vegetable area and not in the fruit section. This chutney needs four days of preparation but is worth it.

Tips

Untoasted sesame oil is cold-pressed from sesame seeds, not an infusion. It is known as *gingelly oil* and is used as a cooking oil in some southern dishes. Do not substitute Chinese toasted sesame oil, as they are dissimilar.

When serving this or any other chutney, use a clean, dry spoon only, as the slightest bit of moisture will cause mold to form. Never replace chutney once removed from jar. Cover and keep at room temperature to serve again later.

W

Sweet Tamarind Chutney

Makes 3 cups (750 mL)

This chutney is an essential element of chaat. The sour tamarind sweetened with jaggery (unrefined brown sugar) and seasoned with cayenne pepper and black salt has a complexity that enhances almost any dish. It is served in many Indian restaurants in North America as a dip for papadums. There are many variations on this recipe so feel free to experiment with proportions and seasoning ingredients.

Tip
This makes a thickish chutney that can be diluted with water for pouring purposes.

7 oz	tamarind brick (½ brick)	212.5 g
1 cup	lightly packed jaggery (gur)	250 mL
1 tsp	cayenne pepper	5 mL
1 tsp	cumin powder	5 mL
1 tsp	ground ginger	5 mL
½ tsp	black salt (kala namak)	2 mL

1. Break tamarind into small pieces. Place in a bowl and pour 2 cups (500 mL) very hot water over top. Soak for 30 minutes. Soften pieces between fingers and pour into a large-holed strainer set over a bowl, taking care that bottom of strainer is suspended in bowl. Mash either with fingers or with back of spoon to extract as much pulp as possible. Scrape off any pulp from bottom of strainer. Discard solids and seeds. Transfer to a saucepan.

2. Add 1 cup (250 mL) water, jaggery, cayenne, cumin, ginger and black salt. Cook over medium-low heat, stirring, until jaggery is dissolved. Simmer until flavors are blended, 3 to 4 minutes.

3. Let cool before serving.

4. Chutney can stored in a glass jar in the refrigerator for up to 1 year. When spooning chutney out of a jar, make sure the spoon is absolutely dry. If even a hint of moisture is introduced, the condiment will grow mold. Also, never return any unused chutney to the jar because once it has been removed, it is exposed to bacteria in the atmosphere. Instead, cover and refrigerate the unused portion.

Garlic Pickle

½ cup	untoasted sesame oil, divided (see Tip, page 423)	125 mL
½ cup	cayenne pepper	125 mL
2 tsp	powdered fenugreek seeds (methi)	10 mL
3 tbsp	salt	45 mL
1 cup	freshly squeezed lime juice	250 mL
1 cup	vertically sliced garlic	250 mL
1½ tsp	dark mustard seeds	7 mL
2	dried Indian red chiles	2
1	sprig fresh curry leaves, stripped (12 to 15 leaves)	1

1. Set aside 2 tbsp (25 mL) of the oil in a small skillet.

2. In a saucepan, heat remaining oil over medium heat. Add cayenne and fenugreek powder. Sauté for 3 minutes.

3. Add salt and lime juice and cook for 3 minutes. Add garlic and reduce heat to low. Cook for 15 minutes.

4. Heat skillet with reserved oil over high heat until a couple of mustard seeds thrown in start to sputter. Add all the mustard seeds and cover quickly. When the seeds stop popping, in a few seconds, uncover, reduce heat to medium and add chiles and curry leaves. Sauté for 30 seconds and pour into garlic mixture. Let cool and transfer to a glass jar with a tight-fitting lid. Serve immediately or store at room temperature for up to 1 year.

Makes 1½ cups (375 mL)
HOT

Serve this mouthwatering condiment in small quantities to accompany grilled or baked chicken or fish. It's not as hot as you might think, notwithstanding the rather intimidating amount of cayenne! To serve, use a fork to lift out garlic and masala, avoiding flooding the plate with excessive oil.

Tip
When spooning pickles out of a jar, make sure the spoon is absolutely dry. If even a hint of moisture is introduced the condiment will grow mold. Also, never return any unused pickles to the jar because once they have been removed, they are exposed to bacteria in the atmosphere. Instead, cover and refrigerate unused portion.

Gujarati Chile Pickle

1 tbsp	sesame seeds	15 mL
1 tbsp	cumin powder	15 mL
15	long hot green Indian chiles or serrano chiles (see Tip, right)	15
¼ cup	oil	50 mL
1 tsp	granulated sugar	5 mL
¾ tsp	salt	4 mL
¼ cup	freshly squeezed lemon juice	50 mL

1. In a dry skillet, toast sesame seeds over medium-low heat, stirring continuously, until golden, 2 to 3 minutes. Stir in cumin powder and cook for 1 minute. Remove from heat and tip into a bowl.

2. Rinse chiles and wipe dry.

3. In a small wok or saucepan, heat oil over medium heat. Add chiles and fry, turning often with tongs, until skins are slightly charred, 3 to 4 minutes. Step back when frying, as chiles will sputter and pop as they fry. Remove with tongs to bowl with sesame mixture.

4. Sprinkle with sugar and salt. Add lemon juice and mix well.

Makes about 1 ½ cups (375 mL)

This is typical of the type of fresh relish served with simple home-style dishes. These are made almost daily in many homes, in small quantities, and can be refrigerated for a day or two at most. Use milder chiles if you prefer, but for many Indians, the hotter, the better.

Tip

Fresh green chiles are available year-round in Indian markets. Serrano chiles are a good substitute.

Prawn Balchow

**Makes 3 cups
(750 mL)**

HOT

This is a famous condiment from Goa. Along the west coast, it is not uncommon to have seafood, such as fish roe, dried fish, shrimp or little clams, made into fiery oil-based pickles.

The seasonings are always assertive, and they are very salty because salt is the preservative in these condiments. Very small portions are eaten to accompany each mouthful. This is one of my all-time favorites.

Tip

When spooning pickles out of a jar, make sure the spoon is absolutely dry. If even a hint of moisture is introduced, the condiment will grow mold. Also, never return any unused pickles to the jar because once they have been removed, they are exposed to bacteria in the atmosphere. Instead, cover and refrigerate the unused portion.

1 lb	prawns or shrimp, peeled and deveined	500 g
¾ tsp	cumin seeds	4 mL
¾ tsp	black peppercorns	4 mL
6	dried Indian red chiles, broken into pieces	6
1½ tsp	turmeric	7 mL
1 cup	mustard oil	250 mL
2 cups	chopped onions	500 mL
1	sprig fresh curry leaves, stripped (12 to 15 leaves)	1
6	large plum (Roma) tomatoes, cut into quarters	6
6	large cloves garlic, partially smashed	6
1	piece (2½ by 2 inches/6 by 5 cm) peeled gingerroot, coarsely julienned	1
3	green chiles, preferably serranos, cut into ½-inch (1 cm) pieces	3
1 tbsp	salt	15 mL
	Cayenne pepper to taste, optional	

1. Rinse prawns and wipe dry thoroughly. Transfer to a food processor. Process, pulsing 3 to 4 times, until coarsely ground. Set aside.

2. In a spice grinder, grind cumin seeds, peppercorns and red chiles to a fine powder. Mix with turmeric and set aside.

3. In a saucepan, heat oil over high heat until smoking. Remove from heat and let cool for 1 minute (see Tip, page 326). Return saucepan to medium heat. Add onions and sauté until golden, 8 to 10 minutes.

4. Add powdered spices and prawns and sauté for 2 minutes. Add curry leaves and sauté for 1 minute. Add tomatoes, garlic, ginger, green chiles and salt. Reduce heat to medium-low. Simmer, uncovered, until tomatoes are soft and mixture (masala) looks well mixed, 6 to 8 minutes. Add cayenne, if desired. Let cool and transfer to sterilized jars. (This pickle will keep in jars in the refrigerator for up to 3 months.)

Chicken Pickle

2 lbs	bone-in skinless chicken pieces	1 kg
1	stick cinnamon, about 4 inches (10 cm) long	1
15	whole cloves	15
4 tsp	coriander powder	20 mL
1 tbsp	cumin powder	15 mL
2½ tsp	turmeric	12 mL
2 tsp	cayenne pepper	10 mL
2 tsp	salt	10 mL
2 cups	oil, divided	500 mL
2 tbsp	minced peeled gingerroot	25 mL
2 tbsp	minced garlic	25 mL
2½ cups	cider vinegar	625 mL
1½ tsp	freshly ground black pepper	7 mL

1. Rinse chicken and pat dry thoroughly. Cut into about 2-inch (5 cm) pieces, including the bone. Place on paper towel–lined baking sheet and refrigerate, uncovered, for several hours to air-dry. Pat dry again. It is essential that chicken not have any moisture at all or pickle will develop mold.

2. In a bowl, mix together cinnamon, cloves, coriander, cumin, turmeric, cayenne and salt. Set aside.

3. In a saucepan, heat 1 cup (250 mL) of the oil over medium heat. Add ginger and garlic and fry for 2 minutes. Add spice mixture and cook for 1 minute. Add chicken and fry until partially cooked, 5 to 7 minutes.

4. Add vinegar. Bring to a gentle boil. Reduce heat to medium-low and cook until chicken is no longer pink inside, 2 to 5 minutes for chicken on the bone, less if using boneless chicken (see Variation, right). Add pepper.

5. In another saucepan, heat remaining 1 cup (250 mL) of oil over high heat until smoking. Remove from heat and let cool completely.

6. When chicken is cool, transfer to wide-mouth jars with the extra masala liquid and oil. Shake or tap jars to allow contents to settle and remove any air bubbles. Pour in cooled oil to cover completely. Refrigerate for at least 24 hours before serving.

7. To serve, remove pieces of chicken with a fork, allowing excess oil to drain. Chicken will be coated with sufficient masala. (Chicken pickle will keep in jars in the refrigerator for up to 3 months.)

Makes about 3½ lbs (1.75 kg)

HOT

I have had this recipe for more than 40 years and made it often when I lived in India. I included it in a "Gifts from an Indian Kitchen" class that I taught several years ago, and it was an instant winner. The enormous amount of oil is a must in all pickles, as it is a preservative, which allows otherwise perishable ingredients, such as chicken to be stored for months.

Tip
Chicken pickle and similar highly seasoned condiments are eaten in small amounts with simple home-style meals, such as lightly seasoned dal, steamed rice and lightly cooked vegetables.

Variation
Although the traditional recipe calls for chicken on the bone, boneless thighs, cut into 1-inch (2.5 cm) pieces, are a good substitute.

Sweets and Beverages

TO THE WESTERNER, INDIAN DESSERTS are esoteric and a little strange. Many claim they are too sweet. All of the above is probably true. None of the usual Western dessert ingredients are used — no eggs, no butter, no cream, no chocolate. Instead, a bewildering variety of lentils, vegetables, nuts, chickpea flour and lots of milk are the essence of Indian sweets. Indians love their sweets, and sweet shops selling milk fudge, nut brittle and an assortment of brightly colored squares and rolls dot every town. Street stalls and hole-in-the-wall places sell specialties that people travel long distances to buy. During the major holidays, sweet shops do an enormous amount of business as gaily wrapped boxes are exchanged — much as Christmas cookies and candy are in North America. Most festivals are associated with particular sweets, and these are either homemade or store-bought and shared with friends and family.

MILK-BASED DESSERTS ARE PERHAPS the most popular in the north and the west. Buffalo milk is preferred over cow's milk because it contains about 12% milk fat. This rich milk is slowly reduced over low heat for several hours until it is semi-solid. The resulting mass is known as *khoya* or *mava* and is the main component of many fudge-like sweets called *burfi*.

IN THE EAST, BENGAL IS JUSTLY FAMOUS for its sweets based on the soft Indian cheese panir (*chenna*). The Bengali sweet tooth is well known, and sweets are a daily treat. The famous Bengali sweet yogurt, mishti doi, also deserves mention. Rich, with a distinctive smoky flavor, and intensely sweet, it is a cross between dessert and yogurt. It is made daily in sweet shops and sold in disposable terra-cotta pots, which add to the special flavor of this incredible sweet.

IN SOUTH INDIA, MILK-BASED DESSERTS are not as concentrated as in the north and are therefore lighter. Their version of milk-based "puddings," known as *payasam,* are soupier and the milk sugars are not as caramelized. Payasams can be made with rice, vermicelli or lentils and are served for special occasions.

Traditionally in India, everyday meals do not end with dessert. There may be fruit, but a must-have dessert is a foreign concept. Only when guests are invited are sweets mandatory.

TEA IS STILL THE HOT BEVERAGE OF choice in India, and hot tea is served with many variations. Most often it is brewed or served with milk, but recently plain tea has gained popularity in the more sophisticated watering holes. Young people, exposed to iced tea in North America, have embraced it — and it is now offered in elegant

Sweets and Beverages

restaurants and hotels. Equally popular are the wide range of sodas of every flavor, some distinctly Indian. Gone are the days of homemade lemonade, which was served to guests when they came to visit. Coffee is popular in the cities and in South India, where it is grown. The way coffee is served in South India is unique. It is brewed to make a strong decoction, and this concentrate is served hot in the small cream pitcher that is part of a coffee service. Very hot milk is served in the coffee pot. A little coffee is poured in the cup, which is then filled with milk and served with plenty of sugar.

Buttermilk, or *lassi* as it is called in India, is a popular drink made of fresh yogurt, ice cubes and water and can be either savory or sweet. Lassi is particularly welcome in summer, as it cools the body.

FRESH FRUIT DRINKS ARE VERY popular, too, and juice centers serve freshly squeezed juices from pomegranates, watermelons, mangoes, guavas and grapes. Fresh-pressed sugarcane juice is another favorite, usually spiked with ginger, which makes a heavenly combination. In the north, *thandai,* a milk drink made with ground almonds, fennel seeds and peppercorns, is a cooling summer drink. In the west and the south, tamarind and green mango, both tart and considered cooling, are made into summer drinks and enjoyed over ice.

Firni

Rice Custard

¼ cup	rice (any variety), ground to a powder	50 mL
4 cups	milk (see Tip, right)	1 L
½ cup	granulated sugar	125 mL
1 tsp	kewra extract (see Tips, page 445)	5 mL
½ tsp	ground cardamom	2 mL
3 tbsp	chopped unsalted pistachios	45 mL

1. Stir rice powder into ½ cup (125 mL) of the milk and set aside.

2. Pour remaining milk into a heavy-bottomed saucepan (do not use a nonstick pan). Stir in sugar and bring to a boil over medium heat. Remove pan from heat and stir in rice powder mixture. Return to medium heat and cook, stirring continuously, until mixture thickens, about 15 minutes.

3. Remove from heat and stir in kewra extract and cardamom. Pour into 6 shallow dessert dishes and let cool to room temperature. Sprinkle pistachios over top and chill for at least 3 to 4 hours.

Serves 6

A light rice pudding, this is a classic dessert from Kashmir, perfumed with kewra (pandanus) extract.

Tip
Any type of milk is acceptable here, including skim or 1%, because rice powder is the thickener.

Besan Ladoo

Chickpea Flour Balls

¾ cup	ghee	175 mL
2 cups	chickpea flour (besan), sifted	500 mL
1 cup	confectioner's (icing) sugar, sifted	250 mL
1 tbsp	ground cardamom	15 mL
2 tbsp	raisins	25 mL

1. In a wok, melt ghee over medium heat. Add chickpea flour all at once and mix well. Reduce heat to medium-low. Cook, stirring continuously, until well browned and aromatic, about 15 minutes.

2. Remove from heat and add sugar, cardamom and raisins. Mix well. Let cool for 15 minutes.

3. Spoon by heaping tablespoonfuls (15 mL) onto baking sheet, at least 2½ inches (6 cm) apart. Mixture will spread slightly. Let rest for 15 minutes until firm. Roll into balls. If mixture is not firm enough to hold its shape, repeat process after 15 minutes. Do not refrigerate to harden. Balls will hold their shape as they rest.

Makes 20

These are a favorite sweet of many Indians, from the north and the south. There are a few minor variations, but two things remain constant — they must be made with ghee, and the chickpea flour must be cooked long and slowly to develop the right toasted flavor. There are no shortcuts.

Badam ki Firni

Almond Rice Custard

Serves 6

*Firni is a classic
milk and ground rice
pudding from Kashmir.
Light and refreshing,
it is quick to make and is
always set in individual
shallow dishes. The
almond flavor in this
version is an interesting
twist.*

Tip

Almond meal is
available in some
specialty food stores.
To make your own,
process 2 tbsp (25 mL)
blanched almonds in
a mini-processor or
blender until ground
to a fine powder.

2½ tbsp	almond meal (see Tip, left)	32 mL
¼ cup	rice flour	50 mL
2½ cups	whole or 2% milk	625 mL
¼ tsp	saffron threads	1 mL
5 to 6 tbsp	granulated sugar	75 to 90 mL
¼ tsp	ground cardamom	1 mL
2 to 3	drops almond extract	2 to 3
2 tbsp	chopped unsalted pistachios	25 mL
1 tbsp	slivered or sliced almonds	15 mL

1. In a bowl, mix together almond meal and rice flour. Set aside.

2. In a saucepan, heat milk over medium heat, stirring occasionally, until it comes to a boil. Transfer ¼ cup (50 mL) to a small bowl and add saffron. Set aside.

3. To the remaining milk, add sugar and stir to dissolve. Remove pan from heat.

4. Pour almond flour mixture in a slow but steady stream into milk, whisking continuously to prevent lumps. Mixture must be lump-free.

5. Return pan to medium-low heat and cook, gently stirring continuously, until mixture reaches the consistency of cake batter, 5 to 7 minutes. Add saffron milk.

6. Stir in cardamom and almond extract. Mix well and pour into 6 shallow individual bowls.

7. Let cool and chill for at least 4 hours or overnight. Garnish with pistachios and almonds before serving.

Gajar ka Halwa
Caramelized Carrot Pudding

1½ lbs	carrots, grated (5 or 6)	750 g
4 cups	whole milk	1 L
1¼ cups	granulated sugar (approx.), divided	300 mL
¼ cup	oil or unsalted butter	50 mL
¼ cup	raisins	50 mL
8 to 10	green cardamom pods	8 to 10
	Whole blanched almonds	
	Edible silver leaf (varak) (see Tips, right), optional	

1. In a large heavy-bottomed saucepan (do not use a nonstick pan) over medium heat, combine carrots and milk. Cook, stirring frequently, until milk is completely absorbed and mixture begins to solidify, about 1 hour.

2. Stir in 1 cup (250 mL) of the sugar, oil and raisins. When sugar is dissolved, check sweetness. Add remaining sugar if needed. Cook, stirring constantly, until mixture begins to leave sides of pan, 15 to 20 minutes.

3. Remove seeds from cardamom pods, discarding pods. Pound seeds and stir into pudding. Serve warm or at room temperature. Before serving, garnish with blanched almonds and top with edible silver leaf, if using (see North Indian Rice Pudding, page 436, for directions on using).

Serves 8

This is a favorite in North India and is particularly good when made with the sweet pink winter carrots grown in that area. The flavor is more delicate than other carrots, and they are juicier. I have never come across this variety in North America.

Tips

This dish freezes well for several months. Thaw and warm in a 200°F (100°C) oven. Sprinkle with additional almonds and top with edible silver, if using.

Silver varak is a very thin film of sterling silver. It is edible and is used to garnish special sweets and rice dishes. It is readily available in Indian markets and cake decorating supply stores.

Kheer

North Indian Rice Pudding

Serves 6 to 8

A traditional North Indian favorite, this dessert depends on the slow reduction of milk, a very important technique in the making of milk desserts. The milk flavor is intensified as natural sugars are concentrated and takes on a complexity that is unique.

Tips

Pudding can be made up to 2 days ahead and refrigerated.

Recipe can be halved. It will take less time to thicken, about 1 hour.

Variation

Saffron Rice Pudding: Heat ½ cup (125 mL) of the milk until very hot. Add 1 tsp (5 mL) saffron and set aside to steep. Instead of pistachios, use ¼ cup (50 mL) slivered blanched almonds. In Step 2, add saffron liquid, 2 tbsp (25 mL) each almonds and raisins along with sugar. Sprinkle with remaining almonds in Step 4.

8 cups	whole milk	2 L
8	green cardamom pods, slightly crushed	8
2 tbsp	long-grain rice	25 mL
4 to 5 tbsp	granulated sugar	60 to 75 mL
3 tbsp	chopped unsalted pistachios, divided	45 mL
1 to 2	sheets edible silver leaf (varak) (see Tips, page 435), optional	1 to 2

1. In a large heavy-bottomed saucepan (do not use a nonstick pan) over medium to medium-low heat, combine milk, cardamom and rice. Bring to a boil. Reduce heat immediately to maintain a gentle boil. This is critical. Every 5 to 6 minutes, a layer of cream and froth will form on top. Gently stir this in and mix well. Periodically scrape bottom of pan to make sure milk is not scorching. Cook until reduced by half. This will take 1½ to 2 hours, stirring every 5 to 6 minutes. (Watch more closely as the mixture reduces. You don't want it to burn.) Remove from heat. Remove cardamom pods, if desired.

2. Stir in sugar to taste and 2 tbsp (25 mL) of the pistachios. Mix well. Let cool.

3. Mix again and pour into serving bowl. Let cool to room temperature. Pudding will be the texture of pancake batter at this point and will thicken when chilled.

4. Garnish with silver leaf sheets, if using, by carefully inverting tissue-backed sheets over surface of pudding. Do not handle sheets directly with your fingers, as they are fragile. Sprinkle with remaining pistachios.

5. Cover bowl with plastic wrap and chill well before serving.

Rose-Scented Bread Pudding

Serves 6 to 8

This unusual Indian bread pudding is a true surprise. It evolved as a result of a rather ordinary dessert, which sounded exotic but was disappointing. I hope you enjoy it as much as my "testers" (a.k.a. family) did!

Tip

Do not use commercial sandwich white bread, as it will get mushy.

- *13-by 9-inch (3 L) baking dish, sprayed with vegetable spray*

6 cups	whole milk	1.5 L
¾ cup	granulated sugar	175 mL
3 tbsp	almond meal	45 mL
½ tsp	seeds of green cardamom pods, coarsely powdered	2 mL
3 to 4	drops almond extract	3 to 4
3 to 4	drops rose extract (see Tips, page 438)	3 to 4
8	slices French loaf, cut ½-inch (1 cm) thick (see Tip, right)	8
	Butter-flavor vegetable spray	
2	large apples, cut into ½-inch (1 cm) wedges, unpeeled if desired	2
2 tbsp	toasted almonds	25 mL

1. In a heavy-bottomed saucepan (do not use a nonstick pan), bring milk to a boil over medium heat. Reduce heat immediately to maintain a gentle boil. This is critical. Every 5 to 6 minutes, a layer of cream and froth will form on top. Gently stir this in and mix well. Cook for 30 minutes, periodically scraping bottom of pan to make sure milk is not scorching.

2. Add sugar and almond meal. Continue to cook in the same way, but stirring more frequently as the mixture thickens. When reduced by half, in about 1½ hours, remove from heat and let cool. Stir in cardamom and almond and rose extracts. The mixture should be like thick cream. This can be done up to 2 days ahead. Cover and refrigerate until ready to use.

3. Preheat oven to 350°F (180°C).

4. Spray a large griddle or skillet lightly with vegetable spray. Mist both sides of sliced bread with spray. Add bread to skillet, in batches as necessary, and toast over medium heat until lightly browned on both sides. Remove, break into pieces and place in prepared dish.

5. Spray apple wedges with vegetable spray and add to skillet. Brown on both sides.

6. Add to bread in prepared dish. Pour milk mixture over top. Sprinkle with toasted almonds and bake until lightly browned, for 30 minutes. Serve warm or at room temperature.

China Grass

Serves 8

This is a light home-style dessert particularly popular with Sindhis. Agar-agar is derived from seaweed and is therefore acceptable to vegetarians. It has the ability to gel without refrigeration and is perfect for a tropical climate.

Tips

Agar-agar is sold in rough noodle-like strands and is available in Asian and Indian markets.

Rose extract (essence) is a commonly used ingredient in special rice dishes and in sweets. It is concentrated and is not to be confused with rose water, which, being water-based, dissipates over time.

• *8-inch (2 L) square glass baking dish*

4¼ cups	whole or 2% milk	1.05 L
Scant ½ tsp	saffron threads	2 mL
½ cup	agar-agar pieces (see Tips, left)	125 mL
¼ cup	granulated sugar	50 mL
3 to 4	drops rose extract, optional (see Tips, left)	3 to 4
2 tbsp	coarsely chopped unsalted pistachios	25 mL

1. In a large heavy-bottomed saucepan (do not use a nonstick pan) over medium to medium-low heat, bring milk to a boil. Reduce heat immediately to maintain a gentle boil. Remove ¼ cup (50 mL) hot milk and stir in saffron. Set aside. Boil remaining milk for 40 to 45 minutes, maintaining a gentle boil. This is critical. Every 5 to 6 minutes a layer of cream and froth will form on top. Gently stir this in and mix well. Periodically scrape bottom of pan to make sure milk is not scorching.

2. Break agar-agar into 2-inch (5 cm) pieces and soak in 1 cup (250 mL) hot water for 10 minutes. Drain off water.

3. When milk is reduced by about one-third, stir in drained agar-agar. Add saffron with soaking milk. Add sugar. Stir until agar-agar and sugar are dissolved. Continue to cook until mixture is thick like heavy cream. Remove from heat and stir in rose extract, if using.

4. Pour into dish. Let cool and when partially set, sprinkle with pistachios. Gently tap nuts into place with a spatula.

5. Chill for 3 hours or overnight. Cut into 2-inch (5 cm) squares to serve.

Kaju Burfi
Cashew Fudge

- 8- or 9-inch (2 or 2.5 L) square baking pan, well greased

¾ cup	granulated sugar	175 mL
1 tsp	ghee or shortening	5 mL
¾ cup	whole or 2% milk	175 mL
1½ cups	unsalted raw cashews (see Tips, page 448)	375 mL
2 tbsp	unsalted pistachios, chopped	25 mL

1. In a heavy nonstick saucepan over medium-high heat, bring ¾ cup (175 mL) water, sugar and ghee to a boil. When sugar is dissolved, add milk. Cook mixture until thick and bubbly, 30 to 40 minutes.

2. Meanwhile, in a food processor, process cashews until the texture of cornmeal, scraping around the base and sides of the bowl periodically. Do not let nuts exude oil.

3. When milk mixture turns creamy and bubbly, place a drop on a greased plate and let cool. Test with thumb and forefinger: if it feels thick and tacky, remove milk from heat and add cashew meal. If not thick enough, continue to cook for a few more minutes and check again. When thick enough, add cashew meal. Stir briskly to mix well. Continue stirring for 3 to 4 minutes until mixture stiffens a little.

4. Pour into prepared pan. Sprinkle and press pistachios on top. Grease knife edge and mark squares. Let cool and cut into squares.

Makes 36

Variations of this traditional sweet are made all over the country. This is my grandmother's recipe and one of the first dishes I learned when I began my culinary adventures.

Tip
Store fudge in an airtight container at room temperature for up to 3 days or in the refrigerator for up to 3 weeks.

Walnut Date Burfi

Makes 20

Dried fruit sweets are generally served in the cooler months, as they are considered to be warming for the body. Rich and fudge-like, this is perfect as part of a tray of bite-size sweets.

Tip

Medjool dates, if available, are preferable. You will need 12 oz (375 g) with or without pits. You need more because they are stickier and become more compressed when rolled. Remove pits. Do not put Medjool dates in processor — chop them by hand.

Variation

To make balls, in Step 4, scoop spoonfuls of mixture and roll into balls instead of spreading in pan. Roll each ball in finely chopped walnuts. Refrigerate until firm.

- *8-inch (2 L) square cake pan, greased with ghee*

3 cups	whole or 2% milk	750 mL
8 oz	chopped dates (see Tip, left)	250 g
2 tsp	ghee or oil	10 mL
1 cup	walnut pieces, coarsely chopped	250 mL
1/3 cup	finely chopped walnuts, divided, optional	75 mL

1. In a heavy saucepan (do not use a nonstick pan), bring milk to a boil over medium to medium-low heat. Reduce heat to maintain a gentle boil. This is critical. As milk foams and rises to the top, every 5 to 6 minutes, stir it back in. Boil gently until reduced by half. This will take about 30 to 35 minutes.

2. Meanwhile, in a food processor, process dates into a paste. Set aside.

3. When milk is sufficiently reduced, stir in dates and reduce heat to low. Add ghee. Cook, stirring continuously, until mixture begins to hold together, 5 to 6 minutes.

4. Stir in half of the walnuts and mix well. Place in prepared pan and pat evenly with a greased spatula. Sprinkle remaining walnuts on top and press into place.

5. Refrigerate overnight to set. Cut into bite-size pieces and serve.

Kheer Makhana

Lotus Seed Puffs in Sweet Milk

Serves 8

Lotus seed puffs are essentially a North Indian ingredient. They are the equivalent of popcorn — light and airy but with no particular flavor. They are all about texture. This dessert from Rajasthan is light and perfect for summer.

8 cups	whole or 2% milk	2 L
2/3 cup	granulated sugar	150 mL
4 cups	lotus seed puffs (phool makhana)	1 L
2 tbsp	chopped unsalted pistachios	25 mL

1. In a large heavy-bottomed saucepan (do not use a nonstick pan), over medium to medium-low heat, bring milk to a boil. Reduce heat immediately to maintain a gentle boil. This is critical. Every 5 to 6 minutes, a layer of cream and froth will form on top. Gently stir this in and mix well. Periodically scrape bottom of pan to make sure milk is not scorching. Boil gently for 45 minutes. Stir in sugar. Continue to boil gently until reduced by one-third, about 1 hour.

2. Meanwhile, in another saucepan, bring 4 cups (1 L) water to a boil over high heat. Add lotus puffs and cook for 2 minutes. Drain thoroughly.

3. Add puffs to milk and cook for 2 minutes. Let cool. Pour into a serving bowl and let chill well. Before serving, sprinkle pistachios over top. Serve in individual bowls.

Pistachio Squares

Serves 8

This heavenly sweet takes me back to my childhood, when my grandmother made these treats for a special occasion. The best-quality pistachios with the brightest green color are essential to duplicate the taste.

• 8- or 9-inch (2 or 2.5 L) square cake pan, greased

2 cups	unsalted raw pistachios	500 mL
1 cup	granulated sugar	250 mL
	Edible silver leaf (varak), optional	

1. Soak pistachios in very hot water to cover for 10 minutes. Drain and rub off skins. Spread on paper towels for 15 minutes to dry. In a food processor, process until the texture of coarse cornmeal.

2. In a saucepan, combine sugar and 1/2 cup (125 mL) water. Dissolve sugar over medium heat and cook for 2 minutes. Stir in ground pistachios and mix well. Cook over medium-low heat, stirring continuously, until mixture begins to form a ball.

3. Transfer to prepared pan and spread quickly with a greased spatula. Garnish with silver leaf, if using, while still warm.

4. Let cool to room temperature. Cut into squares or diamonds.

Badam ka Halva

Almond Halva

- *8-inch (2 L) square cake pan, well greased*

6 tbsp	butter	90 mL
½ cup	fine semolina (sooji or rava)	125 mL
1 cup + 2 tbsp	ground almonds (almond meal)	275 mL
½ cup	granulated sugar	125 mL
1¼ tsp	freshly ground nutmeg	6 mL
1⅓ cups	whole or 2% milk	325 mL
2 tbsp	sliced almonds	25 mL

1. In a heavy saucepan or wok, melt butter over medium heat. Add semolina and stir until golden, 3 to 4 minutes.

2. Add ground almonds, sugar and nutmeg and stir to mix well.

3. Add milk, about ¼ cup (50 mL) at a time, and stir to incorporate. Mixture will thicken and pull away from the sides of the saucepan.

4. Spread evenly in prepared pan. Press sliced almonds into top of halva while still warm. When cool, cut into diamonds or squares. Refrigerate for at least 1 hour before removing from pan.

Makes 20

Indian halvas are not similar to those of the Middle East, which are made with sesame seeds and honey. Halva in India can be the consistency of a very thick pudding (thick enough to allow a spoon to stand up) or fudge-like squares made with an assortment of ingredients, including one made with pistachios.

Tips

Halva can be refrigerated in an airtight container for up to 3 days.

Work quickly once mixture is transferred to pan, as it sets quickly and almonds will fall off if too cool.

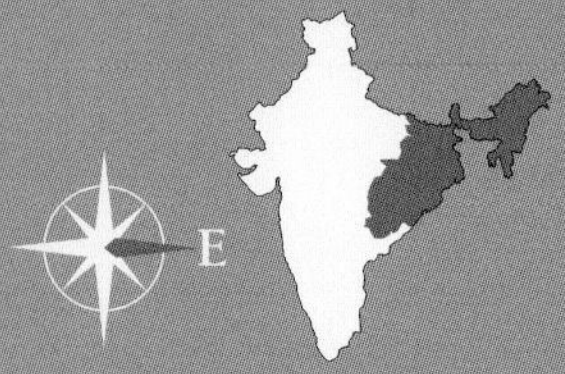

Mishti Doi
Bengali Sweet Yogurt

**Makes about
5 cups (1.25 L)**

*This sweet and slightly
tart yogurt is one of
the jewels of Bengali
cuisine. It is set in
earthenware pots, which
impart a distinctive
earthy flavor that makes
it almost addictive.
The pots are porous and
therefore designed for
one-time use only.*

4 cups	whole milk	1 L
1	can (12 oz/375 mL) evaporated milk, not low-fat	1
2/3 cup	jaggery (gur)	150 mL
1 cup	plain yogurt, at room temperature	250 mL

1. In a large heavy-bottomed saucepan (do not use a nonstick pan), mix together milk and evaporated milk. Bring to a boil over medium heat. Reduce heat immediately to maintain a gentle boil until reduced by about one-third, 20 to 25 minutes. This is critical. Every 5 to 6 minutes, a layer of cream and froth will form on top. Gently stir this in and mix well. Periodically scrape bottom of pan to make sure milk is not scorching

2. Add jaggery and stir until dissolved. Cook for 2 minutes. Let cool until just warm on the inside of the wrist. Stir in yogurt and mix well.

3. Pour into a bowl and place in a warm spot away from drafts to set, 12 to 18 hours. Chill well before serving. (Yogurt will be slightly jiggly when ready and will firm up when chilled.) Cover and refrigerate for up to 3 days.

Rasogolla
Cheese Balls in Syrup

- *Double layer of fine cheesecloth*

Panir

8 cups	whole milk	2 L
3 to 4 tbsp	freshly squeezed lemon juice	45 to 60 mL
2 tsp	fine semolina (sooji or rava)	10 mL
2 cups	granulated sugar	500 mL
½ tsp	kewra extract (see Tips, right)	2 mL

1. *Panir:* Line a large strainer with a double layer of cheesecloth.

2. In a heavy-bottomed saucepan (do not use a nonstick pan), bring milk to a boil over medium heat. Stir periodically to prevent sticking. When milk comes to a boil, add lemon juice. Milk will curdle immediately. Remove from heat and pour into prepared strainer. Gather up ends of cheesecloth, twist to form a ball and tie with string. Tie the ends loosely on kitchen faucet and let drain over sink for at least 3 to 4 hours. Remove from cheesecloth, put in a bowl and cover with plastic wrap. Refrigerate overnight.

3. Break up cheese (panir) with fingers and transfer to a food processor. Pulse until finely crumbled. Add semolina and process for 2 minutes, scraping down sides once. Mixture will be smooth and creamy. Transfer to a bowl. Break off a heaping teaspoon-size (5 mL) portion and, using a light touch, roll into a smooth ball. Repeat with remaining dough to make about 25 balls.

4. In a saucepan, bring sugar and 6 cups (1.5 L) water to a boil over medium-high heat. As soon as sugar dissolves, add extract. Drop balls into syrup. Return to a gentle boil, cover and reduce heat to medium-low. Cook, without lifting lid, for 40 minutes.

5. Remove from heat and transfer immediately to serving bowl. Pour syrup over top. Balls must be floating in syrup. Let cool and serve in individual bowls with plenty of syrup.

Makes 25

This most traditional and popular Bengali sweet is light, refreshing and easy to prepare, but do not change any of the specific instructions. There is a fine line between light-as-a-feather balls and disaster!

Tips

Cheese balls can be refrigerated in syrup for up to 1 week.

Kewra extract is from the pandanus plant, which has long sword-like leaves coming up from the base of the plant. This floral extract is used in meat and rice dishes in the north but is unknown in the south. All extracts should be tightly sealed and can be stored indefinitely in the pantry.

Malpuas

Makes 12 to 14

This is an adaptation of a simple Bengali dessert, which is served in a pool of syrup. I prefer to serve it with sweetened bananas. Malpuas, *also called* Malpuras, *are a breakfast dish for Sindhis, and my grandmother's recipe included the black peppercorns. I find they add a wonderful contrast to the sweet batter. This recipe is a combination of the Sindhi and Bengali versions.*

• *Preheat broiler*

½ cup	all-purpose flour	125 mL
½ cup	chapati flour (atta) or whole wheat flour	125 mL
½ cup	granulated sugar	125 mL
½ tsp	crushed cardamom seeds	2 mL
20	black peppercorns, cracked	20
¾ cup	whole or 2% milk (approx.)	175 mL
	Oil for pan-frying	
8	ripe bananas	8
3 tbsp	crumbled jaggery (gur)	45 mL
	Whipped cream or ice cream, optional	

1. In a bowl, mix together all-purpose and chapati flours, sugar, cardamom and peppercorns. Add enough milk to make a batter slightly thinner than pancake batter. Set aside for 15 minutes.

2. Add enough oil to a skillet to reach ½ inch (1 cm) up the sides and heat over medium heat until very hot. Using a ladle, pour a circle of batter about 3 inches (7.5 cm) in diameter into hot oil. Fry until golden, about 1 minute. Turn and fry other side, about 1 minute. When ready, the edges should be crisp and the centre soft. Do not overcook. Remove with a large-holed strainer and drain on paper towels. Repeat with remaining batter, adding more oil and reheating as necessary between batches.

3. Peel and slice bananas lengthwise. Cut each piece in half. Place in ovenproof dish and sprinkle with crumbled jaggery. Place under broiler and broil until jaggery is melted and bubbly, 2 to 3 minutes.

4. *To serve:* Place 2 malpuas on each plate. Top with 2 to 3 pieces of banana and serve with a dollop of whipped cream or ice cream, if desired.

South Indian Banana Fritters

- *Wok or deep-fryer*
- *Candy/deep-fry thermometer*

¼ cup	parboiled rice	50 mL
3	firm ripe bananas	3
¼ cup	granulated sugar	50 mL
¼ cup	all-purpose flour	50 mL
1	egg	1
	Oil for deep-frying	

1. In a bowl, soak rice in 2 cups (500 mL) water for 2 hours. Drain. Transfer to a blender and blend with 2 to 3 tbsp (25 to 45 mL) water to a smooth paste.

2. In another bowl, mash bananas into a paste with a fork. Add rice paste. Stir in sugar and flour.

3. In a separate bowl, whisk egg. Add half to banana mixture. Discard remaining egg or reserve for another use. Mix well.

4. In a wok or deep-fryer, heat oil to 350°F (180°C). Drop batter by teaspoonfuls (5 mL) into oil, in batches, and fry until golden, about 2 minutes. Remove with a large-holed strainer and drain on paper towels. Serve hot.

Serves 6

Fritters such as these were often served as an after-school snack. A make-ahead treat, they are also a good addition to a school lunch box.

Tip

Fritters can be cooled, covered and refrigerated for up to 4 days and reheated in a microwave oven to freshen them. Although they will be slightly soft, they are still delicious.

Baked Bananas with Coconut and Jaggery

Serves 6

Here the always-available humble banana is transformed into an exotic dessert. Perfect for a brunch table.

Tips

Jaggery is unrefined brown sugar usually made from sugarcane. It is rich tasting, like molasses. Dark brown sugar can be substituted, but the flavor will be altered.

Raw cashews are sweet tasting and in no way resemble roasted cashews. They are always unsalted. There is no substitute. Both jaggery and raw cashews are available in Indian markets.

- *Preheat oven to 375°F (190°C)*
- *Shallow baking dish*

6	firm ripe bananas, preferably lightly spotted	6
½ cup	grated coconut, preferably fresh (or frozen, thawed), divided	125 mL
⅔ cup	grated jaggery (gur) (see Tips, left)	150 mL
3 tbsp	raw cashews (see Tips, left)	45 mL
1 tsp	ground cardamom	5 mL
1 cup	coconut milk	250 mL
1½ tsp	cornstarch	7 mL
2 tbsp	chopped unsalted pistachios	25 mL

1. Peel and cut bananas in half lengthwise. Arrange in single layer in baking dish.

2. In a bowl, mix together coconut, jaggery, cashews and cardamom. Sprinkle evenly over bananas.

3. In a small bowl, stir together coconut milk and cornstarch and gently pour over top.

4. Bake in preheated oven until top is thick and bubbly, about 30 minutes. Garnish with pistachios. Serve at room temperature or chilled.

Jaggery Rice Pudding

Serves 8 to 10

Tapioca and coconut milk add an interesting texture and flavor to this unusual rice pudding from the south.

———— ❧ ————

2 tbsp	tapioca pearls	25 mL
¾ cup	medium- or long-grain rice (not basmati)	175 mL
4	green cardamom pods, cracked open	4
1¾ cups	loosely packed jaggery (gur)	425 mL
1 cup	coconut milk	250 mL
2 tbsp	raisins	25 mL
2 tbsp	chopped raw cashews (see Tips, page 448)	25 mL

1. In a bowl, soak tapioca in 1 cup (250 mL) water for 1 hour. Drain.

2. In a saucepan, combine rice, tapioca, cardamom and 6 cups (1.5 L) water. Bring to a boil over medium-high heat. Reduce heat to low. Cook, partially covered, until steam bubbles appear on surface and almost all the water is absorbed, 16 to 18 minutes.

3. Meanwhile, in a small saucepan over medium heat, melt jaggery with ½ cup (125 mL) water. Keep warm.

4. Stir melted jaggery into rice mixture and cook, stirring occasionally, until absorbed, 6 to 7 minutes.

5. Stir in coconut milk and raisins. Remove from heat and discard cardamom, if desired. Transfer to serving dish while still warm. Sprinkle cashews over top. Serve warm, at room temperature or cold.

Sweet Pongal

Sweet South Indian Khichri

½ tsp	saffron threads	2 mL
3 tbsp	ghee	45 mL
2 tbsp	raw cashews or cashew halves (see Tips, page 448)	25 mL
2 tbsp	raisins	25 mL
⅔ cup	long-grain white rice (not basmati)	150 mL
6 tbsp	yellow mung beans (yellow mung dal)	90 mL
2 tbsp	split yellow peas (channa dal)	25 mL
1 cup + 2 tbsp	dark brown sugar	275 mL
¾ tsp	ground cardamom	4 mL

Serves 6

Pongal *is the South Indian version of* khichri *— the combination of rice and dal cooked together — that is every Indian's basic comfort food. The variations are numerous and, although usually savory, can be sweet as well, as it is here.*

⸎

Tip
Pongal will stiffen as it cools. It can be refrigerated for up to 1 week. Reheat in microwave before serving, as it tastes best slightly warm.

1. In a small bowl, soak saffron in ¼ cup (50 mL) very hot water for 10 minutes.

2. In a small skillet, heat ½ tbsp (7 mL) of the ghee over medium heat. Add cashews and sauté for 1 minute. Add raisins and sauté until cashews are golden and raisins puffed, about 1 minute. Remove with a slotted spoon and set aside.

3. In a wok over medium heat, toast rice and mung dal together, stirring continuously, until rice is opaque and dal is lightly browned, 3 to 4 minutes. At this point there should be a faint aroma. Transfer to a large bowl. Toast channa dal in the same way until golden and aromatic, about 2 minutes. Add to bowl. Add 3 to 4 inches (7.5 to 10 cm) water and swirl fingers through mixture to rinse. Drain and repeat process 3 to 4 times. Drain.

4. Transfer rice mixture to a large saucepan. Add 2½ cups (625 mL) water, remaining ghee and saffron with soaking liquid. Bring to a boil over medium-high heat. Reduce heat to low. Cover and simmer until water is absorbed, about 20 minutes.

5. Sprinkle sugar and cardamom over top. Cover and simmer for 2 minutes. (Mixture will loosen slightly as sugar dissolves.) Stir gently to mix. Cook until sugar is absorbed, for 1 minute. Transfer to serving platter and garnish with fried nuts and raisins.

Pineapple Zarda
Pineapple Sweet Rice

Serves 6 to 8

A refreshing variation on a traditional sweet rice dish, this dessert comes from the distinctive Muslim cuisine of Hyderabad.

½ tsp	saffron threads	2 mL
2 tbsp	ghee or butter	25 mL
¼ cup	raisins	50 mL
¼ cup	raw cashews (see Tips, page 448)	50 mL
¼ cup	sliced almonds	50 mL
4	green cardamom pods, cracked open	4
1	stick cinnamon, about 4 inches (10 cm) long	1
1 cup	long-grain rice (not basmati)	250 mL
¾ cup	granulated sugar	175 mL
2 cups	fresh or drained canned pineapple chunks	500 mL

1. In a bowl, soak saffron in ¼ cup (125 mL) very hot water. Set aside.

2. In a saucepan, melt ghee over medium heat. Add raisins, cashews and almonds and sauté until golden, about 2 minutes. Remove with a slotted spoon and place in a bowl. Set aside.

3. Add cardamom and cinnamon to remaining ghee in the saucepan. Sauté until fragrant, about 1 minute. Stir in rice. Add 1 cup (250 mL) water and increase heat to medium-high. Cover and bring to a boil. Reduce heat to low and cook until water is absorbed, about 6 minutes.

4. In a separate pan, dissolve sugar in 1½ cups (375 mL) water. Bring to a boil. Add to rice along with the saffron liquid and threads. Mix well. Cover and cook over very low heat until liquid is absorbed, about 15 minutes.

5. Stir in pineapple chunks. Cover and cook for 5 minutes. Remove from heat and stir in half of the reserved nut mixture.

6. Sprinkle remaining nut mixture over top for garnish. Serve warm or at room temperature.

Cashew-Stuffed Sweet Bread

2 cups	all-purpose flour	500 mL
½ tsp	baking soda	2 mL
Scant ½ tsp	salt	2 mL
1 cup	whipping (35%) cream	250 mL

Stuffing

½ cup	raw cashews, powdered coarsely (see Tips, page 448)	125 mL
¼ cup	grated coconut, preferably fresh (or frozen, thawed), divided	50 mL
⅔ cup	granulated sugar	150 mL
½ tsp	ground cardamom	2 mL
½ cup	semolina (sooji or rava) (approx.)	125 mL
¼ cup	oil	50 mL

Makes 20

This rich and delicious bread is a wonderful treat with a cup of hot milky tea or coffee. It is also a great addition to a brunch menu.

Tip

When cool, stack three or four together, wrap tightly in foil and place in a resealable plastic bag. Store in the refrigerator for up to 1 week. To serve, warm in microwave.

1. In a food processor, combine flour, baking soda and salt. Pulse twice. With motor running, pour cream in a steady stream through feed tube. Process to form a smooth dough. Transfer to a floured work surface and knead for 1 minute by hand. Place in a bowl, cover and set aside.

2. *Stuffing:* In a skillet over medium-low heat, toast cashew powder, stirring continuously, until aromatic and lightly browned, 2 to 3 minutes. Transfer to a bowl. Add coconut, sugar and cardamom and mix well.

3. Break off a walnut-size piece of dough. Roll into a ball and flatten to ½-inch (1 cm) thick disk. Dust with semolina and roll into a 4-inch (10 cm) circle. Place a heaping tablespoon (15 mL) of the stuffing in center. Spread slightly. Pull edges of dough over filling to enclose, pinching seam on one side. Flatten to a disk and roll out into a 4- to 5-inch (10 to 12.5 cm) circle, dusting with semolina as necessary to prevent sticking.

4. Heat a dry griddle or skillet over medium heat. Add bread, one disk at a time, and cook until brown spots appear. Flip disk and cook other side in the same manner until brown sides appear on this side. Spread ¼ tsp (1 mL) of the oil on top of browned side. Press down with spatula, particularly on the edges. After 1 minute, sprinkle ¼ tsp (1 mL) oil around edges of bread. Tilt skillet to cook underside. Hold down with spatula. Flip oiled side again and cook for 30 seconds. Both sides will be crisp and browned. Transfer to a plate and keep warm. Repeat with remaining dough and filling.

Caramel Custard

Serves 8

This was my father's favorite dessert, and it has remained my lifelong favorite, too! It was often called "hospital pudding" in our home, because hospitals served it almost daily to patients, since it was considered to be very nutritious yet easy on the stomach. This is a lighter version of flan, which is so popular in Latin countries.

Tip

Do not use a deep bowl, because it will be tricky to invert custard without it falling apart. Ideally, custard should fill the bowl almost to the top.

- *Preheat oven to 350ºF (180ºC)*
- *6-cup (1.5 L) metal bowl (preferably stainless steel)*
- *13-by 9-inch (3 L) square pan*

1 ¼ cups	granulated sugar, divided	300 mL
4 cups	whole or 2% milk	1 L
6	eggs	6
½ cup	granulated sugar	125 mL
1 tsp	vanilla extract	5 mL
¼ tsp	salt	1 mL

1. In a metal bowl, melt ¾ cup (175 mL) of the sugar over medium-high heat. Do not stir. As sugar melts and darkens, swirl bowl slowly to coat sides. Sugar should be almost blackened but not burned, and sides should be coated up to about 3 inches (7.5 cm). Set aside to cool.

2. In a saucepan, heat milk over medium heat until a drop on the inner wrist feels very warm. Set aside.

3. In a large bowl, beat together eggs, ½ cup (125 mL) sugar, vanilla and salt. Gradually pour warm milk into eggs in a thin stream, beating continuously until well mixed. Pour through strainer into bowl with caramelized sugar.

4. Place metal bowl in a 13-by 9-inch (3 L) square pan. Add enough boiling water to come halfway up sides of dish. Bake in preheated oven until a toothpick inserted in center comes out clean, about 1 hour and 15 minutes. Custard will be slightly jiggly. Let cool and refrigerate to chill well.

5. *To serve:* Run a sharp knife around custard to loosen. Place a serving dish, about 2 inches (5 cm) deep, on top of bowl. Swiftly invert so custard is upside down in the dish. Spoon syrup over top of custard and serve.

Lagan nu Kastar
Parsi Baked Wedding Custard

- *Preheat oven to 350°F (180°C)*
- *8-inch (2 L) square baking dish*

4 cups	whole or 2% milk	1 L
1 cup	granulated sugar	250 mL
4	eggs	4
6	green cardamom pods, seeds only, coarsely powdered	6
½ tsp	freshly grated nutmeg	2 mL
1 tsp	vanilla extract	5 mL
½ tsp	rose extract (see Tips, page 438)	2 mL
4 tbsp	sliced almonds, divided	60 mL

1. In a large heavy-bottomed saucepan (do not use a nonstick pan) over medium to medium-low heat, bring milk to a boil. Reduce heat immediately to maintain a gentle boil. This is critical. Boil for 30 minutes. Every 5 to 6 minutes a layer of cream and froth will form on top. Gently stir this in and mix well. Periodically scrape bottom of pan to make sure milk is not scorching.

2. Add sugar and continue to boil gently until reduced by about half. Let cool for 5 minutes.

3. In a separate bowl, beat eggs lightly. Add cardamom powder, nutmeg, vanilla and rose extracts and half of the almonds. Gradually, in a thin steady stream, add milk mixture and mix well.

4. Pour into baking dish. Sprinkle with remaining almonds. Bake in preheated oven until top is golden and bubbly, for 30 minutes. Custard will be slightly jiggly and puffy, and will deflate and firm as it cools. Let cool and chill. Cut into squares and serve.

Serves 8 to 10

This unusual flan-like dessert, perfumed with rose and vanilla extracts, is a must at Parsi weddings. It is one of my favorite desserts, and I don't wait for a wedding to serve it.

Biscuit Pudding

Serves 6 to 8

This dish is an Anglo-Indian innovation and was very popular in small restaurants and clubs when I was growing up in Bombay. Maria biscuits are still very popular with tea in India, and I was pleasantly surprised to find Mexicans and Spaniards enjoy them, too.

Tips

Custard powder is essentially a form of flavored cornstarch. It is available in Indian and British markets.

Maria cookies are available in Indian and Latin markets.

• *8-inch (2 L) square glass baking dish*

⅓ cup	custard powder (see Tips, left)	75 mL
6 tbsp	unsweetened cocoa powder	90 mL
6 cups	whole or 2% milk, divided	1.5 L
¾ cup	granulated sugar	175 mL
2 tbsp	instant coffee granules or 1 cup (250 mL) very strong hot coffee	25 mL
2	packages (each 7oz/212.5 g) Maria biscuits or digestive cookies	2
¼ cup	chopped walnuts or pecans	50 mL

1. In a bowl, stir together custard powder, cocoa and 1 cup (250 mL) of the milk. Set aside.

2. Pour remaining milk into a saucepan. Stir in sugar and bring to a boil over medium heat.

3. Drizzle custard mixture into milk and cook, stirring continuously, until thickened to the consistency of pancake batter, about 15 minutes. Let cool.

4. In a small bowl, stir coffee granules into 1 cup (250 mL) boiling water. Set aside.

5. Dip biscuits individually into coffee. Layer in the bottom of baking dish. Fill in any gaps with smaller pieces. Pour half of the custard over the cookies and sprinkle with half of the nuts. Repeat with layers of cookies and custard. Shake dish gently to allow custard to settle. Sprinkle with remaining nuts. Chill for at least 3 hours or for up to 6 hours before serving.

Coconut Pudding with Almonds and Pistachios

1 ½ tbsp	ghee or butter	22 mL
2 tbsp	semolina or cream of wheat (sooji or rava)	25 mL
4 cups	whole or 2% milk	1 L
2 cups	grated coconut, fresh, or frozen, thawed	500 mL
1	can (14 oz/396 g or 300 mL) sweetened condensed milk	1
2 tbsp	chopped raw pistachios	25 mL
2 tbsp	slivered almonds	25 mL

1. In a deep heavy-bottomed saucepan, heat ghee over medium heat. Add semolina and sauté until pale gold, 2 to 3 minutes.

2. Remove from heat. Pour in 1 cup (250 mL) of the milk and whisk to a smooth paste. Pour in remaining milk and whisk until smooth. Return to medium and cook, stirring gently, until reduced by half, 20 to 25 minutes. Stir in coconut and condensed milk. Reduce heat to medium-low and return to simmer. Cook, stirring continuously, until as thick as cake batter, about 10 minutes.

3. Transfer to individual bowls. Sprinkle with nuts and serve chilled.

Serves 6 to 8

If you like coconut, this one's for you.

Tip
Pudding can be made 1 day ahead. Cool, cover with plastic wrap and chill. Sprinkle nuts on just before serving.

Rava Sweet
Semolina Squares

2 tbsp	butter	25 mL
¾ cup	semolina (rava or sooji)	175 mL
2 cups	whole or 2% milk	500 mL
⅔ cup	granulated sugar	150 mL
1 tsp	vanilla extract	5 mL
2 tbsp	slivered unsalted pistachios	25 mL

1. In a wok or saucepan, melt butter over medium heat. Add semolina and sauté for 5 minutes. Do not brown.

2. Remove from heat and gradually whisk in milk. There should be no lumps. Stir in sugar and return to medium heat. Cook, stirring continuously, until thickened, 6 to 8 minutes.

3. Stir in vanilla. Pour into 8-inch (2 L) square baking dish. Press pistachios into top to garnish. Let cool and cut into squares to serve.

Serves 6 to 8

This simple but delicious dessert comes from the Parsi community, who emigrated centuries ago from Persia. It is often served at feasts and celebrations.

Narial ke Ladoo
Coconut Balls

- *Mini paper baking cups*

3 cups	grated coconut, preferably fresh (or frozen, thawed)	750 mL
1½ cups	granulated sugar	375 mL
1 cup	whole or 2% milk	250 mL
¼ cup	oil	50 mL
25	green cardamom pods, seeds only, crushed, or 1½ tsp (7 mL) ground cardamom (see Tips, right)	25

1. In a saucepan over medium heat, mix together coconut, sugar, milk and oil. Cook, stirring frequently, until almost dry, 35 to 40 minutes.

2. Continue cooking, stirring constantly to prevent browning, until mixture is dry enough to hold together, about 10 minutes more.

3. Add cardamom and mix well.

4. Remove from heat and let cool to room temperature.

5. When cool enough to handle but still warm, place 1 tbsp (15 mL) mixture into palm of hand and roll into a ball. Place in paper baking cup. Continue until all the mixture is used. Chill for 2 to 3 hours before serving.

Makes 20 to 22

Coconut sweets are popular along the coast of India, with slight variations. On the west coast, they are often made for festivals and celebrations. This recipe came from my aunt, who often made it for family celebrations.

Tips

Balls can be made up to 2 days ahead for optimum freshness, but they can be stored in the refrigerator in an airtight container for up to 5 days.

Cardamom powder turns the mixture a pale gray, which I personally do not like. Crushed seeds are preferable, as they will leave the coconut mixture a more attractive white.

Variation

In Step 4, divide mixture into 3 portions. Tint 1 portion with 2 drops red food coloring and 1 portion with 2 drops green food coloring. Leave 1 portion white.

Karanji
Coconut Pastries

Makes 15

These sweet-filled pastries are a Maharashtrian speciality, made for festival days like Diwali, the "festival of lights" — one of the most important holidays in India.

❦

- *Wok or deep-fryer*
- *Candy/deep-fry thermometer*

Pastry
1 cup	all-purpose flour	250 mL
1 1/2 tbsp	semolina (sooji or rava)	22 mL
1/4 cup	ghee	50 mL
1/4 cup	whole or 2% milk	50 mL

Filling
1 cup	grated coconut, preferably fresh (or frozen, thawed)	250 mL
1 cup	grated or shaved jaggery, not packed	250 mL
2 tbsp	dark raisins	25 mL
1/2 tsp	green cardamom seeds, powdered	2 mL
	Oil for deep-frying	

1. *Pastry:* Place flour into a bowl. Mix in semolina. Add ghee and rub in with fingertips until mixture resembles bread crumbs. Pour in milk and about 1 tbsp (15 mL) water or enough to make a soft dough. Mix until dough forms a ball. Knead until smooth and elastic, about 5 minutes. Cover and set aside for 30 minutes.

2. *Filling:* In a nonstick skillet over medium heat, toast coconut, stirring continuously, until golden, 5 to 7 minutes. Transfer to a bowl and let cool completely. Add jaggery, raisins and cardamom and mix well. Divide filling into 15 equal portions.

3. *To assemble:* Knead dough again for 1 minute. Roll into a 1 1/2-inch (4 cm) thick rope. Divide into 15 equal portions. Roll each portion into a smooth ball. Cover and set aside. Working with one ball at a time, pat into a 1/2-inch (1 cm) thick disk. Using a light hand, roll into a 4 1/2-inch (11 cm) circle. Place 1 portion of the filling on half of the circle. Gently lift other half of pastry and cover filling. Press edges firmly (you will have a half-moon shape). Carefully lift filled pastry and press edges to seal tightly. This is important or else it will come apart when frying. Continue with the rest of the pastry and filling.

4. In a wok or deep-fryer, heat oil to 350°F (180°C). Add pastry, in batches without crowding, and fry, turning once, until golden, 2 to 3 minutes per batch. Remove with strainer. Drain on paper towels.

5. When cool, serve or transfer to an airtight container and store at room temperature up to 5 days.

Golpapdi

- *Wok*
- *9-inch (2.5 L) square cake pan, greased*

²⁄₃ cup	ghee, divided	150 mL
1 cup	chapati flour (atta)	250 mL
1 cup	loosely packed shaved jaggery (gur)	250 mL
1 ½ tsp	crushed cardamom seeds	7 mL

1. In a wok, melt ½ cup (125 mL) of the ghee over medium heat. Add chapati flour. Reduce heat to medium-low. Cook, stirring continuously to brown evenly, like a roux, until mixture is golden and aromatic, 6 to 8 minutes. Set aside.

2. In another saucepan over medium heat, combine 2 tbsp (25 mL) ghee and jaggery and stir until melted. Pour into flour mixture. Add cardamom and mix well.

3. Turn out into prepared pan and spread evenly. Smooth top with a greased spatula and let cool slightly. Score into diamond shapes and let cool completely. When cool, cut carefully.

Makes 25

This type of sweet is typical of Gujarat. Jaggery is an important ingredient in the cooking of the area and is often used in place of sugar.

Tip
Golpapdi can be stored in an airtight container for up to 1 week at room temperature.

Chickpea Flour and Coconut Fudge

Makes about 36

This simple but delicious sweet is typically the type served with tea or stored in the pantry for unexpected guests.

Tip

Dry unsweetened coconut powder is available in Indian markets. Refrigerate in a resealable freezer bag for up to 2 years.

• 8- or 9-inch (2 or 2.5 L) round or square cake pan, sprayed with vegetable spray

1½ cups	granulated sugar	375 mL
½ cup	ghee	125 mL
½ cup	dry unsweetened coconut powder (see Tip, left)	125 mL
½ cup	chickpea flour (besan)	125 mL
½ cup	whole or 2% milk	125 mL
½ tsp	green cardamom seeds, powdered	2 mL

1. In a nonstick wok or saucepan, combine sugar, ghee, coconut, chickpea flour and milk. Cook over medium-low heat, stirring constantly, until mixture turns the color of butterscotch and begins to form a soft ball as it pulls away from the sides of the wok, about 15 minutes. Stir in cardamom.

2. Pour into prepared pan and shake to even out the mixture. Work quickly, as mixture begins to set almost immediately. Mark into diamond pieces while still warm. Cut when cool and store in an airtight container.

Stewed Apricots with Custard

1 lb	dried Afghani apricots (see Tips, right)	500 g
½ cup	granulated sugar	125 mL

Custard

4 cups	whole or 2% milk, divided	1 L
¾ cup	granulated sugar	175 mL
¼ cup	custard powder (see Tips, right)	50 mL
2 tbsp	sliced almonds	25 mL

1. Soak apricots in hot water to cover by 3 to 4 inches (7.5 to 10 cm) for 30 minutes. Drain.

2. In a saucepan, combine 3 cups (750 mL) water, sugar and apricots and bring to a boil over medium heat. Reduce heat to medium-low. Simmer, stirring gently periodically, until apricots are soft but not mushy, 8 to 10 minutes. Set aside to cool.

3. *Custard:* In a saucepan, bring 3½ cups (875 mL) of the milk and sugar to a boil over medium heat. Stir custard powder into remaining milk to make a smooth paste. Slowly pour into boiling milk, stirring continuously. Cook, stirring, until custard thickens and coats the back of a spoon, 8 to 10 minutes. Remove from heat and let cool. Place plastic wrap on surface of custard and chill for at least 2 hours and for up to 2 days.

4. Divide apricots between 8 dessert bowls. Spoon custard over top and garnish with sliced almonds.

Serves 8

This was a favorite in my family when I was growing up, and I still relish it when I make it with Afghani apricots. These are very different from dried apricots in North America. They are small, grayish and hard with a small pit. They are utterly sweet and sinfully delicious. They are available in Indian markets.

Tips

There's no need to remove the apricot pits. Chew around them discretely and remove from your mouth as you would with cherry pits.

Custard powder is available in Indian and British markets. It was introduced to India by the British, who often used it in place of crème anglaise.

Shaker Para

Sweet Cardamom Scented Crispies

Serves 6 to 8

These scrumptious teatime treats are typical of the snacks from Maharashtra and Gujarat. Serve these with coffee or steaming Masala Chai (see recipe, page 471).

Tip

Store crispies in an airtight container at room temperature for 3 to 4 weeks.

- *Wok or deep-fryer*
- *Candy/deep-fry thermometer*

½ cup	granulated sugar	125 mL
1 ½ cups	all-purpose flour	375 mL
¼ tsp	salt	1 mL
1 ½ tsp	freshly ground green cardamom seeds (12 to 14 pods)	7 mL
2 tbsp	ghee	25 mL
	Oil for deep-frying	

1. In a small saucepan over low heat, melt sugar in 2 tbsp (25 mL) water.

2. In a bowl, combine flour and salt. Sprinkle in cardamom evenly. Rub in ghee. Pour sugar syrup into mixture. Add about 2 tbsp (25 mL) water and mix to make a stiff dough. Knead for 2 to 3 minutes.

3. Divide dough into 4 portions. Keep 3 covered, away from heat. Roll 1 portion into a rectangle ⅛ inch (0.25 cm) thick. Score lengthwise into strips about 1½ inches (4 cm) wide. Cut diagonally across strips to make diamond-shaped pieces.

4. In a wok or deep-fryer, heat oil to 325°F (160°C). Add pieces to oil and fry, in batches, turning to brown evenly, about 3 minutes. Remove with a large-holed strainer and drain on paper towels. Repeat with remaining dough.

Mitha Poha
Sweet Pressed Rice

³⁄₄ cup	pressed rice flakes (thick poha) (see Tips, right)	175 mL
1	can (14 oz/400 mL) unsweetened coconut milk	1
¹⁄₂ cup	milk	125 mL
5 tbsp	granulated sugar	75 mL
2 tbsp	slivered almonds	25 mL
2 tbsp	golden raisins	25 mL
1 tsp	freshly grated nutmeg	5 mL
¹⁄₄ tsp	green cardamom seeds, powdered	1 mL
3 to 4	drops rose extract (see Tips, page 438)	3 to 4
2 tbsp	chopped unsalted pistachios	25 mL

1. Place pressed rice in a strainer and hold under running water while separating gently with fingers. Rinse and drain well. Set aside.

2. In a saucepan over medium heat, bring coconut milk, milk and sugar to a boil, stirring gently. Simmer for 3 minutes.

3. Add rinsed rice flakes, almonds, raisins, nutmeg and cardamom. Stir gently to mix. Simmer for 2 minutes. Remove from heat and let cool slightly. Stir in rose extract. Transfer to a serving dish or into individual bowls and garnish with pistachios. Serve at room temperature or chilled.

Makes about 3 cups (750 mL)

Pressed rice is popular on the west coast and in Bengal. It is usually prepared as a savory snack. In this recipe, it is transformed into a deliciously rich dessert with coconut milk and nuts.

Tips
Poha is dried flattened rice. It is best known in the eat-out-of-hand snack *chevra* from western India, where it is fried and mixed with cashews, raisins, peanuts and spices. It is also used for other savory and sweet dishes like this one.

This dish can be made 1 day ahead. Cover with plastic wrap and refrigerate.

Kheer Seviyan

Vermicelli in Milk

Serves 8

Very fine vermicelli, the only form of noodles used in Indian cuisine, is popular both in North India, where it is made into a sweetened breakfast dish or this marvelous dessert, and in the south, where it is also used in combination with vegetables. This sweet dish, also known as Sheer Khorma, *is eaten by Muslims to break the Ramadan fast on the morning of their Id celebration.*

Tips

Chironji nuts, also known as *charoli,* do not have an English name. They are small flattened seeds, slightly soft and mottled with dark patches. They can be found in small packets in the refrigerated section of a well-stocked Indian grocery store.

Silver varak is a very thin film of sterling silver. It is edible and is used to garnish special sweets and rice dishes.

1 tbsp	raisins	15 mL
1 tbsp	chironji nuts (see Tips, left)	15 mL
1 tbsp	butter, divided	15 mL
+1 tsp		+ 5 mL
6 cups	whole or 2% milk	1.5 L
2	whole cloves	2
2	green cardamom pods, cracked open	2
2 oz	vermicelli (sevian), broken into pieces	60 g
½ cup	granulated sugar	125 mL

Garnish

1 tbsp	blanched slivered almonds	15 mL
1 tbsp	unsalted chopped pistachios	15 mL
	Edible silver varak (see Tips, left), optional	

1. Soak raisins and chironji nuts separately in water for 30 minutes. Drain. Set raisins aside.

2. In a small skillet, heat 1 tsp (5 mL) of the butter over medium heat. Add chironji nuts and sauté for 2 minutes. Remove and set aside.

3. In a large heavy-bottomed saucepan (do not use a nonstick pan) over medium-low heat, bring milk to a boil. Reduce heat immediately to maintain a gentle boil. This is critical. Every 5 to 6 minutes, a layer of cream and froth will form on top. Gently stir this in and mix well. Periodically scrape bottom of pan to make sure milk is not scorching. Boil until reduced by half, 45 minutes to 1 hour.

4. Meanwhile, in a large skillet, melt remaining butter over medium heat. Add cloves and cardamom and sauté for 30 seconds. Reduce heat to medium-low. Add vermicelli and sauté until golden, 2 to 3 minutes. Stir into milk. Add sugar and continue to simmer, stirring occasionally, about 6 minutes. Mixture will be somewhat runny but will continue to thicken to a custard-like consistency as it cools.

5. Stir in raisins and chironji nuts and remove from heat. Pour into serving dish. Top with almonds, pistachios and silver varak, if using. Serve warm, at room temperature or chilled.

Chikki
Peanut Brittle

Serves 6 to 8

Jaggery, unrefined brown sugar, is used extensively in Indian sweets and makes this brittle unique.

Tips

Store brittle in an airtight container at room temperature for up to 1 week in an airtight container. Do not refrigerate.

If you don't have a candy or deep-fry thermometer, test the doneness of the jaggery syrup by dropping a small amount into very cold water. When cooked enough, the syrup should form a hard ball that holds its shape but is still pliable.

- *Wok*
- *Candy/deep-fry thermometer*
- *Rolling pin, greased*
- *Heatproof surface, greased*

1 cup	skinned raw peanuts	250 mL
1 cup	loosely packed jaggery (gur)	250 mL
2 tsp	ghee or butter	10 mL
1½ tsp	granulated sugar	7 mL

1. In a skillet, toast peanuts over medium heat, stirring continuously, until light brown spots appear, 3 to 4 minutes. Let cool and chop coarsely.

2. In a wok over medium-low heat, melt jaggery, ghee and sugar, stirring until jaggery is dissolved. Boil gently until mixture turns golden brown and reaches hard-ball stage, 250°F to 265°F (121°C to 129°C), 3 to 4 minutes (see Tips, left).

3. Immediately add peanuts and remove from heat. Mix quickly and turn out on to a well-oiled heatproof surface (a rimmed baking sheet turned upside down works well). With a well-greased rolling pin, roll quickly, or with a greased spatula, pat rapidly to spread mixture as thin as possible. Let cool and break into pieces.

Thandai

Fennel-Scented Nut and Milk Cooler

2 tbsp	unsalted pistachios	25 mL
2 tbsp	blanched almonds, about 12	25 mL
2 tbsp	raw cashews (see Tips, page 448)	25 mL
1/2 tsp	seeds of green cardamom pods	2 mL
1/2 tsp	freshly grated nutmeg	2 mL
1/2 tsp	fennel seeds (saunf)	2 mL
1/4 tsp	black peppercorns	1 mL
8 cups	whole or 2% milk, divided	2 L
1/2 cup	granulated sugar	125 mL
3	drops rose extract (see Tips, page 438)	3
	Ice cubes	
	Organic rose petals, optional	

1. Soak pistachios in 1/2 cup (125 mL) very hot water for 15 minutes to loosen skins. Rub off skins and dry pistachios thoroughly. Spread on paper towels for 15 minutes to dry further.

2. In a spice grinder, grind together pistachios, almonds, cashews, cardamom, nutmeg, fennel and peppercorns to a powder. Transfer to a bowl. Add 1/3 cup (75 mL) milk and mix to a paste.

3. In a blender, combine sugar, nut paste, 2 cups (500 mL) of the remaining milk and rose extract and blend until smooth.

4. Pour remaining milk into a pitcher. Pour in spiced milk from blender and stir thoroughly. Add 4 to 5 ice cubes to each chilled glass. Pour drink over top and serve. Garnish with rose petals, if using.

Serves 6 to 8

This is a popular summer drink in the north, as it is believed to have a cooling effect on the body. Its Indian name, thandai, *means just that — cooler.*

Tip
Cooler can be prepared up to Step 3 a day ahead, then tightly covered and refrigerated.

Lassi

Serves 4

Lassi is the summer drink in India, either sweet or savory. My personal favorite is definitely the savory version, cool and refreshing with the aroma of freshly ground cumin.

Variation

To make a sweet lassi, omit cumin, salt and pepper. Add 2 to 3 tbsp (25 to 45 mL) sugar.

1 tsp	cumin seeds	5 mL
2 cups	plain yogurt	500 mL
¾ tsp	salt or to taste	4 mL
½ tsp	freshly ground black pepper	2 mL
	Ice cubes	

1. Toast cumin seeds in a small skillet over medium heat, stirring continuously, until seeds turn a shade darker and aromatic, about 3 minutes. Let cool and grind in mortar with pestle or in spice grinder until powdery. Set aside.

2. In a blender, combine yogurt, 2 cups (500 mL) cold water and 1 to 2 cups (250 to 500 mL) ice cubes. Add salt, pepper and half of the cumin powder and blend until smooth.

3. Pour into 4 tall glasses to serve. Sprinkle with remaining cumin to garnish.

Mango Lassi

Serves 4

I had never had mango lassi until I came to the U.S. I prefer to use canned Indian mango purée, as mangoes are seasonal and only the sweetest, fibrous-free ones should be used.

1½ cups	plain yogurt	375 mL
1½ cups	canned Indian mango purée or to taste	375 mL
½ cup	whole or 2% milk	125 mL
	Ice cubes	

1. In a blender, combine yogurt, mango purée, milk and 1 to 2 cups (250 to 500 mL) ice cubes and blend until smooth.

2. Pour into 4 tall glasses to serve.

Masala Chai
Spiced Tea

½ cup	milk	125 mL
2	whole cloves	2
1	green cardamom pod, cracked open	1
1	thin slice peeled gingerroot, about ½ inch (1 cm) round	1
4 to 5	pieces (each 2 inches/5 cm long) lemongrass	4 to 5
2 tsp	Indian black tea leaves	10 mL
2 tsp	granulated sugar or to taste	10 mL

1. In a saucepan over medium-high heat, combine 1½ cups (375 mL) water, milk, cloves, cardamom, ginger and lemongrass. Bring to a boil.

2. Add tea and sugar. Reduce heat to medium and simmer for 2 minutes. Remove from heat, cover and let tea steep for 3 to 4 minutes longer. (If using an electric stove, turn off heat, cover and leave on burner.) Strain into warmed teapot or cups.

Makes 2 cups (500 mL)

This is my favorite recipe for masala chai *(spiced tea), an old Indian tradition. Many variations exist, but basically it is made with black tea leaves and aromatic spices and herbs and is astonishingly soul-satisfying. It is also healing and soothing, depending on the spices used. The addition of ginger is particularly good for a cold or queasy stomach.*

Tip
If making 4 cups (1 L) or more at a time, reduce tea to ¾ tsp (4 mL) per cup.

Cumin Mint Refresher

Serves 4

This cumin-infused tamarind mixture is the liquid filling in the famous Pani Puri chaat *of Mumbai. It doubles as a drink, well known for its digestive properties, and is served in juice glasses at parties and in many Indian restaurants.*

Tip
Beverage can be refrigerated for up to 3 days. Always stir well before serving.

1 cup	mint leaves	250 mL
¼ cup	cilantro, leaves and soft stems	50 mL
1 tsp	chopped green chiles, preferably serranos	5 mL
1 tsp	minced peeled gingerroot	5 mL
5 tbsp	unsalted Thai tamarind purée	75 mL
2½ tsp	black salt (kala namak)	12 mL
2 tsp	toasted cumin seeds, powdered	10 mL
4	mint leaves	4

1. In a blender, combine 1 cup (250 mL) mint, cilantro, chiles and ginger. Spoon tamarind over top. Blend to a paste, scraping down sides of blender a couple of times. Transfer to a pitcher.

2. Add 4 cups (1 L) water, black salt and cumin and stir vigorously to mix well. Refrigerate until chilled, at least 3 hours, preferably 10 to 12 hours. Stir well a couple of times while in the refrigerator as herbs and spices tend to settle.

3. *To serve:* Stir just before serving. Pour into juice glasses. Garnish with mint leaves and serve chilled.

Library and Archives Canada Cataloguing in Publication

Vaswani, Suneeta
    Complete book of Indian cooking : 350 recipes from the regions of India / Suneeta Vaswani.

Includes index.
ISBN 978-0-7788-0175-7 (bound)
ISBN 978-0-7788-0170-2 (pbk.)

    1. Cookery, India. I. Title.

TX724.5.I4V375 2007   641.5954   C2007-902863-2

Sources

Mail Order Sources

Patel Bros.
5815 Hillcroft
Houston, TX 77036
713-784-8332

There are many stores throughout the United States with this name, but they are all independently owned. This one has been in business for more than 20 years and is the primary mail order source for Indians in the southern and southeastern United States.

Kalustyan's
123 Lexington Ave.
New York, NY 10016
800-352-3451
www.kalustyans.com

This famous New York source has been handling international foods for more than half a century.

Penzeys Spices
Multiple locations
414-679-7207 or 800-741-7787
www.penzeys.com

Premier family-owned and -operated spice company with an outstanding mail-order business and retail stores in 21 states. The quarterly catalogs, packed with detailed information and recipes, are worth saving.

Website Shopping

Indian Foods Co.
www.indianfoodsco.com

One-stop shopping for everything from chutneys to herbs and spices to cookbooks.

Get Spice
www.getspice.com

This very easy-to-use website has spices listed with color photos. Kitchen equipment and cookbooks also available.

Ethnic Grocer
www.ethnicgrocer.com

Herbs and spices, oils, sauces, teas and much more are available here. Free catalog available upon request.

Index